Treaty Series

Treaties and international agreements registered or filed and recorded with the Secretariat of the United Nations

VOLUME 3166

Recueil des Traités

Traités et accords internationaux enregistrés ou classés et inscrits au répertoire au Secrétariat de l'Organisation des Nations Unies

United Nations • Nations Unies
New York, 2025

Print ISBN: 978-92-1-003237-7
e-ISBN: 978-92-1-106666-1
ISSN: 0379-8267
e-ISSN: 2412-1495

TABLE OF CONTENTS

I

Treaties and international agreements
registered in January 2017
Nos. 54176 to 54183

TABLE DES MATIÈRES

I

Traités et accords internationaux
enregistrés en janvier 2017
Nos 54176 à 54183

NOTE BY THE SECRETARIAT

Under Article 102 of the Charter of the United Nations, every treaty and every international agreement entered into by any Member of the United Nations after the coming into force of the Charter shall, as soon as possible, be registered with the Secretariat and published by it. Furthermore, no party to a treaty or international agreement subject to registration which has not been registered may invoke that treaty or agreement before any organ of the United Nations. The General Assembly, by resolution 97 (I), established regulations to give effect to Article 102 of the Charter (see text of the regulations, vol. 859, p. VIII; https://treaties.un.org/Pages/Resource.aspx?path=Publication/Regulation/Page1_en.xml).

The terms "treaty" and "international agreement" have not been defined either in the Charter or in the regulations, and the Secretariat follows the principle that it acts in accordance with the position of the Member State submitting an instrument for registration that, so far as that party is concerned, the instrument is a treaty or an international agreement within the meaning of Article 102. Registration of an instrument submitted by a Member State, therefore, does not imply a judgement by the Secretariat on the nature of the instrument, the status of a party or any similar question. It is the understanding of the Secretariat that its acceptance for registration of an instrument does not confer on the instrument the status of a treaty or an international agreement if it does not already have that status, and does not confer upon a party a status which it would not otherwise have.

*

* *

<u>Disclaimer</u>: All authentic texts in the present Series are published as submitted for registration by a party to the instrument. Unless otherwise indicated, the translations of these texts have been made by the Secretariat of the United Nations, for information.

NOTE DU SECRÉTARIAT

Aux termes de l'Article 102 de la Charte des Nations Unies, tout traité ou accord international conclu par un Membre des Nations Unies après l'entrée en vigueur de la Charte sera, le plus tôt possible, enregistré au Secrétariat et publié par lui. De plus, aucune partie à un traité ou accord international qui aurait dû être enregistré mais ne l'a pas été ne pourra invoquer ledit traité ou accord devant un organe de l'Organisation des Nations Unies. Par sa résolution 97 (I), l'Assemblée générale a adopté un règlement destiné à mettre en application l'Article 102 de la Charte (voir texte du règlement, vol. 859, p. IX; https://treaties.un.org/Pages/Resource.aspx?path=Publication/Regulation/Page1_fr.xml).

Les termes « traité » et « accord international » n'ont été définis ni dans la Charte ni dans le règlement, et le Secrétariat a pris comme principe de s'en tenir à la position adoptée à cet égard par l'État Membre qui a présenté l'instrument à l'enregistrement, à savoir que, en ce qui concerne cette partie, l'instrument constitue un traité ou un accord international au sens de l'Article 102. Il s'ensuit que l'enregistrement d'un instrument présenté par un État Membre n'implique, de la part du Secrétariat, aucun jugement sur la nature de l'instrument, le statut d'une partie ou toute autre question similaire. Le Secrétariat considère donc que son acceptation pour enregistrement d'un instrument ne confère pas audit instrument la qualité de traité ou d'accord international si ce dernier ne l'a pas déjà, et qu'il ne confère pas à une partie un statut que, par ailleurs, elle ne posséderait pas.

*

* *

<u>Déni de responsabilité</u> : Tous les textes authentiques du présent Recueil sont publiés tels qu'ils ont été soumis pour enregistrement par l'une des parties à l'instrument. Sauf indication contraire, les traductions de ces textes ont été établies par le Secrétariat de l'Organisation des Nations Unies, à titre d'information.

I

Treaties and international agreements registered in January 2017 Nos. 54176 to 54183

Traités et accords internationaux enregistrés en janvier 2017 Nos 54176 à 54183

No. 54176

Latvia and Kazakhstan

Agreement between the Government of the Republic of Latvia and the Government of the Republic of Kazakhstan on the Exemption of Visa Requirements for Holders of Diplomatic Passports. Riga, 16 September 2011

Entry into force: *4 February 2016, in accordance with article 12*

Authentic texts: *English, Kazakh and Latvian*

Registration with the Secretariat of the United Nations: *Latvia, 4 January 2017*

Not published in print, in accordance with article 12(2) of the General Assembly regulations to give effect to Article 102 of the Charter of the United Nations, as amended, and the publication practice of the Secretariat.

Lettonie et Kazakhstan

Accord entre le Gouvernement de la République de Lettonie et le Gouvernement de la République du Kazakhstan sur l'exemption des formalités de visa pour les titulaires d'un passeport diplomatique. Riga, 16 septembre 2011

Entrée en vigueur : *4 février 2016, conformément à l'article 12*

Textes authentiques : *anglais, kazakh et letton*

Enregistrement au Secrétariat de l'Organisation des Nations Unies : *Lettonie, 4 janvier 2017*

Non disponible en version imprimée, conformément au paragraphe 2 de l'article 12 du règlement de l'Assemblée générale destiné à mettre en application l'Article 102 de la Charte des Nations Unies, tel qu'amendé, et à la pratique du Secrétariat en matière de publication.

No. 54177

Latvia
and
Republic of Moldova

Agreement between the Government of the Republic of Latvia and the Government of the Republic of Moldova for the avoidance of double taxation and the prevention of fiscal evasion with respect to taxes on income and on capital. Riga, 25 February 1998

Entry into force: *24 June 1998 by notification, in accordance with article 28*

Authentic texts: *English, Latvian and Moldovan*

Registration with the Secretariat of the United Nations: *Latvia, 4 January 2017*

Lettonie
et
République de Moldova

Accord entre le Gouvernement de la République de Lettonie et le Gouvernement de la République de Moldova tendant à éviter les doubles impositions et à prévenir la fraude fiscale en matière d'impôts sur le revenu et sur la fortune. Riga, 25 février 1998

Entrée en vigueur : *24 juin 1998 par notification, conformément à l'article 28*

Textes authentiques : *anglais, letton et moldave*

Enregistrement au Secrétariat de l'Organisation des Nations Unies : *Lettonie, 4 janvier 2017*

[TEXT IN ENGLISH – TEXTE EN ANGLAIS]

AGREEMENT
BETWEEN
THE GOVERNMENT OF THE REPUBLIC OF LATVIA
AND THE GOVERNMENT OF THE REPUBLIC OF MOLDOVA
FOR THE AVOIDANCE OF DOUBLE TAXATION
AND THE PREVENTION OF FISCAL EVASION
WITH RESPECT TO TAXES ON INCOME AND ON CAPITAL

The Government of the Republic of Latvia and the Government of the Republic of Moldova,

Desiring to conclude an Agreement for the avoidance of double taxation and the prevention of fiscal evasion with respect to taxes on income and on capital,

have agreed as follows:

Article 1
PERSONAL SCOPE

This Agreement shall apply to persons who are residents of one or both of the Contracting States.

Article 2
TAXES COVERED

1. This Agreement shall apply to taxes on income and on capital imposed on behalf of a Contracting State or of its political subdivisions or local authorities, irrespective of the manner in which they are levied.

2. There shall be regarded as taxes on income and on capital all taxes imposed on total income, on total capital, or on elements of income or of capital, including taxes on gains from the alienation of movable or immovable property, as well as taxes on capital appreciation.

3. The existing taxes to which the Agreement shall apply are in particular:

a) in the Republic of Moldova:
(i) income tax on enterprises (impozitul pe beneficiul (venitul) intreprinderilor;
(ii) income tax on individuals (impozitul pe venitul persoanelor fizice;
(iii) tax on immovable property (impozitul pe proprietati imobiliare;
(hereinafter referred to as "Moldovan tax");

b) in Latvia:

(i) the enterprise income tax (uznemumu ienakuma nodoklis);

(ii) the personal income tax (iedzivotaju ienakuma nodoklis);

(iii) the property tax (ipasuma nodoklis);

(hereinafter referred to as "Latvian tax").

4. This Agreement shall apply also to any identical or substantially similar taxes which are imposed after the date of signature of this Agreement in addition to, or in place of, the existing taxes. The competent authorities of the Contracting States shall notify each other of any significant changes which have been made in their respective taxation laws.

Article 3
GENERAL DEFINITIONS

1. For the purposes of this Agreement, unless the context otherwise requires:

a) the term "Republic of Moldova" means the Republic of Moldova and, when used in geographical sense, means the territory of Moldova including the internal waters, aerial space over which the Republic of Moldova exercises sovereign rights to work mineral and natural resources in accordance to the norms of international law;

b) the term "Latvia" means the Republic of Latvia and, when used in the geographical sense, means the territory of the Republic of Latvia and any other area adjacent to the territorial waters of the Republic of Latvia within which under the laws of Latvia and in accordance with international law, the rights of Latvia may be exercised with respect to the sea bed and its sub-soil and their natural resources;

c) the terms "a Contracting State" and "the other Contracting State" mean Latvia or the Republic of Moldova, as the context requires;

d) the term "person" includes an individual, a company and any other body of persons;

e) the term "company" means any body corporate or any entity which is treated as a body corporate for tax purposes;

f) the terms "enterprise of a Contracting State" and "enterprise of the other Contracting State" mean respectively an enterprise carried on by a resident of a Contracting State and an enterprise carried on by a resident of the other Contracting State;

g) the term "international traffic" means any transport by an aircraft operated by an enterprise of a Contracting State, except when the aircraft is operated solely between places in the other Contracting State;

h) the term "competent authority" means :

(i) in the Republic of Moldova, the Minister of Finance or his authorised representative;

(ii) in Latvia, the Minister of Finance or his authorised representative;

i) the term "national" means:
(i) any individual possessing the nationality of a Contracting State;
(ii) any legal person, partnership or association deriving its status as such from the laws in force in a Contracting State.

2. As regards the application of this Agreement by a Contracting State any term not defined therein shall, unless the context otherwise requires, have the meaning which it has under the law of that Contracting State concerning the taxes to which this Agreement applies.

Article 4
RESIDENT

1. For the purposes of this Agreement, the term "resident of a Contracting State" means any person who, under the laws of that State, is liable to tax therein by reason of his domicile, residence, place of management, place of incorporation or any other criterion of a similar nature. The term also includes the Government of that State itself, its political subdivisions and local authorities. But this term does not include any person who is liable to tax in that State in respect only of income from sources in that State or capital situated therein.

2. Where by reason of the provisions of paragraph 1 of this Article an individual is a resident of both Contracting States, then his status shall be determined as follows:

a) he shall be deemed to be a resident of the State in which he has a permanent home available to him; if he has a permanent home available to him in both States, he shall be deemed to be a resident of the State with which his personal and economic relations are closer (centre of vital interests);

b) if the State in which he has his centre of vital interests cannot be determined, or if he has not a permanent home available to him in either State, he shall be deemed to be a resident of the State in which he has an habitual abode;

c) if he has an habitual abode in both States or in neither of them, he shall be deemed to be a resident of the State of which he is a national;

d) if he is a national of both States or of neither of them, the competent authorities of the Contracting States shall settle the question by mutual agreement.

3. Where by reason of the provisions of paragraph 1 of this Article a person other than an individual is a resident of both Contracting States, the competent authorities of the Contracting States shall endeavour to settle the question by mutual agreement and determine the mode of application of the Agreement to such person. In the absence of such agreement, such person shall not be considered to be a resident of either Contracting State for enjoying benefits under the Agreement.

Article 5

PERMANENT ESTABLISHMENT

1. For the purposes of this Agreement, the term "permanent establishment" means a fixed place of business through which the business of an enterprise is wholly or partly carried on.

2. The term "permanent establishment" includes especially:

a) a place of management;
b) a branch;
c) an office;
d) a factory;
e) a workshop, and
f) a mine, an oil or gas well, a quarry or any other place of extraction of natural resources.

3. a) A building site or construction or installation project constitutes a permanent establishment only if it lasts more than six months;

b) activities carried on offshore in a Contracting State in connection with the exploration or exploitation of the sea bed and sub-soil and their natural resources situated in that State shall be deemed to be carried on through a permanent establishment situated in that State, if such activities are carried on for a period or periods exceeding in the aggregate 30 days in any twelve-month period.

4. Notwithstanding the preceding provisions of this Article, the term "permanent establishment" shall be deemed not to include:

a) the use of facilities solely for the purpose of storage, display or delivery of goods or merchandise belonging to the enterprise;

b) the maintenance of a stock of goods or merchandise belonging to the enterprise solely for the purpose of storage, display or delivery;

c) the maintenance of a stock of goods or merchandise belonging to the enterprise solely for the purpose of processing by another enterprise;

d) the maintenance of a fixed place of business solely for the purpose of purchasing goods or merchandise or of collecting information, for the enterprise;

e) the maintenance of a fixed place of business solely for the purpose of carrying on, for the enterprise, any other activity of a preparatory or auxiliary character;

f) the maintenance of a fixed place of business solely for any combination of activities mentioned in sub-paragraphs a) to e) of this paragraph, provided that the overall activity of the fixed place of business resulting from this combination is of a preparatory or auxiliary character.

5. Notwithstanding the provisions of paragraphs 1 and 2 of this Article, where a person - other than an agent of an independent status to whom paragraph 6 of this Article applies - is acting on behalf of an enterprise and has, and habitually exercises, in a Contracting State an authority to conclude contracts in the name of the enterprise, that enterprise shall be deemed to have a permanent establishment in that State in respect of any activities which that person undertakes for the enterprise, unless the activities of such person are limited to those mentioned in paragraph 4 of this Article which, if exercised through a fixed place of business, would not make this fixed place of business a permanent establishment under the provisions of that paragraph.

6. An enterprise shall not be deemed to have a permanent establishment in a Contracting State merely because it caries on business in that State through a broker, general commission agent or any other agent of an independent status, provided that such persons are acting in the ordinary course of their business.

7. The fact that a company which is a resident of a Contracting State controls or is controlled by a company which is a resident of the other Contracting State, or which carries on business in that other State (whether through a permanent establishment or otherwise), shall not of itself constitute either company a permanent establishment of the other.

Article 6

INCOME FROM IMMOVABLE PROPERTY

1. Income derived by a resident of a Contracting State from immovable property (including income from agriculture or forestry) situated in the other Contracting State may be taxed in that other State.

2. The term "immovable property" shall have the meaning which it has under the law of the Contracting State in which the property in question is situated. The term shall in any case include property accessory to immovable property, livestock and equipment used in agriculture and forestry, rights to which the provisions of general law respecting landed property apply, any option or similar right to acquire immovable property, usufruct of immovable property and rights to variable or fixed payments as consideration for the working of, or the right to work, mineral deposits, sources and other natural resources, rights to assets to be produced by the exploration or exploitation of the sea bed and sub-soil and their natural resources, including rights to interests in or to the benefit of such assets. Aircraft shall not be regarded as immovable property.

3. The provisions of paragraph 1 of this Article shall apply to income derived from the direct use, letting, or use in any other form of immovable property, as well as income from the alienation of immovable property.

4. Where the ownership of shares or other corporate rights in a company entitles the owner of such shares or corporate rights to the enjoyment of immovable property held by the company, the income from direct use, letting, or use in any other form of such right to enjoyment may be taxed in the Contracting State in which the immovable property is situated.

5. The provisions of paragraphs 1, 3 and 4 of this Article shall also apply to the income from immovable property of an enterprise and to income from immovable property used for the performance of independent personal services.

Article 7

BUSINESS PROFITS

1. The profits of an enterprise of a Contracting State shall be taxable only in that State unless the enterprise carries on business in the other Contracting State through a permanent establishment situated therein. If the enterprise carries on business as aforesaid, the profits of the enterprise may be taxed in the other State but only so much of them as is attributable to that permanent establishment.

2. Subject to the provisions of paragraph 3 of this Article, where an enterprise of a Contracting State carries on business in the other Contracting State through a permanent establishment situated therein, there shall in each Contracting State be attributed to that permanent establishment the profits which it might be expected to make if it were a distinct and separate enterprise engaged in the same or similar activities under the same or similar conditions and dealing wholly independently with the enterprise of which it is a permanent establishment.

3. In determining the profits of a permanent establishment, there shall be allowed as deductions expenses which are incurred for the purposes of the permanent establishment, including executive and general administrative expenses so incurred, whether in the State in which the permanent establishment is situated or elsewhere. However, no such deduction shall be allowed in respect of amounts, if any, paid (otherwise than towards reimbursement of actual expenses) by the permanent establishment to the enterprise or any of its offices, by way of royalties, fees or other similar payments in return for the use of patents or other rights, or by way of commission, for specific services performed or for management, or, except in case of a banking enterprise, by way of interest on moneys lent to the permanent establishment by the enterprise.

4. Insofar as it has been customary in a Contracting State to determine the profits to be attributed to a permanent establishment on the basis of an apportionment of the total profits of the enterprise to its various parts, nothing in paragraph 2 of this Article shall preclude that Contracting State from determining the profits to be taxed by such an apportionment as may be customary; the method of apportionment adopted shall, however, be such that the result shall be in accordance with the principles contained in this Article.

5. No profits shall be attributed to a permanent establishment by reason of the mere purchase by that permanent establishment of goods or merchandise for the enterprise.

6. For the purposes of the preceding paragraphs of this Article, the profits to be attributed to the permanent establishment shall be determined by the same method year by year unless there is good and sufficient reason to the contrary.

7. Where profits include items of income, which are dealt with separately in other Articles of this Agreement, then the provisions of those Articles shall not be affected by the provisions of this Article.

Article 8

AIR TRANSPORT

1. Profits of an enterprise of a Contracting State from the operation of aircraft in international traffic shall be taxable only in that State.

2. The provisions of paragraph 1 of this Article shall also apply to profits from the participation in a pool, a joint business or an international operating agency.

Article 9

ASSOCIATED ENTERPRISES

1. Where
   a) an enterprise of a Contracting State participates directly or indirectly in the management, control or capital of an enterprise of the other Contracting State, or

b) the same persons participate directly or indirectly in the management, control or capital of an enterprise of a Contracting State and an enterprise of the other Contracting State,

and in either case conditions are made or imposed between the two enterprises in their commercial or financial relations which differ from those which would be made between independent enterprises, then any profits which would, but for those conditions, have accrued to one of the enterprises, but, by reason of those conditions, have not so accrued, may be included in the profits of that enterprise and taxed accordingly.

2. Where a Contracting State includes in the profits of an enterprise of that State - and taxes accordingly - profits on which an enterprise of the other Contracting State has been charged to tax in that other State and the profits so included are profits which would have accrued to the enterprise of the first-mentioned State if the conditions made between the two enterprises had been those which would have been made between independent enterprises, then that other State shall make an appropriate adjustment to the amount of the tax charged therein on those profits. In determining such adjustment, due regard shall be had to the other provisions of this Agreement and the competent authorities of the Contracting States shall if necessary consult each other.

Article 10
DIVIDENDS

1. Dividends paid by a company which is a resident of a Contracting State to a resident of the other Contracting State may be taxed in that other State.

2. However, such dividends may also be taxed in the Contracting State of which the company paying the dividends is a resident and according to the laws of that State, but if the recipient is the beneficial owner of the dividends the tax so charged shall not exceed 10 per cent of the gross amount of the dividends.

This paragraph shall not affect the taxation of the company in respect of the profits out of which the dividends are paid.

3. The term "dividends" as used in this Article means income from shares or other rights, not being debt-claims, participating in profits, as well as income from other corporate rights which is subjected to the same taxation treatment as income from shares by the laws of the State of which the company making the distribution is a resident.

4. The provisions of paragraphs 1 and 2 of this Article shall not apply if the beneficial owner of the dividends, being a resident of a Contracting State, carries on business in the other Contracting State of which the company paying the dividends is a resident, through a permanent establishment situated therein, or performs in that other State independent personal services from a fixed base situated therein, and the holding in respect of which the dividends are paid is effectively connected with such permanent establishment or fixed base. In such case the provisions of Article 7 or Article 14 of this Agreement, as the case may be, shall apply.

5. Where a company which is a resident of a Contracting State derives profits or income from the other Contracting State, that other State may not impose any tax on the dividends paid by the company, except insofar as such dividends are paid to a resident of that other State or insofar as the holding in respect of which the dividends are paid is effectively connected with a permanent establishment or a fixed base situated in that other State, nor subject the company's undistributed profits to a tax on the company's undistributed profits, even if the dividends paid or the undistributed profits consist wholly or partly of profits or income arising in such other State.

Article 11
INTEREST

1. Interest arising in a Contracting State and paid to a resident of the other Contracting State may be taxed in that other State.

2. However, such interest may also be taxed in the Contracting State in which it arises and according to the laws of that State, but if the recipient is the beneficial owner of the interest the tax so charged shall not exceed 10 per cent of the gross amount of the interest.

3. Notwithstanding the provisions of paragraph 2 of this Article interest arising in a Contracting State, derived and beneficially owned by the Government of the other Contracting State, including political subdivisions and local authorities thereof, the Central (National) Bank or any financial institution wholly owned by that Government, or interest derived on loans guaranteed by that Government shall be exempt from tax in the first-mentioned State.

4. The term "interest" as used in this Article means income from debt-claims of every kind, whether or not secured by mortgage, and in particular, income from government securities and income from bonds or debentures, including premiums and prizes attaching to such securities, bonds or debentures. Penalty charges for late payment shall not be regarded as interest for the purpose of this Article.

5. The provisions of paragraphs 1, 2 and 3 of this Article shall not apply if the beneficial owner of the interest, being a resident of a Contracting State, carries on business in the other Contracting State in which the interest arises, through a permanent establishment situated therein, or performs in that other State independent personal services from a fixed base situated therein, and the debt-claims in respect of which the interest is paid is effectively connected with such permanent establishment or fixed base. In such case the provisions of Article 7 or Article 14 of this Agreement, as the case may be, shall apply.

6. Interest shall be deemed to arise in a Contracting State when the payer is a resident of that State. Where, however, the person paying the interest, whether he is a resident of a Contracting State or not, has in a Contracting State a permanent establishment or a fixed base in connection with which the indebtedness on which the interest is paid was incurred, and such interest is borne by such permanent establishment or fixed base, then such interest shall be deemed to arise in the State in which the permanent establishment or fixed base is situated.

7. Where, by reason of a special relationship between the payer and the beneficial owner or between both of them and some other person, the amount of the interest, having regard to the debt-claim for which it is paid, exceeds the amount which would have been agreed upon by the payer and the beneficial owner in the absence of such relationship, the provisions of this Article shall apply only to the last-mentioned amount. In such case, the excess part of the payments shall remain taxable according to the laws of each Contracting State, due regard being had to the other provisions of this Agreement.

Article 12

ROYALTIES

1. Royalties arising in a Contracting State and paid to a resident of the other Contracting State may be taxed in that other State.

2. However, such royalties may also be taxed in the Contracting State in which they arise and according to the laws of that State, but if the recipient is the beneficial owner of the royalties, the tax so charged shall not exceed 10 per cent of the gross amount of the royalties.

3. The term "royalties" as used in this Article means payments of any kind received as a consideration for the use of, or the right to use, any copyright of literary, artistic or scientific work including cinematograph films and films or tapes for radio or television broad-casting, any patent, trade mark, design or model, plan, secret formula or process, or for the use of, or the right to use industrial, commercial or scientific equipment, or for information concerning industrial, commercial or scientific experience.

4. The provisions of paragraphs 1 and 2 of this Article shall not apply if the beneficial owner of the royalties, being a resident of a Contracting State, carries on business in the other Contracting State in which the royalties arise, through a permanent establishment situated therein, or performs in that other State independent personal services from a fixed base situated therein, and the right or property in respect of which the royalties are paid is effectively connected with such permanent establishment or fixed base. In such case the provisions of Article 7 or Article 14 of this Agreement, as the case may be, shall apply.

5. Royalties shall be deemed to arise in a Contracting State when the payer is a resident of that State. Where, however, the person paying the royalties, whether he is a resident of a Contracting State or not, has in a Contracting State a permanent establishment or a fixed base in connection with which the liability to pay the royalties was incurred, and such royalties are borne by such permanent establishment or fixed base, then such royalties shall be deemed to arise in the State in which the permanent establishment or fixed base is situated.

6. Where, by reason of a special relationship between the payer and the beneficial owner or between both of them and some other person, the amount of the royalties, having regard to the use, right or information for which they are paid, exceeds the amount which would have been agreed upon by the payer and the beneficial owner in the absence of such relationship, the provisions of this Article shall apply only to the last-mentioned amount. In such case, the excess part of the payments shall remain taxable according to the laws of each Contracting State, due regard being had to the other provisions of this Agreement.

Article 13
CAPITAL GAINS

1. Gains derived by a resident of a Contracting State from the alienation of immovable property referred to in Article 6 of this Agreement and situated in the other Contracting State or shares in a company the assets of which consist mainly of such property may be taxed in that other State.

2. Gains from the alienation of movable property forming part of the business property of a permanent establishment which an enterprise of a Contracting State has in the other Contracting State or of movable property pertaining to a fixed base available to a resident of a Contracting State in the other Contracting State for the purpose of performing independent personal services, including such gains from the alienation of such a permanent establishment (alone or with the whole enterprise) or of such fixed base, may be taxed in that other State.

3. Gains derived by an enterprise of a Contracting State from the alienation of aircraft operated in international traffic by that enterprise or movable property pertaining to the operation of such aircraft, shall be taxable only in that State.

4. Gains from the alienation of any property other than that referred to in paragraphs 1, 2 and 3 of this Article, shall be taxable only in the Contracting State of which the alienator is a resident.

Article 14

INDEPENDENT PERSONAL SERVICES

1. Income derived by an individual who is a resident of a Contracting State in respect of professional services or other activities of an independent character shall be taxable only in that State unless he has a fixed base regularly available to him in the other Contracting State for the purpose of performing his activities. If he has such a fixed base, the income may be taxed in the other Contracting State but only so much of it as is attributable to that fixed base. For this purpose, where an individual who is a resident of a Contracting State stays in the other Contracting State for a period or periods exceeding in the aggregate 183 days in any twelve-month period commencing or ending in the fiscal year concerned, he shall be deemed to have a fixed base regularly available to him in that other State and the income that is derived from his activities referred to above that are performed in that other State shall be attributable to that fixed base.

2. The term "professional services" includes especially independent scientific, literary, artistic, educational or teaching activities as well as the independent activities of physicians, lawyers, engineers, architects, dentists and accountants.

Article 15

DEPENDENT PERSONAL SERVICES

1. Subject to the provisions of Articles 16, 18 and 19 of this Agreement, salaries, wages and other similar remuneration derived by a resident of a Contracting State in respect of an employment shall be taxable only in that State unless the employment is exercised in the other Contracting State. If the employment is so exercised, such remuneration as is derived therefrom may be taxed in that other State.

2. Notwithstanding the provisions of paragraph 1 of this Article, remuneration derived by a resident of a Contracting State in respect of an employment exercised in the other Contracting State shall be taxable only in the first-mentioned State if:

a) the recipient is present in the other State for a period or periods not exceeding in the aggregate 183 days in any twelve month period commencing or ending in the fiscal year concerned, and

b) the remuneration is paid by, or on behalf of, an employer who is not a resident of the other State, and

c) the remuneration is not borne by a permanent establishment or a fixed base which the employer has in the other State.

3. Notwithstanding the preceding provisions of this Article, remuneration derived in respect of an employment exercised aboard an aircraft operated in international traffic by an enterprise of a Contracting State may be taxed in that State.

Article 16
DIRECTORS' FEES

Directors' fees and other similar payments derived by a resident of a Contracting State in his capacity as a member of the board of directors or any other similar organ of a company which is a resident of the other Contracting State may be taxed in that other State.

Article 17
ARTISTES AND SPORTSMEN

1. Notwithstanding the provisions of Articles 14 and 15 of this Agreement, income derived by a resident of a Contracting State as an entertainer, such as a theatre, motion picture, radio or television artiste, or a musician, or as a sportsman, from his personal activities as such exercised in the other Contracting State, may be taxed in that other State.

2. Where income in respect of personal activities exercised by an entertainer or a sportsman in his capacity as such accrues not to the entertainer or sportsman himself but to another person, that income may, notwithstanding the provisions of Articles 7, 14 and 15 of this Agreement, be taxed in the Contracting State in which the activities of the entertainer or sportsman are exercised.

3. The provisions of paragraphs 1 and 2 of this Article shall not apply to income derived from activities exercised in a Contracting State by an entertainer or a sportsman if the visit to that State is wholly or mainly supported by public funds of one or both of the Contracting States or their political subdivisions or local authorities thereof. In such case, the income shall be taxable only in the Contracting State of which the entertainer or sportsman is a resident.

Article 18

PENSIONS

Subject to the provisions of paragraph 2 of Article 19 of this Agreement, pensions and other similar remuneration paid to a resident of a Contracting State in consideration of past employment shall be taxable only in that State.

Article 19

GOVERNMENT SERVICE

1. a) Salaries, wages and other similar remuneration, other than a pension, paid by a Contracting State or a political subdivision or a local authority thereof to an individual in respect of services rendered to that State, subdivision or authority shall be taxable only in that State.

b) However, such salaries, wages and other similar remuneration shall be taxable only in the other Contracting State if the services are rendered in that State and the individual is a resident of that State who:

(i) is a national of that State; or

(ii) did not become a resident of that State solely for the purpose of rendering the services.

2. a) Any pension paid by, or out of funds created by, a Contracting State or a political subdivision or a local authority thereof to an individual in respect of services rendered to that State, subdivision or authority shall be taxable only in that State.

b) However, such pension shall be taxable only in the other Contracting State if the individual is a resident of, and a national of, that State.

3. The provisions of Articles 15, 16 and 18 of this Agreement shall apply to salaries, wages and other similar remuneration, and to pensions, in respect of services rendered in connection with a business carried on by a Contracting State or a political subdivision or a local authority thereof.

Article 20
STUDENTS

Payments which a student, an apprentice or a trainee who is or was immediately before visiting a Contracting State a resident of the other Contracting State and who is present in the first-mentioned State solely for the purpose of his education or training receives for the purpose of his maintenance, education or training shall not be taxed in that State, provided that such payments arise from sources outside that State.

Article 21
OTHER INCOME

1. Items of income of a resident of a Contracting State, wherever arising, not dealt with in the foregoing Articles of this Agreement shall be taxable only in that State.

2. The provisions of paragraph 1 of this Article shall not apply to income, other than income from immovable property as defined in paragraph 2 of Article 6 of this Agreement, if the recipient of such income, being a resident of a Contracting State, carries on business in the other Contracting State through a permanent establishment situated therein, or performs in that other State independent personal services from a fixed base situated therein, and the right or property in respect of which the income is paid is effectively connected with such permanent establishment or fixed base. In such case the provisions of Article 7 or Article 14 of this Agreement, as the case may be, shall apply.

Article 22
CAPITAL

1. Capital represented by immovable property referred to in Article 6 of this Agreement, owned by a resident of a Contracting State and situated in the other Contracting State, may be taxed in that other State.

2. Capital represented by movable property forming part of the business property of a permanent establishment which an enterprise of a Contracting State has in the other Contracting State or by movable property pertaining to a fixed base available to a resident of a Contracting State in the other Contracting State for the purpose of performing independent personal services, may be taxed in that other State.

3. Capital represented by aircraft operated in international traffic by an enterprise of a Contracting State and by movable property pertaining to the operation of such aircraft, shall be taxable only in that State.

4. All other elements of capital of a resident of a Contracting State shall be taxable only in that State.

Article 23

ELIMINATION OF DOUBLE TAXATION

1. In the case of a resident of the Republic of Moldova double taxation shall be avoided as follows: where a resident of the Republic of Moldova derives income or owns capital, which in accordance with the provisions of this Agreement, may be taxed in Latvia, the Republic of Moldova shall allow:

a) as a deduction from the tax on income of that resident, an amount equal to the income tax paid in Latvia;

b) as a deduction from the tax on the capital of that resident, an amount equal to the capital tax paid in Latvia.

Such deduction, in either case shall not, however, exceed that part of the income tax or capital tax in the Republic of Moldova, as computed before the deduction is given, which is attributable, as the case may be, to the income or capital which may be taxed in Latvia.

2. In the case of resident of Latvia, double taxation shall be avoided as follows:

a) where a resident of Latvia derives income or owns capital which, in accordance with this Agreement, may be taxed in the Republic of Moldova, unless a more favourable treatment is provided in its domestic law, Latvia shall allow:

(i) as a deduction from the tax on the income of that resident, an amount equal to the income tax paid thereon in the Republic of Moldova;

(ii) as a deduction from the tax on the capital of that resident, an amount equal to the capital tax paid thereon in the Republic of Moldova.

Such deduction in either case shall not, however, exceed that part of the income or capital tax in Latvia, as computed before the deduction is given, which is attributable, as the case may be, to the income or the capital which may be taxed in the Republic of Moldova.

b) For the purposes of subparagraph a) of this paragraph, where a company that is a resident of Latvia receives a dividend from a company that is a resident of the Republic of Moldova in which it owns at least 10 per cent of its shares having full voting rights, the tax paid in the Republic of Moldova shall include not only the tax paid on dividend, but also the tax paid on the underlying profits of the company out of which the dividend was paid.

Article 24

NON-DISCRIMINATION

1. Nationals of a Contracting State shall not be subjected in the other Contracting State to any taxation or any requirement connected therewith, which is other or more burdensome than the taxation and connected requirements to which nationals of that other State in the same circumstances, in particular with respect to residence, are or may be subjected. This provision shall, notwithstanding the provisions of Article 1 of this Agreement, also apply to persons who are not residents of one or both of the Contracting States.

2. Stateless persons who are residents of a Contracting State shall not be subjected in either Contracting State to any taxation or any requirement connected therewith, which is other or more burdensome than the taxation and connected requirements to which nationals of the State concerned in the same circumstances are or may be subjected.

3. The taxation on a permanent establishment which an enterprise of a Contracting State has in the other Contracting State shall not be less favourably levied in that other State than the taxation levied on enterprises of that other State carrying on the same activities. This provision shall not be construed as obliging a Contracting State to grant to residents of the other Contracting State any personal allowances, reliefs and reductions for taxation purposes on account of civil status or family responsibilities which it grants to its own residents.

4. Except where the provisions of paragraph 1 of Article 9, paragraph 7 of Article 11, or paragraph 6 of Article 12 of this Agreement, apply, interest, royalties and other disbursements paid by an enterprise of a Contracting State to a resident of the other Contracting State shall, for the purpose of determining the taxable profits of such enterprise, be deductible under the same conditions as if they had been paid to a resident of the first-mentioned State. Similarly, any debts of an enterprise of a Contracting State to a resident of the other Contracting State shall, for the purpose of determining the taxable capital of such enterprise, be deductible under the same conditions as if they had been contracted to a resident of the first-mentioned State.

5. Enterprises of a Contracting State, the capital of which is wholly or partly owned or controlled, directly or indirectly, by one or more residents of the other Contracting State, shall not be subjected in the first-mentioned State to any taxation or any requirement connected therewith which is other or more burdensome than the taxation and connected requirements to which other similar enterprises of the first-mentioned State are or may be subjected.

6. The provisions of this Article shall, notwithstanding the provisions of Article 2 of this Agreement, apply to taxes of every kind and description.

Article 25

MUTUAL AGREEMENT PROCEDURE

1. Where a person considers that the actions of one or both of the Contracting States result or will result for him in taxation not in accordance with the provisions of this Agreement, he may, irrespective of the remedies provided by the domestic law of those States, present his case to the competent authority of the Contracting State of which he is a resident or, if his case comes under paragraph 1 of Article 24, to that of the Contracting State of which he is a national. The case must be presented within three years from the first notification of the action resulting in taxation not in accordance with the provisions of the Agreement.

2. The competent authority shall endeavour, if the objection appears to it to be justified and if it is not itself able to arrive at a satisfactory solution, to resolve the case by mutual agreement with the competent authority of the other Contracting State, with a view to the avoidance of taxation which is not in accordance with the Agreement. Any agreement reached shall be implemented notwithstanding any time limits in the domestic law of the Contracting States.

3. The competent authorities of the Contracting States shall endeavour to resolve by mutual agreement any difficulties or doubts arising as to the interpretation or application of this Agreement. They may also consult together for the elimination of double taxation in cases not provided for in the Agreement.

4. The competent authorities of the Contracting States may communicate with each other directly for the purpose of reaching an agreement in the sense of the preceding paragraphs.

Article 26
EXCHANGE OF INFORMATION

1. The competent authorities of the Contracting States shall exchange such information as is necessary for carrying out the provisions of this Agreement or of the domestic laws of the Contracting States concerning taxes covered by the Agreement insofar as the taxation thereunder is not contrary to the Agreement. The exchange of information is not restricted by Article 1. Any information received by a Contracting State shall be treated as secret in the same manner as information obtained under the domestic laws of that State and shall be disclosed only to persons or authorities (including courts and administrative bodies) involved in the assessment or collection of, the enforcement or prosecution in respect of, or the determination of appeals in relation to, the taxes covered by the Agreement. Such persons or authorities shall use the information only for such purposes. They may disclose the information in public court proceedings or in judicial decisions.

2. In no case shall the provisions of paragraph 1 of this Article be construed so as to impose on a Contracting State the obligation:

a) to carry out administrative measures at variance with the laws and administrative practice of that or of the other Contracting State;

b) to supply information which is not obtainable under the laws or in the normal course of the administration of that or of the other Contracting State;

c) to supply information which would disclose any trade, business, industrial, commercial or professional secret or trade process, or information, the disclosure of which would be contrary to public policy (ordre public).

Article 27

MEMBERS OF DIPLOMATIC MISSIONS AND CONSULAR POSTS

Nothing in this Agreement shall affect the fiscal privileges of members of diplomatic missions or consular posts under the general rules of international law or under the provisions of special agreements.

Article 28

ENTRY INTO FORCE

1. The Contracting States shall notify each other through diplomatic channels that their constitutional requirements for the entry into force of this Agreement have been complied with.

2. This Agreement shall enter into force on the date of the later of the notifications referred to in paragraph 1 of this Article and its provisions shall have effect in both Contracting States:

a) in respect of taxes withheld at source, on income derived on or after the first day of January in the calendar year next following the year in which the Agreement enters into force;

b) in respect of other taxes on income and taxes on capital, for taxes chargeable for any fiscal year beginning on or after the first day of January in the calendar year next following the year in which the Agreement enters into force.

Article 29
TERMINATION

This Agreement shall remain in force until terminated by one of the Contracting States. Either Contracting State may terminate the Agreement, through diplomatic channels, by giving written notice of termination at least six months before the end of any calendar year. In such event, the Agreement shall cease to have effect in both Contracting States:

a) in respect of taxes withheld at source, on income derived on or after the first day of January in the calendar year next following the year in which the notice has been given;

b) in respect of other taxes on income and taxes on capital, for taxes chargeable for any fiscal year beginning on or after the first day of January in the calendar year next following the year in which the notice has been given.

In witness whereof, the undersigned, duly authorised thereto, have signed this Agreement.

Done in duplicate at ....Riga.......... this ...25th...... day of ...February............... 1998........., in the Latvian, Moldovan and English languages, all three texts being equally authentic. In the case of divergence of interpretation the English text shall prevail.

For the Government of the Republic of Latvia

For the Government of the Republic of Moldova

[TEXT IN LATVIAN – TEXTE EN LETTON]

LATVIJAS REPUBLIKAS VALDĪBAS UN MOLDOVAS REPUBLIKAS VALDĪBAS

LĪGUMS

PAR NODOKĻU DUBULTĀS UZLIKŠANAS UN NODOKĻU

NEMAKSĀŠANAS NOVĒRŠANU ATTIECĪBĀ UZ IENĀKUMA

UN KAPITĀLA NODOKĻIEM

Latvijas Republikas valdība un Moldovas Republikas valdība, apliecinādamas vēlēšanos noslēgt Līgumu par nodokļu dubultās uzlikšanas un nodokļu nemaksāšanas novēršanu attiecībā uz ienākuma un kapitāla nodokļiem,

vienojas:

1.pants
Līguma darbības sfēra

Šis Līgums attiecas uz personām, kas ir vienas Līgumslēdzējas Valsts vai abu Līgumslēdzēju Valstu rezidenti.

2.pants
Nodokļi, uz kuriem attiecas Līgums

1. Šis Līgums attiecas uz ienākuma un kapitāla nodokļiem, ko neatkarīgi no to iekasēšanas veida iekasē Līgumslēdzējas Valsts vai arī tās politiski administratīvo vienību vai pašvaldību vārdā.

2. Par ienākuma un kapitāla nodokļiem uzskatāmi visi nodokļi, ar kuriem apliek kopējo ienākumu, kopējo kapitālu vai ienākuma vai kapitāla daļu, arī nodoklis, ar kuru apliek kustamā vai nekustamā īpašuma atsavināšanas rezultātā gūto ienākumu un kapitāla vērtības pieaugumu.

3. Esošie nodokļi, uz kuriem attiecas šis Līgums, konkrēti ir šādi:

a) Moldovas Republikā:
(i) uzņēmumu ienākuma nodoklis;
(ii) fizisko personu ienākuma nodoklis;
(iii) nekustamā īpašuma nodoklis;
(turpmāk - Moldovas nodokļi);

b) Latvijā:
(i) uzņēmumu ienākuma nodoklis;
(ii) iedzīvotāju ienākuma nodoklis;
(iii) īpašuma nodoklis;
(turpmāk — Latvijas nodokļi).

4. Šis Līgums tiks piemērots arī visiem identiskiem vai pēc būtības līdzīgiem nodokļiem, kuri tiks ieviesti Līgumslēdzējā Valstī pēc šī Līguma parakstīšanas datuma, papildinot vai aizstājot esošos nodokļus. Abu Līgumslēdzēju Valstu kompetentajām iestādēm ir savstarpēji jāinformē vienai otra par jebkuriem būtiskiem grozījumiem šo valstu nodokļu likumdošanas aktos.

3.pants.
Vispārīgās definīcijas

1. Ja no konteksta neizriet citādi, šajā Līgumā:

a) jēdziens "Moldovas Republika" nozimē Moldovas Republiku, un, lietots ģeogrāfiskā nozimē, tas apzimē Moldovas teritoriju, kas ietver iekšzemes ūdeņus, gaisa telpu, kurā saskaņā ar starptautisko tiesību normām Moldovas Republika realizē savas suverēnās tiesības izstrādāt minerālos un dabas resursus;

b) jēdziens "Latvija" nozimē Latvijas Republiku, un, lietots ģeogrāfiskā nozimē, tas apzimē Latvijas Republikas teritoriju un jebkuru citu Latvijas Republikas teritoriālajiem ūdeņiem piegulošu teritoriju, kurā saskaņā ar Latvijas likumdošanas aktiem un starptautiskajām tiesībām var tikt istenotas Latvijas tiesības uz jūras un zemes dzilēm un tur esošajiem dabas resursiem;

c) jēdzieni "Ligumslēdzēja Valsts" un "otra Ligumslēdzēja Valsts" atkaribā no konteksta apzimē Latviju vai Moldovas Republiku;

d) jēdziens "persona" apzimē fizisko personu, sabiedribu un jebkuru citu personu kopumu;

e) jēdziens "sabiedriba" apzimē jebkuru apvienotu veidojumu vai jebkuru vienibu, kas nodokļu aplikšanas nolūkos tiek uzskatita par apvienotu veidojumu;

f) jēdzieni "Ligumslēdzējas Valsts uzņēmums" un "otras Ligumslēdzējas Valsts uzņēmums" attiecigi apzimē uzņēmumu, ko vada Ligumslēdzējas Valsts rezidents, un uzņēmumu, ko vada otras Ligumslēdzējas Valsts rezidents;

g) jēdziens "starptautiskā satiksme" apzimē jebkurus pārvadājumus ar gaisa transportu, ko veic Ligumslēdzējas Valsts uzņēmums, izņemot tos gadijumus, kad gaisa transporta lidzekļi pārvietojas vienigi otras Ligumslēdzējas Valsts iekšienē;

h) jēdziens "kompetentās iestādes" apzimē:
(i) Moldovas Republikā - Finansu ministru vai viņa pilnvaroto pārstāvi;
(ii) Latvijā - Finansu ministru vai viņa pilnvaroto pārstāvi;

i) jēdziens "pilsonis" apzimē:
(i) jebkuru fizisko personu, kas ir Ligumslēdzējas Valsts pilsonis;
(ii) jebkuru juridisko personu, ligumsabiedribu vai asociāciju, kuras statuss izriet no Ligumslēdzējā Valsti spēkā esošajiem likumdošanas aktiem.

2. Piemērojot šo Ligumu, Ligumslēdzēja Valsts lietos jebkuru jēdzienu, kas šeit nav definēts, tikai tādā nozimē, ja vien no konteksta neizriet citādi, kādā tas lietots šis Ligumslēdzējas Valsts likumdošanas aktos attiecibā uz nodokļiem, uz kuriem attiecas šis Ligums.

4.pants
Rezidents

1. Šajā Līgumā jēdziens "Līgumslēdzējas Valsts rezidents" apzīmē jebkuru personu, kas saskaņā ar šīs valsts likumdošanas aktiem ir pakļauta aplikšanai ar nodokļiem, pamatojoties uz tās pastāvīgo dzīvesvietu, rezidenci, faktiskās vadības atrašanās vietu, inkorporācijas (reģistrācijas) vietu vai jebkuru citu līdzīga rakstura kritēriju. Jēdziens ietver arī šīs valsts valdību, tās politiski administratīvās vienības un pašvaldības. Bet šis jēdziens neietver personas, kurām tiek uzlikti nodokļi šajā valstī tikai attiecībā uz to ienākumiem no šajā valstī esošajiem avotiem vai izvietotā kapitāla.

2. Ja saskaņā ar šī panta 1.punkta noteikumiem fiziskā persona ir abu Līgumslēdzēju Valstu rezidents, tās statuss tiks noteikts šādā veidā:

a) šī persona tiks uzskatīta par rezidentu tajā valstī, kurā atrodas tās pastāvīgā dzīvesvieta; ja tās pastāvīgā dzīvesvieta ir abās valstīs, šī persona tiks uzskatīta par tās valsts rezidentu, ar kuru tai ir ciešākas personiskās vai ekonomiskās attiecības (vitālo interešu centrs);

b) ja nav iespējams noteikt valsti, kurā šai personai ir vitālo interešu centrs, vai arī ja tai nav pastāvīgas dzīvesvietas nevienā no abām valstīm, šī persona tiks uzskatīta par tās valsts rezidentu, kura tai ir ierastā mītnes zeme;

c) ja šai personai ierastā mītnes zeme ir abas valstis vai nav neviena no tām, tā tiks uzskatīta par tās valsts rezidentu, kuras pilsonis ir šī persona;

d) ja šī persona ir pilsonis abās valstīs vai nevienā no šīm valstīm, tad Līgumslēdzēju Valstu kompetentās iestādes izšķir šo jautājumu, savstarpēji vienojoties.

3. Ja saskaņā ar šī panta 1.punkta nosacījumiem persona, kas nav fiziskā persona, ir abu Līgumslēdzēju Valstu rezidents, Līgumslēdzēju Valstu kompetentām iestādēm jācenšas izšķirt šo jautājumu, savstarpēji vienojoties, un noteikt šī Līguma piemērošanas veidu šādai personai. Ja šāda vienošanās nav tikusi panākta, šāda persona netiks uzskatīta ne par vienas Līgumslēdzējas Valsts rezidentu, kas varētu baudīt šī Līguma priekšrocības.

5.pants
Pastāvīgā pārstāvniecība

1. Šajā Līgumā jēdziens "pastāvīgā pārstāvniecība" nozīmē noteiktu vietu, kur uzņēmumi pilnīgi vai daļēji veic uzņēmējdarbību.

2. Jēdziens "pastāvīgā pārstāvniecība" ietver:

a) uzņēmuma vadības atrašanās vietu;

b) filiāli;

c) kantori;

d) fabriku;

e) darbnīcu;

f) šahtu, naftas vai gāzes ieguves vietu, akmeņlauztuves vai jebkuru citu dabas resursu ieguves vietu.

3. a) Būvlaukums vai montāžas vai instalācijas projekts tiks uzskatīts par pastāvīgo pārstāvniecību tikai tad, ja tas ilgst vairāk nekā sešus mēnešus;

b) darbība Līgumslēdzējas Valsts šelfa zonā, kas saistīta ar šīs valsts jūras un zemes dziļu un tur esošo dabas resursu pētīšanu un izmantošanu, tiks uzskatīta par tādu darbību, kas veikta, izmantojot šajā valstī esošo pastāvīgo pārstāvniecību, ja šādas darbības ilgums pārsniedz laika posmu, vai laika posmus, kopumā 30 dienas jebkurā 12 mēnešu ilgā periodā.

4. Neatkarīgi no šī panta iepriekšējo punktu noteikumiem jēdziens "pastāvīgā pārstāvniecība" neietver:

a) ēku un iekārtu izmantošanu tikai un vienīgi uzņēmumam piederošo preču vai izstrādājumu uzglabāšanai, demonstrēšanai vai piegādēm;

b) uzņēmumam piederošos preču vai izstrādājumu krājumus, kas paredzēti tikai un vienīgi uzglabāšanai, demonstrēšanai vai piegādēm;

c) uzņēmumam piederošos preču vai izstrādājumu krājumus, kas paredzēti tikai un vienīgi pārstrādei citā uzņēmumā;

d) pastāvīgu darbības vietu, kas paredzēta tikai un vienīgi preču vai izstrādājumu iepirkšanai vai informācijas vākšanai uzņēmuma vajadzībām;

e) pastāvīgu darbības vietu, kas paredzēta tikai un vienīgi tam, lai veiktu uzņēmuma labā jebkurus citus priekšdarbus vai palīgdarbību;

f) pastāvīgu darbības vietu, kas paredzēta tikai un vienīgi tam, lai veiktu šī punkta no "a" līdz "e" apakšpunktā minētās darbības jebkurā kombinācijā, ar nosacījumu, ka kopējam darbības veidam ir priekšdarbu vai palīgdarbības raksturs.

5. Neatkarīgi no šī panta 1. un 2. punkta noteikumiem, ja persona, uz kuru neattiecas šī panta 6. punktā minētais neatkarīgā aģenta statuss, darbojas uzņēmuma labā un parasti izmanto tai piešķirtās pilnvaras noslēgt līgumus šī uzņēmuma vārdā Līgumslēdzējā Valstī, tiks uzskatīts, ka šim uzņēmumam ir pastāvīgā pārstāvniecība šajā valstī attiecībā uz jebkuru šīs personas veikto darbību uzņēmuma labā šajā valstī, izņemot gadījumus, kad pastāvīgo darbības vietu, kuru izmanto šī persona, veicot šī panta 4.punktā minēto darbību, nevar uzskatīt par pastāvīgo pārstāvniecību saskaņā ar šī panta 4. punkta noteikumiem.

6. Tiks uzskatīts, ka uzņēmumam nav pastāvīgās pārstāvniecības Līgumslēdzējā Valstī, ja uzņēmums veic uzņēmējdarbību šajā valstī, vienīgi izmantojot starpnieku, tirdzniecības aģentu vai jebkuru citu neatkarīgu aģentu, ar nosacījumu, ka šīs personas veic savu parasto uzņēmējdarbību.

7. Fakts, ka sabiedrība — Līgumslēdzējas Valsts rezidents kontrolē sabiedrību, kura ir otras Līgumslēdzējas Valsts rezidents vai kura veic uzņēmējdarbību šajā otrā valstī (izmantojot pastāvīgo pārstāvniecību vai kādā citā veidā), vai ir pakļauta šādas sabiedrības kontrolei, pats par sevi nepārvērš vienu no šīm sabiedrībām par otras sabiedrības pastāvīgo pārstāvniecību.

6.pants
Ienākums no nekustamā īpašuma

1. Ienākumus, ko gūst Līgumslēdzējas Valsts rezidents no nekustamā īpašuma (arī ienākumus no lauksaimniecības un mežkopības), kas atrodas otrā Līgumslēdzējā Valstī, var aplikt ar nodokļiem šajā otrā valstī.

2. Jēdzienam "nekustamais īpašums" būs tāda nozīme, kāda tam ir tās Līgumslēdzējas Valsts likumdošanas aktos, kurā atrodas minētais īpašums. Jebkurā gadījumā šis jēdziens nozīmēs īpašumu, kas ir piederīgs nekustamajam īpašumam, mājlopus un iekārtas, ko izmanto lauksaimniecībā un mežkopībā, tiesības, kuras vispārējā likumdošanā ir attiecināmas uz īpašumu, kas atrodas uz zemes, jebkuras nekustamā īpašuma pirkšanas un pārdošanas tiesību izmantošanas tiesības, vai līdzīgas tiesības iegūt nekustamo īpašumu, nekustamā īpašuma uzufruktu un tiesības uz mainīga lieluma vai pastāvīgiem maksājumiem par tiesībām izmantot vai par derīgo izrakteņu, avotu un citu dabas resursu izmantošanu, tiesības uz īpašumu, kas var tikt radīts, veicot jūras un zemes dziļu un tur esošo dabas resursu pētīšanu un izmantošanu, ieskaitot tiesības uz līdzdalību īpašumā vai peļņā, kuru var gūt šis īpašums. Par nekustamo īpašumu netiks uzskatītas lidmašīnas.

3. Šī panta 1. punkta noteikumi tiks piemēroti attiecībā uz ienākumu no nekustamā īpašuma tiešas izmantošanas, izīrēšanas vai izmantošanas citā veidā, kā arī attiecībā uz ienākumu, ko iegūst, atsavinot nekustamo īpašumu.

4. Ja sabiedrības akcijas vai citas tiesības dod to īpašniekam tiesības uz sabiedrības nekustamā īpašuma izmantošanu, tad ienākumu no šo tiesību tiešas izmantošanas, iznomāšanas vai lietošanas jebkādā citā veidā var aplikt ar nodokļiem tajā Līgumslēdzējā Valstī, kurā atrodas šis nekustamais īpašums.

5. Šī panta 1., 3. un 4. punkta noteikumi tiks piemēroti arī attiecībā uz ienākumu no uzņēmuma nekustamā īpašuma, kā arī attiecībā uz ienākumu no nekustamā īpašuma, kas tiek izmantots neatkarīgu individuālu pakalpojumu sniegšanai.

7.pants
Uzņēmējdarbības peļņa

1. Līgumslēdzējas Valsts uzņēmuma peļņa tiks aplikta ar nodokļiem tikai šajā valstī, izņemot gadījumus, kad uzņēmums veic uzņēmējdarbību otrā Līgumslēdzējā Valstī, izmantojot tur esošo pastāvīgo pārstāvniecību. Ja uzņēmums veic uzņēmējdarbību minētajā veidā, uzņēmuma peļņu var aplikt ar nodokļiem otrā valstī, bet tikai to peļņas daļu, kas attiecas uz šo pastāvīgo pārstāvniecību.

2. Saskaņā ar šī panta 3. punkta noteikumiem, ja Līgumslēdzējas Valsts uzņēmums veic uzņēmējdarbību otrā Līgumslēdzējā Valstī, izmantojot tur esošo pastāvīgo pārstāvniecību, katrā Līgumslēdzējā Valstī uz šo pastāvīgo pārstāvniecību attiecināms tāds peļņas daudzums, kādu šī pārstāvniecība varētu gūt, ja nepārprotami būtu atsevišķs uzņēmums, kas veic vienādu vai līdzīgu uzņēmējdarbību vienādos vai līdzīgos apstākļos un darbojas pilnīgi neatkarīgi no šī uzņēmuma.

3. Nosakot pastāvīgās pārstāvniecības peļņu, tiks pieļauta pastāvīgās pārstāvniecības izdevumu atskaitīšana no summas, kuru apliek ar nodokļiem. Šie izdevumi var būt pārstāvniecības operatīvie un vispārējie administratīvie izdevumi, kas radušies vai nu valstī, kur atrodas pastāvīgā pārstāvniecība, vai citur. Tomēr šādi atskaitījumi netiks atļauti attiecībā uz maksājumiem, kurus pastāvīgā pārstāvniecība izmaksā (kuri ir citādi kā faktisko izdevumu atmaksa) uzņēmumam vai jebkurai citai tā daļai, kā autoratlīdzības, maksas vai cita veida līdzīgus maksājumus par patentu vai citu tiesību izmantošanu, vai kā komisijas maksu par īpašu pakalpojumu sniegšanu vai vadības pakalpojumiem vai, izņemot uzņēmumu - banku procentu maksājumus, par naudas summām, kuras pastāvīgajai pārstāvniecībai ir aizdevis uzņēmums.

4. Ja Līgumslēdzējā Valstī peļņu, kas attiecināma uz pastāvīgo pārstāvniecību, nosaka, uzņēmuma kopīgo peļņu proporcionāli sadalot starp tā struktūrvienībām, šī panta 2.punkts neaizliedz Līgumslēdzējai Valstij kā parasti noteikt apliekamās peļņas daļu pēc šī principa; tomēr šī sadales metode jālieto tā, lai rezultāts atbilstu šajā pantā ietvertajiem principiem.

5. Uz pastāvīgo pārstāvniecību netiks attiecināta peļņa tikai tāpēc vien, ka tā ir iegādājusies sava uzņēmuma vajadzībām preces vai izstrādājumus.

6. Lai piemērotu ši panta iepriekšējo punktu, peļņa, ko attiecina uz pastāvīgo pārstāvniecību, katru gadu ir jānosaka ar vienu un to pašu metodi, izņemot gadījumus, kad ir pietiekams pamats rīkoties citādi.

7. Ja peļņā ir ietverti citos ši Līguma pantos atsevišķi aplūkotie ienākuma veidi, ši panta noteikumi neietekmēs šo citu pantu noteikumus.

8.pants
Gaisa transports

1. Līgumslēdzējas Valsts uzņēmuma peļņa no gaisa transporta izmantošanas starptautiskajā satiksmē tiks aplikta ar nodokļiem tikai šajā valstī.

2. Šī panta 1. punkta noteikumi attiecas arī uz peļņu, kas gūta no piedalīšanās pulā, kopējā uzņēmējdarbībā vai starptautiskās satiksmes transporta uzņēmumā.

9.pants
Saistītie uzņēmumi

1. Gadījumos, kad:

a) Līgumslēdzējas Valsts uzņēmums tieši vai netieši piedalās otras Līgumslēdzējas Valsts uzņēmuma vadībā vai kontrolē vai tam pieder daļa no ši uzņēmuma kapitāla; vai

b) vienas un tās pašas personas tieši vai netieši piedalās Līgumslēdzējas Valsts uzņēmuma vadībā vai kontrolē vai tām pieder daļa kapitāla šajā uzņēmumā un vienlaikus citā otrās Līgumslēdzējas Valsts uzņēmumā,

un šo divu uzņēmumu komerciālās un finansu attiecības tiek veidotas vai nodibinātas pēc noteikumiem, kas atšķiras no tiem noteikumiem, kuri būtu spēkā starp diviem neatkarīgiem (savstarpēji nesaistītiem) uzņēmumiem, jebkura peļņa, kas veidotos vienam no uzņēmumiem, bet iepriekšminēto radīto noteikumu ietekmē nav izveidojusies, var tikt iekļauta ši uzņēmuma peļņā un atbilstoši aplikta ar nodokļiem.

2. Ja Līgumslēdzēja Valsts iekļauj šīs valsts uzņēmuma peļņā un attiecīgi apliek ar nodokļiem to peļņu, attiecībā uz kuru otras Līgumslēdzējas Valsts uzņēmums ir ticis aplikts ar nodokļiem šajā otrā valstī, un ši iekļautā peļņa ir tāda peļņa, kuru būtu guvis pirmās Līgumslēdzējas Valsts uzņēmums, ja attiecības starp šiem diviem uzņēmumiem būtu bijušas tādas, kādas pastāvētu starp diviem pilnīgi neatkarīgiem uzņēmumiem, tad otrai valstij ir jāizdara atbilstošas korektīvas attiecībā uz nodokļa lielumu, ar kuru tiek aplikta ši peļņa otrā valstī. Nosakot šīs korektīvas, jāņem vērā citi ši Līguma noteikumi un, ja nepieciešams, jārīko Līgumslēdzēju Valstu kompetento iestāžu konsultācijas.

10.pants
Dividendes

1. Dividendes, ko sabiedrība — Līgumslēdzējas Valsts rezidents izmaksā otras Līgumslēdzējas Valsts rezidentam, var aplikt ar nodokļiem šajā otrā valstī.

2. Tomēr šīs dividendes var arī aplikt ar nodokļiem atbilstoši attiecīgās valsts likumdošanas aktiem tajā Līgumslēdzējā Valstī, kuras rezidents ir sabiedrība, kas izmaksā dividendes, bet, ja dividenžu saņēmējs ir šo dividenžu īstenais īpašnieks, nodoklis nedrīkst pārsniegt 10% no dividenžu bruto apjoma.

Šis punkts neietekmēs sabiedrības aplikšanu ar nodokļiem attiecībā uz peļņu, no kuras tiek izmaksātas dividendes.

3. Jēdziens "dividendes" šajā pantā nozīmē ienākumu no akcijām vai citām tādām tiesībām piedalīties peļņas sadalē, kuras nav parādsaistības, kā arī ienākumu no citām korporatīvām tiesībām, kurš ir pakļauts tādai pašai aplikšanas procedūrai kā ienākums no akcijām saskaņā ar tās valsts likumdošanas aktiem, kuras rezidents ir sabiedrība, kas veic šo sadali.

4. Šī panta 1. un 2. punkta noteikumi netiks piemēroti, ja dividenžu īstenais īpašnieks, būdams Līgumslēdzējas Valsts rezidents, veic uzņēmējdarbību otrā Līgumslēdzējā Valstī, izmantojot tur esošo pastāvīgo pārstāvniecību, vai arī sniedz otrā valstī neatkarīgus individuālos pakalpojumus, izmantojot tur izvietoto pastāvīgo bāzi, ja sabiedrība, kura izmaksā dividendes, ir šīs otras valsts rezidents un ja līdzdalība, par kuru tiek izmaksātas dividendes, ir faktiski saistīta ar pastāvīgo pārstāvniecību vai pastāvīgo bāzi. Šajā gadījumā atbilstoši apstākļiem piemērojami šī Līguma 7. vai 14. panta noteikumi.

5. Ja sabiedrība — Līgumslēdzējas Valsts rezidents gūst peļņu vai ienākumus no otras Līgumslēdzējas Valsts, šī otra valsts nedrīkst aplikt ne ar kādu nodokli šīs sabiedrības izmaksātās dividendes, izņemot gadījumus, kad dividendes tiek izmaksātas otras valsts rezidentam vai kad līdzdalība, par kuru tiek izmaksātas dividendes, ir faktiski saistīta ar pastāvīgo pārstāvniecību vai pastāvīgo bāzi, kas atrodas otrā valstī, ne arī aplikt ar nesadalītās peļņas nodokli sabiedrības nesadalīto peļņu pat tādā gadījumā, ja izmaksātās dividendes vai nesadalītā peļņa pilnīgi vai daļēji sastāv no otrā valstī gūtās peļņas vai ienākuma.

11.pants
Procenti

1. Procentus, kas rodas Līgumslēdzējā Valstī un tiek izmaksāti otras Līgumslēdzējas Valsts rezidentam, var aplikt ar nodokļiem šajā otrā valstī.

2. Tomēr šos procentus var arī aplikt ar nodokļiem atbilstoši attiecīgās valsts likumdošanas aktiem tajā Līgumslēdzējā Valstī, kurā tie rodas; ja procentu saņēmējs ir šo procentu īstenais īpašnieks, nodoklis nedrīkst pārsniegt 10 procentus no šo procentu kopapjoma.

3. Šī panta 2. punkta noteikumi netiks piemēroti, ja procentus, kas rodas vienā Līgumslēdzējā Valstī, saņem otras Līgumslēdzējas Valsts valdība, kā arī tās politiski administratīvās vienības un pašvaldības, centrālā (nacionālā) banka vai jebkura cita šai valdībai pilnīgi piederoša finansu institūcija, kura ir šo procentu īstenā īpašniece, vai arī procenti, kas saņemti par šīs valdības garantētajiem aizdevumiem, netiks aplikti ar nodokļiem pirmajā minētajā valstī.

4. Šajā pantā lietotais jēdziens "procenti" nozīmē ienākumu no jebkura veida parādsaistībām neatkarīgi no to nodrošinājuma ar galvojumu, jo sevišķi ienākumu no valdības vērtspapīriem, ienākumu no obligācijām un parādzīmēm, ieskaitot prēmijas un balvas par šiem vērtspapīriem, obligācijām vai parādzīmēm. Soda naudas, kas saņemtas par laikā neveiktajiem maksājumiem, netiks uzskatītas par procentiem, uz kuriem attiecas šis pants.

5. Šī panta 1., 2. un 3. punkta noteikumi netiks piemēroti, ja persona — procentu īstenā īpašniece, būdama Līgumslēdzējas Valsts rezidents, veic uzņēmējdarbību otrā Līgumslēdzējā Valstī, kurā šie procenti rodas, izmantojot tur esošo pastāvīgo pārstāvniecību, vai arī sniedz šajā otrā valstī neatkarīgus individuālos pakalpojumus, izmantojot tur izvietoto pastāvīgo bāzi, un parādsaistības, uz kuru pamata tiek maksāti procenti, ir faktiski saistītas ar šo pastāvīgo pārstāvniecību vai pastāvīgo bāzi. Šajā gadījumā atbilstoši apstākļiem piemērojami šī Līguma 7. vai 14. panta noteikumi.

6. Ja procentu maksātājs ir šīs valsts rezidents, tiks uzskatīts, ka procenti rodas šajā valstī. Tomēr, ja persona, kas izmaksā procentus, neatkarīgi no tā, vai šī persona ir Līgumslēdzējas Valsts rezidents vai nav, izmanto Līgumslēdzējā Valstī esošo pastāvīgo pārstāvniecību vai tur izvietoto pastāvīgo bāzi, sakarā ar kuru radušās parādsaistības, par kurām tiek maksāti procenti, un šos procentus izmaksā pastāvīgā pārstāvniecība vai pastāvīgā bāze, tiks uzskatīts, ka šie procenti rodas tajā valstī, kurā atrodas pastāvīgā pārstāvniecība vai pastāvīgā bāze.

7. Ja sakarā ar īpašām attiecībām starp procentu maksātāju un procentu īsteno īpašnieku vai starp viņiem abiem un kādu trešo personu procentu summa, kas attiecas uz parādsaistībām, uz kuru pamata tā tiek izmaksāta, pārsniedz summu, par kādu būtu varējuši vienoties procentu maksātājs un procentu īstenais īpašnieks, ja starp viņiem nebūtu minēto īpašo attiecību, tad šī panta noteikumi tiks piemēroti tikai attiecībā uz pēdējo minēto summu. Šajā gadījumā atlikusī maksājumu daļa tiek aplikta ar nodokļiem atbilstoši katras Līgumslēdzējas Valsts likumdošanas aktiem ar nosacījumu, ka tiek ievēroti pārējie šī Līguma noteikumi.

12.pants
Autoratlīdzība

1. Autoratlīdzību, kas rodas Līgumslēdzējā Valstī un tiek izmaksāta otras Līgumslēdzējas Valsts rezidentam, var aplikt ar nodokļiem šajā otrā valstī.

2. Tomēr šo autoralīdzību var aplikt ar nodokļiem atbilstoši attiecīgās valsts likumdošanas aktiem tajā Līgumslēdzējā Valstī, kurā tā rodas. Ja autoratlīdzības saņēmējs ir šis autoratlīdzības īstenais īpašnieks, nodoklis nedrīkst pārsniegt 10 procentus no autoratlīdzības kopapjoma.

3. Jēdziens "autoratlīdzība" šajā pantā nozīmē jebkāda veida maksājumus, ko saņem kā atlīdzību par jebkuru autortiesību izmantošanu vai par tiesībām izmantot autortiesības uz literāru, mākslas vai zinātnisku darbu, ieskaitot kinofilmas un filmas, vai arī ierakstus radio un televīzijas pārraidēm, uz jebkuru patentu, preču zīmi, dizainu vai modeli, plānu, slepenu formulu vai procesu, vai par rūpnieciskas, komerciālas vai zinātniskas iekārtas izmantošanu, vai par tiesībām to izmantot, vai par informāciju attiecībā uz rūpniecisku, komerciālu vai zinātnisku darbību un pieredzi.

4. Šī panta 1. un 2. punkta nosacījumi netiks piemēroti, ja šo maksājumu īstenais īpašnieks, būdams Līgumslēdzējas Valsts rezidents, veic uzņēmējdarbību otrā Līgumslēdzējā Valstī, kurā rodas autoratlīdzība, izmantojot tur esošo pastāvīgo pārstāvniecību, vai šajā otrā valstī sniedz neatkarīgus individuālos pakalpojumus, izmantojot tur izvietoto pastāvīgo bāzi, un ja tiesības vai īpašums, uz kuriem attiecas autoratlīdzības maksājumi, ir faktiski saistīti ar šo pastāvīgo pārstāvniecību vai pastāvīgo bāzi. Šajā gadījumā atbilstoši apstākļiem piemērojami šī Līguma 7. vai 14. panta noteikumi.

5. Ja autoratlīdzības maksātājs ir Līgumslēdzējas Valsts rezidents, tiks uzskatīts, ka autoratlīdzība rodas šajā valstī. Tomēr, ja persona, kas izmaksā autoratlīdzību, neatkarīgi no tā, vai šī persona ir Līgumslēdzējas Valsts rezidents vai nav, izmanto Līgumslēdzējā Valstī esošo pastāvīgo pārstāvniecību vai tur izvietoto pastāvīgo bāzi, sakarā ar kuru radušās saistības izmaksāt autoratlīdzību, un šo autoratlīdzību izmaksā pastāvīgā pārstāvniecība vai pastāvīgā bāze, tiks uzskatīts, ka autoratlīdzība rodas tajā valstī, kurā atrodas pastāvīgā pārstāvniecība vai pastāvīgā bāze.

6. Ja sakarā ar īpašām attiecībām starp autoratlīdzības maksātāju un autoratlīdzības īsteno īpašnieku vai starp viņiem abiem un kādu trešo personu autoratlīdzības summa, kas attiecas uz tiesībām, izmantošanu vai informāciju, pārsniedz autoratlīdzības summu, par kādu būtu varējuši vienoties maksātājs un īstenais īpašnieks, ja starp viņiem nebūtu minēto īpašo attiecību, tad šī panta noteikumi tiks piemēroti tikai attiecībā uz pēdējo minēto summu. Šajā gadījumā maksājumu daļa, kas pārsniedz šo summu, tiek aplikta ar nodokļiem atbilstoši katras Līgumslēdzējas Valsts likumdošanas aktiem ar nosacījumu, ka tiek ievēroti pārējie šī Līguma noteikumi.

13.pants
Kapitāla pieaugums

1. Ienākumu, ko gūst Līgumslēdzējas Valsts rezidents, atsavinot šī Līguma 6.pantā minēto otrā Līgumslēdzējā Valstī esošo nekustamo īpašumu vai tādas sabiedrības akcijas, kuras aktīvi sastāv galvenokārt no šāda īpašuma, var aplikt ar nodokļiem šajā otrā valstī.

2. Pieaugumu (kapitāla), kas gūts par kustamā īpašuma, kas ir Līgumslēdzējas Valsts uzņēmuma pastāvīgās pārstāvniecības otrā Līgumslēdzējā Valstī komercīpašuma daļa, atsavināšanu vai par kustamā īpašuma, kas ir piederīgs Līgumslēdzējas Valsts rezidenta pastāvīgajai bāzei otrā Līgumslēdzējā Valstī, kura izveidota neatkarīgo individuālo pakalpojumu sniegšanai, atsavināšanu, ieskaitot pieaugumu (kapitāla) no šādas pastāvīgās pārstāvniecības (atsevišķi vai kopā ar visu uzņēmumu) atsavināšanas vai šādas pastāvīgās bāzes atsavināšanas, var aplikt ar nodokļiem otrā Līgumslēdzējā Valstī.

3. Kapitāla pieaugums, ko gūst Līgumslēdzējas Valsts uzņēmums, par šī uzņēmuma starptautiskajā satiksmē izmantoto gaisa transporta līdzekļu atsavināšanu, vai par šo gaisa transporta līdzekļu izmantošanai piederīgā kustamā īpašuma atsavināšanu, tiks aplikts ar nodokļiem tikai šajā valstī.

4. Kapitāla pieaugums, kas gūts par jebkura tāda īpašuma atsavināšanu, kas atšķiras no šī panta 1., 2. un 3. punktā minētā īpašuma, tiks aplikts ar nodokļiem tikai tajā Līgumslēdzējā Valstī, kuras rezidents ir šī īpašuma atsavinātājs.

14.pants
Neatkarīgie individuālie pakalpojumi

1. Līgumslēdzējas Valsts rezidenta - fiziskās personas ienākumi, kas gūti, sniedzot profesionālus pakalpojumus vai veicot cita veida neatkarīgu darbību, tiks aplikti ar nodokļiem tikai šajā valstī, izņemot gadījumus, kad šī persona savas darbības vajadzībām izmanto tai regulāri pieejamu pastāvīgo bāzi otrā Līgumslēdzējā Valstī. Ja tiek izmantota šāda pastāvīgā bāze, ienākumus var aplikt ar nodokļiem arī otrā Līgumslēdzējā Valstī, bet tikai tik lielā mērā, kādā tie ir attiecināmi uz šo pastāvīgo bāzi. Šī panta piemērošanai, gadījumā, kad Līgumslēdzējas Valsts rezidents - fiziskā persona uzturas otrā Līgumslēdzējā Valstī laika posmu vai laika posmus, kuri kopumā pārsniedz 183 dienas jebkurā 12 mēnešu periodā, kas sākas vai beidzas attiecīgajā finansu gadā, tad tiks uzskatīts, ka šī persona izmanto regulāri pieejamu pastāvīgo bāzi otrā Līgumslēdzējā Valstī, un ienākums, kas gūts par otrā valstī veiktajām iepriekšminētajām darbībām, tiks attiecināts uz šo pastāvīgo bāzi.

2. Jēdziens "profesionālie pakalpojumi" nozīmē neatkarīgu zinātnisko, literāro, māksliniecisko, izglītojošo vai pedagoģisko darbību, kā arī ārsta, jurista, inženiera, arhitekta, zobārsta un grāmatveža neatkarīgu darbību.

15.pants
Atkarīgie individuālie pakalpojumi

1. Saskaņā ar šī Līguma 16., 18. un 19. panta noteikumiem darba alga, samaksa un cita līdzīga veida atlīdzība, ko saņem Līgumslēdzējas Valsts rezidents par savu darbu, tiks aplikta ar nodokļiem tikai šajā valstī, ja vien algots darbs netiek veikts otrā Līgumslēdzējā Valstī. Ja algots darbs tiek veikts otrā Līgumslēdzējā Valstī, par to saņemto atlīdzību var aplikt ar nodokļiem šajā otrā valstī.

2. Neatkarīgi no šī panta 1. punkta noteikumiem atlīdzība, kuru Līgumslēdzējas Valsts rezidents saņem par algotu darbu, kas tiek veikts otrā Līgumslēdzējā Valstī, tiks aplikta ar nodokli tikai pirmajā minētajā valstī, ja:

a) atlīdzības saņēmējs ir atradies otrā valstī ne vairāk kā 183 dienas jebkurā 12 mēnešu laika posmā, kas sākas vai beidzas attiecīgajā finanšu gadā; un

b) atlīdzību maksā darba devējs, kas nav otras valsts rezidents, vai cita persona tāda darba devēja vārdā; un

c) atlīdzību neizmaksā pastāvīgā pārstāvniecība vai pastāvīgā bāze, ko darba devējs izmanto otrā valstī.

3. Neatkarīgi no šī panta iepriekšminētajiem noteikumiem atlīdzību par darbu, kas tiek veikts, strādājot uz Līgumslēdzējas Valsts uzņēmuma gaisa transporta līdzekļiem starptautiskajā satiksmē, var aplikt ar nodokli šajā valstī.

16.pants
Direktoru atalgojums

Direktoru atalgojumu un citus līdzīgus maksājumus, kurus saņem Līgumslēdzējas Valsts rezidents kā sabiedrības, kas ir otras Līgumslēdzējas Valsts rezidents, direktoru padomes vai citas līdzīgas institūcijas loceklis, var aplikt ar nodokļiem otrā Līgumslēdzējā Valstī.

17.pants
Mākslinieki un sportisti

1. Neatkarīgi no šī Līguma 14. un 15. panta noteikumiem ienākumus, ko gūst Līgumslēdzējas Valsts rezidents kā izpildītājmākslinieks, piemēram, kā teātra, kino, radio vai televīzijas aktieris, kā mūziķis vai arī kā sportists par savu individuālo darbību otrā Līgumslēdzējā Valstī, var aplikt ar nodokļiem šajā otrā valstī.

2. Ja mākslinieka vai sportista ienākumi par viņa individuālo darbību attiecīgajā jomā tiek maksāti nevis pašam māksliniekam vai sportistam, bet citai personai, šos ienākumus neatkarīgi no šī Līguma 7., 14. un 15. panta noteikumiem var aplikt ar nodokļiem tajā Līgumslēdzējā Valstī, kurā tiek veikta izpilditājmākslinieka vai sportista darbība.

3. Šī panta 1. un 2. punkta noteikumi netiks piemēroti attiecībā uz ienākumu, kuru Līgumslēdzējā Valstī gūst izpilditājmākslinieks vai sportists, ja viņa darbība šajā valstī tiek pilnīgi vai galvenokārt finansēta no vienas vai abu Līgumslēdzēju Valstu, to politiski administratīvo vienību vai pašvaldību sabiedriskajiem fondiem, vai šo darbību pilnīgi vai galvenokārt finansē viena vai abas Līgumslēdzējas Valstis, to politiski administratīvās vienības vai pašvaldības. Šajā gadījumā ienākums tiks aplikts ar nodokļiem tikai tajā Līgumslēdzējā Valstī, kuras rezidents ir šis mākslinieks vai sportists.

18.pants
Pensijas

Saskaņā ar šī Līguma 19. panta 2. punktu pensijas un cita veida līdzīga atlīdzība par iepriekš veikto algoto darbu, ko saņem Līgumslēdzējas Valsts rezidents, tiks aplikta ar nodokļiem tikai šajā valstī.

19.pants
Valsts dienests

1. a) Alga, izpeļņa un cita līdzīga atlīdzība, kura nav pensija un kuru fiziskajai personai izmaksā Līgumslēdzēja Valsts, tās politiski administratīvā vienība vai pašvaldība par šai valstij, vienībai vai pašvaldībai sniegtajiem pakalpojumiem, tiks aplikta ar nodokļiem tikai šajā valstī.

   b) Tomēr šī alga, izpeļņa un cita līdzīga atlīdzība tiks aplikta ar nodokļiem tikai otrā Līgumslēdzējā Valstī, ja pakalpojumi ir sniegti šajā otrā valstī un šī fiziskā persona ir tāds šīs valsts rezidents, kas:

      (i) ir šīs valsts pilsonis; vai
      (ii) nav kļuvis par šīs valsts rezidentu tikai un vienīgi ar mērķi sniegt pakalpojumus.

2. a) Jebkura pensija, ko fiziskajai personai izmaksā Līgumslēdzēja Valsts, tās politiski administratīvā vienība vai pašvaldība, vai ko izmaksā no šīs Līgumslēdzējas Valsts, politiski administratīvās vienības vai pašvaldības izveidotiem fondiem par pakalpojumiem, ko šī persona sniegusi šai valstij, vienībai vai pašvaldībai, tiks aplikta ar nodokļiem tikai šajā valstī.

b) Tomēr šī pensija tiks aplikta ar nodokļiem tikai otrā Līgumslēdzējā Valstī, ja šī fiziskā persona ir šīs otras valsts rezidents un pilsonis.

3. Algai, izpeļņai, citai līdzīgai atlīdzībai un pensijai, ko saņem par pakalpojumiem, kas sniegti sakarā ar Līgumslēdzējas Valsts vai tās pašvaldības veikto uzņēmējdarbību, ir jāpiemēro šī Līguma 15., 16. un 18. panta noteikumi.

20. pants
Studenti

Maksājumi, kurus uzturēšanās, studiju vai stažēšanās vajadzībām saņem students, māceklis vai stažieris, kas ir, vai tieši pirms ierašanās Līgumslēdzējā Valstī bija, otras Līgumslēdzējas Valsts rezidents un kas atrodas pirmajā minētajā valstī vienīgi ar nolūku studēt vai stažēties, netiks aplikti ar nodokļiem šajā valstī, ja šie maksājumi rodas ārpus šīs valsts.

21.pants
Citi ienākumi

1. Šī Līguma iepriekšējos pantos neaplūkotie Līgumslēdzējas Valsts rezidenta citi ienākumi neatkarīgi no to rašanās vietas tiks aplikti ar nodokļiem tikai šajā valstī.

2. Šī panta 1. punkta noteikumi netiks piemēroti ienākumam, kas nav ienākums no šī Līguma 6. panta 2. punktā definētā nekustamā īpašuma, ja šī ienākuma saņēmējs, būdams Līgumslēdzējas Valsts rezidents, veic uzņēmējdarbību otrā Līgumslēdzējā Valstī, izmantojot tur esošo pastāvīgo pārstāvniecību, vai sniedz šajā otrā valstī neatkarīgus individuālos pakalpojumus, izmantojot tur izvietoto pastāvīgo bāzi, un ja tiesības vai īpašums, par ko tiek saņemts šis ienākums, ir faktiski saistīti ar šo pastāvīgo pārstāvniecību vai pastāvīgo bāzi. Šajā gadījumā atbilstoši apstākļiem piemērojami šī Līguma 7. vai 14. panta noteikumi.

22.pants
Kapitāls

1. Kapitālu, ko pārstāv šī Līguma 6. pantā minētais Līgumslēdzējas Valsts rezidenta nekustamais īpašums, kas atrodas otrā Līgumslēdzējā Valstī, var aplikt ar nodokļiem šajā otrā valstī.

2. Kapitālu, ko pārstāv kustamais īpašums, kas veido daļu no otrā Līgumslēdzējā Valstī esošās Līgumslēdzējas Valsts uzņēmuma pastāvīgās pārstāvniecības īpašuma, vai kapitālu, ko pārstāv kustamais īpašums, kas ir piederīgs Līgumslēdzējas Valsts rezidenta pastāvīgajai bāzei otrā Līgumslēdzējā Valstī, kura tiek izmantota neatkarīgu individuālo pakalpojumu sniegšanai, var aplikt ar nodokļiem šajā otrā valstī.

3. Kapitāls, ko pārstāv gaisa transporta līdzekļi, kurus Līgumslēdzējas Valsts uzņēmums izmanto starptautiskajā satiksmē, kā arī kustamais īpašums, kas piederīgs šo gaisa transporta līdzekļu izmantošanai, tiks aplikts ar nodokļiem tikai šajā valstī.

4. Visi pārējie Līgumslēdzējas Valsts rezidenta kapitāla elementi tiks aplikti ar nodokļiem tikai šajā valstī.

23.pants
Nodokļu dubultās uzlikšanas novēršana

1. Attiecībā uz Moldovas Republikas rezidentiem nodokļu dubultā uzlikšana tiks novērsta šādā veidā: gadījumā, kad Moldovas Republikas rezidents gūst ienākumus vai viņam pieder kapitāls, kuru saskaņā ar šī Līguma noteikumiem var aplikt ar nodokļiem Latvijā, Moldovas Republikai jāatļauj:

a) samazināt šī rezidenta ienākuma nodokli par nodokļa daļu, kas ir vienāda ar Latvijā samaksāto ienākuma nodokli;

b) samazināt šī rezidenta kapitāla nodokli par nodokļa daļu, kas ir vienāda ar Latvijā samaksāto kapitāla nodokli.

Šie samazinājumi tomēr nekādā gadījumā nedrīkst pārsniegt tādu ienākuma nodokļa vai kapitāla nodokļa daļu, kas ir aprēķināta Moldovas Republikā pirms šī samazinājuma piemērošanas, kura atkarībā no apstākļiem ir attiecināma uz ienākumu vai kapitālu, kuru var aplikt ar nodokļiem Latvijā;

2. Attiecībā uz Latvijas rezidentiem nodokļu dubultā uzlikšana tiks novērsta šādā veidā:

a) gadījumā, kad Latvijas rezidents gūst ienākumus vai viņam pieder kapitāls, kuru saskaņā ar šī Līguma noteikumiem var aplikt ar nodokļiem Moldovas Republikā, ja vien Latvijas Republikas iekšējās likumdošanas akti nenodrošina labvēlīgākus noteikumus, Latvijas Republikai jāatļauj:

(i) samazināt šī rezidenta ienākuma nodokli par nodokļa daļu, kas ir vienāda ar Moldovas Republikā samaksāto ienākuma nodokli;

(ii) samazināt šī rezidenta kapitāla nodokli par nodokļa daļu, kas ir vienāda ar Moldovas Republikā samaksāto kapitāla nodokli.

Šie samazinājumi tomēr nekādā gadījumā nedrīkst pārsniegt tādu ienākuma nodokļa vai kapitāla nodokļa daļu, kas ir aprēķināta Latvijas Republikā pirms šī samazinājuma piemērošanas, kura atkarībā no apstākļiem ir attiecināma uz ienākumu vai kapitālu, kuru var aplikt ar nodokļiem Moldovas Republikā;

b) lai piemērotu šī punkta a) apakšpunktu, ja sabiedrība - Latvijas Republikas rezidents saņem dividendes no sabiedrības - Moldovas Republikas rezidenta un šajā sabiedrībā Latvijas Republikas rezidentam pieder vismaz 10 procenti akciju ar pilnām balsstiesībām, Moldovas Republikā samaksātajā nodoklī tiks ietverts ne tikai nodoklis, ar kuru apliek dividendes, bet arī nodoklis, ar kuru apliek sabiedrības peļņu, no kuras tiek izmaksātas dividendes.

24.pants
Diskriminācijas nepieļaušana

1. Līgumslēdzējas Valsts pilsoņi otrā Līgumslēdzējā Valstī netiks pakļauti aplikšanai ar nodokļiem vai jebkurām ar tiem saistītajām prasībām, it īpaši attiecībā uz rezidenci, kas atšķiras no aplikšanas ar nodokļiem vai ar tiem saistītajām prasībām, kurām tiek vai var tikt pakļauti otras valsts pilsoņi tādos pašos apstākļos, vai kas ir apgrūtinošākas. Šis noteikums neatkarīgi no šī Līguma 1. panta noteikumiem attiecas arī uz personām, kas nav vienas Līgumslēdzējas Valsts vai abu Līgumslēdzēju Valstu rezidenti.

2. Bezvalstnieki, kas ir Līgumslēdzējas Valsts rezidenti, nevienā no Līgumslēdzējām Valstīm netiks pakļauti aplikšanai ar nodokļiem vai jebkurām ar tiem saistītām prasībām, kas ir citādi vai apgrūtinošāki nekā tādi, kam tiek vai var tikt pakļauti attiecīgās valsts pilsoņi tādos pašos apstākļos.

3. Līgumslēdzējas Valsts uzņēmuma pastāvīgo pārstāvniecību, kuru tas izmanto otrā Līgumslēdzējā Valstī, nevar aplikt ar nodokļiem šajā otrā valstī mazāk labvēlīgi, nekā tiktu aplikti ar nodokļiem otras valsts uzņēmumi, kas veic tāda paša veida darbību. Šo noteikumu nedrīkst iztulkot tādējādi, ka tas uzliktu Līgumslēdzējai Valstij pienākumu piešķirt otras Līgumslēdzējas Valsts rezidentiem jebkādas personiskas atlaides, atvieglojumus vai samazinājumus attiecībā uz aplikšanu ar nodokļiem, kādus šī valsts piešķir saviem rezidentiem, ņemot vērā viņu civilstāvokli vai ģimenes saistības.

4. Izņemot gadījumus, kad piemērojami šī Līguma 9. panta 1. punkta, 11. panta 7.punkta vai 12.panta 6.punkta noteikumi, procenti, autoratlīdzība un citi maksājumi, ko Līgumslēdzējas Valsts uzņēmums izmaksā otras Līgumslēdzējas Valsts rezidentam, nosakot šī uzņēmuma apliekamo peļņu, ir jāatskaita no šīs peļņas pēc tādiem pašiem noteikumiem kā tad, ja tie tiktu izmaksāti pirmās minētās valsts rezidentam. Tāpat arī Līgumslēdzējas Valsts uzņēmuma parādi otras Līgumslēdzējas Valsts rezidentam, nosakot šāda uzņēmuma apliekamā kapitāla vērtību, ir jāatskaita pēc tādiem pašiem noteikumiem kā tad, ja tie attiektos uz pirmās minētās valsts rezidentu.

5. Līgumslēdzējas Valsts uzņēmumus, kuru kapitāls pilnīgi vai daļēji pieder vienam vai vairākiem otras Līgumslēdzējas Valsts rezidentiem vai kurus šie rezidenti tieši vai netieši kontrolē, pirmajā minētajā valstī nevar pakļaut aplikšanai ar nodokļiem vai jebkurām ar tiem saistītajām prasībām, kas atšķiras no aplikšanas ar nodokļiem un ar tiem saistītajām prasībām, kurām tiek vai var tikt pakļauti līdzīgi pirmās minētās valsts uzņēmumi, vai kas ir apgrūtinošākas.

6. Šī panta noteikumi neatkarīgi no šī Līguma 2. panta noteikumiem attiecas uz visu veidu nodokļiem.

25.pants
Savstarpējās saskaņošanas procedūra

1. Ja persona uzskata, ka vienas Līgumslēdzējas Valsts vai abu Līgumslēdzēju Valstu rīcība izraisa vai var izraisīt šīs personas aplikšanu ar nodokļiem, kas neatbilst šī Līguma noteikumiem, šī persona var neatkarīgi no šo valstu iekšējās likumdošanas noteikumiem, kas paredz novērst šādu aplikšanu ar nodokļiem, iesniegt savu jautājumu izskatīšanai tās Līgumslēdzējas Valsts kompetentām iestādēm, kuras rezidents ir šī persona, vai arī, ja jautājums attiecas uz šī Līguma 24. panta 1. punktu, tās Līgumslēdzējas Valsts kompetentām iestādēm, kuras pilsonis ir šī persona. Jautājums jāiesniedz izskatīšanai triju gadu laikā no pirmā paziņojuma par rīcību, kas izraisījusi aplikšanu ar nodokļiem neatbilstoši šī Līguma noteikumiem.

2. Kompetentās iestādes pienākums ir censties atrisināt šo jautājumu, ja tā uzskata, ka sūdzība ir pamatota, un, ja šī iestāde pati nespēj panākt apmierinošu risinājumu, tai jāmēģina atrisināt jautājumu, savstarpēji vienojoties ar otras Līgumslēdzējas Valsts kompetentajām iestādēm, lai novērstu šim Līgumam neatbilstošu aplikšanu ar nodokļiem. Katra šāda panāktā vienošanās ir jāizpilda neatkarīgi no Līgumslēdzējas Valsts iekšējās likumdošanas aktos noteiktajiem termiņiem.

3. Līgumslēdzēju Valstu kompetentajām iestādēm ir jācenšas savstarpējas saskaņošanas gaitā atrisināt jebkurus sarežģījumus vai novērst šaubas, kas var rasties, skaidrojot vai piemērojot šo Līgumu. Tās var arī savstarpēji konsultēties, lai novērstu nodokļu dubulto uzlikšanu gadījumos, kādi nav paredzēti šajā Līgumā.

4. Līgumslēdzēju Valstu kompetentās iestādes var tieši sazināties viena ar otru, lai panāktu vienošanos iepriekšējos punktos minētajos jautājumos.

26.pants
Informācijas apmaiņa

1. Līgumslēdzēju Valstu kompetentajām iestādēm ir jāapmainās ar informāciju, kas nepieciešama šī Līguma noteikumu izpildīšanai vai ar šajā Līgumā ietvertajiem nodokļiem saistīto Līgumslēdzēju Valstu iekšējās likumdošanas aktu prasību izpildei tiktāl, ciktāl šie likumi nav pretrunā ar šo Līgumu. Līguma 1. pants neierobežo informācijas apmaiņu. Jebkura informācija, ko saņem Līgumslēdzēja Valsts, ir jāuzskata par slepenu tāpat kā informācija, kas tiek iegūta saskaņā ar šīs valsts likumdošanas aktiem un var tikt izpausta tikai tām personām vai varas iestādēm (arī tiesas un administratīvajām iestādēm), kas ir iesaistītas nodokļu, uz kuriem attiecas šis Līgums, aprēķināšanā, iekasēšanā, piespiedu līdzekļu lietošanā vai apsūdzības celšanā, lietu iztiesāšanā vai apelāciju izskatīšanā. Šīm personām vai varas iestādēm šī informācija jālieto vienīgi iepriekšminētajos nolūkos. Tās drīkst izpaust šo informāciju tiesas prāvā vai tiesas lēmumos.

2. Nekādā gadījumā šī panta 1. punkta noteikumus nedrīkst iztulkot tādējādi, ka tie uzliktu Līgumslēdzējai Valstij pienākumu:

a) veikt administratīvus pasākumus, kas nesaskan ar vienas vai otras Līgumslēdzējas Valsts likumdošanas aktiem vai administratīvo praksi;

b) sniegt informāciju, kas nav pieejama saskaņā ar vienas vai otras Līgumslēdzējas Valsts likumdošanas aktiem vai administratīvo praksi;

c) sniegt informāciju, kas var atklāt jebkuru tirdzniecības, komerciālo, ražošanas vai profesionālo noslēpumu vai tirdzniecības procesu, vai arī sniegt informāciju, kuras izpaušana būtu pretrunā ar sabiedrības interesēm (ordre public).

27.pants

Diplomātisko un konsulāro pārstāvniecību personāls

Nekas šajā Līgumā nedrīkst ietekmēt diplomātisko misiju vai konsulāro pārstāvniecību personāla fiskālās privilēģijas, kuras tam piemērojamas saskaņā ar starptautiskajām tiesībām vai īpašiem līgumiem.

28.pants
Stāšanās spēkā

1. Līgumslēdzējām Valstīm diplomātisko notu apmaiņas ceļā ir jāpaziņo otrai par to, ka ir izpildītas šo valstu konstitucionālās prasības, kas attiecas uz šī Līguma spēkā stāšanos.

2. Šis Līgums stāsies spēkā ar šī panta pirmajā punktā minētā pēdējā paziņojuma datumu, un tā noteikumi abās Līgumslēdzējās Valstīs tiks piemēroti:

a) attiecībā uz nodokļiem, ko ietur izmaksas brīdī, sākot ar ienākumu, ko gūst janvāra pirmajā dienā vai pēc janvāra pirmās dienas tajā kalendārajā gadā, kas seko gadam, kurā šis Līgums stājas spēkā;

b) attiecībā uz pārējiem ienākuma un kapitāla nodokļiem, sākot ar nodokļiem, kas maksājami jebkurā finansu gadā, kurš sākas, janvāra pirmajā dienā vai pēc janvāra pirmās dienas, tajā kalendārajā gadā, kas seko gadam, kurā šis Līgums stājas spēkā.

29.pants
Darbības izbeigšana

Šis Līgums ir spēkā tik ilgi, kamēr Līgumslēdzēja Valsts tā darbību izbeidz. Katra Līgumslēdzēja Valsts var izbeigt šī Līguma darbību, diplomātiskā ceļā iesniedzot rakstisku notu par izbeigšanu vismaz sešus mēnešus pirms jebkura kalendārā gada beigām. Šajā gadījumā Līguma darbība abās Līgumslēdzējās Valstīs tiks izbeigta:

a) attiecībā uz nodokļiem, ko iekasē izmaksas brīdī, sākot ar ienākumu, ko gūst janvāra pirmajā dienā vai pēc janvāra pirmās dienas tajā kalendārajā gadā, kas seko gadam, kurā ir iesniegta attiecīgā nota;

b) attiecībā uz pārējiem ienākuma un kapitāla nodokļiem, sākot ar nodokļiem, kas maksājami jebkurā finansu gadā, kurš sākas janvāra pirmajā dienā vai pēc janvāra pirmās dienas tajā kalendārajā gadā, kas seko gadam, kurā ir iesniegta attiecīgā nota.

Šo apliecinot, apakšā parakstījušies, būdami pienācīgi pilnvaroti, šo Ligumu ir parakstījuši.

Ligums noslēgts Rīgā 1998 gada 25.02. divos eksemplāros, katrs no tiem latviešu, moldāvu un angļu valodās. Visi trīs teksti ir vienlīdz autentiski. Atšķirīgas interpretācijas gadījumā noteicošais ir teksts angļu valodā.

Latvijas Republikas
valdības vārdā

Moldovas Republikas
valdības vārdā

[TEXT IN MOLDOVAN – TEXTE EN MOLDAVE]

A C O R D

ÎNTRE

GUVERNUL REPUBLICII LETONIA

ŞI GUVERNUL REPUBLICII MOLDOVA

PENTRU EVITAREA DUBLEI IMPUNERI ŞI PREVENIREA EVAZIUNII FISCALE CU PRIVIRE LA IMPOZITELE PE VENIT ŞI PE CAPITAL

Guvernul Republicii Letonia și Guvernul Republicii Moldova,

dorind să încheie un Acord pentru evitarea dublei impuneri și prevenirea evaziunii fiscale cu privire la impozitele pe venit și pe capital,

au convenit după cum urmează :

Articolul 1
PERSOANE VIZATE

Prezentul Acord se va aplica persoanelor care sînt rezidente ale unuia sau ale ambelor State Contractante.

Articolul 2
IMPOZITE VIZATE

1. Prezentul Acord se va aplica impozitelor pe venit și pe capital, stabilite în numele unui Stat Contractant sau subdiviziunilor sale politice sau autorităților locale, indiferent de modul în care sînt percepute.

2. Vor fi considerate impozite pe venit și pe capital toate impozitele, stabilite pe venitul total, pe capitalul total, sau pe elementele de venit sau de capital, inclusiv impozitele pe cîștigurile din înstrăinarea proprietății mobiliare sau imobiliare, precum și impozitele asupra creșterii capitalului.

3. Impozitele existente asupra cărora se va aplica Acordul, în particular sînt:

a) în Republica Moldova:
(i) impozitul pe beneficiul (venitul) întreprinderilor;
(ii) impozitul pe venitul persoanelor fizice;
(iii) impozitul pe proprietăți imobiliare;
(în continuare "impozitul moldovenesc");

b) în Letonia:
(i) impozitul pe venitul întreprinderilor;
(ii) impozitul pe venitul persoanelor fizice;
(iii) impozitul pe proprietate;
(în continuare "impozitul leton").

4. Prezentul Acord se va aplica, de asemenea, oricăror impozite identice sau în esență similare, care sînt stabilite după data semnării prezentului Acord, în plus, sau în locul impozitelor existente. Autoritățile competente ale Statelor Contractante se vor

informa reciproc asupa oricăror modificări importante aduse în legislațiile lor fiscale.

Articolul 3
DEFINIȚII GENERALE

1. În sensul prezentului Acord, în măsura în care contextul nu cere o interpretare diferită:

a) termenul "Republica Moldova" înseamnă Republica Moldova si folosit în sens geografic, înseamnă teritoriul Moldovei, inclusiv apele interne si spațiul aerian, asupra cărora Republica Moldova își exercită drepturile sale suverane la exploatarea resurselor minerale si naturale, conform normelor dreptului internațional;

b) termenul "Letonia" înseamnă Republica Letonă si folosit în sens geografic, înseamnă teritoriul Republicii Letone și orice altă suprafață atribuită apelor teritoriale ale Republicii Letonia, potrivit legislației Letoniei si în conformitate cu legislația internațională, drepturile Letoniei pot fi exercitate asupra țărmului maritim, subsolul lui si asupra resurselor lor naturale.

c) expresiile "un Stat Contractant" și "celălalt Stat Contractant" înseamnă Republica Moldova sau Letonia, după cum cere contextul;

d) termenul "persoană" include o persoană fizică, o companie si orice altă asociere de persoane;

e) termenul "companie" înseamnă orice asociere corporativă sau orice entitate care este considerată ca o asociere corporativă în scopul impozitării;

f) expresiile "întreprindere a unui Stat Contractant" și "întreprindere a celuilalt Stat Contractant" înseamnă, respectiv, o întreprindere exploatată de un rezident al unui Stat Contractant și o întreprindere exploatată de un rezident al celuilalt Stat Contractant;

g) expresia "trafic internațional" înseamnă orice transport efectuat cu o navă aeriană exploatată de o întreprindere a unui Stat Contractant, cu excepția cazului, cînd nava aeriană este exploatată numai între locuri situate în celălalt Stat Contractant;

h) expresia "autoritate competentă" înseamnă:

(i) în Republica Moldova, Ministrul Finanțelor sau reprezentantul său autorizat;

(ii) în Letonia, Ministrul Finanțelor sau reprezentantul său autorizat;

i) expresia "persoană națională" înseamnă:

(i) orice persoană fizică care are cetățenia unui Stat Contractant;

(ii) orice persoană juridică, parteneriat sau asociație care au primit acest statut în baza legislației în vigoare a unui Stat Contractant;

2. În ce privește aplicarea prezentului Acord de un Stat Contractant, orice termen care nu este altfel definit va avea, dacă contextul nu cere o interpretare diferită, înțelesul pe care îl are în cadrul legislației acestui Stat Contractant cu privire la impozitele la care prezentul Acord se aplică.

Articolul 4
REZIDENT

1. În sensul prezentului Acord, expresia "rezident al unui Stat Contractant" înseamnă orice persoană care, potrivit legislației acestui Stat, este supusă impunerii conform domiciliului său, reședinței, locului conducerii, locului de încorporare sau oricărui alt criteriu de natură similară. Expresia va include, de asemenea, însuși Guvernul acestui Stat, subdiviziunile lui politice și autoritățile lui locale. Totuși, această expresie nu include orice persoană care este supusă impozitării în acest Stat numai pentru faptul, că obține venituri din surse aflate în acest Stat sau deține capital situat acolo.

2. Cînd, în conformitate cu prevederile paragrafului 1 al acestui articol, o persoană fizică este rezidentă a ambelor State Contractante, atunci statutul său va fi determinat după cum urmează:

a) aceasta va fi considerată rezidentă a Statului în care are o locuință permanentă la dispoziția sa; dacă ea dispune de o locuință permanentă la dispoziția sa în ambele State, va fi considerată rezidentă a Statului cu care legăturile sale personale si economice sînt mai strînse (centrul intereselor vitale);

b) dacă Statul, în care această persoană are centrul intereselor sale vitale, nu poate fi determinat, sau dacă ea nu dispune de o locuință permanentă la dispoziția sa în nici unul din State, atunci ea va fi considerată rezidentă a Statului în care locuieşte în mod obişnuit;

c) dacă această persoană locuieste în mod obişnuit în ambele State sau în nici unul dintre ele, ea va fi considerată rezidentă a Statului a cărui cetățenie o are;

d) dacă această persoană are cetățenia ambelor State sau a nici unuia dintre ele, autoritățile competente ale Statelor Contractante vor rezolva problema de comun acord.

3. Cînd, potrivit prevederilor paragrafului 1 al acestui articol, o persoană, alta decît o persoană fizică, este rezidentă a ambelor State Contractante, autoritățile competente ale Statelor Contractante se vor strădui să rezolve problema de comun acord şi să determine modul de aplicare a Acordului față de această persoană. În lipsa unui asemenea acord, această persoană nu va fi considerată rezidentă a nici unuia din Statele Contractante în sensul Acordului.

Articolul 5
REPREZENTANȚĂ PERMANENTĂ

1. În sensul prezentului Acord, expresia "reprezentanță permanentă" înseamnă un loc fix de afaceri prin care o întreprindere îşi desfăşoară în întregime sau parțial activitatea sa.

2. Expresia "reprezentanță permanentă", include în special:

a) un loc de conducere;
b) o sucursală;
c) un birou;
d) o uzină;
e) un atelier, şi
f) o mină, o sondă petrolieră sau de gaze, o carieră sau orice alt loc de extracție a resurselor naturale.

3. a) Un şantier de construcție, o construcție sau un proiect de instalație constituie o reprezentanță permanentă numai, cînd durează pentru o perioadă mai mare de şase luni.

b) activitățile ofşore desfăşurate într-un Stat Contractant în legătură cu explorarea sau exploatarea țărmului maritim, subsolului și resurselor lor naturale situate în acest Stat, vor fi considerate ca fiind desfășurate printr-o reprezentanță permanentă situată în acest Stat, dacă asemenea activități sînt desfășurate pentru o perioadă sau perioade ce depășesc în total 30 zile în orice perioadă de douăsprezece luni.

4. Independent de prevederile precedente ale acestui articol, expresia "reprezentanță permanentă" va fi considerată, că nu include:

a) folosirea de instalații, exclusiv, în scopul depozitării, expunerii sau livrării de produse sau mărfuri aparținînd întreprinderii;

b) menținerea unui stoc de produse sau mărfuri aparținînd întreprinderii, exclusiv, în scopul depozitării, expunerii sau livrării;

c) menținerea unui stoc de produse sau mărfuri aparținînd întreprinderii, exclusiv, în scopul prelucrării de către o altă întreprindere;

d) menținerea unui loc fix de afaceri, exclusiv, în scopul cumpărării de produse sau mărfuri sau colectării de informații pentru întreprindere;

e) menținerea unui loc fix de afaceri, exclusiv, în scopul efectuării pentru întreprindere a oricărei alte activități cu caracter pregătitor sau auxiliar;

f) menținerea unui loc fix de afaceri, exclusiv, pentru orice combinare de activități menționate în subparagrafele a) la e) ale acestui paragraf, cu condiția, că întreaga activitate a locului fix de afaceri, ce rezultă din acestă combinare, să aibă un caracter pregătitor sau auxiliar.

5. Independent de prevederile paragrafelor 1 și 2 ale acestui articol, cînd o persoană, alta decît un agent cu statut independent căruia i se aplică prevederile paragrafului 6 al acestui articol, desfășoară activitate în numele unei întreprinderi, are și, ca regulă, exercită în Statul Contractant împuternicirea de a încheia contracte în numele întreprinderii, această întreprindere va fi considerată ca avînd o reprezentanță permanentă în acest Stat, referitor la orice activități efectuate de această persoană pentru întreprindere, cu excepția cazului, cînd activitățile acestei persoane sînt limitate de cele menționate în paragraful 4 al acestui articol, care, fiind exercitate printr-un loc fix de afaceri, nu transformă acest loc fix

de afaceri într-o reprezentanță permanentă potrivit prevederilor acestui paragraf.

6. O întreprindere nu va fi considerată, că are o reprezentanță permanentă într-un Stat Contractant, numai prin faptul, că aceasta exercită activitate de afaceri în acest Stat printr-un broker, agent comisionar general sau orice alt agent cu statut independent, cu condiția, ca aceste persoane să acționeze în cadrul activității lor obișnuite.

7. Faptul, că o companie care este rezidentă a unui Stat Contractant controlează sau este controlată de o companie care este rezidentă a celuilalt Stat Contractant sau care exercită activitate de afaceri în acel celălalt Stat (printr-o reprezentanță permanentă sau în alt mod), nu este suficient pentru a face una din aceste companii o reprezentanță permanentă a celeilalte.

Articolul 6
VENITURI DIN PROPRIETĂȚI IMOBILIARE

1. Veniturile, obținute de un rezident al unui Stat Contractant din proprietăți imobiliare (inclusiv venitul din agricultură sau din exploatări forestiere) situate în celălalt Stat Contractant, pot fi impuse în acel celălalt Stat.

2. Expresia "proprietăți imobiliare" va avea înțelesul care este atribuit de legislația Statului Contractant în care proprietățile în cauză sînt situate. Expresia va include, în orice caz, accesoriile proprietății imobiliare, inventarul viu și echipamentul utilizat în agricultură și exploatări forestiere, drepturile asupra cărora se aplică prevederile dreptului comun cu privire la proprietatea funciară, orice opțiune sau drept similar pentru acumularea proprietății imobiliare, uzufructul proprietății imobiliare și drepturile la rente variabile sau fixe pentru exploatarea sau dreptul la exploatarea zăcămintelor minerale, izvoarelor și altor resurse naturale, drepturile la active ce apar în urma explorării sau exploatării țărmului maritim, subsolului și resurselor lor naturale, inclusiv drepturile la dobînzi sau la beneficierea acestor active. Navele aeriene nu vor fi considerate proprietăți imobiliare.

3. Prevederile paragrafului 1 al acestui articol se vor aplica veniturilor, obținute din exploatarea directă, din darea în arendă sau din folosirea în orice altă formă a proprietății imobiliare, precum și veniturilor, obținute din înstrăinarea proprietății imobiliare.

4. Cînd deținerea acțiunilor sau altor drepturi corporative în entitățile unei companii care este proprietarul acestor acțiuni sau drepturilor corporative la utilizarea proprietății imobiliare deținută de companie, veniturile din folosirea directă, darea în arendă, sau folosirea în orice altă formă a acestor drepturi la utilizare, pot fi impuse în Statul Contractant în care este situată proprietatea imobiliară.

5. Prevederile paragrafelor 1, 3 și 4 ale acestui articol se vor aplica, de asemenea, veniturilor din proprietăți imobiliare a unei întreprinderi și veniturilor din proprietăți imobiliare folosite pentru prestarea serviciilor personale independente.

Articolul 7
PROFITURI DIN ACTIVITĂȚI DE AFACERI

1. Profiturile unei întreprinderi a unui Stat Contractant vor fi impuse numai în acest Stat, în afară de cazul, cînd întreprinderea exercită activitate de afaceri în celălalt Stat Contractant printr-o reprezentanță permanentă situată acolo. Dacă întreprinderea exercită activitate de afaceri în așa mod, profiturile întreprinderii pot fi impuse în celălalt Stat, dar numai partea atribuibilă acelei reprezentanțe permanente.

2. Sub rezerva prevederilor paragrafului 3 al acestui articol, cînd o întreprindere a unui Stat Contractant exercită activitate de afaceri în celălalt Stat Contractant printr-o reprezentanță permanentă situată acolo, atunci se atribuie în fiecare Stat Contractant, acelei reprezentanțe permanente, profiturile care le-ar fi putut obține, dacă ar fi constituit o întreprindere distinctă și separată, exercitînd activități identice sau similare în condiții identice sau similare și tratînd cu toată independența cu întreprinderea a cărei reprezentanță permanentă este.

3. La determinarea profiturilor unei reprezentanțe permanente vor fi admise la scădere cheltuielile, ce pot fi dovedite ca fiind efectuate pentru scopurile reprezentanței permanente, inclusiv cheltuielile de conducere și cheltuielile generale de administrare efectuate, indiferent de faptul, că s-au efectuat în Statul în care se află situată reprezentanța permanentă sau în altă parte. Totuși, o asemenea scădere nu se admite la plățile efectuate (altfel decît pentru rambursarea cheltuielilor actuale) de către reprezentanța permanentă întreprinderii sau oricărui din oficiile sale, privind redevențele, onorariile, sau alte plăți similare pentru folosirea patentelor sau altor drepturi, sau a comisioanelor, pentru servicii specifice prestate sau pentru administrare sau, cu excepția, cazului

unei întreprinderi bancare, cu privire la dobînda din împrumutul acordat reprezentanței permanente de către întreprindere.

4. În măsura, in care într-un Stat Contractant se practică ca profitul, care se atribuie unei reprezentanțe permanente, să fie determinat prin repartizarea profitului total al întreprinderii în diversele sale părți componente, nici o prevedere a paragrafului 2 al acestui articol nu va împiedica acest Stat Contractant să determine profitul impozabil, în conformitate cu repartizarea obișnuită; metoda de repartizare adoptată va fi, totusi, aceea prin care rezultatul va fi în concordanță cu principiile enunțate în acest articol.

5. Nici un profit nu se va atribui unei reprezentanțe permanente numai pentru faptul, că această reprezentanță permanentă cumpără produse sau mărfuri pentru întreprindere.

6. În sensul paragrafelor precedente ale acestui articol, profiturile, care se atribuie reprezentanței permanente, vor fi determinate în fiecare an prin aceeasi metodă, în afară de cazul, cînd există motive temeinice si suficiente de a proceda altfel.

7. Cînd profiturile includ elemente de venit, care sînt tratate separat în alte articole ale prezentului Acord, atunci prevederile acestor articole nu vor fi afectate de prevederile acestui articol.

Articolul 8
TRANSPORTUL AERIAN

1. Profiturile unei întreprinderi a unui Stat Contractant, obținute din exploatarea în trafic internațional a navelor aeriene, vor fi impuse numai în acest Stat.

2. Prevederile paragrafului 1 al acestui articol se vor aplica, de asemenea, profiturilor obținute din participarea la un pool, la o exploatare în comun sau la o agenție internațională de transporturi.

Articolul 9
ÎNTREPRINDERI ASOCIATE

1. Cînd.

a) o întreprindere a unui Stat Contractant participă direct sau indirect la conducerea, controlul sau la capitalul unei întreprinderi a celuilalt Stat Contractant, sau

b) aceleași persoane participă, direct sau indirect, la conducerea, controlul sau la capitalul unei întreprinderi a unui Stat Contractant și a unei întreprinderi a celuilalt Stat Contractant,
și fie într-un caz, fie în celălalt, cele două întreprinderi sînt legate în relațiile lor financiare sau comerciale prin condiții acceptate sau impuse, care diferă de acelea, care ar fi fost stabilite între întreprinderi independente, atunci orice profituri, care fără aceste condiții ar fi fost calculate de una din întreprinderi, dar nu au putut fi calculate în fapt, datorită acestor condiții, pot fi incluse în profiturile acestei întreprinderi și impozitate în consecință.

2. Cînd un Stat Contractant include în profiturile unei întreprinderi aparținînd acestui Stat și impune, în consecință, profiturile asupra cărora o întreprindere a celuilalt Stat Contractant a fost supusă impozitării în acel celălalt Stat și profiturile astfel incluse sînt profituri, care ar fi revenit întreprinderii primului Stat menționat, dacă condițiile stabilite între cele două întreprinderi ar fi fost acelea, care ar fi fost stabilite între întreprinderi independente, atunci acel celălalt Stat va proceda la modificarea corespunzătoare a sumei impozitului, stabilit asupra acestor profituri. La efectuarea unor astfel de modificări se va ține cont de celelalte prevederi ale prezentului Acord și, în caz de necesitate, autoritățile competente ale Statelor Contractante se vor consulta reciproc.

Articolul 10
DIVIDENDE

1. Dividendele plătite de o companie, care este rezidentă a unui Stat Contractant, unui rezident al celuilalt Stat Contractant, pot fi impuse în acel celălalt Stat.

2. Totuși, aceste dividende pot fi, de asemenea, impuse în Statul Contractant în care este rezidentă compania plătitoare de dividende și potrivit legislației acestui Stat, dar dacă primitorul este beneficiarul efectiv al dividendelor, impozitul astfel stabilit nu va depăși 10 la sută din suma brută a dividendelor.

Acest paragraf nu va afecta impunerea companiei în ce privește profiturile din care se plătesc dividendele.

3. Termenul "dividende", folosit în acest articol, înseamnă veniturile provenind din acțiuni sau alte drepturi, care nu sînt titluri de creanță, din participarea la profituri, precum și veniturile din alte drepturi corporative, care sînt supuse aceluiași regim de

impunere ca veniturile din acțiuni, de către legislația Statului, în care este rezidentă compania distribuitoare a dividendelor.

4. Prevederile paragrafelor 1 și 2 ale acestui articol nu se vor aplica dacă beneficiarul efectiv al dividendelor, fiind un rezident al unui Stat Contractant, desfășoară activitate de afaceri în celălalt Stat Contractant, în care compania plătitoare de dividende este rezidentă, printr-o reprezentanță permanentă situată acolo, sau desfășoară în acel celălalt Stat servicii personale independente printr-o bază fixă situată acolo, iar deținerea drepturilor generatoare de dividende în legătură cu care dividendele sînt plătite, este efectiv legată de o asemenea reprezentanță permanentă sau bază fixă. În această situație se vor aplica prevederile articolului 7 sau articolului 14 al prezentului Acord, după caz.

5. Cînd o companie rezidentă a unui Stat Contractant obține profituri sau venituri din celălalt Stat Contractant, acel celălalt Stat nu poate percepe nici un impozit asupra dividendelor plătite de companie, cu excepția cazului, cînd asemenea dividende sînt plătite unui rezident al acelui celuilalt Stat sau cînd deținerea drepturilor generatoare de dividende, în legătură cu care dividendele sînt plătite, este efectiv legată de o reprezentanță permanentă sau o bază fixă situată în acel celălalt Stat, nici să supună profiturile nedistribuite ale companiei unui impozit asupra profiturilor nedistribuite, chiar dacă dividendele plătite sau profiturile nedistribuite reprezintă în întregime sau în parte profituri sau venituri provenind din acel celălalt Stat.

Articolul 11
DOBÎNZI

1. Dobînzile, provenind dintr-un Stat Contractant și plătite unui rezident al celuilalt Stat Contractant, pot fi impuse în acel celălalt Stat.

2. Totuși, aceste dobînzi pot fi, de asemenea, impuse în Statul Contractant din care provin și potrivit legislației acestui Stat, dar dacă primitorul este beneficiarul efectiv al dobînzilor, impozitul astfel stabilit nu va depăși 10 la sută din suma brută a dobînzilor.

3. Independent de prevederile paragrafului 2 al acestui articol, dobînzile provenind într-un Stat Contractant, obținute și deținute de către Guvernul celuilalt Stat Contractant, inclusiv subdiviziunile politice și autoritățile locale ale acestuia, Banca

Centrală (Națională) sau orice instituție financiară ce complet aparține acelui Guvern, sau dobînzile din împrumuturile garantate de acel Guvern vor fi scutite de impunere în primul Stat menționat.

4. Termenul "dobînzi", astfel cum este folosit în acest articol, înseamnă venituri din titluri de creanță de orice natură, însoțite sau nu de garanții ipotecare, și, în special, venituri din hîrtii de valoare guvernamentale și venituri din titluri de creanță sau obligațiuni, inclusiv primele și premiile legate, de asemenea, hîrtii de valoare, titluri de creanță sau obligațiuni. Penalitățile pentru plata cu întîrziere nu sînt considerate dobînzi în sensul acestui articol.

5. Prevederile paragrafelor 1, 2 și 3 ale acestui articol nu se vor aplica, dacă beneficiarul efectiv al dobînzilor, fiind un rezident al unui Stat Contractant, desfășoară activitate de afaceri în celălalt Stat Contractant, din care provin dodînzile, printr-o reprezentanță permanentă situată acolo, sau prestează în acel celălalt Stat servicii personale independente printr-o bază fixă situată acolo, și creanța în legătură cu care sînt plătite dobînzile este efectiv legată de o asemenea reprezentanță permanentă sau bază fixă. În această situație se vor aplica prevederile articolului 7 sau articolului 14 al prezentului Acord, după caz.

6. Dobînzile se consideră, că provin dintr-un Stat Contractant, cînd plătitorul este un rezident al acestui Stat. Totuși, cînd plătitorul dobînzilor, fie că este sau nu rezident al unui Stat Contractant, are într-un Stat Contractant o reprezentanță permanentă sau o bază fixă, în legătură cu care a fost contractată creanța generatoare de dobînzi și aceste dobonzi se suportă de acea reprezentanță permanentă sau bază fixă, atunci aceste dobînzi vor fi considerate, că provin din Statul, în care este situată reprezentanța permanentă sau baza fixă.

7. Cînd datorită relațiilor speciale existente între plătitor și beneficiarul efectiv sau între ambii si o altă persoană, suma dobînzilor, ținînd cont de creanța pentru care sînt plătite, depășește suma care s-ar fi convenit între plătitor și beneficiarul efectiv în lipsa unor astfel de relații, prevederile acestui articol se vor aplica numai la această ultimă sumă menționată. În acest caz, partea excedentară a plăților va fi impozitată potrivit legislației fiecărui Stat Contractant, ținînd cont de celelalte prevederi ale prezentului Acord.

Articolul 12
REDEVENȚE

1. Redevențele, provenind dintr-un Stat Contractant și plătite unui rezident al celuilalt Stat Contractant, pot fi impuse în acel celălalt Stat.

2. Totuși, aceste redevențe pot fi, de asemenea, impuse în Statul Contractant din care provin si potrivit legislației acestui Stat, dar dacă primitorul este beneficiarul efectiv al redevențelor, impozitul astfel stabilit nu va depăși 10 la sută din suma brută a redevențelor.

3. Termenul "redevențe" folosit în acest articol înseamnă plăți de orice natură, primite pentru folosirea sau concesionarea oricărui drept de autor asupra unei opere literare, artistice sau științifice, inclusiv asupra filmelor de cinematograf și filmelor sau benzilor folosite pentru emisiunile de radio sau televiziune, orice patent, marcă de comerț, desen sau model, plan, formulă secretă sau procedeu, sau pentru folosirea sau concesionarea oricărui echipament industrial, comercial sau științific, sau pentru informații referitoare la experiența în domeniul industrial, comercial sau științific.

4. Prevederile paragrafelor 1 și 2 ale acestui articol nu se vor aplica dacă beneficiarul efectiv al redevențelor, fiind un rezident al unui Stat Contractant, desfășoară activitate de afaceri în celălalt Stat Contractant din care provin redevențele, printr-o reprezentanță permanentă situată acolo sau prestează în acel celălalt Stat servicii personale independente printr-o bază fixă situată acolo, iar dreptul sau proprietatea pentru care se plătesc redevențele sînt efectiv legate de o asemenea reprezentanță permanentă sau bază fixă. În această situație se vor aplica prevederile articolului 7 sau articolului 14 al prezentului Acord, după caz.

5. Redevențele vor fi considerate, că provin dintr-un Stat Contractant, cînd plătitorul este un rezident al acestui Stat. Totuși, cînd plătitorul redevențelor, fie că este sau nu rezident al unui Stat Contractant, are într-un Stat Contractant o reprezentanță permanentă sau o bază fixă de care este legată obligația de a plăti redevențe, și aceste redevențe sînt suportate de o asemenea reprezentanță permanentă sau baza fixă, atunci aceste redevențe sînt considerate ca provenind din Statul în care este situată reprezentanța permanentă sau baza fixă.

6. Cînd, datorită relaţiilor speciale existente între plătitor şi beneficiarul efectiv sau între ambii şi o altă persoană, suma redevenţelor avînd în vedere utilizarea, dreptul sau informaţia pentru care sînt plătite, depăşeşte suma care ar fi fost convenită între plătitor şi beneficiarul efectiv în lipsa unor astfel de relaţii, prevederile acestui articol se vor aplica numai la această ultimă sumă menţionată. În acest caz, partea excedentară a plăţilor va fi impusă potrivit legislaţiei fiecărui Stat Contractant, ţinînd seama de celelalte prevederi ale prezentului Acord.

Articolul 13
CÎŞTIGURI DE CAPITAL

1. Cîştigurile, obţinute de un rezident al unui Stat Contractant din înstrăinarea proprietăţii imobiliare, astfel cum este definită în articolul 6 al prezentului Acord şi situată în celălalt Stat Contractant sau acţiunilor companiei activul căreia constă în special din aşa proprietăţi, pot fi impuse în acel celălalt Stat.

2. Cîştigurile provenite din înstrăinarea proprietăţii mobiliare, făcînd parte din activul unei reprezentanţe permanente pe care o întreprindere a unui Stat Contractant o are în celălalt Stat Contractant sau a proprietăţii mobiliare, ţinînd de o bază fixă de care dispune un rezident al unui Stat Contractant în celălalt Stat Contractant pentru prestarea serviciilor personale independente, inclusiv cîştigurile, provenind din înstrăinarea unei asemenea reprezentanţe permanente (singură sau cu întreaga întreprindere) sau a acelei baze fixe, pot fi impuse în acel celălalt Stat.

3. Cîştigurile, obţinute de o întreprindere a unui Stat Contractant din înstrăinarea navelor aeriene exploatate în trafic internaţional de această întreprindere sau a proprietăţii mobiliare, ce ţine de exploatarea acestor nave aeriene, vor fi impozitate numai în acest Stat.

4. Cîştigurile, provenite din înstrăinarea oricărei proprietăţi, alta decît cea la care se face referire în paragrafele 1, 2 şi 3 ale acestui articol, vor fi impuse numai în Statul Contractant, în care este rezident cel care înstrăinează.

Articolul 14
SERVICII PERSONALE INDEPENDENTE

1. Veniturile, obţinute de o persoană fizică rezidentă a unui Stat Contractant din exercitarea serviciilor profesionale sau a altor activităţi cu caracter independent, vor fi impuse numai în acest

Stat, dacă nu dispune în mod obişnuit, în celălalt Stat Contractant de o bază fixă la dispoziţia sa pentru exercitarea activităţilor sale. Dacă dispune de o astfel de bază fixă, veniturile pot fi impuse în celălalt Stat Contractant, dar numai partea, care este atribuibilă acelei baze fixe. În acest scop, cînd o persoană fizică rezidentă a unui Stat Contractant este prezentă în celălalt Stat Contractant pentru o perioadă sau perioade ce depăsesc în total 183 zile în orice perioadă de douăsprezece luni ce se începe sau se termină în anul fiscal interesat, ea va fi considerată ca avînd o bază fixă regular la dispoziţia sa în acel celălalt Stat si veniturile obţinute din activităţile sale, la care ne referim mai sus care sînt prestate în acel celălalt Stat se vor atribui acelei baze fixe.

2. Expresia "servicii profesionale" cuprinde în special activităţile independente de ordin ştiinţific, literar, artistic, educativ sau pedagogic, precum şi exercitarea independentă a profesiilor de medic, avocat, inginer, arhitect, dentist şi contabil.

Articolul 15
SERVICII PERSONALE DEPENDENTE

1. Sub rezerva prevederilor articolelor 16, 18 şi 19 ale prezentului Acord, salariile, sîmbriile si alte remuneraţii similare, obţinute de un rezident al unui Stat Contractant pentru o activitate salariată, vor fi impuse numai în acest Stat, în afară de cazul, cînd activitatea salariată este exercitată în celălalt Stat Contractant. Dacă activitatea salariată este exercitată în acest mod, remuneraţiile primite pot fi impuse în acel celălalt Stat.

2. Independent de prevederile paragrafului 1 al acestui articol, remuneraţiile, obţinute de un rezident al unui Stat Contractant pentru o activitate salariată exercitată în celălalt Stat Contractant, vor fi impuse numai în primul Stat menţionat dacă:

a) primitorul este prezent în celălalt Stat pentru o perioadă sau perioade care nu depăşesc în total 183 zile în orice perioadă de douăsprezece luni ce se începe sau se termină în anul fiscal interesat, si

b) remuneraţiile sînt plătite de o persoană sau în numele unei persoane care angajează şi care nu este rezidentă a celuilalt Stat, şi

c) remuneraţiile nu sînt suportate de o reprezentanţă permanentă sau de o bază fixă pe care cel care angajează le are în celălalt Stat.

3. Independent de prevederile precedente ale acestui articol, remunerațiile, primite pentru o activitate salariată exercitată la bordul unei nave aeriene exploatate în trafic internațional de o întreprindere a unui Stat Contractant, pot fi impuse în acest Stat.

Articolul 16
REMUNERAȚIILE DIRECTORILOR

Remunerațiile directorilor și alte plăți similare, primite de un rezident al unui Stat Contractant în calitatea sa de membru al Consiliului de Administrație sau a oricărui organ similar a unei companii care este rezidentă a celuilalt Stat Contractant, pot fi impuse în acel celălalt Stat.

Articolul 17
ARTIȘTI ȘI SPORTIVI

1. Independent de prevederile articolului 14 și articolului 15 ale prezentului Acord, veniturile, obținute de un rezident al unui Stat Contractant în calitate de artist de spectacol cum sînt artiștii de teatru, de film, de radio sau televiziune ori ca interpreți muzicali, sau ca sportivi, din activitatea lor personală desfășurată în celălalt Stat Contractant, pot fi impuse în acel celălalt Stat.

2. Cînd veniturile în legătură cu activitățile personale desfășurate de un artist de spectacol sau un sportiv nu revin artistului de spectacol sau sportivului, ci unei alte persoane, acele venituri, independent de prevederile articolelor 7, 14 și 15 ale prezentului Acord, pot fi impuse în Statul Contractant, în care sînt exercitate activitățile artistului de spectacol sau sportivului.

3. Prevederile paragrafelor 1 si 2 ale acestui articol nu se vor aplica față de veniturile obținute din activități desfășurate într-un Stat Contractant de un artist de spectacol sau un sportiv, dacă vizita în acest Stat este pe deplin sau parțial finanțată din fondurile publice ale unuia sau ale ambelor State Contractante, subdiviziunilor politice sau autorităților locale ale acestora. În această situație, veniturile se vor impozita numai în Statul Contractant al cărui rezident este artistul de spectacol sau sportivul.

Articolul 18
PENSIILE

Sub rezerva prevederilor paragrafului 2 al articolului 19 al prezentului Acord, pensiile și alte remunerații similare, plătite unui rezident al unui Stat Contractant pentru munca salariată desfăşurată în trecut, vor fi impozitate numai în acest Stat.

Articolul 19
FUNCŢII GUVERNAMENTALE

1. a) Salariile, simbriile şi alte remuneraţii similare, altele decit pensia, plătite de un Stat Contractant, de o subdiviziune politică sau de o autoritate locală a acestuia, unei persoane fizice pentru serviciile prestate acestui Stat, subdiviziunii sau autorităţii, vor fi impozitate numai în acest Stat.

b) Totuşi, aceste salarii, simbrii şi alte remuneraţii similare vor fi impozitate numai în celălalt Stat Contractant, dacă serviciile sînt prestate în acel Stat şi persoana fizică este rezidentă a acelui Stat, şi

(i) are cetăţenia acelui Stat; sau

(ii) nu a devenit rezidentă a acelui Stat, numai în scopul prestării serviciilor.

2. a) Orice pensii plătite de, sau din fonduri create de un Stat Contractant, de o subdiviziune politică sau de o autoritate locală a acestuia, unei persoane fizice pentru serviciile prestate acestui Stat, subdiviziunii sau autorităţii, vor fi impozitate numai în acest Stat.

b) Totuşi, aceste pensii vor fi impozitate numai în celălalt Stat Contractant, dacă persoana fizică este rezidentă şi are cetăţenia acestui Stat.

3. Prevederile articolelor 15, 16 si 18 ale prezentului Acord, se vor aplica salariilor, simbriilor şi altor remuneraţii simiulare, si pensiilor, pentru serviciile prestate în legătură cu o activitate de afaceri desfăşurată de un Stat Contractant, de o subdiviziune politică sau de o autoritate locală a acestuia.

Articolul 20
STUDENŢI

Plăţile primite de un student, un practicant, sau un instructor în scopul întreţinerii, educării sau instruirii, care este sau a fost imediat înainte de sosirea sa într-un Stat Contractant rezident al celuilalt Stat Contractant şi care este prezent în primul Stat menţionat în scopul educării sau instruirii sale, vor fi scutite de impozit în acest Stat, cu condiția, ca aceste plăți să fie primite din surse aflate în afara acestui Stat.

Articolul 21
ALTE VENITURI

1. Elementele de venit ale unui rezident al unui Stat Contractant, independent de sursa de proveniență, care nu sînt tratate în articolele precedente ale prezentului Acord, vor fi impuse numai în acest Stat.

2. Prevederile paragrafului 1 al acestui articol nu se vor aplica asupra veniturilor, altele decît veniturile, provenind din proprietăți imobiliare asa cum sînt definite în paragraful 2 al articolului 6 al prezentului Acord, dacă primitorul unor astfel de venituri, fiind un rezident al unui Stat Contractant desfășoară activitate de afaceri în celălalt Stat Contractant printr-o reprezentanță permanentă situată acolo, sau exercită în acel celălalt Stat servicii personale independente printr-o bază fixă situată acolo și dreptul sau proprietatea în legătură cu care venitul este plătit sînt efectiv legate de o asemenea reprezentanță permanentă sau bază fixă. În această situație se vor aplica prevederile articolului 7 sau articolului 14, după caz.

Articolul 22
CAPITALUL

1. Capitalul reprezentat de proprietăți imobiliare, astfel cum sînt definite în articolul 6 al prezentului Acord, deținut de un rezident al unui Stat Contractant și situat în celălalt Stat Contractant, poate fi impus în acel celălalt Stat.

2. Capitalul reprezentat de proprietăți mobiliare, făcînd parte din activul unei reprezentanțe permanente pe care o întreprindere a unui Stat Contractant o are în celălalt Stat Contractant sau de proprietăți mobiliare, aparținînd unei baze fixe ce se află la dispoziția unui rezident al unui Stat Contractant în celălalt Stat Contractant pentru prestarea serviciilor personale independente, poate fi impus în acel celălalt Stat.

3. Capitalul, reprezentat de nave aeriene exploatate în trafic internațional de o întreprindere a unui Stat Contractant, și de proprietăți mobiliare, ce țin de exploatarea unor asemenea nave aeriene, va fi impus numai în acest Stat.

4. Toate celelalte elemente de capital ale unui rezident al unui Stat Contractant vor fi impozitate numai în acest Stat.

Articolul 23
ELIMINAREA DUBLEI IMPUNERI

1. În cazul unui rezident al Republicii Moldova dubla impunere se va elimina în felul următor:

Cînd un rezident al Republicii Moldova obține venit sau deține capital, care conform prevederilor prezentului Acord, poate fi impus în Letonia, Republica Moldova va permite:

a) o scădere din impozitul pe venit al acestui rezident o suma egală cu impozitul pe venit plătit în Letonia;

b) o scădere din impozitul pe capital al acestui rezident o suma egală cu impozitul pe capital plătit în Letonia;

Această scădere, în orice caz, nu poate depăși partea impozitului pe venit sau pe capital în Republica Moldova, calculată pînă la scădere, care se atribuie, în dependență de caz, venitului sau capitalului care poate fi impus în Letonia.

2. În cazul unui rezident al Letoniei, dubla impunere se va elimina în felul următor:

a) cînd un rezident al Letoniei obține venit sau deține capital care, în conformitate cu prezentul Acord, poate fi impus în Republica Moldova, în afară de cazul, cînd se prevede de legislația ei internă o impozitare mai favorabilă, Letonia va permite:

(i) o scădere din impozitul pe venit al acestui rezident o sumă egală cu impozitul pe venit plătit în Republica Moldova;

(ii) o scădere din impozitul pe capital al acestui rezident o sumă egală cu impozitul pe capital plătit în Republica Moldova;

Această scădere, în orice caz, nu poate depăși partea impozitului pe venit sau pe capital în Letonia, calculată pînă la scădere, care se atribuie, în dependență de caz, venitului sau capitalului care poate fi impus în Republica Moldova;

b) În sensul subparagrafului a) al acestui paragraf, cînd o companie rezidentă a Letoniei primește dividende de la o companie rezidentă a Republicii Moldova, în care deține cel puțin 10 la sută din acțiunile ei și avînd drepturi depline la vot, impozitul plătit în Republica Moldova va include nu numai impozitul plătit pe dividende, dar și impozitul pe profiturile companiei care este distribuitoare a dividendelor.

Articolul 24
NEDISCRIMINAREA

1. Persoanele naționale ale unui Stat Contractant nu vor fi supuse în celălalt Stat Contractant la nici o impozitare sau obligație legată de aceasta, diferită sau mai împovărătoare decît impozitarea sau obligatia la care sînt sau pot fi supuse persoanele naționale ale celuilalt Stat, aflate în aceeași situație, în special, în privința residenției. Independent de prevederile articolului 1 al prezentului Acord, această prevedere se va aplica, de asemenea, persoanelor care nu sînt rezidente ale unuia sau ale ambelor State Contractante.

2. Persoanele fără cetățenie, rezidente ale unui Stat Contractant, nu vor fi supuse în nici unul din Statele Contractante oricăror impozitări sau oricăror obligațiuni legate de ea, diferite sau mai împovărătoare, decît impozitarea sau obligațiunea, la care sînt sau pot fi supuse persoanele naționale ale Statului în condiții similare.

3. Impunera unei reprezentanțe permanente, pe care o întreprindere a unui Stat Contractant o are în celălalt Stat Contractant, nu va fi stabilită în condiții mai puțin favorabile în acel celălalt Stat, decît impunerea stabilită întreprinderilor acelui celuilalt Stat care desfășoară aceleași activități. Această prevedere nu va fi interpretată ca obligînd un Stat Contractant să acorde rezidenților celuilalt Stat Contractant nici o deducere, înlesnire sau reducere cu titlu personal pe baza statutului civil sau obligațiilor familiare în ce privește impunerea, ce se pot acorda rezidenților săi.

4. Cu excepția cazului, cînd se aplică prevederile paragrafului 1 al articolului 9, paragrafului 7 al articolului 11 sau paragrafului 6 al articolului 12 al prezentului Acord, dobînzile, redevențele și alte plăți efectuate de o întreprindere a unui Stat Contractant unui rezident al celuilalt Stat Contractant, se vor deduce, în scopul determinării profiturilor impozabile ale unei asemenea întreprinderi, în aceleași condiții ca și cum ar fi fost plătite unui rezident al primului Stat menționat. În mod similar, orice datorii ale unei întreprinderi a unui Stat Contractant față de un rezident al celuilalt Stat Contractant, se vor deduce, în scopul determinării

capitalului impozabil al acestei întreprinderi, ca și cînd ar fi fost contactate față de un rezident al primului Stat menționat.

5. Întreprinderile unui Stat Contractant, ale căror capital este integral sau parțial deținut sau controlat în mod direct sau indirect, de unul sau mai mulți rezidenți ai celuilalt Stat Contractant, nu vor fi supuse în primul Stat menționat, nici unei impuneri sau nici unei obligații legate de aceasta, care să fie diferită sau mai împovărătoare decît impunerea și obligația la care sînt sau pot fi supuse alte întreprinderi similare ale primului Stat menționat.

6. Independent de prevederile articolului 2 al prezentului Acord, prevederile acestui articol se vor aplica impozitelor de orice tip și fel.

Articolul 25
PROCEDURA AMIABILĂ

1. Cînd o persoană consideră, că datorită măsurilor luate de unul sau de ambele State Contractante rezultă sau va rezulta pentru ea o impozitare, care nu este conformă cu prevederile prezentului Acord, ea poate, indiferent de căile de atac prevăzute de legislația internă a acestor State, să supună cazul său autorității competente a Statului Contractant a cărui rezidentă este sau, dacă situația sa se încadrează în prevederile paragrafului 1 al articolului 24, acelui Stat Contractant al cărui persoană națională este. Cazul trebuie prezentat în decurs de trei ani de la prima notificare a acțiunii din care rezultă că impunerea nu este în conformitate cu prevederile Acordului.

2. Autoritatea competentă se va strădui, dacă reclamația pare întemeiată și dacă ea însăși nu este în măsură să ajungă la o soluționare corespunzătoare, să rezolve cazul pe calea unei înțelegeri amiabile cu autoritatea competentă a celuilalt Stat Contractant, în vederea evitării unei impozitări, care nu este în conformitate cu Acordul. Orice înțelegere realizată va fi aplicată, indiferent de perioada de prescripție prevăzută în legislația internă a Statelor Contractante.

3. Autoritățile competente ale Statelor Contractante se vor strădui să rezolve pe calea înțelegerii amiabile orice dificultăți sau dubii rezultate ca urmare a interpretării sau aplicării Acordului. De asemenea, se pot consulta reciproc pentru evitarea dublei impuneri în cazurile neprevăzute de Acord.

4. Autoritățile competente ale Statelor Contractante pot comunica direct între ele, în scopul realizării unei înțelegeri, în sensul paragrafelor precedente.

Articolul 26
SCHIMB DE INFORMAȚII

1. Autoritățile competente ale Statelor Contractate vor face schimb de informații necesare aplicării prevederilor prezentului Acord sau ale legislației interne ale Statelor Contractante referitoare la impozitele vizate de Acord, în măsura în care impozitarea la care se referă nu este contrară Acordului. Schimbul de informații nu este limitat de articolul 1. Orice informație obținută de un Stat Contractant va fi tratată ca secret în același mod ca și informația obținută, conform prevederilor legislației interne a acestui Stat, și va fi dezvăluită numai persoanelor sau autorităților (inclusiv la instanțe judecătorești și organe administrative) însărcinate cu stabilirea sau încasarea, aplicarea sau urmărirea, sau soluționarea contestațiilor cu privire la impozitele care fac obiectul Acordului. Asemenea persoane sau autorități vor folosi informația numai în aceste scopuri. Acestea pot dezvălui informația în procedurile judecătoresti sau deciziile judiciare.

2. Prevederile paragrafului 1 al acestui articol nu vor impune în nici un caz unui Stat Contractant obligația:

a) de a lua măsuri administrative contrare legislației și practicii administrative a acestui sau a celuilalt Stat Contractant;

b) de a furniza informații, care nu pot fi obținute pe baza legislației sau în cadrul practicii administrative normale a acestui sau a celuilalt Stat Contractant;

c) de a furniza informații, care ar dezvălui un secret de afaceri, industrial, comercial sau profesional, sau un procedeu de fabricație sau informație a căror divulgare ar fi contrară ordinei publice.

Articolul 27
MEMBRII MISIUNILOR DIPLOMATICE ȘI POSTURILOR CONSULARE

Prevederile prezentului Acord nu vor afecta privilegiile fiscale de care beneficiază membrii misiunilor diplomatice sau posturilor consulare în virtutea regulilor generale ale dreptului internațional sau a prevederilor unor acorduri speciale.

Articolul 28
INTRAREA ÎN VIGOARE

1. Statele Contractante se vor informa reciproc pe canale diplomatice despre încheierea procedurilor lor constuționale necesare intrării în vigoare a prezentului Acord.

2. Prezentul Acord va intra în vigoare la data ultimei înștiințări la care se referă paragraful 1 al acestui articol și prevederile lui se vor aplica în ambele State Contractante:

a) în ce privește impozitul reținut la sursă la venitul obținut la sau după prima zi a lunii ianuarie a anului calendaristic, imediat următor anului, în care Acordul a intrat în vigoare;

b) în ce privește celelalte impozite pe venit și pe capital, pentru orice an fiscal ce se începe la sau după prima zi a lunii ianuarie a anului calendaristic, imediat următor anului, în care Acordul a intrat în vigoare.

Articolul 29
DENUNȚAREA

Prezentul Acord va rămîne în vigoare pînă atunci, cînd un Stat Contractant nu îl va denunța. Fiecare Stat Contractant poate denunța acțiunea Acordului pe canale diplomatice, înaintînd o notă de denunțare scrisă, cu cel puțin șase luni pînă la finele oricărui an calendaristic. În această situație Acordul va înceta să aibă efect în ambele State Contractante:

a) în ce privește impozitul reținut la sursă la venitul obținut la sau după prima zi a lunii ianuarie a anului calendaristic, imediat următor anului, în care a fost remisă nota de denunțare;

b) în ce privește celelalte impozite pe venit și pe capital pentru orice an fiscal ce se începe la sau după prima zi a lunii ianuarie a anului calendaristic, imediat următor anului, în care a fost remisă nota de denunțare.

Drept care, subsemnații autorizați au semnat prezentul Acord.

Întocmit în dublu exemplar la Riga la 25 02 1998, în limbile letonă, moldovenească și engleză, toate trei texte fiind egal autentic. În cazul divergentelor de interpretare textul în limba engleză va prevala.

Valdis Birkavs

Pentru Guvernul
Republicii Letonia

I. Lurcean

Pentru Guvernul
Republicii Moldova

[TRANSLATION IN FRENCH – TRADUCTION EN FRANÇAIS]

ACCORD ENTRE LE GOUVERNEMENT DE LA RÉPUBLIQUE DE LETTONIE ET LE GOUVERNEMENT DE LA RÉPUBLIQUE DE MOLDOVA TENDANT À ÉVITER LES DOUBLES IMPOSITIONS ET À PRÉVENIR LA FRAUDE FISCALE EN MATIÈRE D'IMPÔTS SUR LE REVENU ET SUR LA FORTUNE

Le Gouvernement de la République de Lettonie et le Gouvernement de la République de Moldova,

Désireux de conclure un Accord tendant à éviter les doubles impositions et à prévenir la fraude fiscale en matière d'impôts sur le revenu et sur la fortune,

Sont convenus de ce qui suit :

Article premier. Personnes visées

Le présent Accord s'applique aux personnes qui sont résidentes de l'un des États contractants ou des deux États contractants.

Article 2. Impôts visés

1. Le présent Accord s'applique aux impôts sur les revenus et sur la fortune prélevés pour le compte d'un État contractant, de ses subdivisions politiques ou de ses collectivités locales, quel que soit le système de perception.

2. Sont considérés comme impôts sur le revenu et sur la fortune les impôts perçus sur le revenu total, sur la fortune totale, ou sur des éléments du revenu ou de la fortune, y compris les impôts sur les gains provenant de l'aliénation de biens mobiliers ou immobiliers ainsi que les impôts sur les gains en capital.

3. Les impôts actuels auxquels s'applique l'Accord sont notamment :

a) En République de Moldova :

i) L'impôt sur les sociétés (impozitul pe beneficiul (venitul) intreprinderilor) ;

ii) L'impôt sur le revenu (impozitul pe venitul persoanelor fizice) ;

iii) L'impôt foncier (impozitul pe proprietati imobiliare) ;

(ci-après dénommés « impôt moldave ») ;

b) En Lettonie :

i) L'impôt sur les sociétés (uznemumu ienakuma nodoklis) ;

ii) L'impôt sur le revenu (iedzivotaju ienakuma nodoklis) ;

iii) L'impôt foncier (ipasuma nodoklis) ;

(ci-après dénommés « impôt letton »).

4. Le présent Accord s'applique aussi aux impôts de nature identique ou analogue qui seraient établis après la signature de l'Accord et qui s'ajouteraient aux impôts actuels ou qui les remplaceraient. Les autorités compétentes des États contractants se communiquent les modifications significatives apportées à leur législation fiscale respective.

Article 3. Définitions générales

1. Aux fins du présent Accord, à moins que le contexte n'exige une interprétation différente :

a) L'expression « République de Moldova » désigne la République de Moldova et, lorsqu'il est employé dans un sens géographique, le territoire de Moldova en ce compris les eaux intérieures et l'espace aérien sur lesquels la République de Moldova exerce des droits souverains d'exploitation des minerais et des ressources naturelles conformément aux normes du droit international ;

b) Le terme « Lettonie » désigne la République de Lettonie et, lorsqu'il est employé dans un sens géographique, le territoire de la République de Lettonie et toute autre zone adjacente aux eaux territoriales de la République de Lettonie au sein de laquelle, en vertu de la législation lettone et conformément au droit international, la Lettonie exerce ses droits à l'égard des fonds marins, de leurs sous-sols et de leurs ressources naturelles ;

c) Les expressions « l'un des États contractants » et « l'autre État contractant » désignent, selon le contexte, la Lettonie ou la République de Moldova ;

d) Le terme « personne » comprend les personnes physiques, les sociétés et autres groupements de personnes ;

e) Le terme « société » désigne toute personne morale ou toute entité qui est considérée comme une personne morale aux fins d'imposition ;

f) Les expressions « entreprise d'un État contractant » et « entreprise de l'autre État contractant » désignent respectivement une entreprise exploitée par un résident d'un État contractant et une entreprise exploitée par un résident de l'autre État contractant ;

g) L'expression « trafic international » désigne tout transport effectué par un aéronef exploité par une entreprise d'un État contractant, sauf lorsque l'aéronef n'est exploité qu'entre des points situés dans l'autre État contractant ;

h) L'expression « autorité compétente » désigne :

i) Pour la République de Moldova, le Ministre des finances ou son représentant autorisé ;

ii) Pour la Lettonie, le Ministre des finances ou son représentant autorisé ;

i) Le terme « ressortissant » désigne :

i) Toute personne physique qui possède la nationalité ou la citoyenneté d'un État contractant ;

ii) Toute personne morale, société de personnes ou association constituée conformément à la législation en vigueur dans un État contractant.

2. Pour l'application du présent Accord par un État contractant, toute expression ou tout terme qui n'y est pas défini a, sauf si le contexte exige une interprétation différente, le sens que lui attribue à ce moment, le droit de cet État contractant concernant les impôts auxquels s'applique l'Accord.

Article 4. Résident

1. Au sens du présent Accord, l'expression « résident d'un État contractant » désigne toute personne qui, selon la législation de cet État, est assujettie à l'impôt dans cet État, en raison de son domicile, de sa résidence, de son siège de direction, de son lieu de constitution, ou de tout autre critère de nature analogue. L'expression s'applique également au Gouvernement de cet État, à ses subdivisions politiques et à ses collectivités locales. Toutefois, cette expression ne comprend pas les personnes qui ne sont assujetties à l'impôt dans cet État que pour les revenus de sources situées dans cet État ou pour la fortune qui y est située.

2. Lorsque, selon les dispositions du paragraphe 1 du présent article, une personne physique est un résident des deux États contractants, sa situation est réglée de la manière suivante :

a) Cette personne est considérée comme résidente de l'État où elle dispose d'un foyer d'habitation permanent ; si elle dispose d'un foyer d'habitation permanent dans les deux États, elle est considérée comme résidente de l'État avec lequel ses liens personnels et économiques sont les plus étroits (centre des intérêts vitaux) ;

b) Si l'État où cette personne a ses intérêts vitaux ne peut pas être déterminé, ou si elle ne dispose d'un foyer d'habitation permanent dans aucun des États, elle est considérée comme résidente de l'État où elle séjourne de façon habituelle ;

c) Si cette personne séjourne de façon habituelle dans les deux États ou si elle ne séjourne de façon habituelle dans aucun d'eux, elle est considérée comme résidente de l'État dont elle possède la nationalité ;

d) Si cette personne possède la nationalité des deux États ou si elle ne possède la nationalité d'aucun d'eux, les autorités compétentes des États contractants tranchent la question d'un commun accord.

3. Lorsque, selon les dispositions du paragraphe 1 du présent article, une personne autre qu'une personne physique est résidente des deux États contractants, les autorités compétentes s'efforcent de trancher la question par voie d'accord amiable et arrêtent les modalités d'application de l'Accord à ladite personne. À défaut d'un tel accord, cette personne n'est pas considérée comme un résident de l'un ou l'autre État contractant et ne peut être admise au bénéfice des mesures prévues par l'Accord.

Article 5. Établissement stable

1. Au sens du présent Accord, l'expression « établissement stable » désigne une installation fixe d'affaires par l'intermédiaire de laquelle l'entreprise exerce tout ou partie de son activité.

2. L'expression « établissement stable » comprend notamment :

a) Un siège de direction ;

b) Une succursale ;

c) Un bureau ;

d) Une usine ;

e) Un atelier ; et

f) Une mine, un puits de pétrole ou de gaz, une carrière ou tout autre lieu d'extraction de ressources naturelles.

3. a) Un chantier de construction, ou un projet de construction ou d'installation constitue un établissement stable seulement s'il dure plus de six mois ;

b) Les activités exercées au large des côtes d'un État contractant dans le cadre de l'exploration ou de l'exploitation des fonds et du sous-sol marins ainsi que de leurs ressources naturelles situées dans cet État sont réputées être exercées par l'intermédiaire d'un établissement stable situé dans cet État si lesdites activités sont exercées pendant une période ou des périodes dépassant au total 30 jours au cours de toute période de 12 mois.

4. Nonobstant les dispositions précédentes du présent article, il est considéré que l'expression « établissement stable » ne comprend pas :

a) L'utilisation d'installations aux seules fins de stockage, d'exposition ou de livraison de biens ou de marchandises appartenant à l'entreprise ;

b) L'exploitation d'un stock de biens ou de marchandises appartenant à l'entreprise aux seules fins de stockage ou d'exposition ;

c) L'exploitation d'un stock de biens ou de marchandises appartenant à l'entreprise aux seules fins de transformation par une autre entreprise ;

d) L'exploitation d'une installation fixe d'affaires aux seules fins d'acheter des marchandises ou de réunir des informations pour l'entreprise ;

e) L'exploitation d'une installation fixe d'affaires aux seules fins d'exercer, pour l'entreprise, toute autre activité de caractère préparatoire ou auxiliaire ;

f) L'exploitation d'une installation fixe d'affaires aux seules fins d'exercice cumulé d'activités mentionnées aux alinéas a) à e) du présent paragraphe, à condition que l'activité d'ensemble de l'installation fixe d'affaires résultant de ce cumul garde un caractère préparatoire ou auxiliaire.

5. Nonobstant les dispositions des paragraphes 1 et 2 du présent article, lorsqu'une personne – autre qu'un agent jouissant d'un statut indépendant auquel s'applique le paragraphe 6 – agit pour le compte d'une entreprise, et dispose dans un État contractant de pouvoirs qu'elle y exerce habituellement, lui permettant de conclure des contrats au nom de cette entreprise, celle-ci est considérée comme ayant un établissement stable dans cet État pour toutes les activités que cette personne entreprend pour cette entreprise, à moins que les activités de cette personne ne soient limitées à celles qui sont énumérées au paragraphe 4 du présent article et qui, si elles étaient exercées par l'intermédiaire d'une installation fixe d'affaires, ne permettraient pas de faire de cette installation fixe un établissement selon les dispositions de ce paragraphe.

6. Une entreprise n'est pas considérée comme ayant un établissement stable dans un État contractant du seul fait qu'elle y exerce son activité par l'entremise d'un courtier, d'un commissionnaire général ou de tout autre agent jouissant d'un statut indépendant, à condition que ces personnes agissent dans le cadre ordinaire de leur activité.

7. Le fait qu'une société qui est résidente d'un État contractant contrôle ou est contrôlée par une société qui est résidente de l'autre État contractant ou qui y exerce son activité (que ce soit par l'intermédiaire d'un établissement stable ou non) ne suffit pas, en lui-même, à faire de l'une quelconque de ces sociétés un établissement stable de l'autre.

Article 6. Revenus immobiliers

1. Les revenus qu'un résident d'un État contractant tire de biens immobiliers (y compris les revenus des exploitations agricoles ou forestières) situés dans l'autre État contractant sont imposables dans cet autre État.

2. L'expression « biens immobiliers » a le sens que lui attribue le droit de l'État contractant où les biens considérés sont situés. L'expression comprend en tout cas les accessoires, le cheptel et le matériel des exploitations agricoles et forestières, les droits auxquels s'appliquent les dispositions du droit privé concernant la propriété foncière, toute option ou droit analogue sur les biens immobiliers, l'usufruit des biens immobiliers et les droits à des paiements variables ou fixes pour l'exploitation ou la concession de l'exploitation de gisements minéraux, sources et autres ressources naturelles, les droits sur les biens issus de l'exploration ou de l'exploitation des fonds et du sous-sol marins et de leurs ressources naturelles, y compris les droits sur les participations dans ces biens ou aux bénéfices de ces biens. Les aéronefs ne sont pas considérés comme des biens immobiliers.

3. Les dispositions du paragraphe 1 du présent article s'appliquent aux revenus provenant de l'exploitation directe, de la location ou de l'affermage, ainsi que de toute autre forme d'exploitation de biens immobiliers, ainsi qu'aux revenus provenant de l'aliénation de biens immobiliers.

4. Lorsque la propriété d'actions ou d'autres parts sociales d'une société confère au propriétaire de ces actions ou de ces parts sociales la jouissance de biens immobiliers détenus par la société, les revenus provenant de l'exploitation directe, de la location ou de l'affermage, ainsi que de toute autre forme d'exploitation de ce droit de jouissance sont imposables dans l'État contractant dans lequel les biens immobiliers sont situés.

5. Les dispositions des paragraphes 1, 3 et 4 du présent article s'appliquent également aux revenus provenant des biens immobiliers d'une entreprise ainsi qu'aux revenus des biens immobiliers servant à l'exercice d'une profession indépendante.

Article 7. Bénéfices des entreprises

1. Les bénéfices d'une entreprise d'un État contractant ne sont imposables que dans cet État, sauf si l'entreprise exerce son activité dans l'autre État contractant par l'intermédiaire d'un établissement stable qui y est situé. Si l'entreprise exerce son activité d'une telle façon, les bénéfices de l'entreprise sont imposables dans l'autre État, mais uniquement dans la mesure où ils sont imputables audit établissement stable.

2. Sous réserve des dispositions du paragraphe 3 du présent article, lorsqu'une entreprise d'un État contractant exerce son activité dans l'autre État contractant par l'intermédiaire d'un établissement stable qui y est situé, il est imputé à cet établissement stable, dans chaque État contractant, les bénéfices qu'il aurait pu réaliser s'il avait constitué une entreprise distincte exerçant des activités identiques ou analogues dans des conditions identiques ou analogues et traitant en toute indépendance avec l'entreprise dont il constitue un établissement stable.

3. Pour déterminer les bénéfices d'un établissement stable, sont admises en déduction les dépenses relatives aux fins poursuivies par cet établissement stable, y compris les dépenses de direction et les frais généraux d'administration ainsi enregistrés, soit dans l'État où est situé cet établissement stable, soit ailleurs. Toutefois, aucune déduction n'est admise pour les sommes qui seraient, le cas échéant, versées (à d'autres titres que le remboursement des frais) par l'établissement stable à l'entreprise ou à l'un quelconque de ses bureaux, comme redevances, honoraires ou autres paiements similaires, pour l'usage de brevets ou d'autres droits, ou comme commission, pour des

services précis fournis ou pour une activité de direction ou, sauf dans le cas d'une entreprise bancaire, comme intérêts sur des sommes prêtées à l'établissement stable par l'entreprise.

4. S'il est d'usage, dans un État contractant, de déterminer les bénéfices imputables à un établissement stable sur la base d'une répartition des bénéfices totaux de l'entreprise entre ses diverses composantes, aucune disposition du paragraphe 2 du présent article n'empêche cet État contractant de déterminer les bénéfices imposables selon la répartition en usage ; la méthode de répartition adoptée doit cependant être telle que le résultat obtenu soit conforme aux principes énoncés dans le présent article.

5. Aucun bénéfice n'est imputable à un établissement stable du seul fait que celui-ci a acheté des biens ou des marchandises pour l'entreprise.

6. Aux fins des paragraphes précédents du présent article, les bénéfices à imputer à l'établissement stable sont déterminés chaque année selon la même méthode, sauf s'il existe des motifs valables et suffisants de procéder autrement.

7. Lorsque les bénéfices comprennent des éléments de revenu traités séparément dans d'autres articles du présent Accord, les dispositions de ces articles ne sont pas affectées par les dispositions du présent article.

Article 8. Navigation aérienne

1. Les bénéfices d'une entreprise d'un État contractant provenant de l'exploitation, en trafic international, d'aéronefs ne sont imposables que dans cet État.

2. Les dispositions du paragraphe 1 du présent article s'appliquent aussi aux bénéfices provenant de la participation à un consortium, à une coentreprise ou à un organisme international d'exploitation.

Article 9. Entreprises associées

1. Lorsque :

a) Une entreprise d'un État contractant participe directement ou indirectement à la direction, au contrôle ou au capital d'une entreprise de l'autre État contractant ; ou que

b) Les mêmes personnes participent directement ou indirectement à la direction, au contrôle ou au capital d'une entreprise d'un État contractant et d'une entreprise de l'autre État contractant ;

et que, dans l'un et l'autre cas, les deux entreprises sont, dans leurs relations commerciales ou financières, liées par des conditions convenues ou imposées qui diffèrent de celles qui seraient convenues entre des entreprises indépendantes, les bénéfices qui, sans ces conditions, auraient été réalisés par l'une des entreprises, mais n'ont pu l'être en fait à cause de ces conditions, peuvent être inclus dans les bénéfices de cette entreprise et imposés en conséquence.

2. Lorsqu'un État contractant inclut dans les bénéfices d'une entreprise de cet État, et impose en conséquence, des bénéfices sur lesquels une entreprise de l'autre État contractant a été imposée dans cet autre État, et que les bénéfices ainsi inclus sont des bénéfices qui auraient été réalisés par l'entreprise du premier État si les conditions convenues entre les deux entreprises avaient été celles qui auraient été convenues entre des entreprises indépendantes, alors cet autre État procède à un ajustement approprié du montant de l'impôt qui y a été perçu sur ces bénéfices. Pour déterminer cet

ajustement, il est tenu compte des autres dispositions de l'Accord et, si c'est nécessaire, les autorités compétentes des États contractants se consultent.

Article 10. Dividendes

1. Les dividendes payés par une société qui est résidente d'un État contractant à un résident de l'autre État contractant sont imposables dans cet autre État.

2. Toutefois, ces dividendes sont aussi imposables dans l'État contractant dont la société qui paie les dividendes est un résident, et selon la législation de cet État, mais si la personne qui reçoit les dividendes en est le bénéficiaire effectif, l'impôt ainsi établi ne peut excéder 10 % du montant brut des dividendes.

Le présent paragraphe n'affecte pas l'imposition de la société au titre des bénéfices qui servent au paiement des dividendes.

3. Le terme « dividendes » employé dans le présent article désigne les revenus provenant d'actions ou autres parts bénéficiaires à l'exception des créances, ainsi que les revenus d'autres parts sociales soumis au même régime fiscal que les revenus d'actions par la législation de l'État dont la société distributrice est un résident.

4. Les dispositions des paragraphes 1 et 2 du présent article ne s'appliquent pas lorsque le bénéficiaire effectif des dividendes, résident d'un État contractant, exerce, dans l'autre État contractant dont la société qui paie les dividendes est un résident, soit une activité industrielle ou commerciale par l'intermédiaire d'un établissement stable qui y est situé, soit une profession indépendante au moyen d'une base fixe qui y est située, et que la participation génératrice des dividendes s'y rattache effectivement. Dans ces cas, les dispositions de l'article 7 ou de l'article 14 du présent Accord, suivant le cas, sont applicables.

5. Lorsqu'une société qui est résidente d'un État contractant tire des bénéfices ou des revenus de l'autre État contractant, cet autre État ne peut percevoir aucun impôt sur les dividendes payés par la société, sauf dans la mesure où ces dividendes sont payés à un résident de cet autre État ou dans la mesure où la participation génératrice des dividendes se rattache effectivement à un établissement stable ou à une base fixe situés dans cet autre État, ni prélever aucun impôt, au titre de l'imposition des bénéfices non distribués, sur les bénéfices non distribués de la société, même si les dividendes payés ou les bénéfices non distribués consistent en tout ou en partie en bénéfices ou en revenus provenant de cet autre État.

Article 11. Intérêts

1. Les intérêts provenant d'un État contractant et payés à un résident de l'autre État contractant sont imposables dans cet autre État.

2. Toutefois, ces intérêts sont aussi imposables dans l'État contractant d'où ils proviennent et selon la législation de cet État, mais si la personne qui reçoit les intérêts en est le bénéficiaire effectif, l'impôt ainsi établi ne peut excéder 10 % du montant brut des intérêts.

3. Nonobstant les dispositions du paragraphe 2 du présent article, les intérêts provenant d'un État contractant et dont le bénéficiaire effectif est le Gouvernement de l'autre État contractant, y compris l'une de ses subdivisions politiques et collectivités locales, sa Banque centrale (nationale) ou toute institution financière entièrement détenue par ce Gouvernement, ou provenant de prêts garantis par ce Gouvernement, sont exonérés d'impôt dans le premier État contractant.

4. Le terme « intérêts » employé dans le présent article désigne les revenus des créances de toute nature, assorties ou non de garanties hypothécaires, et notamment les revenus des fonds publics et des obligations d'emprunts, y compris les primes et lots attachés à ces titres. Les pénalisations pour paiement tardif ne sont pas considérées comme des intérêts au sens du présent article.

5. Les dispositions des paragraphes 1, 2 et 3 du présent article ne s'appliquent pas lorsque le bénéficiaire effectif des intérêts, résident d'un État contractant, exerce dans l'autre État contractant d'où proviennent les intérêts soit une activité industrielle ou commerciale par l'intermédiaire d'un établissement stable qui y est situé, soit une profession indépendante au moyen d'une base fixe qui y est située, et que la créance génératrice des intérêts se rattache effectivement à cet établissement stable ou à cette base fixe. Dans ces cas, les dispositions de l'article 7 ou de l'article 14 du présent Accord, suivant le cas, sont applicables.

6. Les intérêts sont considérés comme provenant d'un État contractant lorsque le débiteur est un résident de cet État. Toutefois, lorsque le débiteur des intérêts, qu'il soit ou non résident d'un État contractant, a dans un État contractant un établissement stable ou une base fixe pour lesquels la dette donnant lieu au paiement des intérêts a été contractée et qui supportent la charge de ces intérêts, ceux-ci sont considérés comme provenant de l'État où l'établissement stable, ou la base fixe, est situé.

7. Lorsque, en raison de relations spéciales existant entre le débiteur et le bénéficiaire effectif ou que l'un et l'autre entretiennent avec de tierces personnes, le montant des intérêts, compte tenu de la créance pour laquelle ils sont payés, excède celui dont seraient convenus le débiteur et le bénéficiaire effectif en l'absence de pareilles relations, les dispositions du présent article ne s'appliquent qu'à ce dernier montant. Dans ce cas, la partie excédentaire des paiements reste imposable selon la législation de chaque État contractant et compte tenu des autres dispositions du présent Accord.

Article 12. Redevances

1. Les redevances générées dans un État contractant et payées à un résident de l'autre État contractant sont imposables dans cet autre État.

2. Toutefois, ces redevances sont aussi imposables dans l'État contractant d'où elles proviennent et selon la législation de cet État, mais si la personne qui reçoit les redevances en est le bénéficiaire effectif, l'impôt ainsi établi ne peut excéder 10 % du montant brut des redevances.

3. Le terme « redevances » employé dans le présent article désigne les rémunérations de toute nature payées pour l'usage ou la concession de l'usage d'un droit d'auteur sur une œuvre littéraire, artistique ou scientifique, y compris les films cinématographiques, et les films ou bandes pour les émissions radiophoniques ou télévisées, d'un brevet, d'une marque de fabrique ou de commerce, d'un dessin ou d'un modèle, d'un plan, d'une formule ou d'un procédé secrets, ainsi que pour l'usage ou la concession de l'usage d'un équipement industriel, commercial ou scientifique et pour des informations ayant trait à une expérience acquise dans le domaine industriel, commercial ou scientifique.

4. Les dispositions des paragraphes 1 et 2 du présent article ne s'appliquent pas lorsque le bénéficiaire effectif des redevances, résident d'un État contractant, exerce dans l'autre État contractant source des redevances soit une activité industrielle ou commerciale par l'intermédiaire d'un établissement stable qui y est situé soit une profession indépendante au moyen d'une base fixe qui y est située, et que le droit ou le bien générateur des redevances se rattache effectivement à cet

établissement stable ou cette base fixe. Dans ces cas, les dispositions de l'article 7 ou de l'article 14 du présent Accord, suivant le cas, sont applicables.

5. Les redevances sont considérées comme provenant d'un État contractant lorsque le débiteur est un résident de cet État. Toutefois, lorsque le débiteur des redevances, qu'il soit ou non résident d'un État contractant, a dans un État contractant un établissement stable ou une base fixe pour lesquels l'engagement donnant lieu aux redevances a été contracté et qui supportent la charge de ces redevances, celles-ci sont considérées comme provenant de l'État où l'établissement stable ou la base fixe sont situés.

6. Lorsque, en raison de relations spéciales existant entre le débiteur et le bénéficiaire effectif ou que l'un et l'autre entretiennent avec de tierces personnes, le montant des redevances, compte tenu de la prestation pour laquelle elles sont payées, excède celui dont seraient convenus le débiteur et le bénéficiaire effectif en l'absence de pareilles relations, les dispositions du présent article ne s'appliquent qu'à ce dernier montant. Dans ce cas, la partie excédentaire des paiements reste imposable selon la législation de chaque État contractant et compte tenu des autres dispositions du présent Accord.

Article 13. Gains en capital

1. Les gains qu'un résident d'un État contractant tire de l'aliénation de biens immobiliers visés à l'article 6 du présent Accord et situés dans l'autre État contractant ou de parts d'une société dont l'actif est principalement constitué de tels biens sont imposables dans cet autre État.

2. Les gains issus de l'aliénation de biens meubles qui font partie de l'actif d'un établissement stable qu'une entreprise d'un État contractant a dans l'autre État contractant, ou de biens meubles qui appartiennent à une base fixe dont un résident d'un État contractant dispose dans l'autre État contractant pour l'exercice d'une profession indépendante, y compris de tels gains dégagés par l'aliénation de cet établissement stable (seul ou avec l'ensemble de l'entreprise) ou de cette base fixe, sont imposables dans cet autre État.

3. Les gains d'une entreprise d'un État contractant provenant de l'aliénation d'aéronefs exploités en trafic international par cette entreprise ou de biens meubles affectés à leur exploitation ne sont imposables que dans cet État.

4. Les gains provenant de l'aliénation de tous biens autres que ceux visés aux paragraphes 1, 2 et 3 du présent article ne sont imposables que dans l'État contractant dont le cédant est un résident.

Article 14. Professions indépendantes

1. Les revenus qu'une personne physique qui est un résident d'un État contractant tire d'une profession libérale ou d'autres activités de caractère indépendant ne sont imposables que dans cet État à moins qu'elle ne dispose de façon habituelle dans l'autre État contractant d'une base fixe pour l'exercice de ses activités. Si elle dispose d'une telle base, les revenus sont imposables dans l'autre État contractant, mais uniquement dans la mesure où ils sont imputables à ladite base fixe. À cette fin, lorsqu'une personne physique qui est un résident d'un État contractant séjourne dans l'autre État contractant pendant une période ou des périodes excédant au total 183 jours au cours de toute période de 12 mois commençant ou se terminant au cours de l'année fiscale considérée, elle est considérée comme disposant régulièrement d'une base fixe dans cet autre État et les revenus qui proviennent de ses activités visées ci-dessus et qui sont exercées dans cet autre État sont imputables à cette base fixe.

2. L'expression « profession indépendante » se rapporte notamment aux activités indépendantes d'ordre scientifique, littéraire, artistique, éducatif ou pédagogique, ainsi qu'aux activités indépendantes des médecins, avocats, ingénieurs, architectes, dentistes et comptables.

Article 15. Professions dépendantes

1. Sous réserve des dispositions des articles 16, 18 et 19 du présent Accord, les salaires, traitements et autres rémunérations similaires qu'un résident d'un État contractant reçoit au titre d'un emploi salarié ne sont imposables que dans cet État, à moins que l'emploi ne soit exercé dans l'autre État contractant. Si l'emploi y est exercé, les rémunérations reçues à ce titre sont imposables dans cet autre État.

2. Nonobstant les dispositions du paragraphe 1 du présent article, les rémunérations qu'un résident d'un État contractant reçoit au titre d'un emploi salarié exercé dans l'autre État contractant ne sont imposables que dans le premier État si :

a) Le bénéficiaire séjourne dans l'autre État pendant une période ou des périodes n'excédant pas au total 183 jours au cours de toute période de 12 mois commençant ou s'achevant pendant l'année fiscale considérée ; et

b) Les rémunérations sont payées par un employeur ou pour le compte d'un employeur qui n'est pas un résident de l'autre État ; et

c) La charge des rémunérations n'est pas supportée par un établissement stable ou une base fixe que l'employeur a dans l'autre État.

3. Nonobstant les dispositions précédentes du présent article, les rémunérations reçues au titre d'un emploi salarié exercé à bord d'un aéronef exploité en trafic international par une entreprise d'un État contractant sont imposables dans cet État.

Article 16. Tantièmes et rémunérations du personnel de direction de haut niveau

Les tantièmes, jetons de présence et autres rétributions similaires qu'un résident d'un État contractant reçoit en sa qualité de membre du conseil d'administration ou d'un organe similaire d'une société qui est résidente de l'autre État contractant sont imposables dans cet autre État.

Article 17. Artistes et athlètes

1. Nonobstant les dispositions des articles 14 et 15 du présent Accord, les revenus qu'un résident d'un État contractant tire de ses activités personnelles exercées dans l'autre État contractant en tant qu'artiste du spectacle – artiste de théâtre, de cinéma, de la radio ou de la télévision ou musicien – ou en tant qu'athlète sont imposables dans cet autre État.

2. Lorsque les revenus d'activités qu'un artiste du spectacle ou un athlète exerce personnellement et en cette qualité sont attribués non pas à l'artiste du spectacle ou à l'athlète lui-même mais à une autre personne, ces revenus sont, nonobstant les dispositions des articles 7, 14 et 15 du présent Accord, imposables dans l'État contractant où les activités de l'artiste du spectacle ou de l'athlète sont exercées.

3. Les dispositions des paragraphes 1 et 2 du présent article ne s'appliquent pas aux revenus provenant d'activités exercées dans un État contractant par un artiste du spectacle ou un athlète si son séjour dans cet État est financé entièrement ou principalement par des fonds publics d'un des

États contractants ou des deux États contractants, ou de leurs subdivisions politiques ou collectivités locales. Dans ce cas, les revenus ne sont imposables que dans l'État contractant dont l'artiste de spectacle ou l'athlète est un résident.

Article 18. Pensions

Sous réserve des dispositions du paragraphe 2 de l'article 19 du présent Accord, les pensions et autres émoluments de cette nature versés à un résident d'un État contractant au titre d'un emploi antérieur ne sont imposables que dans cet État.

Article 19. Fonction publique

1. a) Les traitements, salaires et autres rémunérations analogues, autres que les pensions, payés par un État contractant ou l'une de ses subdivisions politiques ou collectivités locales à une personne physique au titre de services fournis à cet État, à cette subdivision ou à cette collectivité ne sont imposables que dans cet État ;

   b) Toutefois, ces traitements, salaires et autres rémunérations analogues ne sont imposables que dans l'autre État contractant si les services sont exécutés dans cet État et si la personne physique est un résident de cet État qui :

      i) Possède la nationalité de cet État ; ou

      ii) N'est pas devenu un résident de cet État à seule fin d'exécuter les services en question.

2. a) Toute pension versée par un État contractant ou l'une de ses subdivisions politiques ou collectivités locales, soit directement soit par prélèvement sur des fonds qu'ils ont constitués, à une personne physique au titre de services fournis à cet État ou à cette subdivision ou collectivité, ne sont imposables que dans cet État ;

   b) Toutefois, ces pensions ne sont imposables que dans l'autre État contractant si la personne physique est résidente de cet État et en possède la nationalité.

3. Les dispositions des articles 15, 16 et 18 du présent Accord s'appliquent aux salaires, traitements et autres rémunérations ainsi qu'aux pensions payées au titre de services fournis dans le cadre d'une activité industrielle ou commerciale exercée par un État contractant ou l'une de ses subdivisions politiques ou collectivités locales.

Article 20. Étudiants

Les sommes qu'un étudiant, stagiaire ou apprenti, qui est ou qui était immédiatement avant d'aller vivre dans un État contractant un résident de l'autre État contractant et qui séjourne dans le premier État à seule fin d'y poursuivre ses études ou sa formation, reçoit pour couvrir ses frais d'entretien, d'études ou de formation ne sont pas imposables dans cet État, à condition qu'elles proviennent de sources situées en dehors de cet État.

Article 21. Autres revenus

1. Les éléments du revenu d'un résident d'un État contractant, d'où qu'ils proviennent, qui ne sont pas traités dans les articles précédents du présent Accord ne sont imposables que dans cet État.

2. Les dispositions du paragraphe 1 du présent article ne s'appliquent pas aux revenus autres que les revenus provenant de biens immobiliers, tels qu'ils sont définis au paragraphe 2 de l'article 6 du présent Accord, lorsque le bénéficiaire de tels revenus, résident d'un État contractant, exerce dans l'autre État contractant soit une activité industrielle ou commerciale par l'intermédiaire d'un établissement stable qui y est situé, soit une profession indépendante au moyen d'une base fixe qui y est située, et que le droit ou le bien générateur des revenus s'y rattache effectivement. Dans ces cas, les dispositions de l'article 7 ou de l'article 14 du présent Accord, suivant le cas, sont applicables.

Article 22. Fortune

1. La fortune constituée par des biens immobiliers visés à l'article 6 du présent Accord, que possède un résident d'un État contractant et qui sont situés dans l'autre État contractant, est imposable dans cet autre État.

2. La fortune constituée par les biens meubles qui font partie de l'actif d'un établissement stable qu'une entreprise d'un État contractant a dans l'autre État contractant, ou par les biens meubles qui appartiennent à une base fixe dont un résident d'un État contractant dispose dans l'autre État contractant pour l'exercice d'une profession indépendante, est imposable dans cet autre État.

3. La fortune constituée par des aéronefs exploités en trafic international par une entreprise d'un État contractant ou des biens meubles affectés à leur exploitation ne sont imposables que dans cet État.

4. Tous les autres éléments de la fortune d'un résident d'un État contractant ne sont imposables que dans cet État.

Article 23. Élimination des doubles impositions

1. S'agissant des résidents de la République de Moldova, les doubles impositions sont éliminées comme suit : lorsqu'un résident de la République de Moldova reçoit des revenus ou possède de la fortune qui, conformément aux dispositions du présent Accord, sont imposables en Lettonie, la République de Moldova accorde :

a) Sur l'impôt qu'elle perçoit sur les revenus de ce résident, une déduction d'un montant égal à l'impôt sur le revenu payé en Lettonie ;

b) Sur l'impôt qu'elle perçoit sur la fortune de ce résident, une déduction d'un montant égal à l'impôt sur la fortune payé en Lettonie.

Dans l'un ou l'autre cas, cette déduction ne peut toutefois excéder la fraction de l'impôt sur le revenu ou de l'impôt sur la fortune en République de Moldova, calculé avant déduction, correspondant selon le cas aux revenus ou à la fortune imposables en Lettonie.

2. S'agissant des résidents de Lettonie, les doubles impositions sont éliminées comme suit :

a) Lorsqu'un résident de Lettonie reçoit des revenus ou possède de la fortune qui, conformément aux dispositions du présent Accord, sont imposables en République de

Moldova, à moins qu'un traitement plus favorable ne soit prévu par sa législation interne, la Lettonie accorde :

i) Sur l'impôt qu'elle perçoit sur les revenus de ce résident, une déduction d'un montant égal à l'impôt sur le revenu payé en République de Moldova ;

ii) Sur l'impôt qu'elle perçoit sur la fortune de ce résident, une déduction d'un montant égal à l'impôt sur la fortune payé en République de Moldova.

Dans l'un ou l'autre cas, cette déduction ne peut toutefois excéder la fraction de l'impôt sur le revenu ou sur la fortune en Lettonie, calculé avant déduction, correspondant selon le cas aux revenus ou à la fortune imposables en République de Moldova ;

b) Aux fins de l'alinéa a) du présent paragraphe, lorsqu'une société qui est résidente de la Lettonie reçoit des dividendes d'une société qui est résidente de la République de Moldova et dans laquelle elle détient au moins 10 % des actions avec plein droit de vote, l'impôt payé en République de Moldova comprend non seulement l'impôt payé sur les dividendes, mais également l'impôt payé sur les bénéfices de la société servant au paiement des dividendes.

Article 24. Non-discrimination

1. Les ressortissants d'un État contractant ne sont soumis dans l'autre État contractant à aucune imposition ou obligation correspondante, qui est autre ou plus lourde que celles auxquelles sont ou pourront être assujettis les ressortissants de cet autre État qui se trouvent dans la même situation. La présente disposition s'applique aussi, nonobstant les dispositions de l'article premier du présent Accord, aux personnes qui ne sont pas des résidents d'un État contractant ou des deux États contractants.

2. Les apatrides qui sont des résidents d'un État contractant ne sont soumis dans l'un ou l'autre État contractant à aucune imposition ou obligation correspondante qui est autre ou plus lourde que celles auxquelles sont ou pourront être assujettis les ressortissants de l'État concerné qui se trouvent dans la même situation.

3. L'imposition d'un établissement stable qu'une entreprise d'un État contractant a dans l'autre État contractant n'est pas établie dans cet autre État d'une façon moins favorable que l'imposition des entreprises de cet autre État qui exercent la même activité. La présente disposition ne peut être interprétée comme obligeant un État contractant à accorder aux résidents de l'autre État contractant les déductions personnelles, abattements et réductions d'impôt en fonction de la situation ou des charges de famille qu'il accorde à ses propres résidents.

4. À moins que les dispositions du paragraphe 1 de l'article 9, du paragraphe 7 de l'article 11 ou du paragraphe 6 de l'article 12 du présent Accord ne soient applicables, les intérêts, redevances et autres montants payés par une entreprise d'un État contractant à un résident de l'autre État contractant sont déductibles, pour la détermination des bénéfices imposables de cette entreprise, dans les mêmes conditions que s'ils avaient été payés à un résident du premier État. De même, les dettes d'une entreprise d'un État contractant envers un résident de l'autre État contractant sont déductibles, pour la détermination de la fortune imposable de cette entreprise, dans les mêmes conditions que si elles avaient été contractées envers un résident du premier État.

5. Les entreprises d'un État contractant dont le capital est en totalité ou en partie, directement ou indirectement, détenu ou contrôlé par un ou plusieurs résidents de l'autre État contractant, ne

sont soumises dans le premier État à aucune imposition ou obligation correspondante, qui est autre ou plus lourde que celles auxquelles sont ou pourront être assujetties les autres entreprises similaires du premier État.

6. Les dispositions du présent article s'appliquent, nonobstant les dispositions de l'article 2 du présent Accord, aux impôts de toute nature ou dénomination.

Article 25. Procédure amiable

1. Lorsqu'une personne estime que les mesures prises par un État contractant ou par les deux États contractants entraînent ou entraîneront pour elle une imposition non conforme aux dispositions du présent Accord, elle peut, indépendamment des recours prévus par le droit interne de ces États, soumettre son cas à l'autorité compétente de l'État contractant dont elle est un résident ou, si son cas relève du paragraphe 1 de l'article 24, à celle de l'État contractant dont elle possède la nationalité. Le cas doit être soumis dans un délai de trois ans à partir de la première notification des mesures qui entraînent une imposition non conforme aux dispositions de l'Accord.

2. L'autorité compétente s'efforce, si la réclamation lui paraît fondée et si elle n'est pas elle-même en mesure d'y apporter une solution satisfaisante, de résoudre le cas par voie d'accord amiable avec l'autorité compétente de l'autre État contractant, en vue d'éviter une imposition non conforme à l'Accord. L'accord est appliqué quels que soient les délais prévus par le droit interne des États contractants.

3. Les autorités compétentes des États contractants s'efforcent, par voie d'accord amiable, de résoudre les difficultés ou de dissiper les doutes auxquels peuvent donner lieu l'interprétation ou l'application du présent Accord. Elles peuvent aussi se concerter en vue d'éliminer les doubles impositions dans les cas non prévus par l'Accord.

4. Les autorités compétentes des États contractants communiquent directement entre elles en vue de parvenir à un accord au sens des paragraphes précédents.

Article 26. Échange de renseignements

1. Les autorités compétentes des États contractants échangent les renseignements nécessaires pour appliquer les dispositions du présent Accord ou celles de la législation interne des États contractants relative aux impôts visés par l'Accord, dans la mesure où l'imposition qu'elle prévoit n'est pas contraire à l'Accord. L'échange de renseignements n'est pas restreint par l'article premier. Les renseignements reçus par un État contractant sont tenus secrets de la même manière que les renseignements obtenus en application de la législation interne de cet État, et ils ne sont communiqués qu'aux personnes ou autorités (y compris les tribunaux et organes administratifs) concernées par l'établissement ou le recouvrement des impôts visés dans le présent Accord, par les procédures ou poursuites concernant ces impôts, ou par les décisions sur les recours relatifs à ces impôts. Ces personnes ou autorités n'utilisent ces renseignements qu'à ces fins, mais peuvent faire état de ces renseignements au cours d'audiences publiques de tribunaux ou dans des jugements.

2. Les dispositions du paragraphe 1 du présent article ne peuvent en aucun cas être interprétées comme imposant à un État contractant l'obligation :

a) De prendre des mesures administratives dérogeant à sa législation et à sa pratique administrative ou à celles de l'autre État contractant ;

b) De fournir des renseignements qui ne pourraient être obtenus sur la base de sa législation ou dans le cadre de sa pratique administrative normale ou de celles de l'autre État contractant ;

c) De fournir des renseignements qui révéleraient un secret commercial, industriel, professionnel ou un procédé commercial ou des renseignements dont la communication serait contraire à l'ordre public.

Article 27. Membres de missions diplomatiques et de postes consulaires

Rien dans le présent Accord ne porte atteinte aux privilèges fiscaux dont bénéficient les agents diplomatiques ou les fonctionnaires consulaires en vertu soit des règles générales du droit des gens, soit des dispositions d'accords particuliers.

Article 28. Entrée en vigueur

1. Les États contractants s'informent mutuellement, par la voie diplomatique, de l'accomplissement des procédures constitutionnelles requises pour l'entrée en vigueur du présent Accord.

2. Le présent Accord entre en vigueur à la date de la dernière des notifications visées au paragraphe 1 du présent article, et ses dispositions sont applicables dans les deux États contractants :

a) En ce qui concerne les impôts retenus à la source, aux revenus perçus à compter du 1er janvier, inclus, de l'année civile suivant immédiatement celle de l'entrée en vigueur de l'Accord ;

b) En ce qui concerne les autres impôts sur le revenu et impôts sur la fortune, aux impôts dus pour tout exercice fiscal commençant à partir du 1er janvier, inclus, de l'année civile suivant immédiatement celle de l'entrée en vigueur de l'Accord.

Article 29. Dénonciation

Le présent Accord demeure en vigueur tant qu'il n'a pas été dénoncé par l'un des États contractants. Chaque État contractant peut dénoncer l'Accord en envoyant un préavis écrit, par la voie diplomatique, au moins six mois avant la fin de chaque année civile. Dans ce cas, l'Accord cesse d'être applicable dans les deux États contractants :

a) En ce qui concerne les impôts retenus à la source, aux revenus perçus à compter du 1er janvier, inclus, de l'année civile suivant immédiatement celle au cours de laquelle la notification est faite ;

b) En ce qui concerne les autres impôts sur le revenu et impôts sur la fortune, aux impôts dus pour tout exercice fiscal commençant à partir du 1er janvier de l'année civile suivant immédiatement celle au cours de laquelle la notification est faite.

EN FOI DE QUOI, les soussignés, à ce dûment autorisés, ont signé le présent Accord.

FAIT à Riga, le 25 février 1998, en double exemplaire en langues lettone, moldave et anglaise, les trois textes faisant également foi. En cas de divergence d'interprétation, le texte anglais prévaut.

Pour le Gouvernement de la République de Lettonie :

[VALDIS BIRKAVS]

Pour le Gouvernement de la République de Moldova :

[JONS LESANU]

No. 54178

Latvia
and
Portugal

Agreement between the Republic of Latvia and the Portuguese Republic concerning the International Transport of Passengers and Goods by Road. Warsaw, 20 May 1999

Entry into force: *20 November 2000 by notification, in accordance with article 19*

Authentic texts: *English, Latvian and Portuguese*

Registration with the Secretariat of the United Nations: *Latvia, 4 January 2017*

Lettonie
et
Portugal

Accord entre la République de Lettonie et la République portugaise relatif au transport international de passagers et de marchandises par route. Varsovie, 20 mai 1999

Entrée en vigueur : *20 novembre 2000 par notification, conformément à l'article 19*

Textes authentiques : *anglais, letton et portugais*

Enregistrement au Secrétariat de l'Organisation des Nations Unies : *Lettonie, 4 janvier 2017*

[TEXT IN ENGLISH – TEXTE EN ANGLAIS]

AGREEMENT

between the Republic of Latvia and the Portuguese Republic Concerning the International Transport of Passengers and Goods by Road

The Republic of Latvia and the Portuguese Republic, hereinafter referred to as the "Contracting Parties";

wishing to contribute to the development of the transport of passengers and goods by road between the two countries, as well as in transit through their territories;

taking into account the need to establish at an European level a policy directed towards the progressive liberalization of transport services, in connection with harmonization of competition conditions, environmental protection and safety in road traffic;

Have agreed as follows:

I INTRODUCTORY PROVISIONS

Article 1
Scope

Without prejudice to the provisions of paragraph 2 of article 7, this Agreement entitles carriers established in either Contracting Party to transport passengers or goods by road between the territories of the Contracting Parties or in transit through them.

Article 2
Definitions

For the purpose of this Agreement:

a) a *"carrier"* is any physical or juridical person duly authorized either in the Republic of Latvia or in the Portuguese Republic:

1) to engage in the international transport of passengers or goods by road for hire or reward;

2) to perform transport on his own account;

b) a *"vehicle"* is:

1) in the case of transport of passengers, any motor vehicle intended for carriage of passengers with more than 9 seats – including the driver's seat – as well as trailers for transport of passenger luggage, provided that the trailer is registered in the same Contracting Party as the motor vehicle;

2) in the case of transport of goods, any lorry, tractor, trailer or semi-trailer, as well as any articulated vehicle or a combination of lorry and trailer, provided that at least the motor vehicle is registered in the territory of either Contracting Party;

c) *"transit"* is the transport performed by a carrier established in one of the Contracting Parties through the territory of the other Contracting Party without taking or leaving there any passengers or goods.

II TRANSPORT OF PASSENGERS

Article 3
Types of Services

1) The transport services of passengers to be performed under the provisions of this Agreement may be:

a) regular services;

b) shuttle services;

c) occasional services.

2. *"Regular services"* are services which provide for the carriage of passengers on specified routes, according to previously determined itinerary, schedule, fares and stopping points for collecting and setting down passengers.

3. *"Shuttle services"* are services whereby, by means of several outward and return journeys, groups of passengers assembled in advance are carried from the same area of departure to the same area of destination.

"Area of departure" and *"area of destination"* mean respectively the place where the journey begins and the place where the journey ends, as well as, in each case, all localities within a radius of 50 kms.

Besides transport, shuttle services should include the accomodation of passengers in the area of destination for a period of at least two nights.

Without prejudice to the provisions of paragraph 3 b) of article 4 of this Agreement, in shuttle services:

- each group of passengers having made the outward journey together is carried back to the starting point together in a later journey;
- passengers shall not be collected or set down outside the areas of departure and destination;
- the first return journey and the last outward journey are empty runs.

4. *"Occasional services"* are services which do not fall within the definition of regular services nor within the definition of shuttle services.

Article 4
Regime of Authorization

1. Apart from the exceptions referred to in paragraph 1 of article 5, any passenger transport services performed under this Agreement are subject to an authorization granted by the competent authority of the other Contracting Party on the basis of reciprocity.

2. In what regards regular services:

a) the establishment of a regular service, as well as the modification of the operating conditions thereof, will be authorized by common agreement between the competent authorities of the Contracting Parties, provided that an approval is obtained from the competent authorities of the transit countries, whenever necessary;

b) an authorization granted by the competent authority of a Contracting Party will be valid only in that part of the route which is situated in the territory of the same Contracting Party;

c) in principle, the authorization for each regular service will be granted on a basis of reciprocity;

d) the term of validity of an authorization cannot exceed five years.

3. In what concerns shuttle services:

a) the term of validity of an authorization cannot exceed six months;

b) authorization may be granted to allow for:

- in a given percentage, passengers having been carried in the outward journey within a certain group to be carried in the return journey within another group;
- passengers to be taken or set down at a maximum of three places outside the areas of departure and three places outside the area of destination.

Article 5
Transport Services Exempted from Authorization

1. The following occasional services do not require authorization:

a) *"closed door tours"*, i.e., services whereby the same vehicle carries the same group of passengers throughout the journey and brings them back to the place of departure, provided that the place of departure and destination is situated in the territory of the Contracting Party where the vehicle is registered;

b) services involving a laden journey from a place of departure situated in the territory of the Contracting Party where the vehicle is registered to a place of destination situated in the territory of the other Contracting Party, followed by an empty journey back to the place of departure;

c) services including an unladen journey entering the territory of the other Contracting Party, followed by a laden journey, provided that all passengers are picked up in the same place and:

- that they are grouped by a transport contract concluded before they enter the territory of the other Contracting Party; or

- that they have been previously carried by the same undertaking to the territory of the other Contracting Party; or
- that have been invited to come to the territory of the Contracting Party where the carrier is established, the costs of transport being at the charge of the person responsible for the invitation;

d) unladen runs of a passenger vehicle sent to replace a vehicle which has broken down in another country, in order to continue the carriage of passengers under cover of the waybill of the broken down vehicle.

2. Services exempted from authorization under the provisions of paragraph 1 of this article shall be carried out under cover of a control document to be established in the Protocol referred to in article 17 of this Agreement.

III TRANSPORT OF GOODS

Article 6
Regime of Authorization

1. Apart from the exceptions referred to in paragraph 3 of this article, the transport of goods for hire or reward or on own account performed under the provisions of this Agreement by a carrier established in the country of one of the Contracting Parties, by means of a motor vehicle registered in the same country, is subject to an authorization granted by the competent authority of the other Contracting Party.

2. The competent authorities of both Contracting Parties may agree on the following two types of authorizations:

a) journey authorizations, valid for one journey;or

b) multijourney authorizations, valid for the number of journeys indicated thereon;

the term of validity of which is from the 1st of January up to the 31st of January of the coming year.

3. The following transports are exempted from authorization:

a) transport of goods by motor vehicles whose Total Permissible Laden Weight (TPLW), including trailers, does not exceed 6 tons, or whose permitted payload, including trailers, does not exceed 3.5 tons;

b) transport of goods to or from airports, in cases where air services are diverted;

c) transport of vehicles which are damaged or have broken down and the transport of breakdown repair vehicles;

d) unladen runs by a goods vehicle sent to replace a vehicle which has broken down in another country and also the return run, after repair, of the vehicle that had broken down;

e) transport of spare parts and provisions for ocean-going ships and aircraft;

f) transport of medical supplies and equipment needed for emergencies, particularly in response to natural disasters;

g) transport of works and objects for fairs and exhibitions;

h) transport for non commercial purposes of material, accessories and animals to or from theatrical, musical, film, sportive, circus performances or fairs, as well as transport of material intended for radio recordings or for film or television production;

i) transport of mail as public service;

j) funereal transport.

Article 7
Authorization Quotas

1. Authorizations shall be issued by the competent authority of the Contracting Party where the vehicle is registered, within the limits of the quota fixed annually by common agreement between the competent authorities of the Contracting Parties.

2. A part of the quota referred to in paragraph 1 of this article, to be fixed by common agreement between the competent authorities of the Contracting Parties, may be used by carriers established in the territory of one of the Contracting Parties to perform transports between the territory of the other Contracting Party and a third country.

IV GENERAL PROVISIONS

Article 8
Cabotage

This Agreement does not entitle a carrier established in one of the Contracting Parties to collect passengers or to load goods in the territory of the other Contracting Party for transport within the same territory, except in cases where a special authorization is granted by the competent authority of the latter Contracting Party.

Article 9
Fiscal and Customs Regime

1. Vehicles which are registered in the territory of one Contracting Party and are temporarily imported into the territory of the other Contracting Party to perform transport services in accordance with this Agreement shall be exempt, according to the reciprocity principle, from taxes on vehicles and transport services as well as from user charges.

2. The provision of paragraph 1 of this article does not apply to tolls related to the use of motorways, bridges and other infrastructures, which shall be levied on the basis of the principle of non discrimination.

3. In transports carried out under this Agreement the temporary admission of vehicles of one Contracting Party into the territory of the other Contracting Party is exempted from customs duties.

4. For transports carried out under this Agreement the exemption from import duties as well as other charges will be mutually granted to:

a) fuel contained in the normal tanks of the vehicles;

b) lubricants in the necessary quantity to ensure their maintenance during the journey.

5. Each Contracting Party shall allow the temporary admission, with total relief of import duties and other charges and the waving of garanty submission, of spare parts meant for repairing the vehicle performing international transport operations under the present Agreement, provided that the non used parts or those having been replaced shall be re-exported or destroyed, in accordance with the provisions in force in the territory of the respective Contracting Party.

Article 10
Weight and Dimensions of Vehicles

1. In what concerns weights and dimensions of vehicles, each Contracting Party undertakes not to submit vehicles registered in the territory of the other Contracting Party to more severe conditions than those that are imposed on vehicles registered in its own country.

2. When the weight and/or the dimensions of a vehicle exceed the maximum limits admissible in the territory of the other Contracting Party, a special authorization is required from the respective authority of the same Contracting Party.

3. The authorization referred to in paragraph 2 of this article will be granted only for the carriage of goods of abnormal weight and/or dimensions.

4. Whenever the authorization stipulates that the vehicle must use a specific itinerary, it shall be valid only for that itinerary.

Article 11
Intransferableness

Authorizations, as required under the provisions of this Agreement, are personal and intransferable. They may be used only by the carrier in whose name they have been issued.

Article 12
Sanctions

1. If a carrier or his driving personnel, when in the territory of the other Contracting Party, infringe the provisions of this Agreement or the laws and regulations applicable in that territory, the competent authority of the country where the carrier is established shall, at request of the competent authority of the other Contracting Party, adopt one of the following measures:

a) issue a warning; or

b) withdraw, on a temporary or permanent basis, partially or totally, the right to perform transports under the provisions of this Agreement in the territory of the country where the infringement has been committed.

2. The competent authority having requested the adoption of a sanction shall be informed as soon as possible about its effective adoption.

3. The provisions of this article shall apply without prejudice to any sanction provided for by the laws and regulations in force in the Contracting Party in whose territory the infringement was committed.

Article 13
Authorization and Control Document Forms

The forms for authorizations and control documents as required by this Agreement shall be established by common agreement between the competent authorities of the Contracting Parties mentioned in article 16 and in the Protocol referred to in article 17.

Article 14
Control

The authorizations - or a certified copy thereof in the case of regular passenger services - as well as any control document required under the provisions of this Agreement shall be carried inside the vehicle and be presented at request of representatives of the control authorities.

Article 15
Suppletive Provisions

The laws and regulations of both Contracting Parties shall apply in all matters that are not regulated by the provisions of this Agreement or of other international agreements which are binding for the Republic of Latvia and the Portuguese Republic.

Article 16
Competent Authorities

1. The competent authorities for implementing this Agreement are:

a) in the Republic of Latvia:
Road Transport Department
Ministry of Transport;

b) in the Portuguese Republic:
Direcção-Geral de Transportes Terrestres
Ministry of Equipment, Planning and Territorial Administration.

2. The competent authorities of both Contracting Parties shall contact each other directly.

Article 17
Implementation of the Agreement

1. The competent authorities of the Contracting Parties referred to in paragraph 1 of article 16 shall by common agreement define the conditions for implementing this Agreement in a Protocol to be signed by them.

2. The Joint Committee mentioned in Article 18 of this Agreement is competent to modify the Protocol.

Article 18
Joint Committee

1. Representatives of the competent authorities mentioned in article 16 of this Agreement shall form a Joint Committee in order to ensure the correct implementation of this Agreement and to settle as soon as possible all unresolved issues. In case of necessity, representatives of other institutions may be invited to participate at the Joint Committee meetings.

2. At request of the competent authority of either Contracting Party, the Joint Committe shall hold its meetings alternately in the territories of both Contracting Parties.

V FINAL PROVISIONS

Article 19
Entry into Force

This Agreement shall enter into force on the date of the last notification, if all constitutional formalities required by the Contracting Parties have been complied with.

Article 20
Duration

1. This Agreement is concluded for an indefinite period of time.

2. Either Contracting Party may inform the other Contracting Party by means of diplomatic notes, at least three months before the end of each calendar year, of its intention to terminate this Agreement. In this case, the Agreement will cease to be in force from the first of January of the following year.

DONE in Warsaw, on May "20", 1999, in two originals, each in Latvian, Portuguese and English languages, all texts being equally authentic. In case of divergence of interpretation, the Englisn text of the Agreement shall prevail.

For the Republic of Latvia:	For the Portuguese Republic:

[TEXT IN LATVIAN – TEXTE EN LETTON]

Latvijas Republikas
un
Portugāles Republikas

NOLĪGUMS

par pasažieru un kravu starptautiskajiem pārvadājumiem ar autotransportu

Latvijas Republika un Portugāles Republika (turpmāk – Līgumslēdzējas Puses),

lai veicinātu pasažieru un kravu starptautiskos pārvadājumus ar autotransportu starp abām valstīm, kā arī tranzītā cauri to teritorijām;

vadoties no nepieciešamības izstrādāt Eiropas līmenim atbilstošu politiku, kas vērsta uz aizvien plašāku transporta pakalpojumu liberalizāciju saistībā ar konkurences apstākļu harmonizāciju, vides aizsardzību un ceļu satiksmes drošību,

vienojās par sekojošo:

I. IEVADA NOTEIKUMI

1.pants
Darbības sfēra

Saskaņā ar šī Nolīguma noteikumiem, neietekmējot 7.panta 2.punkta nosacījumus, jebkuras Līgumslēdzējas Puses valstī reģistrētiem pārvadātājiem ir tiesības veikt pasažieru vai kravu starptautiskos pārvadājumus ar autotransportu starp Līgumslēdzēju Pušu valstu teritorijām vai tranzītā cauri tām.

2.pants
Definīcijas

Šī Nolīguma ietvaros:

a) *"pārvadātājs"* ir jebkura fiziska vai juridiska persona, kura vai nu Latvijas Republikā vai Portugāles Republikā ir tiesīga veikt:

1) pasažieru vai kravu starptautiskos pārvadājumus pēc nomas līguma vai par atlīdzību;

2) pārvadājumus savām vajadzībām;

b) *"autotransporta līdzeklis"* ir:

1) saistībā ar pasažieru pārvadājumiem - jebkurš motorizēts autotransporta līdzeklis, kas paredzēts pasažieru pārvadāšanai un kurā ir vairāk kā 9 sēdvietas, autovadītāja vietu ieskaitot, kā arī tam piekabinātas piekabes pasažieru bagāžas pārvadāšanai, ar noteikumu, ka piekabe reģistrēta tās pašas Līgumslēdzējas Puses valstī, kurā reģistrēts motorizētais autotransporta līdzeklis;

2) saistībā ar kravu pārvadājumiem - jebkurš kravas automobilis, vilcējs, piekabe vai puspiekabe, kā arī jebkura kravas automobiļa vai vilcēja kombinācija ar piekabi vai puspiekabi, ar noteikumu, ka vismaz motorizētais autotransporta līdzeklis ir reģistrēts vienas vai otras Līgumslēdzējas Puses valsts teritorijā;

c) *"tranzīts"* ir pārvadājumu veids, kad vienas Līgumslēdzējas Puses valstī reģistrēts pārvadātājs, šķērsojot otras Līgumslēdzējas Puses valsts teritoriju, tajā neuzņem vai neizlaiž pasažierus vai neizkrauj vai neiekrauj kravu.

II. PASAŽIERU PĀRVADĀJUMI

3.pants
Pārvadājumu veidi

1. Saskaņā ar šī Nolīguma noteikumiem atļauts veikt šādus pasažieru pārvadājumus:

a) regulārus pārvadājumus;

b) sistemātiskus turp un atpakaļ pārvadājumus;

c) neregulārus pārvadājumus.

2. *"Regulāri pārvadājumi"* ir pārvadājumi, kurus veicot, pasažieri tiek pārvadāti noteiktos maršrutos atbilstoši iepriekš saskaņotiem kustības sarakstiem un braukšanas tarifiem ar noteiktām pieturvietām pasažieru iekāpšanai un izkāpšanai.

3. *"Sistemātiski turp un atpakaļ pārvadājumi"* ir pārvadājumi, kuros iepriekš izveidotas pasažieru grupas tiek pārvadātas atkārtotos turp un atpakaļ braucienos no vienas un tās pašas brauciena sākuma vietas uz vienu un to pašu brauciena galapunktu.

Ar *"brauciena sākuma vietu"* un *"brauciena galapunktu"* jāsaprot attiecīgi vieta, kur brauciens sākas, un vieta, kas ir brauciena mērķis, kā arī apkārtne 50 km rādiusā ap šīm vietām.

Veicot sistemātiskus turp un atpakaļ pārvadājumus, papildus transporta pakalpojumiem jānodrošina arī pasažieru izmitināšana braucienu galapunktā vismaz uz divām diennaktīm.

Ievērojot šī Nolīguma 4.panta 3.b) punkta noteikumus, sistemātisku turp un atpakaļ pārvadājumu veikšanas laikā:

- katra pasažieru grupa tādā pašā sastāvā, kādā tā veikusi braucienu turp, kādā no sekojošiem braucieniem jāatved atpakaļ brauciena sākuma vietā;
- nav atļauts uzņemt vai izlaist pasažierus ārpus brauciena sākuma vietas vai tā galapunkta;
- pirmais atpakaļbrauciens un pēdējais turpbrauciens jāveic bez pasažieriem.

4. *"Neregulāri pārvadājumi"* ir pārvadājumi, kas neatbilst ne regulāro pārvadājumu, ne sistemātisko turp un atpakaļ pārvadājumu nosacījumiem.

4.pants
Atļauju režīms

1. Izņemot 5.panta 1.punktā minētos gadījumus, visiem pasažieru pārvadājumiem, kas tiek veikti saskaņā ar šo Nolīgumu, nepieciešamas atļaujas, kuras izsniedz otras Līgumslēdzējas Puses kompetentā institūcija, balstoties uz savstarpīguma principa.

2. Attiecībā uz regulāriem pārvadājumiem:

a) to uzsākšanai, kā arī esošo regulāro pārvadājumu nosacījumu maiņas gadījumā nepieciešama atļauja, ko izdevušas Līgumslēdzēju Pušu kompetentās institūcijas, savstarpēji vienojoties un, ja nepieciešams, saņemot tranzītvalstu kompetento institūciju piekrišanu;

b) vienas Līgumslēdzējas Puses kompetentās institūcijas izdota atļauja ir derīga tikai tai maršruta daļai, kas atrodas šīs Līgumslēdzējas Puses valsts teritorijā;

c) atļauja regulāriem pārvadājumiem tiek izdota, ievērojot savstarpējās vienlīdzības principu;

d) atļaujas derīguma termiņš nedrīkst pārsniegt piecus gadus.

3. Attiecībā uz sistemātiskiem turp un atpakaļ pārvadājumiem:

a) atļaujas derīguma termiņš nedrīkst pārsniegt sešus mēnešus;

b) atļauja var piešķirt tiesības:

- noteikta procentuālā apjoma ietvaros pārvadāt pasažierus, kuri turp braukuši vienas grupas sastāvā, bet atgriežas atpakaļ citas grupas sastāvā;
- uzņemt vai izlaist pasažierus ārpus brauciena sākuma vietas un galapunkta ne vairāk kā trijās vietās.

5.pants
Pārvadājumi, kuriem atļauja nav nepieciešama

1. Atļauja nav nepieciešama šādiem neregulāriem pārvadājumiem:

a) *"braucieniem ar slēgtām durvīm"* - kad visa brauciena laikā ar vienu un to pašu autotransporta līdzekli tiek pārvadāta viena un tā pati pasažieru grupa un tā tiek atvesta atpakaļ brauciena sākuma vietā, turklāt brauciena sākuma vieta un tā galapunkts atrodas tās Līgumslēdzējas Puses valsts teritorijā, kurā autotransporta līdzeklis reģistrēts;

b) ja brauciens ar pasažieriem sākas vietā, kas atrodas tās Līgumslēdzējas Puses valsts teritorijā, kurā autotransporta līdzeklis reģistrēts, un beidzas otras Līgumslēdzējas Puses valsts teritorijā, turklāt autotransporta līdzeklis atgriežas brauciena sākuma vietā bez pasažieriem;

c) ja pēc iebraukšanas otras Līgumslēdzējas Puses valsts teritorijā bez pasažieriem seko brauciens ar pasažieriem, ar noteikumu, ka visi pasažieri tiek uzņemti vienā vietā un ka:

- šī pasažieru grupa sastādīta, pamatojoties uz pārvadājuma līgumu, kas noslēgts pirms šo pasažieru iebraukšanas otras Līgumslēdzējas Puses valsts teritorijā; vai
- šis pats pārvadātājs viņus iepriekš aizvedis uz otras Līgumslēdzējas Puses valsts teritoriju; vai
- pasažieri ielūgti ierasties tās Līgumslēdzējas Puses valsts teritorijā, kur pārvadātājs reģistrēts, ar noteikumu, ka pārvadājuma izdevumu segšana ir par ielūgumu atbildīgās personas pārziņā;

d) pasažieru autotransporta līdzekļiem bez pasažieriem gadījumos, kad tie nosūtīti, lai nomainītu otrā valstī bojātu autotransporta līdzekli un turpinātu pasažieru pārvadājumu, izmantojot bojātā autotransporta līdzekļa brauciena formulāru.

2. Veicot pārvadājumus, kuriem saskaņā ar šī panta 1.punkta nosacījumiem atļauja nav nepieciešama, nepieciešams kontroles dokuments, kura forma un saturs noteikts šī Nolīguma 17.pantā minētajā Protokolā.

III. KRAVU PĀRVADĀJUMI

6.pants
Atļauju režīms

1. Izņemot šī panta 3.punktā minētos gadījumus, kravu pārvadājumiem pēc nomas līguma vai par atlīdzību vai savām vajadzībām, ko saskaņā ar šī Nolīguma noteikumiem veic vienas Līgumslēdzējas Puses valstī reģistrēts pārvadātājs ar šajā pašā valstī reģistrētu autotransporta līdzekli, nepieciešama otras Līgumslēdzējas Puses kompetentas institūcijas izdota atļauja.

2. Līgumslēdzēju Pušu kompetentās institūcijas var vienoties par šādu divu veidu atļaujām:

a) atļaujas vienam braucienam; vai

b) atļaujas vairākiem braucieniem, kuru skaits attiecīgi norādīts.

Atļauju derīguma termiņš ir no 1.janvāra līdz nākamā gada 31.janvārim.

3. Atļaujas nav nepieciešamas šādiem pārvadājumiem:

a) kravu pārvadājumiem ar motorizētiem autotransporta līdzekļiem, kuru pilnā masa, piekabes ieskaitot, nepārsniedz 6 tonnas vai kuru celtspēja, piekabes ieskaitot, nepārsniedz 3,5 tonnas;

b) kravu pārvadājumiem uz vai no lidostām gadījumos, kad lidmašīna spiesta novirzīties no kursa;

c) bojātu vai avarējušu autotransporta līdzekļu pārvadāšanai un tehniskās palīdzības autotransporta līdzekļu braucieniem;

d) autotransporta līdzekļa braucienam bez kravas, kas nosūtīts, lai nomainītu citā valstī bojātu autotransporta līdzekli, kā arī bojātā autotransporta līdzekļa braucienam atpakaļ pēc remonta veikšanas;

e) rezerves daļu un pārtikas krājumu pārvadājumiem, kas paredzēti okeānu kuģiem un lidmašīnām;

f) medikamentu un medicīnisko iekārtu pārvadājumiem, kas nepieciešami palīdzības sniegšanai nelaimes gadījumos, īpaši dabas katastrofu gadījumos;

g) gadatirgiem un izstādēm paredzētu priekšmetu un piederumu pārvadājumiem;

h) piederumu, iekārtu un dzīvnieku pārvadājumiem nekomerciālos nolūkos, kas paredzēti teātra, mūzikas, kino, cirka izrādēm un sporta pasākumiem vai gadatirgiem, kā arī radio un televīzijas raidījumu ierakstiem vai filmu veidošanai;

i) pasta pārvadājumiem kā valsts pakalpojumam;

j) bēru pārvadājumiem.

7.pants
Atļauju kvotas

1. Atļaujas, par kuru kvotām Līgumslēdzēju Pušu kompetentās institūcijas katru gadu savstarpēji vienojas, izsniedz tās Līgumslēdzējas Puses valsts kompetentā institūcija, kurā autotransporta līdzeklis reģistrēts.

2. Šī panta 1.punktā minētās atļauju kvotas daļu, par kuru Līgumslēdzēju Pušu kompetentās institūcijas savstarpēji vienojas, vienas Līgumslēdzējas Puses valstī reģistrēti pārvadātāji var izmantot pārvadājumu veikšanai starp otras Līgumslēdzējas Puses valsts teritoriju un trešo valsti.

IV. VISPĀRĪGIE NOTEIKUMI

8.pants
Kabotāžas pārvadājumi

Saskaņā ar šī Nolīguma noteikumiem vienas Līgumslēdzējas Puses valstī reģistrētiem pārvadātājiem nav atļauts otras Līgumslēdzējas Puses valsts teritorijā uzņemt pasažierus vai iekraut kravu nogādāšanai citā vietā šīs pašas valsts teritorijā, izņemot gadījumus, kad šīs Līgumslēdzējas Puses kompetentā institūcija ir izsniegusi speciālu atļauju.

9.pants
Finansu un muitas noteikumi

1. Vienas Līgumslēdzējas Puses valsts teritorijā reģistrēti autotransporta līdzekļi, kas uz laiku iebraukuši otras Līgumslēdzējas Puses valsts teritorijā, lai veiktu pārvadājumus saskaņā ar šo Nolīgumu, tiek abpusēji atbrīvoti no nodokļu maksājumiem, kas saistīti ar autotransporta līdzekli un ar pārvadājumu veikšanu, kā arī no ceļu lietotāja nodevas.

2. Šī panta 1.punktā minētais atbrīvojums neattiecas uz nodevām par maksas autoceļu, tiltu un citu infrastruktūru lietošanu, kuri iekasējami, pamatojoties uz nediskriminējošiem nosacījumiem.

3. Vienas Līgumslēdzējas Puses autotransporta līdzekļi, kas uz laiku iebraukuši otras Līgumslēdzējas Puses valsts teritorijā, lai veiktu pārvadājumus saskaņā ar šo Nolīgumu, tiek atbrīvoti no muitas nodevas.

4. Veicot pārvadājumus saskaņā ar šo Nolīgumu, no ievednodevas, kā arī citiem maksājumiem abpusēji tiek atbrīvota:

a) degviela, kas atrodas autotransporta līdzekļu standarta tvertnēs;

b) smērvielas tādā daudzumā, kāds nepieciešams, lai nodrošinātu autotransporta līdzekļu apkopi brauciena laikā.

5. Katra Līgumslēdzēja Puse atļauj ievest uz laiku rezerves daļas, kas paredzētas to autotransporta līdzekļu remontam, kas veic starptautiskos pārvadājumus saskaņā ar šo Nolīgumu, atbrīvojot tās no ievednodevām un citiem maksājumiem, kā arī pieprasot tās uzrādīt, ar noteikumu, ka neizmantotās vai nomainītās detaļas ir jāizved vai jāiznīcina saskaņā ar šīs Līgumslēdzējas Puses valsts teritorijā spēkā esošajiem noteikumiem.

10.pants
Autotransporta līdzekļu svars un izmēri

1. Attiecībā uz autotransporta līdzekļu svaru un izmēriem katra Līgumslēdzēja Puse apņemas neizvirzīt otras Līgumslēdzējas Puses valsts teritorijā reģistrētiem autotransporta līdzekļiem augstākas prasības par tām, kas noteiktas savā valstī reģistrētiem autotransporta līdzekļiem.

2. Ja autotransporta līdzekļa svars un/vai izmēri pārsniedz otras Līgumslēdzējas Puses valsts teritorijā noteiktās pieļaujamās normas, nepieciešama šīs Līgumslēdzējas Puses kompetentās institūcijas speciāla atļauja.

3. Šī panta 2.punktā minētā atļauja tiek izsniegta tikai tādiem kravu pārvadājumiem, kad svars un/vai izmēri pārsniedz noteiktās normas.

4. Ja šajā atļaujā noteikts, ka attiecīgais autotransporta līdzeklis drīkst pārvietoties tikai noteiktā maršrutā, tad šī atļauja derīga tikai braucienam šajā maršrutā.

11.pants
Atļaujas izmantošanas tiesības

Atļaujas, kas nepieciešamas pārvadājumu veikšanai saskaņā ar šī Nolīguma nosacījumiem un izsniegtas noteiktai personai, nav nododamas citām personām. Šīs atļaujas var izmantot tikai tas pārvadātājs, kuram tās izsniegtas.

12.pants
Sankcijas

1. Ja pārvadātājs vai viņa autotransporta līdzekļa apkalpe otras Līgumslēdzējas Puses valsts teritorijā pārkāpj šī Nolīguma noteikumus vai tur spēkā esošos likumus vai citus normatīvos aktus, tad tās valsts kompetentā institūcija, kurā autotransporta līdzeklis reģistrēts, pēc otras Līgumslēdzējas Puses kompetentās institūcijas pieprasījuma piemēro vienu no šādām sankcijām:

a) izsaka pārvadātājam brīdinājumu vai

b) atņem uz laiku vai pavisam, daļēji vai pilnīgi tiesības veikt pārvadājumus saskaņā ar šo Nolīgumu tās valsts teritorijā, kur pārkāpums noticis.

2. Kompetentā institūcija, kas pieprasījusi piemērot kādu no sankcijām, iespējami ātri jāinformē par šīs sankcijas piemērošanu.

3. Šī panta noteikumi neierobežo nevienu likumīgu sankciju, ko var piemērot saskaņā ar tās Līgumslēdzējas Puses valsts likumiem un citiem normatīvajiem aktiem, kuras teritorijā pārkāpums noticis.

13.pants
Atļauju un kontroles dokumentu forma

Atļauju un kontroles dokumentu formu, kas nepieciešami saskaņā ar šo Nolīgumu, savstarpēji vienojoties, nosaka Līgumslēdzēju Pušu kompetentās institūcijas, kas minētas 16.pantā un saskaņā ar 17.pantu sastādītajā Protokolā.

14.pants
Kontrole

Atļaujai vai pasažieru regulāro pārvadājumu gadījumā – to apstiprinātai kopijai, kā arī jebkuram citam kontroles dokumentam, kas paredzēts šajā Nolīgumā, jāatrodas autotransporta līdzeklī, un tie jāuzrāda pēc kontrolējošo institūciju pārstāvju pieprasījuma.

15.pants
Papildnoteikumi

Gadījumos, ko neregulē ne šī Nolīguma, ne arī citu, Latvijas Republikai un Portugāles Republikai saistošu starptautisko līgumu noteikumi, piemērojami Līgumslēdzēju Pušu valstu nacionālie likumi un noteikumi.

16.pants
Kompetentās institūcijas

1. Kompetentās institūcijas šī Nolīguma piemērošanai ir:

a) Latvijas Republikā:
Satiksmes ministrija
Autosatiksmes departaments;

b) Portugāles Republikā:
Apgādes, plānošanas un teritoriālās pārvaldes ministrija
Sauszemes transporta direkcija.

2. Abu Līgumslēdzēju Pušu kompetentās institūcijas savstarpēji sazinās tieši.

17.pants
Nolīguma piemērošana

1. 16.panta 1.punktā minētās Līgumslēdzēju Pušu kompetentās institūcijas savstarpēji vienojas par šī Nolīguma piemērošanas kārtību, sastādot Protokolu, ko paraksta šo kompetento institūciju pārstāvji.

2. Šī Nolīguma 18.pantā minētai Kopējai komisijai ir tiesības grozīt šī Protokola saturu.

18.pants
Kopējā komisija

1. Lai nodrošinātu pareizu šī Nolīguma piemērošanu un iespējami ātri atrisinātu visas ar to saistītās problēmas, šī Nolīguma 16.pantā minēto kompetento institūciju pārstāvji izveido Kopējo komisiju. Nepieciešamības gadījumā Kopējās komisijas sēdēs var pieaicināt citu institūciju pārstāvjus.

2. Kopējās Komisijas sēdes notiek pēc vienas vai otras Līgumslēdzējas Puses kompetentās institūcijas ierosinājuma pārmaiņus abu Līgumslēdzēju Pušu valstu teritorijās.

V. NOSLĒGUMA NOTEIKUMI

19.pants
Stāšanās spēkā

Šis Nolīgums stājas spēkā dienā, kad saņemts pēdējais paziņojums, ko Līgumslēdzējas Puses nosūta viena otrai par to, ka visas konstitucionālās prasības, lai Nolīgums stātos spēkā, ir izpildītas.

20.pants
Darbības ilgums

1. Šis Nolīgums tiek noslēgts uz nenoteiktu laiku.

2. Jebkura Līgumslēdzēja Puse ne vēlāk kā trīs mēnešus pirms katra kalendārā gada beigām pa diplomātiskajiem kanāliem var informēt otru Līgumslēdzēju Pusi par savu nodomu pārtraukt šī Nolīguma darbību. Šajā gadījumā Nolīguma darbība tiek pārtraukta, sākot ar sekojošā gada 1. janvāri.

Parakstīts Varšavā 1999.gada "20." maijā divos oriģināleksemplāros, katrs latviešu, portugāļu un angļu valodā, turklāt visi teksti ir autentiski. Atšķirīgas interpretācijas gadījumā noteicošais ir Nolīguma teksts angļu valodā.

Latvijas Republikas vārdā:	Portugāles Republikas vārdā:
[signature]	[signature]

[TEXT IN PORTUGUESE – TEXTE EN PORTUGAIS][1]

ACORDO
ENTRE
A REPÚBLICA DA LETÓNIA
E
A REPÚBLICA PORTUGUESA
RELATIVO A TRANSPORTES INTERNACIONAIS RODOVIÁRIOS
DE PASSAGEIROS E MERCADORIAS

A República da Letónia e a República Portuguesa, de ora em diante designados por "Partes Contratantes";

desejosos de contribuir para o desenvolvimento do transporte rodoviário de passageiros e mercadorias entre os dois países, bem como em trânsito através dos respectivos territórios;

considerando a necessidade de estabelecer, a nível europeu, uma política orientada para a progressiva liberalização dos serviços de transportes, articulada com a harmonização das condições de concorrência, a protecção do ambiente e a segurança no tráfego rodoviário;

Acordaram no seguinte:

SECÇÃO I
DISPOSIÇÕES INTRODUTÓRIAS

Artigo 1º

Âmbito

Sem prejuízo do disposto no nº 2 do seu Artigo 7º, o presente Acordo confere aos transportadores estabelecidos em qualquer das Partes Contratantes o direito de

[1] Published as submitted – Publié tel que soumis.

transportar passageiros ou mercadorias por estrada entre os territórios das Partes Contratantes ou em trânsito através desses territórios.

Artigo 2º

Definições

Para efeitos do presente Acordo:

a) entende-se por "transportador" qualquer pessoa física ou moral que esteja devidamente autorizada, quer na República da Letónia, quer na República Portuguesa;

1) a exercer a actividade de transporte internacional rodoviário de passageiros ou de mercadorias por conta de outrem;

2) a efectuar transportes por conta própria;

b) entende-se por "veículo":

1) no caso do transporte de passageiros, qualquer veículo a motor destinado ao transporte de passageiros, com mais de 9 lugares sentados, incluindo o lugar do condutor, bem como reboques destinados ao transporte de bagagem, na condição de o reboque e o veículo a motor estarem matriculados no território da mesma Parte Contratante;

2) no caso do transporte de mercadorias, qualquer camião, tractor, reboque ou semi-reboque, bem como qualquer veículo articulado ou conjunto camião-reboque, na condição de pelo menos o veículo a motor estar matriculado no território de uma das Partes Contratantes;

c) entende-se como "em trânsito" o transporte efectuado por um transportador estabelecido numa das Partes Contratantes através do território da outra Parte Contratante sem aí tomar nem largar quaisquer passageiros ou mercadorias.

SECÇÃO II

TRANSPORTE DE PASSAGEIROS

Artigo 3°

Tipos de serviços

1. Os serviços de transporte de passageiros a efectuar ao abrigo do presente Acordo podem ser:

a) serviços regulares;

b) serviços de lançadeira;

c) serviços ocasionais.

2. "Serviços regulares" são serviços que asseguram o transporte de passageiros em percursos especificados, de acordo com itinerário, frequência, horário, tarifas e pontos de paragem para o embarque e o desembarque de passageiros previamente determinados.

3. "Serviços de lançadeira" são serviços em que, por meio de várias viagens de ida e de volta, grupos de passageiros previamente constituídos são transportados da mesma área de partida para a mesma área de destino.

Por "área de partida" e "área de destino" entende-se, respectivamente, o local em que a viagem se inicia e o local em que a viagem termina, bem como, em ambos os casos, todas as localidades situadas dentro de um raio de 50 kms.

Os serviços de lançadeira deverão compreender, além do transporte, o alojamento dos passageiros na área de destino por período de, pelo menos, duas noites.

Sem prejuízo do disposto na alínea b) do nº 3 do Artigo 4º deste Acordo, nos serviços de lançadeira:

- cada grupo de passageiros que hajam efectuado juntos a viagem de ida é reconduzido subsequentemente, também em conjunto, ao ponto de origem;

- não poderão ser tomados nem largados passageiros fora das áreas de partida e destino;

- a primeira viagem de volta e a última viagem de ida são efectuadas em vazio.

4. "Serviços ocasionais" são serviços que não correspondem à definição de serviços regulares nem à definição de serviços de lançadeira.

Artigo 4º
Regime de autorização

1. Sem prejuízo das excepções referidas no nº 1 do Artigo 5º, quaisquer serviços de transporte de passageiros efectuados ao abrigo do presente Acordo estão sujeitos a uma autorização concedida pela autoridade competente da outra Parte Contratante, numa base de reciprocidade.

2. No que respeita a serviços regulares:

a) o estabelecimento de um serviço regular, bem como a alteração das respectivas condições de exploração, será autorizado de comum acordo pelas Partes Contratantes, na condição de se obter, quando for caso disso, a aprovação das autoridades competentes dos países de trânsito;

b) uma autorização concedida pela autoridade competente de uma Parte Contratante só será válida para a parte do percurso que esteja situada no território dessa mesma Parte Contratante;

c) em princípio, a autorização para cada serviço regular será concedida numa base de reciprocidade;

d) o prazo de validade de uma autorização não pode exceder cinco anos.

3. No que respeita a serviços de lançadeira:

a) o prazo de validade de uma autorização não poderá exceder seis meses;

b) poderá ser concedida uma autorização que permita que:

- numa determinada percentagem, passageiros que foram transportados na viagem de ida incluídos num certo grupo sejam transportados na viagem de volta integrados num outro grupo;

- possam ser tomados ou largados passageiros num número máximo de três lugares fora das área de partida e de três lugares fora da área de destino.

Artigo 5º

Serviços de transporte isentos do regime de autorização

1. Não necessitam de autorização os seguintes serviços ocasionais:

a) "circuitos em portas fechadas", isto é, serviços em que um mesmo veículo transporta um mesmo grupo de passageiros em toda a viagem, reconduzindo-os ao ponto de partida, desde que o local de partida e destino esteja situado no território da Parte Contratante em que o veículo estiver matriculado;

b) serviços que comportem uma viagem em carga de um local de partida situado no território da Parte Contratante em que o veículo estiver matriculado para um local de destino situado no território da outra Parte Contratante, seguida de uma viagem de retorno em vazio para o local de partida;

c) serviços que comportem uma viagem de entrada em vazio no território da outra Parte Contratante, seguida de uma viagem em carga, desde que todos os passageiros sejam tomados no mesmo lugar e que:

- sejam agrupados por contrato de transporte celebrado antes da sua entrada no território da outra Parte Contratante; ou

- tenham sido anteriormente transportados pela mesma empresa para o território da outra Parte Contratante; ou

- tenham sido convidados a deslocar-se ao território da Parte Contratante onde o transportador esteja estabelecido, sendo o preço do transporte suportado pela entidade que tenha formulado o convite.

d) as viagens em vazio de um veículo de passageiros enviado para substituir um veículo avariado num outro país, a fim de prosseguir o transporte de passageiros ao abrigo da folha itinerária do veículo avariado.

2. Os serviços isentos de autorização nos termos do nº 1 do presente artigo serão efectuados a coberto de um documento de controlo a ser definido no Protocolo a que se refere o artigo 17º do presente Acordo.

SECÇÃO III
TRANSPORTE DE MERCADORIAS

Artigo 6º

Regime de autorização

1. Sem prejuízo das excepções referidas no nº 3 do presente artigo, o transporte de mercadorias por conta de outrem ou por conta própria efectuado ao abrigo do disposto no presente Acordo por um transportador estabelecido numa das Partes Contratantes por meio de um veículo a motor matriculado nessa mesma Parte Contratante está sujeito a autorização concedida pela autoridade competente da outra Parte Contratante.

2. As autoridades competentes das duas Partes Contratantes poderão, de comum acordo, estabelecer os seguintes tipos de autorizações:

a) autorizações por viagem, válidas para uma só viagem; ou

b) autorizações a prazo, válidas para o número de viagens nelas indicado, com validade de 1 de Janeiro a 31 de Janeiro do ano seguinte.

3. Estão isentos de autorização os seguintes transportes:

a) transporte de mercadorias por meio de veículos a motor cujo Peso Máximo Autorizado (PTAC), incluindo os reboques, não exceda 6 toneladas, ou cuja carga útil, incluindo reboques, não exceda 3,5 toneladas;

b) transporte de mercadorias de ou para aeroportos, em casos de desvio de serviços aéreos;

c) transporte de veículos danificados ou avariados, assim como o transporte de veículos destinados à sua reparação;

d) viagens em vazio efectuadas por um veículo enviado para substituir um veículo avariado noutro país, bem como a viagem de regresso, depois da reparação, do veículo que tinha sofrido avaria;

e) transporte de peças sobressalentes e de mantimentos destinados a navios de mar alto e a aviões;

f) transporte de artigos e equipamentos médicos necessários em situações de emergência, particularmente para acorrer a desastres naturais;

g) transporte de obras e objectos destinados a feiras e exposições;

h) transporte sem fins comerciais de material, acessórios e animais de ou para actividades teatrais, musicais, cinematográficas, desportivas, circenses ou feiras, bem como transporte de material destinados a gravações radiofónicas ou a produções cinematográficas ou televisivas;

i) transporte de correio como serviço público;

j) transportes funerários.

Artigo 7º

Contingentamento

1. As autorizações serão emitidas pela autoridade competente da Parte Contratante de matrícula do veículo, dentro dos limites do contingente fixado anualmente de comum acordo entre as autoridades competentes das Partes Contratantes.

2. Uma parte do contingente referido no nº 1 do presente artigo, a ser determinada de comum acordo pelas autoridades competentes das Partes Contratantes, poderá ser utilizada por transportadores estabelecidos numa das Partes Contratantes para efectuar transportes entre o território da outra Parte Contratante e um terceiro país.

SECÇÃO IV
DISPOSIÇÕES GERAIS

Artigo 8º

Cabotagem

O presente Acordo não confere a um transportador estabelecido numa das Partes Contratantes o direito de recolher passageiros ou carregar mercadorias no território da outra Parte Contratante para os transportar dentro desse mesmo território, com excepção dos casos em que seja concedida uma autorização especial para esse efeito pela autoridade competente desta última Parte Contratante.

Artigo 9º

Regime fiscal e aduaneiro

1. Os veículos matriculados no território de uma Parte Contratante e que sejam temporariamente importados no território da outra Parte Contratante para efectuar serviços de transporte em conformidade com o presente Acordo serão isentos, de acordo com o princípio da reciprocidade, de impostos sobre veículos e serviços de transporte, bem como de direitos de uso.

2. O disposto no nº 1 do presente artigo não se aplica a portagens relacionadas com a utilização de auto-estradas, pontes e outras infra-estruturas, as quais serão cobradas com base no princípio da não discriminação.

3. Nos transportes efectuados ao abrigo do presente Acordo, é permitida a importação temporária de veículos de uma Parte Contratante no território da outra Parte contratante, sem pagamento de direitos.

4. No caso dos transportes efectuados ao abrigo do presente Acordo, é concedida mutuamente franquia dos direitos de importação e de outras imposições:

   a) ao carburante contido nos reservatórios normais dos veículos que os efectuem;

   b) aos lubrificantes na quantidade necessária para a sua manutenção durante a viagem.

5. Cada Parte Contratante autorizará a importação temporária, com suspensão total de direitos de importação e de outras imposições e dispensa de prestação de garantia, de peças sobresselentes destinadas à reparação dos

veículos que efectuem transportes internacionais ao abrigo do presente Acordo, sob condição de as peças não utilizadas ou as que tiverem sido substituídas serem reexportadas ou destruídas, em conformidade com as disposições em vigor no território da respectiva Parte Contratante.

Artigo 10º

Pesos e dimensões dos veículos

1. No que respeita a pesos e dimensões dos veículos, cada uma das Partes Contratantes compromete-se a não sujeitar os veículos matriculados no território da outra Parte Contratante a condições mais restritivas do que as que são impostas aos veículos matriculados no seu próprio país.

2. No caso de o peso e/ou as dimensões de um veículo excederem os limites máximos admitidos no território da outra Parte Contratante, é exigida uma autorização especial da autoridade competente dessa mesma Parte Contratante.

3. As autorizações referidas no nº 2 do presente artigo serão concedidas exclusivamente para o transporte de mercadorias de peso e/ou dimensões excepcionais.

4. Sempre que a autorização estipule que o veículo deve utilizar um itinerário específico, a autorização será exclusivamente válida para esse itinerário.

Artigo 11°

Intransmissibilidade

As autorizações exigíveis nos termos do presente Acordo são pessoais e intransmissíveis. Poderão ser utilizadas apenas pelo transportador em cujo nome foram emitidas.

Artigo 12°

Regime sancionatório

1. No caso de um transportador ou o seu pessoal de condução infringir, no território da outra Parte Contratante, as disposições do presente Acordo ou as leis e regulamentos aplicáveis nesse território, a autoridade competente do país em que o transportador está estabelecido deverá, a pedido da autoridade competente da outra Parte Contratante, adoptar uma das seguintes medidas:

   a) emitir uma advertência; ou

   b) retirar, temporária ou definitivamente, parcial ou totalmente, o direito de efectuar transportes ao abrigo do presente Acordo, no território da Parte Contratante em que foi cometida a infracção.

2. A autoridade competente que tiver requerido a adopção de uma sanção será informada logo que possível de que a sanção foi realmente adoptada.
3. O disposto no presente artigo aplicar-se-á sem prejuízo de quaisquer sanções previstas nas leis e regulamentos em vigor na Parte Contratante em cujo território foi cometida a infracção.

Artigo 13º

Modelos de impressos de autorização e de documento de controlo

Os modelos de impressos de autorização e de documentos de controlo exigidos pelo presente Acordo serão estabelecidos de comum acordo pelas autoridades competentes das Partes Contratantes referidas no artigo 16º e no Protocolo referido no artigo 17º.

Artigo 14º

Fiscalização

As autorizações - ou respectiva cópia certificada no caso dos serviços regulares de passageiros - bem como todos os documentos de controlo exigíveis nos termos do presente Acordo, deverão ser conservados a bordo do veículo e ser apresentados aos agentes de fiscalização sempre que estes o solicitem.

Artigo 15º

Disposições supletivas

As leis e regulamentos de ambas as Partes Contratantes aplicar-se-ão em todos os casos não regulados pelas disposições do presente Acordo ou de outros acordos internacionais a que a Letónia e Portugal estejam obrigados.

Artigo 16º

Autoridades competentes

1. As autoridades competentes para a implementação deste Acordo são as seguintes :

a) Na República da Letónia:
Departamento de Transportes Rodoviários
Ministério dos Transportes

b) Na República Portuguesa
Direcção-Geral de Transportes Terrestres
Ministério do Equipamento, do Planeamento e da Administração do Território

2. As autoridades competentes de ambas as Partes Contratantes contactarão directamente entre si.

Artigo 17º

Implementação do Acordo

1. As autoridades competentes das Partes Contratantes, referidas no nº 1 do artigo 16º, definirão, de comum acordo, as condições de implementação do presente Acordo num Protocolo que será por elas assinado.

2. A Comissão Mista a que se refere o artigo 18º do presente Acordo é competente para alterar o Protocolo.

Artigo 18º

Comissão Mista

1. As Partes Contratantes instituem uma Comissão Mista, composta por representantes seus, com o fim de assegurar a correcta implementação do

presente Acordo e de regular com a celeridade possível todas as questões por resolver. Em caso de necessidade, poderão ser convidados a participar nas reuniões da Comissão Mista representantes de outras instituições.

2. A pedido da autoridade competente de uma das Partes Contratantes, a Comissão Mista realizará as suas reuniões alternadamente nos territórios das duas Partes Contratantes.

SECÇÃO V

DISPOSIÇÕES FINAIS

Artigo 19º

Entrada em vigor

1. As Partes Contratantes notificar-se-ão mutuamente, através dos canais diplomáticos, de que foram cumpridas as condições necessárias, nos termos das respectivas legislações nacionais, para a entrada em vigor do presente Acordo.

2. O presente Acordo entrará em vigor na data da última notificação de se encontrarem cumpridas as formalidades constitucionais exigidas em cada uma das Partes Contratantes.

Artigo 20º
Período de validade

1. O presente Acordo é válido por um período de tempo indefinido.

2. Uma Parte Contratante poderá informar a outra Parte Contratante, através de notas diplomáticas, pelo menos três meses antes do fim de cada ano civil, acerca da sua intenção de denunciar o presente Acordo. Nesse caso, o presente Acordo deixará de vigorar a partir de 1 de Janeiro do ano seguinte.

Feito em VARSÓVIA, em 20 Maio 1999, em três versões originais em línguas letã, portuguesa e inglesa, todos os textos fazendo fé por igual. Em caso de divergência de interpretação, prevalecerá a versão inglesa do Acordo.

PELA
REPÚBLICA DA LETÓNIA

PELA
REPÚBLICA PORTUGUESA

[TRANSLATION IN FRENCH – TRADUCTION EN FRANÇAIS]

ACCORD ENTRE LA RÉPUBLIQUE DE LETTONIE ET LA RÉPUBLIQUE PORTUGAISE RELATIF AU TRANSPORT INTERNATIONAL DE PASSAGERS ET DE MARCHANDISES PAR ROUTE

La République de Lettonie et la République portugaise, ci-après dénommées « Parties contractantes »,

Désireuses de contribuer au développement du transport routier de passagers et de marchandises entre leurs deux pays, ainsi qu'en transit à travers leurs territoires,

Tenant compte de la nécessité d'établir, au niveau européen, une politique orientée vers la libéralisation progressive des services de transport, dans un contexte d'harmonisation des conditions de concurrence, de protection de l'environnement et de sécurité routière,

Sont convenues de ce qui suit :

I. DISPOSITIONS INTRODUCTIVES

Article premier. Champ d'application

Sans préjudice des dispositions du paragraphe 2 de l'article 7, le présent Accord donne le droit aux transporteurs établis sur le territoire de l'une ou l'autre Partie contractante de transporter par la route des passagers ou des marchandises entre les territoires des Parties contractantes ou en transit à travers lesdits territoires.

Article 2. Définitions

Aux fins du présent Accord :

a) Le terme « transporteur » désigne toute personne physique ou morale dûment autorisée soit en République de Lettonie, soit en République portugaise :

1) À se livrer au transport international de passagers ou de marchandises par route, pour compte d'autrui ;

2) À effectuer des transports pour compte propre ;

b) Le terme « véhicule » désigne :

1) Dans le cas du transport de passagers, tout véhicule à moteur destiné au transport de passagers comportant plus de neuf sièges, y compris celui du conducteur, ainsi que les remorques destinées au transport de bagages de passagers, à condition que la remorque soit immatriculée sur le territoire de la même Partie contractante que le véhicule à moteur ;

2) Dans le cas du transport de marchandises, tout camion, tracteur, toute remorque ou semi-remorque, ainsi que tout véhicule articulé ou ensemble camion-remorque, à condition que le véhicule à moteur au moins soit immatriculé sur le territoire de l'une ou l'autre Partie contractante ;

c) Le terme « transit » désigne le transport effectué par un transporteur établi sur le territoire de l'une des Parties contractantes à travers le territoire de l'autre Partie contractante sans prendre ni déposer de passagers ou de marchandises sur son trajet.

II. Transport de passagers

Article 3. Types de services

1. Les services de transport de passagers pouvant être effectués en vertu des dispositions du présent Accord sont les suivants :

   a) Les services réguliers ;

   b) Les services de navette ;

   c) Les services occasionnels.

2. L'expression « services réguliers » désigne les services de transport de passagers sur des itinéraires spécifiés conformément à des horaires, à des tarifs et à des arrêts, où les passagers peuvent monter et descendre, prédéterminés.

3. L'expression « services de navette » désigne les services par lesquels des groupes de passagers préconstitués sont acheminés depuis la même zone de départ vers la même zone de destination en répétant plusieurs voyages aller et retour.

Les expressions « zone de départ » et « zone de destination » désignent respectivement le lieu où le voyage commence et celui où il se termine, ainsi que, dans chaque cas, les localités situées dans un rayon de 50 kilomètres.

En plus du transport, les services de navette doivent inclure l'hébergement des passagers dans la zone de destination pendant au moins deux nuits.

Sans préjudice des dispositions de l'alinéa b) du paragraphe 3 de l'article 4 du présent Accord, en ce qui concerne les services de navette :

- Les membres d'un groupe de passagers ayant effectué ensemble le voyage aller sont ramenés ensemble au point de départ lors d'un voyage ultérieur ;
- Les passagers ne sont pas embarqués ni déposés en dehors des zones de départ et de destination ;
- Le premier voyage de retour et le dernier voyage aller sont effectués à vide.

4. L'expression « services occasionnels » désigne les services qui n'entrent pas dans la définition des services réguliers ni dans celle des services de navette.

Article 4. Régime d'autorisation

1. En dehors des exceptions visées au paragraphe 1 de l'article 5, tout service de transport de passagers exécuté en vertu du présent Accord est soumis à une autorisation accordée par l'autorité compétente de l'autre Partie contractante selon le principe de réciprocité.

2. En ce qui concerne les services réguliers :

   a) La mise en place d'un service régulier, ainsi que la modification de ses conditions d'exploitation, sera autorisée d'un commun accord entre les autorités compétentes des

Parties contractantes, à condition que les autorités compétentes des pays de transit donnent leur accord, lorsque cela est nécessaire ;

b) Une autorisation accordée par l'autorité compétente d'une Partie contractante ne sera valable que pour la partie de l'itinéraire qui est située sur le territoire de cette Partie contractante ;

c) L'autorisation sera en principe accordée pour chaque service régulier selon le principe de réciprocité ;

d) La durée de validité d'une autorisation ne peut dépasser cinq ans.

3. En ce qui concerne les services de navette :

a) La durée de validité d'une autorisation ne peut dépasser six mois ;

b) Une autorisation peut être accordée pour :

- Permettre, selon un pourcentage déterminé, à des passagers ayant été acheminés à l'aller avec un certain groupe d'être acheminés au retour avec un autre groupe ;
- Permettre d'embarquer ou de déposer des passagers dans trois lieux, au maximum, situés en dehors des zones de départ et dans trois lieux, au maximum, situés en dehors de la zone de destination.

Article 5. Services de transport dispensés d'autorisation

1. Les services occasionnels suivants ne nécessitent pas d'autorisation :

a) Les « circuits à portes fermées », c'est-à-dire les services pour lesquels le même véhicule sert à transporter le même groupe de passagers tout au long du trajet et à les ramener au lieu de départ, à condition que les lieux de départ et de destination soient situés sur le territoire de la Partie contractante où le véhicule est immatriculé ;

b) Les services impliquant un voyage en charge depuis un lieu de départ situé sur le territoire de la Partie contractante où est immatriculé le véhicule jusqu'à un lieu de destination situé sur le territoire de l'autre Partie contractante, suivi d'un retour à vide jusqu'au lieu de départ ;

c) Les services impliquant un voyage à vide sur le territoire de l'autre Partie contractante, suivi d'un voyage en charge, à condition que tous les passagers soient embarqués au même endroit et :

- Qu'ils constituent un groupe formé dans le cadre d'un contrat de transport conclu avant leur arrivée sur le territoire de l'autre Partie contractante ; ou
- Qu'ils aient préalablement été transportés par la même entreprise sur le territoire de l'autre Partie contractante ; ou
- Qu'ils aient été invités à se rendre sur le territoire de la Partie contractante où le transporteur est établi, les frais de transport étant à la charge de la personne qui les invite ;

d) Les trajets à vide d'un véhicule de transport de passagers envoyé pour remplacer un véhicule en panne dans un autre pays, afin de poursuivre l'opération de transport de passagers sous le couvert de la feuille de route du véhicule en panne.

2. Les services dispensés d'autorisation en vertu des dispositions du paragraphe 1 du présent article sont exécutés sous le couvert d'un document de contrôle devant être établi dans le protocole visé à l'article 17 du présent Accord.

III. Transport de marchandises

Article 6. Régime d'autorisation

1. En dehors des exceptions visées au paragraphe 3 du présent article, les opérations de transport de marchandises pour compte d'autrui ou pour compte propre effectuées en vertu des dispositions du présent Accord par un transporteur établi dans le pays de l'une des Parties contractantes, au moyen d'un véhicule à moteur immatriculé dans ce même pays, sont soumis à une autorisation accordée par l'autorité compétente de l'autre Partie contractante.

2. Les autorités compétentes des deux Parties contractantes peuvent convenir des deux types d'autorisations suivants :

a) Les autorisations de voyage, valables pour un seul voyage ; ou

b) Les autorisations permettant d'effectuer plusieurs voyages, valables pour le nombre de voyages indiqué sur celles-ci ;

dont la durée de validité s'étend du 1er au 31 janvier de l'année suivante.

3. Les opérations de transport suivantes sont dispensées d'autorisation :

a) Le transport de marchandises par des véhicules à moteur dont le poids total autorisé en charge (PTAC), y compris les remorques, n'excède pas 6 tonnes, ou dont la charge utile, y compris les remorques, n'excède pas 3,5 tonnes ;

b) Le transport de marchandises au départ ou en provenance d'aéroports, dans les cas où les services aériens ont été détournés ;

c) Le transport de véhicules endommagés ou en panne ainsi que le transport des véhicules de réparation ;

d) Le transport à vide par un véhicule de transport de marchandises envoyé pour remplacer un véhicule en panne dans un autre pays, ainsi que le retour, après réparation, du véhicule tombé en panne ;

e) Le transport de pièces détachées et d'approvisionnements pour les navires de mer et les aéronefs ;

f) Le transport de fournitures et d'équipements médicaux nécessaires pour les urgences, particulièrement pour faire face aux catastrophes naturelles ;

g) Le transport d'œuvres et d'objets pour les foires et les expositions ;

h) Le transport à des fins non commerciales de matériel, d'accessoires et d'animaux à destination ou en provenance de représentations théâtrales, musicales, cinématographiques, d'évènements sportifs, de cirques ou de foires, ainsi que le transport de matériel destiné à des enregistrements radiophoniques ou de production cinématographique ou télévisée ;

i) Le transport de courrier en tant que service public ;

j) Le transport funéraire.

Article 7. Quotas d'autorisations

1. Les autorisations sont délivrées par l'autorité compétente de la Partie contractante sur le territoire de laquelle le véhicule est immatriculé, dans les limites du quota fixé annuellement d'un commun accord entre les autorités compétentes des Parties contractantes.

2. Une partie du quota visé au paragraphe 1 du présent article, à fixer d'un commun accord entre les autorités compétentes des Parties contractantes, peut être utilisée par les transporteurs établis sur le territoire d'une des Parties contractantes pour effectuer des opérations de transport entre le territoire de l'autre Partie contractante et celui d'un pays tiers.

IV. DISPOSITIONS GÉNÉRALES

Article 8. Cabotage

Le présent Accord n'autorise pas un transporteur établi sur le territoire de l'une des Parties contractantes à prendre des passagers ou à charger des marchandises sur le territoire de l'autre Partie contractante pour les transporter à l'intérieur de ce même territoire, sauf dans les cas où une autorisation spéciale est accordée par l'autorité compétente de cette dernière Partie contractante.

Article 9. Régime fiscal et douanier

1. Les véhicules immatriculés sur le territoire d'une Partie contractante et importés temporairement sur le territoire de l'autre Partie contractante afin d'exécuter des services de transport conformément au présent Accord sont exemptés, selon le principe de réciprocité, des taxes sur les véhicules et les services de transport ainsi que des redevances d'usage.

2. Les dispositions du paragraphe 1 du présent article ne s'appliquent pas aux droits de péages liés à l'utilisation des autoroutes, ponts et autres infrastructures, dont la perception repose sur le principe de non-discrimination.

3. L'admission temporaire des véhicules d'une Partie contractante sur le territoire de l'autre Partie contractante dans le cadre des opérations de transport effectuées en vertu du présent Accord est exemptée de droits de douane.

4. L'exemption de droits d'importation et d'autres redevances dans le cadre des opérations de transport effectuées en vertu du présent Accord est mutuellement accordée :

a) Au carburant contenu dans les réservoirs d'origine des véhicules ;

b) À la quantité de lubrifiants nécessaire pour assurer l'entretien des véhicules pendant le transport.

5. Chaque Partie contractante autorise l'admission temporaire, en exonération totale des droits d'importation et autres redevances et sans obligation de présenter une garantie, des pièces détachées destinées à la réparation du véhicule effectuant des opérations de transport international dans le cadre du présent Accord, à condition que les pièces non utilisées ou celles qui ont été remplacées soient réexportées ou détruites, conformément aux dispositions en vigueur sur le territoire de la Partie contractante concernée.

Article 10. Poids et gabarit des véhicules

1. En matière de poids et de gabarit des véhicules, chacune des Parties contractantes s'engage à ne pas soumettre les véhicules immatriculés sur le territoire de l'autre Partie contractante à des conditions plus restrictives que celles imposées aux véhicules immatriculés sur son propre territoire.

2. Si le poids et/ou le gabarit d'un véhicule dépasse les limites maximales autorisées sur le territoire de l'autre Partie contractante, une autorisation spéciale est requise de la part de l'autorité compétente de cette Partie contractante.

3. L'autorisation visée au paragraphe 2 du présent article ne sera accordée que pour le transport de marchandises de poids et/ou de dimensions exceptionnels.

4. Lorsque l'autorisation indique que le véhicule doit emprunter un itinéraire précis, cette autorisation n'est valable que pour cet itinéraire.

Article 11. Non-transférabilité

Les autorisations requises en vertu du présent Accord sont personnelles et intransférables. Elles ne peuvent être utilisées que par le transporteur au nom duquel elles ont été délivrées.

Article 12. Sanctions

1. Si un transporteur ou son personnel de conduite, lorsqu'il se trouve sur le territoire de l'autre Partie contractante, enfreint les dispositions du présent Accord ou les lois et règlements applicables sur ce territoire, l'autorité compétente du pays où le transporteur est établi prend, à la demande de l'autorité compétente de l'autre Partie contractante, l'une des mesures suivantes :

   a) Émettre un avertissement ; ou

   b) Retirer, à titre temporaire ou permanent, partiellement ou totalement, le droit d'effectuer des opérations de transport en vertu des dispositions du présent Accord sur le territoire du pays où l'infraction a été commise.

2. L'autorité compétente qui a demandé qu'une sanction soit prise est informée dans les meilleurs délais de l'adoption effective de ladite sanction.

3. Les dispositions du présent article s'appliquent sans préjudice de toute sanction prévue par les lois et règlements en vigueur dans la Partie contractante sur le territoire de laquelle l'infraction a été commise.

Article 13. Formulaires d'autorisation et des documents de contrôle

Les formulaires pour les autorisations et les documents de contrôle requis par le présent Accord sont établis d'un commun accord entre les autorités compétentes des Parties contractantes mentionnées à l'article 16 et dans le protocole visé à l'article 17.

Article 14. Contrôle

Les autorisations, ou une copie certifiée conforme à celles-ci dans le cas de services réguliers de transport de passagers, ainsi que tout document de contrôle requis en vertu des dispositions du présent Accord doivent se trouver à l'intérieur du véhicule et être présentés à la demande des représentants des autorités de contrôle.

Article 15. Dispositions complémentaires

Les lois et règlements des deux Parties contractantes s'appliquent à toutes les questions qui ne sont pas régies par les dispositions du présent Accord ou d'autres accords internationaux qui sont contraignants pour la République de Lettonie et la République portugaise.

Article 16. Autorités compétentes

1. Les autorités compétentes chargées de la mise en œuvre du présent Accord sont :
   a) En République de Lettonie :
   Département du transport routier
   Ministère des transports ;
   b) En République portugaise :
   Direction générale des transports terrestres
   Ministère de l'équipement, de la planification et de l'administration territoriale.
2. Les autorités compétentes des deux Parties contractantes communiquent directement entre elles.

Article 17. Mise en œuvre de l'Accord

1. Les autorités compétentes des Parties contractantes visées au paragraphe 1 de l'article 16 définissent d'un commun accord les conditions de mise en œuvre du présent Accord dans un protocole qu'elles signeront.

2. Le Comité mixte mentionné à l'article 18 du présent Accord est compétent pour modifier le protocole.

Article 18. Comité mixte

1. Un Comité mixte, composé de représentants des autorités compétentes mentionnées à l'article 16 du présent Accord, est créé afin d'assurer la bonne mise en œuvre du présent Accord et de régler dans les meilleurs délais toutes les questions non résolues. Au besoin, des représentants d'autres institutions peuvent être invités à participer aux réunions du Comité mixte.

2. À la demande de l'autorité compétente de l'une ou l'autre Partie contractante, le Comité mixte se réunit alternativement sur le territoire des deux Parties contractantes.

V. DISPOSITIONS FINALES

Article 19. Entrée en vigueur

[1. Les Parties contractantes se notifient mutuellement, par la voie diplomatique, l'accomplissement des formalités nécessaires, conformément à leur législation nationale, à l'entrée en vigueur du présent Accord.

2.][1] Le présent Accord entre en vigueur à la date de la dernière des notifications confirmant l'accomplissement des procédures constitutionnelles requises par les Parties contractantes.

Article 20. Durée

1. Le présent Accord est conclu pour une durée indéterminée.

2. L'une ou l'autre Partie contractante peut informer l'autre Partie contractante, au moyen de notes diplomatiques et au moins trois mois avant la fin de chaque année civile, de son intention de dénoncer le présent Accord. Dans ce cas, l'Accord cesse d'être en vigueur à compter du 1er janvier de l'année suivante.

FAIT à Varsovie, le 20 mai 1999, en deux originaux, chacun en langues lettonne, portugaise et anglaise, tous les textes faisant également foi. En cas de divergence d'interprétation, le texte anglais de l'Accord prévaut.

Pour la République de Lettonie :
[ANATOLIJS GORBUNOVS]

Pour la République portugaise :
[ANTONIO GUILHERMINO RODRIGUES]

[1] Le texte entre crochets ne figure que dans le texte authentique en portugais.

No. 54179

Latvia and Slovakia

Air Services Agreement between the Government of the Republic of Latvia and the Government of the Slovak Republic (with annex). Riga, 9 April 1998

Entry into force: *27 October 1998 by notification, in accordance with article 23*

Authentic text: *English*

Registration with the Secretariat of the United Nations: *Latvia, 4 January 2017*

Lettonie et Slovaquie

Accord relatif aux services aériens entre le Gouvernement de la République de Lettonie et le Gouvernement de la République slovaque (avec annexe). Riga, 9 avril 1998

Entrée en vigueur : *27 octobre 1998 par notification, conformément à l'article 23*

Texte authentique : *anglais*

Enregistrement au Secrétariat de l'Organisation des Nations Unies : *Lettonie, 4 janvier 2017*

[TEXT IN ENGLISH – TEXTE EN ANGLAIS]

AIR SERVICES AGREEMENT
between
The Government of the Republic of Latvia
and
The Government of the Slovak Republic

The Government of the Republic of Latvia and the Government of the Slovak Republic, hereinafter referred to as "the Contracting Parties";

Being parties to the Convention on International Civil Aviation opened for signature at Chicago on 7 December 1944;

Desiring to conclude an Agreement in conformity with and supplementary to the said Convention for the purpose of establishing scheduled air services between and beyond their respective territories;

Have agreed as follows:

Article 1
DEFINITIONS

1. For the purposes of this Agreement, unless the context otherwise requires:

a) the term *"Chicago Convention"* means the Convention on International Civil Aviation opened for signature at Chicago on 7 December 1944, and includes any Annex adopted under Article 90 of that Convention and any amendment of the Annexes and Convention adopted under Articles 90 and 94 thereof so far as those Annexes and amendments have been adopted by both Contracting Parties;

b) the term *"aeronautical authorities"* means, in the case of the Republic of Latvia, the Ministry of Transport, and in the case of the Slovak Republic, the Ministry of Transport, Posts and Telecommunications - Department of Civil Aviation, or, in both cases, any other person or body authorized to perform any functions at present exercised by the said aeronautical authorities;

c) the term *"designated airline"* means an airline which has been designated and authorized in accordance with Article 4 of this Agreement;

d) the terms *"territory"*, *"air service"*, *"international air service"*, *"airline"* and *"stop for non-traffic purposes"* have the meanings respectively assigned to them in Articles 2 and 96 of the Chicago Convention;

e) the term *"Annex"* means the Annex to this Agreement or as amended in accordance with the provisions of paragraph 2 of Article 19 of this Agreement;

f) the term *"agreed services"* means scheduled air services on the routes specified in the Annex to this Agreement for the carriage of passengers, cargo and mail, separately or in combination;

g) the term "tariff" means the prices to be charged for the carriage of passengers, baggage or cargo (excluding mail), including any significant additional benefits to be furnished or made available in conjunction with such carriage, and the commission to be paid on the sales of tickets for the carriage of persons, or on corresponding transactions for the carriage of cargo. It includes also the conditions that govern the applicability of the price for carriage or the payment of commission.

2. The Annex forms an integral part of this Agreement and all references to this Agreement shall include reference to the Annex unless otherwise provided.

3. Titles given to the Articles of this Agreement are for reference purposes only.

Article 2
GRANT OF TRAFFIC RIGHTS

1. Each Contracting Party grants to the other Contracting Party the following rights in respect of the international air services:

a) the right to fly across its territory without landing;

b) the right to make stops in its territory for non-traffic purposes.

2. Each Contracting Party grants to the other Contracting Party the rights specified in this Agreement for the purpose of operating international air services on the routes specified in the Annex to this Agreement. Such services and routes are hereinafter called *"the agreed services"* and *"the specified routes"* respectively.

While operating an agreed service on a specified route an airline designated by each Contracting Party shall enjoy, in addition to the rights specified in paragraph 1 of this Article, the right to make stops in the territory of the other Contracting Party at the points specified for that route in the Annex for the purpose of taking up and/or putting down international traffic in passengers, baggage, cargo and mail, separately or in combination on a commercial basis..

3. Nothing in paragraph 2 of this Article shall be deemed to confer on a designated airline of one Contracting Party the right of taking on, in the territory of the other Contracting Party, passengers, cargo and mail carried for remuneration or hire and destined for another point in the territory of that other Contracting Party.

Article 3
RECOGNITION OF CERTIFICATES AND LICENCES

1. Certificate of airworthiness, certificates of competency and licences issued or rendered valid by one of the Contracting Parties shall, during the period of their validity, be recognized as valid by the other Contracting Party, provided that the requirements under which such certificates or licences were issued or rendered valid are equal to or above the minimum standards which may be established pursuant to the Convention.

2. Each Contracting Party reserves the right, however, to refuse to recognize as valid, for the purpose of flights over its own territory, certificate of competency and licences granted to or rendered valid for its own nationals by the other Contracting Party or by any other State.

Article 4
DESIGNATION OF AIRLINES
AND OPERATING AUTHORIZATION

1. Each Contracting Party shall have the right to designate in writing to the other Contracting Party one or several airlines for the purpose of operating the agreed services on the specified routes.

2. Each Contracting Party shall have the right to withdraw or alter such designation.

3. On receipt of such written designation the aeronautical authorities of the other Contracting Party shall, subject to the provisions of paragraph 4 of this Article and paragraph 1 of Article 5, without delay grant to each designated airline the appropriate operating authorization.

4. The aeronautical authorities of one Contracting Party may require an airline designated by the other Contracting Party to satisfy them that it is qualified to fulfill the conditions prescribed under the laws and regulations normally and reasonably applied to the operation of international air services by such authorities in conformity with the provisions of the Chicago Convention.

5. When an airline has been so designed and authorized it may begin at any time to operate the agreed services, provided that the airline complies with all applicable provisions of this Agreement, including those relating to tariffs.

Article 5
REFUSAL, REVOCATION OR SUSPENSION OF OPERATING AUTHORIZATION

1. The aeronautical authorities of each Contracting Party shall have the right to refuse to grant or to revoke an operating authorization or to suspend the exercise of the rights specified in Article 2 of this Agreement by an airline designated by the other Contracting Party, or to impose such conditions as they may deem necessary on the exercise of those rights:

a) in any case when the designated airline can not prove that substantial ownership and effective control of that airline are vested in the Contracting Party designating the airline or in its nationals; or

b) in case of failure by that airline to comply with the laws and/or regulations of the Contracting Party granting the rights; or

c) in case the airline otherwise fails to operate in accordance with the conditions prescribed under this Agreement.

2. Unless immediate revocation, suspension or imposition of the conditions mentioned in paragraph 1 of this Article is essential to prevent further infringements of laws and/or regulations, such right shall be exercised only after consultations with the aeronautical authorities of the other Contracting Party. Such consultations shall begin within a period of fifteen (15) days from the date of a request for consultations.

Article 6
AIR TRAFFIC CHARGES

Fees and charges for the use of airports and other aviation facilities imposed by the competent authorities in the territory of either Contracting Party on the aircraft of any airline of the other Contracting Party shall not be higher than those imposed on aircraft of a national airline engaged in similar international air services.

Article 7
EXEMPTION FROM CUSTOMS DUTIES, TAXES AND OTHER CHARGES

1. Aircraft operated on international air services by a designated airline of one Contracting Party, as well as their regular equipment, spare parts, supplies of fuel and lubricants, aircraft stores (including food, beverages and tobacco) on board such aircraft shall be exempted from all customs duties, taxes and other similar charges on arriving in the territory of the other Contracting Party, provided such equipment, spare parts, supplies and stores remain on board the aircraft up to such time as they are re-exported or are used or consumed by such aircraft on flights over that territory.

2. There shall also be exempt from the customs duties, taxes and charges referred to in paragraph 1 of this Article, with the exception of charges based on the cost of the service provided:

a) aircraft stores taken on board in the territory of one Contracting Party within reasonable limits, for use on an outbound aircraft engaged in an international air service of a designated airline of the other Contracting Party;

b) spare parts, including engines, introduced into the territory of one Contracting Party for the maintenance or repair of aircraft engaged in an international air service of a designated airline of the other Contracting Party;

c) fuel, lubricants and consumable technical supplies introduced into or supplied in the territory of one Contracting Party for use in an international air service of a designated airline of the other Contracting Party, even when these supplies are to be used on the part of the journey performed over the territory of the other Contracting Party, in which territory they are taken on board.

3. Materials referred to in paragraph 2 of this Article may be required to be kept under Customs supervision or control.

4. The regular airborne equipment, as well as the materials, supplies and spare parts normally retained on board aircraft operated by a designated airline of one Contracting Party, may be unloaded in the territory of the other Contracting Party only with the approval of the customs authorities of that Contracting Party. In such case, they may be placed under the supervision of the said authorities up to such time as they are re-exported or otherwise disposed of in accordance with customs regulations.

5. Necessary airline documents, such as timetables, air tickets and air waybills, intended for the use of a designated airline of one Contracting Party and introduced into the territory of the other Contracting Party, shall be exempted from customs duties and similar charges in the latter territory.

6. Baggage and cargo in direct transit across the territory of a Contracting Party shall be exempted from customs duties, fees and other similar charges not based on the cost of services on arrival or departure.

Article 8
CAPACITY PROVISIONS

1. The designated airlines of the Contracting Parties shall have fair and equal opportunity to operate the agreed services on any route specified in the Annex to this Agreement.

2. In operating the agreed services the designated airline or airlines of each Contracting Party shall take into account the interests of the designated airline or airlines of the other Contracting Party so as not to affect unduly the services which the latter provide on the whole or any part of the same routes.

3. The agreed services provided by the designated airlines of the Contracting Parties shall retain as their primary objective the provision, at a reasonable load factor, of capacity adequate to the current and reasonably anticipated requirements for the carriage of passengers and cargo, including mail, coming from or destined for the territory of the Contracting Party which has designated the airline(s).

4. The right to take up or discharge on the agreed services international traffic destined for and coming from third countries at a point or points on the routes specified in the Annex to this Agreement shall be exercised in accordance with the general principles of orderly development of international air transport and shall be subject to the general principle that capacity should be related to:

a) the traffic requirements between the country of origin and the countries of ultimate destination of the traffic;

b) the requirements of through airline operations; and

c) the traffic requirements of the area through which the airline passes, after taking account of local and regional services.

Article 9
APPROVAL OF TRAFFIC PROGRAMMES

1. The airline or airlines designated by one Contracting Party shall submit its or their traffic programmes (for the Summer and Winter Traffic periods) for approval to the aeronautical authorities of the other Contracting Party at least thirty (30) days prior to the beginning of the operation. The programme shall include in particular the timetables, the frequency of the services and the types of aircraft to be used. The aeronautical authorities shall give their decision on such traffic programme submissions within twenty (20) days from the date the airline concerned submits its programme for approval.

2. Each alteration in the traffic programme as well as requests for permission to operate additional flights shall be submitted by the airline or airlines designated by one Contracting Party for approval to the aeronautical authorities of the other Contracting Party. Such requests for alteration or for additional flights shall be dealt with promptly by the aeronautical authorities.

Article 10
INFORMATION AND STATISTICS

The aeronautical authorities of either Contracting Party shall supply to the aeronautical authorities of the other Contracting Party, at their request, such information and statistics relating to traffic carried on the agreed services by the designated airline or airlines of the first Contracting Party to and from the territory of the other Contracting Party as may normally be prepared and submitted to its national aeronautical authorities. Any additional statistical traffic data which the aeronautical authorities of one Contracting Party may desire shall, upon request, be a subject of mutual discussion and agreement between the aeronautical authorities of the two Contracting Parties.

Article 11
TARIFFS

1. The tariffs on any agreed service shall be established at reasonable levels, due regard being paid to all relevant factors, including cost of operation, reasonable profit, characteristics of service (such as standards of speed and accommodation), the interests of users and the tariffs of other airlines for any part of the specified route. These tariffs shall be fixed in accordance with the following provisions of this Article.

2. The tariffs referred to in paragraph 1 of this Article may be agreed between the designated airlines concerned in respect of each of the specified routes. However, inter-airline consultations shall not be a mandatory requirement for the filing and establishment of tariffs.

3. Each tariff shall be filed for the approval of the aeronautical authorities of both Contracting Parties at least thirty (30) days (or such shorter period as the aeronautical authorities of both Contracting Parties may agree) before the proposed date of its introduction.

4. Each proposed tariff may be approved by the aeronautical authorities of either Contracting Party at any time. In the absence of such approval it will be treated as having been approved by the aeronautical authorities of a Contracting Party unless within twenty (20) days after the date of filing the aeronautical authorities of that Contracting Party have served on the aeronautical authorities of the other Contracting Party written notice of disapproval of the proposed tariff. If, however, either of the aeronautical authorities gives such written notice of disapproval the aeronautical authorities may at the request of either try to determine the tariff by agreement.

5. If the aeronautical authorities cannot determine a tariff under the provisions of paragraph 4 of this Article the dispute may at the request of either be settled in accordance with the provisions of Article 18 of this Agreement.

6. Each tariff established in accordance with the provisions of this Article shall remain in force until it has been replaced by a new tariff determined in accordance with the provisions of this Article. Unless otherwise agreed by the aeronautical authorities of both Contracting Parties a tariff shall not have its validity extended by virtue of this paragraph for more than twelve (12) months after the date on which it would otherwise have expired.

Article 12
FAIR COMPETITION

1. There shall be fair and equal opportunity for the designated airlines of both Contracting Parties to participate in international air transportation covered by this Agreement.

2. Each Contracting Party shall, where necessary, take all appropriate action within its jurisdiction to eliminate all forms of discrimination or unfair competitive practices adversely affecting the competitive position of the airlines of the other Contracting Party.

Article 13
COMMERCIAL ACTIVITIES

1. The designated airline or airlines of each Contracting Party shall have the right to maintain in the territory of the other Contracting Party, within the scope of the laws and regulations in force therein, such offices and administrative, commercial and technical personnel as may be necessary for the requirements of the designated airline concerned.

2. The designated airlines of the Contracting Parties shall be free to sell air transport services on their own transportation documents in the territories of both Contracting Parties, either directly or through an agent, in any currency. Each Contracting Party shall refrain from restricting the right of the designated airline(s) of the other Contracting Party to sell, and of any person to purchase such transportation.

3. Each Contracting Party shall, on a reciprocal basis, allow each designated airline of the other Contracting Party to perform its own handling of passengers, baggage and cargo (self-handling) in the territory of the first Contracting Party. This right is subject to capacity limitations at the airport concerned and does not include air-side ground handling services (aircraft ground handling).

Article 14
TRANSFER OF FUNDS

1. The designated airlines of the Contracting Parties shall be free to transfer the excess of the receipts over expenditure in the territory of the sale.

2. Such transfers shall be effected in a freely convertible currency at the official rate of exchange and shall not, with the exception of normal banking charges and procedures, be subject to any charge, limitation, imposition or delay.

3. If payments between the Contracting Parties are regulated by a special agreement, this special agreement shall apply.

Article 15
AVIATION SECURITY

1. Consistent with their rights and obligations under international law, the Contracting Parties reaffirm that their obligation to each other to protect the security of civil aviation against acts of unlawful interference forms an integral part of this Agreement. Without limiting the generality of their rights and obligations under international law, the Contracting Parties shall in particular act in conformity with the provisions of the Convention on Offences and Certain Other Acts Committed on Board Aircraft, signed at Tokyo on 14 September 1963, the Convention for the Suppression of Unlawful Seizure of Aircraft, signed at the Hague on 16 December 1970 and the Convention for the Suppression of Unlawful Acts against the Safety of Civil Aviation, signed at Montreal on 23 September 1971.

2. The Contracting Parties shall provide upon request all necessary assistance to each other to prevent acts of unlawful seizure of civil aircraft and other unlawful acts against the safety of such aircraft, their passengers and crew, airports and air navigation facilities, and any other threat to the security of civil aviation.

3. The Contracting Parties shall act in conformity with the aviation security provisions and technical requirements established by the International Civil Aviation Organization and designated as Annexes to the Chicago Convention to the extent that such security provisions and requirements are applicable to the Contracting Parties; they shall require that operators of aircraft of their registry or operators of aircraft who have their principal place of business or permanent residence in their territory act in conformity with such aviation security provisions.

4. Each Contracting Party agrees that such operators of aircraft may be required to observe the aviation security provisions and requirements referred to in paragraph 3 above required by the other Contracting Party for entry into, departure from, or while within the territory of that other Contracting Party shall ensure that adequate measures are effectively applied within it's territory to protect the aircraft and to inspect passengers, crew, carry-on items, baggage, cargo and aircraft stores prior to and during boarding or loading. Each Contracting Party shall also give sympathetic consideration to any request from the other Contracting Party for reasonable special security measures to meet a particular threat.

5. When an incident or threat of an incident of unlawful seizure of civil aircraft or other unlawful acts against the safety of such aircraft, their passengers and crew, airports or air navigation facilities occurs, the Contracting Parties shall assist each other by facilitating communications and other appropriate measures intended to terminate rapidly and safely such incident or threat thereof.

Article 16
APPLICATION OF LAWS AND REGULATIONS

1. The laws and regulations of one Contracting Party relating to the entry into, or departure from its territory of aircraft engaged in international air services or to the operation and navigation of such aircraft while the said territory shall apply to the designated airline or airlines of the other Contracting Party.

2. The laws and regulations of one Contracting Party governing entry to, stay in or departure from its territory of passengers, crew, cargo or mail, such as formalities regarding entry, exit, emigration, immigration, customs, currency, health and quarantine shall apply to passengers, crew, cargo and mail carried by the aircraft of the designated airline or airlines of the other Contracting Party, while they are within the said territory.

3. Passengers, baggage and cargo in direct transit across the territory of either Contracting Party and not leaving the area of the airport reserved for such purposes shall, except in respect of security measures against acts of violence and air piracy, be subject to no more than a simplified control.

4. In case a carried passenger fails to comply with laws and regulations for enter into the country of other Contracting Party an airline is obliged to transport him back on costs of this airline.

Article 17
CONSULTATIONS

In a spirit of close co-operation the aeronautical authorities of the Contracting Parties shall consult each other from time to time with a view to ensuring the implementation of and satisfactory compliance with the provisions of this Agreement.

Article 18
SETTLEMENT OF DISPUTES

1. If any dispute arises between the Contracting Parties relating to the interpretation or application of this Agreement, the Contracting Parties shall, in the first place, endeavour to settle it by negotiation.

2. If the Contracting Parties fail to reach a settlement by negotiation, they may agree to refer the dispute for decision to some person or body; if they do not so agree, the dispute shall, at the request of either Contracting Party, be submitted for decision to a tribunal of three arbitrators, one to be nominated by each Contracting Party and the third to be appointed by the two so nominated. Each of the Contracting Parties shall nominate an arbitrator within a period of sixty (60) days from the date of receipt by either Contracting Party from the other of a notice through diplomatic channels requesting arbitration of the dispute by such a tribunal, and the third arbitrator shall be appointed within a further period of sixty (60) days. If either of the Contracting Parties fails to nominate an arbitrator within the period specified, the President of the Council of the International Civil Aviation Organization may at the request of either Contracting Party appoint an arbitrator or arbitrators as the case requires. In all cases, the third arbitrator shall be a national of a third State and shall act as President of the arbitral tribunal.

3. The Contracting Parties shall comply with any decision given under paragraph 2 of this Article.

4. The expenses of the arbitration shall be equally shared between the Contracting Parties.

Article 19
AMENDMENTS

1. If either of the Contracting Parties considers it desirable to modify any provision of this Agreement, it may request consultations with the other Contracting Party. Such consultations shall begin within a period of sixty (60) days from the date of the request, unless both Contracting Parties agree to an extension of this period. Any modification agreed in such consultations shall be approved by each Contracting Party in accordance with its legal procedures and shall enter into force on the first day of the second month after the Contracting Parties have notified each other that these procedures have been complied with.

2. Notwithstanding the provision of paragraph 1 of this Article, amendments relating only to the Annex may be agreed upon between the aeronautical authorities of the Contracting Parties and shall become effective as agreed between them.

Article 20
TERMINATION

1. The validity of this Agreement is for unlimited period.

2. Either Contracting Party may at any time give notice to the other Contracting Party of its decision to terminate this Agreement. Such notice shall simultaneously be communicated to the International Civil Aviation Organization.

3. In such case this Agreement shall terminate twelve (12) months after the date of receipt of the notice by the other Contracting Party. In the absence of acknowledgement of receipt by the other Contracting Party, notice shall be deemed to have been received fourteen (14) days after the receipt of the notice by the International Civil Aviation Organization.

Article 21
MULTILATERAL CONVENTIONS

If a general multilateral air convention enters into force in respect of both Contracting Parties, the provisions of such convention shall prevail. Consultations in accordance with Article 17 of this Agreement may be held with a view to determining the extent to which this Agreement is affected by the provisions of the said multilateral convention.

Article 22
REGISTRATION WITH ICAO

This Agreement and any amendments thereto shall be registered with the International Civil Aviation Organization.

Article 23
ENTRY INTO FORCE

This Agreement shall enter into force as soon as the Contracting Parties have notified one another by exchange of notes of the completion of their respective constitutional formalities.

Done at Riga this 9th day of April, 1998, in duplicate in the English language, both texts being equally authentic.

For the Government of the Republic of Latvia:	For the Government of the Slovak Republic:
Valdis Birkavs	

ANNEX
to the Air Services Agreement
between
the Government of the Republic of Latvia
and the Government of the Slovak Republic

ROUTE SCHEDULE

1. SCHEDULE 1

Routes to be operated by the designated airline of the Republic of Latvia:

From	Intermediate Points	To	Points Beyond
Points in Latvia	**To be specified**	**Points in Slovakia**	**To be specified**
Any points		Any points	

2. SCHEDULE 2

Routes to be operated by the designated airline of the Slovak Republic:

From	Intermediate Points	To	Points Beyond
Points in Slovakia	**To be specified**	**Points in Latvia**	**To be specified**
Any points		Any points	

3. No fifth freedom traffic rights shall be exercised between intermediate points or points beyond and the territory of the other Contracting Party unless an agreement to that effect is made between the two Aeronautical Authorities of the Contracting Parties.

[TRANSLATION IN FRENCH – TRADUCTION EN FRANÇAIS]

ACCORD RELATIF AUX SERVICES AÉRIENS ENTRE LE GOUVERNEMENT DE LA RÉPUBLIQUE DE LETTONIE ET LE GOUVERNEMENT DE LA RÉPUBLIQUE SLOVAQUE

Le Gouvernement de la République de Lettonie et le Gouvernement de la République slovaque, ci-après dénommés « Parties contractantes »,

Étant parties à la Convention relative à l'aviation civile internationale, ouverte à la signature à Chicago le 7 décembre 1944,

Désireux de conclure un accord complémentaire et conforme à ladite Convention en vue d'établir et d'exploiter des services aériens réguliers entre leurs territoires respectifs et au-delà,

Sont convenus de ce qui suit :

Article premier. Définitions

1. Aux fins du présent Accord, sauf exigence contraire due au contexte :
   a) L'expression « Convention de Chicago » désigne la Convention relative à l'aviation civile internationale, ouverte à la signature à Chicago le 7 décembre 1944, et inclut toute annexe adoptée conformément à l'article 90 de ladite Convention, ainsi que de tout amendement des annexes et de la Convention entré en vigueur en application des articles 90 et 94, dans la mesure où ces annexes et amendements ont été adoptés par les deux Parties contractantes ;
   b) L'expression « autorités aéronautiques » désigne, en ce qui concerne la République de Lettonie, le Ministère des transports et, en ce qui concerne la République slovaque, le Département de l'aviation civile du Ministère des transports, des postes et des télécommunications, ou, dans les deux cas, toute personne ou tout organisme habilité à remplir les fonctions actuellement exercées par lesdites autorités aéronautiques ;
   c) L'expression « compagnie aérienne désignée » désigne une compagnie aérienne qui a été désignée et autorisée conformément à l'article 4 du présent Accord ;
   d) Le terme « territoire » et les expressions « service aérien », « service aérien international », « compagnie aérienne » et « escale à des fins non commerciales » ont le sens que leur donnent respectivement les articles 2 et 96 de la Convention de Chicago ;
   e) Le terme « annexe » désigne l'annexe au présent Accord, éventuellement amendée conformément aux dispositions du paragraphe 2 de l'article 19 du présent Accord ;
   f) L'expression « services convenus » désigne les services aériens réguliers assurés sur les routes spécifiées dans l'annexe au présent Accord pour le transport de passagers, de marchandises et de courrier, conjointement ou séparément ;
   g) Le terme « tarif » désigne les prix à acquitter pour le transport de passagers, de bagages ou de marchandises (à l'exclusion du courrier), y compris toute prestation supplémentaire importante fournie ou mise à disposition à l'occasion dudit transport, ainsi que la commission à verser sur la vente des billets pour le transport de personnes

ou sur les transactions correspondantes pour le transport de marchandises. Ce terme comprend également les conditions qui régissent l'applicabilité du prix du transport ou du paiement de la commission.

2. L'annexe fait partie intégrante du présent Accord et toute référence à l'Accord inclut l'annexe, sauf indication contraire.

3. Les intitulés des articles du présent Accord ne sont donnés qu'à titre indicatif.

Article 2. Octroi de droits de trafic

1. Chaque Partie contractante accorde à l'autre Partie contractante les droits suivants en ce qui concerne les services aériens internationaux :

a) Le droit de survoler son territoire sans y atterrir ;

b) Le droit d'y effectuer des escales à des fins non commerciales.

2. Chaque Partie contractante accorde à l'autre Partie contractante les droits visés au présent Accord aux fins de l'exploitation des services aériens internationaux sur les routes spécifiées dans l'annexe du présent Accord. Ces services et routes sont respectivement dénommés ci-après « services convenus » et « routes spécifiées ».

Dans l'exploitation d'un service convenu sur une route spécifiée, toute compagnie aérienne désignée par chaque Partie contractante jouit, outre les droits visés au paragraphe 1 du présent article, du droit de faire escale sur le territoire de l'autre Partie contractante aux points spécifiés à l'annexe pour ladite route, en vue d'embarquer ou de débarquer, en trafic international, des passagers, des bagages, des marchandises et du courrier, séparément ou ensemble, sur une base commerciale.

3. Aucune disposition du paragraphe 2 du présent article ne peut être interprétée comme conférant à une compagnie aérienne désignée d'une Partie contractante le droit d'embarquer, sur le territoire de l'autre Partie contractante, des passagers, des marchandises et du courrier pour les transporter, contre rémunération ou en vertu d'un contrat de location, à destination d'un autre point du territoire de cette autre Partie contractante.

Article 3. Reconnaissance des certificats, brevets et licences

1. Les certificats de navigabilité, les brevets d'aptitude et les licences délivrés ou validés par une Partie contractante sont, pendant leur période de validité, reconnus valables par l'autre Partie contractante, sous réserve que les conditions qui ont régi la délivrance ou la validation de ces certificats, brevets ou licences sont égales ou supérieures aux normes minimales éventuellement fixées conformément à la Convention.

2. Toutefois, chaque Partie contractante se réserve le droit de ne pas reconnaître, pour le survol de son propre territoire, les brevets d'aptitude et les licences validés ou délivrés à ses propres ressortissants par l'autre Partie contractante ou tout autre État.

Article 4. Désignation des compagnies aériennes et autorisation d'exploitation

1. Chaque Partie contractante a le droit de désigner par écrit à l'autre Partie contractante une ou plusieurs compagnies aériennes pour exploiter les services convenus sur les routes spécifiées.

2. Chaque Partie contractante a le droit de retirer ou de modifier cette désignation.

3. Dès réception de cette désignation écrite et sous réserve des dispositions du paragraphe 4 du présent article et du paragraphe 1 de l'article 5, les autorités aéronautiques de l'autre Partie contractante accordent sans délai à chaque compagnie aérienne désignée l'autorisation d'exploitation appropriée.

4. Les autorités aéronautiques d'une Partie contractante peuvent exiger d'une compagnie aérienne désignée par l'autre Partie la preuve qu'elle est à même de respecter les conditions prescrites par les lois et règlements que ces autorités appliquent normalement et raisonnablement à l'exploitation des services aériens internationaux conformément aux dispositions de la Convention de Chicago.

5. Lorsqu'une compagnie aérienne a été ainsi désignée et autorisée, elle peut commencer à exploiter à tout moment les services convenus, à condition qu'elle se conforme à toutes les dispositions applicables du présent Accord, y compris celles qui ont trait aux tarifs.

Article 5. Refus, révocation ou suspension d'autorisation d'exploitation

1. Les autorités aéronautiques de chaque Partie contractante ont le droit de refuser, d'accorder ou de révoquer une autorisation d'exploitation, ou de suspendre l'exercice des droits visés à l'article 2 du présent Accord par une compagnie aérienne désignée par l'autre Partie contractante ou d'imposer toute condition qu'elles peuvent juger nécessaire à l'exercice de ces droits :

a) Lorsque la compagnie aérienne désignée ne peut pas prouver que la propriété substantielle ou le contrôle effectif de cette compagnie aérienne est détenu par la Partie contractante qui l'a désignée ou de ressortissants de cette Partie ; ou

b) Lorsque cette compagnie aérienne omet de se conformer aux lois et/ou règlements de la Partie contractante qui accorde les droits ; ou

c) Lorsque la compagnie aérienne omet, de toute autre manière, de conformer son exploitation aux conditions prescrites par le présent Accord.

2. À moins que des mesures immédiates de révocation, de suspension ou d'imposition de conditions, conformément aux dispositions du paragraphe 1 du présent article, ne soient indispensables pour éviter de nouvelles infractions aux lois et/ou règlements, ce droit n'est exercé qu'après des consultations avec les autorités aéronautiques de l'autre Partie contractante. Ces consultations se tiennent dans un délai de 15 jours à compter de la date de la demande de consultations.

Article 6. Redevances de trafic aérien

Les taxes et redevances pour l'utilisation des aéroports et autres installations aéronautiques imposées par les autorités compétentes sur le territoire de l'une des Parties contractantes sur les aéronefs de toute compagnie aérienne de l'autre Partie contractante ne doivent pas être supérieures à celles imposées sur les aéronefs d'une compagnie aérienne nationale assurant des services aériens internationaux similaires.

Article 7. Exonération des droits de douane, taxes et autres redevances

1. Les aéronefs exploités en service aérien international par une compagnie aérienne désignée d'une Partie contractante, ainsi que leur équipement ordinaire, les pièces de rechange, les approvisionnements en carburant et lubrifiants et les provisions de bord (y compris les denrées

alimentaires, les boissons et le tabac) se trouvant à bord desdits aéronefs, sont exemptés de tous droits de douane, taxes et autres redevances similaires à leur entrée sur le territoire de l'autre Partie contractante, à condition que ces équipements, pièces de rechange et provisions restent à bord des aéronefs jusqu'à leur réexportation ou leur utilisation ou leur consommation par ledit aéronef pendant le survol du territoire en question.

2. Sont également exonérés des droits de douane, des taxes et des redevances visés au paragraphe 1 du présent article, à l'exception des redevances basées sur le coût des services fournis :

a) Les provisions de bord embarquées sur le territoire d'une Partie contractante, dans des limites raisonnables, pour être utilisées à bord des aéronefs en partance, assurant des services aériens internationaux d'une compagnie aérienne désignée de l'autre Partie contractante ;

b) Les pièces de rechange, y compris les moteurs, introduites sur le territoire d'une Partie contractante pour l'entretien ou la réparation des aéronefs en partance, assurant des services aériens internationaux d'une compagnie aérienne désignée de l'autre Partie contractante ;

c) Le carburant, les lubrifiants et les fournitures à usage technique consommables introduits ou fournis sur le territoire d'une Partie contractante afin d'être utilisés dans le cadre d'un service aérien international par une compagnie aérienne désignée de l'autre Partie contractante, même lorsque ces fournitures sont destinées à être utilisées sur la fraction du voyage effectuée au-dessus du territoire de l'autre Partie contractante dans laquelle ils ont été pris à bord.

3. Il peut être exigé que les équipements visés au paragraphe 2 du présent article soient placés sous la surveillance ou le contrôle des autorités douanières.

4. L'équipement ordinaire, ainsi que le matériel, les fournitures et les pièces de rechange conservés habituellement à bord des aéronefs exploités par une compagnie aérienne désignée d'une Partie contractante ne peuvent être déchargés sur le territoire de l'autre Partie contractante qu'avec l'accord des autorités douanières de cette Partie contractante. Dans ce cas, ils peuvent être placés sous la surveillance desdites autorités jusqu'à leur réexportation ou jusqu'à ce qu'il en soit autrement disposé conformément avec la réglementation douanière.

5. Les documents nécessaires, tels que les horaires, billets et connaissements aériens, destinés à être utilisés par une compagnie aérienne désignée d'une Partie contractante et introduits sur le territoire de l'autre Partie contractante sont exonérés de droits de douane et de redevances analogues sur ce territoire.

6. Les bagages et les marchandises en transit direct à travers le territoire d'une Partie contractante sont exonérés des droits de douane, des taxes et autres redevances analogues qui ne sont pas dus au titre d'une prestation de services à l'arrivée et au départ.

Article 8. Dispositions relatives à la capacité

1. Les compagnies aériennes désignées des Parties contractantes ont la possibilité équitable et égale d'assurer les services convenus sur les routes spécifiées dans l'annexe au présent Accord.

2. Lors de l'exploitation des services convenus, les compagnies aériennes désignées de chaque Partie contractante doivent tenir compte des intérêts des compagnies aériennes désignées de l'autre Partie contractante de façon à ne pas affecter indûment les services que cette dernière fournit sur la totalité ou sur une partie quelconque des mêmes routes.

3. Les services convenus exploités par les compagnies aériennes désignées des Parties contractantes ont toujours pour objectif premier d'offrir, à un coefficient de remplissage raisonnable, une capacité adaptée aux besoins actuels et prévisibles en matière de transport de passagers et de marchandises, y compris le courrier, en provenance ou à destination du territoire de la Partie contractante qui a désigné ces compagnies aériennes.

4. Le droit d'embarquer ou de débarquer, au cours des services convenus, du trafic international à destination ou en provenance de pays tiers à un ou plusieurs points sur les routes spécifiées dans l'annexe au présent Accord est exercé conformément aux principes généraux du développement ordonné des transports aériens internationaux, et il est soumis au principe général selon lequel la capacité doit être liée :

a) Aux besoins de trafic entre le pays d'origine et les pays de destination finale du trafic ;

b) Aux besoins en matière d'exploitation de services qui se poursuivent au-delà de points situés sur le territoire des Parties ; et

c) Aux besoins de trafic de la région traversée par les compagnies aériennes, en tenant compte des services locaux et régionaux.

Article 9. Approbation des programmes de trafic aérien

1. Les compagnies aériennes désignées par une Partie contractante soumettent pour approbation, aux autorités aéronautiques de l'autre Partie contractante et au plus tard 30 jours avant le début des services, leurs programmes de vols (pour les saisons de trafic d'été et d'hiver). Le programme comprend notamment les horaires, la fréquence des services et le type d'aéronefs utilisés. Les autorités aéronautiques communiquent leur décision sur ces programmes dans les 20 jours qui suivent la date à laquelle la compagnie aérienne concernée présente son programme pour approbation.

2. Les compagnies aériennes désignées d'une Partie contractante soumettent aux autorités aéronautiques de l'autre Partie contractante, pour approbation, toute demande de modification de leurs programmes ou d'autorisation de vols supplémentaires. Lesdites autorités aéronautiques traitent ces demandes dans les meilleurs délais.

Article 10. Renseignements et statistiques

Les autorités aéronautiques d'une Partie contractante communiquent à celles de l'autre Partie contractante, à leur demande, les renseignements et statistiques concernant le trafic transporté sur les services convenus à destination et en provenance du territoire de l'autre Partie contractante par toute compagnie aérienne désignée de la première Partie contractante, qui peuvent être normalement préparés et soumis à ses autorités aéronautiques nationales. Toutes données statistiques supplémentaires sur le trafic que les autorités aéronautiques d'une Partie contractante peuvent solliciter font, sur demande, l'objet d'une discussion et d'un accord entre les autorités aéronautiques des deux Parties contractantes.

Article 11. Tarifs

1. Les tarifs des services convenus sont établis à des taux raisonnables, en tenant dûment compte de tous les facteurs pertinents, y compris les frais d'exploitation, la réalisation d'un bénéfice raisonnable, les caractéristiques des services offerts (tels que vitesse et types d'installation), les

intérêts des usagers et les tarifs appliqués par d'autres compagnies aériennes exploitant toute autre partie de la route spécifiée. Ces tarifs sont établis conformément aux dispositions suivantes du présent article.

2. Les tarifs visés au paragraphe 1 du présent article peuvent être convenus entre les compagnies aériennes désignées concernées pour chacune des routes spécifiées. Toutefois, les consultations entre compagnies aériennes ne sont pas obligatoires pour le dépôt et l'établissement des tarifs.

3. Chaque tarif est déposé auprès des autorités aéronautiques des deux Parties contractantes pour approbation au moins 30 jours (ou une période plus courte selon ce dont conviennent les autorités aéronautiques des deux Parties contractantes) avant la date proposée de son introduction.

4. Chaque tarif proposé peut être approuvé à tout moment par les autorités aéronautiques de l'une ou l'autre des Parties contractantes. En l'absence d'une telle approbation, il sera considéré comme ayant été approuvé par les autorités aéronautiques d'une Partie contractante, à moins que, dans les 20 jours suivant la date de dépôt, les autorités aéronautiques de cette Partie contractante n'aient envoyé aux autorités aéronautiques de l'autre Partie contractante une notification écrite signifiant leur désapprobation du tarif proposé. Toutefois, si l'une ou l'autre des autorités aéronautiques donne une telle notification écrite de désapprobation, les autorités aéronautiques peuvent, à la demande de l'une ou l'autre, essayer de déterminer le tarif d'un commun accord.

5. Si les autorités aéronautiques ne parviennent pas à déterminer un tarif en vertu des dispositions du paragraphe 4 du présent article, le différend peut être réglé, à la demande de l'une ou l'autre, conformément aux dispositions de l'article 18 du présent Accord.

6. Chaque tarif établi conformément aux dispositions du présent article demeure en vigueur jusqu'à ce qu'il soit remplacé par un nouveau tarif, déterminé conformément aux dispositions du présent article. Sauf accord contraire entre les autorités aéronautiques des deux Parties contractantes, la validité d'un tarif ne peut pas être prolongée, en vertu du présent paragraphe, de plus de 12 mois après la date à laquelle il aurait normalement expiré.

Article 12. Concurrence loyale

1. Les compagnies aériennes désignées des deux Parties contractantes jouissent de possibilités équitables et égales de participer aux activités du transport aérien international qui font l'objet du présent Accord.

2. Chaque Partie contractante prend, s'il y a lieu, toutes les mesures appropriées relevant de sa compétence afin d'éliminer toute forme de discrimination ou de concurrence déloyale susceptible de porter préjudice à la position concurrentielle des compagnies aériennes désignées de l'autre Partie contractante.

Article 13. Activités commerciales

1. Toute compagnie aérienne désignée d'une Partie contractante a le droit de maintenir sur le territoire de l'autre Partie contractante, dans le cadre des dispositions législatives et réglementaires en vigueur dans celui-ci, les bureaux et le personnel administratif, commercial et technique dont elle peut avoir besoin.

2. Les compagnies aériennes désignées des Parties contractantes sont libres de vendre des services de transport aérien sur leurs propres titres de transport sur le territoire des deux Parties

contractantes, directement ou par l'intermédiaire d'un agent, dans une monnaie quelconque. Chaque Partie contractante se garde de restreindre le droit des compagnies aériennes désignées de l'autre Partie contractante de vendre des services de transport, ainsi que le droit de toute personne d'acheter ces services.

3. Chaque Partie contractante autorise, sur une base de réciprocité, chaque compagnie aérienne désignée de l'autre Partie contractante à exécuter ses propres services pour la gestion des passagers, des bagages et des marchandises (services propres) sur le territoire de la première Partie contractante. Ce droit est soumis aux limitations de capacité de l'aéroport concerné et ne comprend pas les services d'escale côté piste (services d'escale pour les aéronefs).

Article 14. Transfert de fonds

1. Les compagnies aériennes désignées des Parties contractantes sont libres de transférer l'excédent de recettes par rapport aux dépenses sur le territoire où la vente a eu lieu.

2. Ces transferts sont effectués dans une monnaie librement convertible, au taux de change officiel, et sans frais, limitation, impôt, ni retard, à l'exception des frais et des procédures bancaires normales.

3. Si les paiements entre les Parties contractantes sont réglementés par un accord particulier, celui-ci est applicable.

Article 15. Sûreté de l'aviation

1. Conformément à leurs droits et obligations en vertu du droit international, les Parties contractantes réaffirment que leur obligation mutuelle de protéger l'aviation civile contre des actes d'intervention illicite, pour en assurer la sûreté, font partie intégrante du présent Accord. Sans limiter la généralité de leurs droits et obligations en vertu du droit international, les Parties contractantes agissent, en particulier, conformément aux dispositions de la Convention relative aux infractions et à certains autres actes survenant à bord des aéronefs, signée à Tokyo le 14 septembre 1963, de la Convention pour la répression de la capture illicite d'aéronefs, signée à La Haye le 16 décembre 1970, et de la Convention pour la répression des actes illicites dirigés contre la sécurité de l'aviation civile, signée à Montréal le 23 septembre 1971.

2. Les Parties contractantes s'accordent mutuellement, sur demande, toute l'assistance nécessaire pour prévenir les actes de capture illicite d'aéronefs civils et autres actes illicites dirigés contre la sécurité de ces aéronefs, de leurs passagers et de leurs équipages, des aéroports et des installations de navigation aérienne, ainsi que toute autre menace pour la sûreté de l'aviation civile.

3. Les Parties contractantes agissent conformément aux dispositions relatives à la sûreté de l'aviation et aux exigences techniques établies par l'Organisation de l'aviation civile internationale et qui sont désignées comme annexes à la Convention de Chicago, dans la mesure où ces dispositions et exigences relatives à la sûreté leur sont applicables ; elles exigent en outre des exploitants d'aéronefs immatriculés par elles ou des exploitants d'aéronefs qui ont leur établissement principal ou leur résidence permanente sur leur territoire qu'ils se conforment à ces dispositions relatives à la sûreté de l'aviation.

4. Chaque Partie contractante convient que ces exploitants d'aéronefs peuvent être tenus de respecter les dispositions en matière de sûreté de l'aviation et les exigences visées au paragraphe 3 ci-dessus que l'autre Partie contractante prescrit pour l'entrée, le séjour sur son territoire ou pour la sortie de celui-ci. Chaque Partie veille à ce que des mesures adéquates soient appliquées

effectivement sur son territoire pour protéger les aéronefs et assurer l'inspection des passagers, des équipages, des bagages à main, des autres bagages, des marchandises et des provisions de bord avant et pendant l'embarquement ou le chargement. Chaque Partie contractante examine aussi avec bienveillance toute demande que lui adresse l'autre Partie contractante en vue d'obtenir que des mesures spéciales de sûreté raisonnables soient prises pour faire face à une menace particulière.

5. En cas d'incident ou de menace d'incident de capture illicite d'aéronefs civils ou d'autres actes illicites contre la sécurité de ces aéronefs, de leurs passagers et de leur équipage, des aéroports ou des installations de navigation aérienne, les Parties contractantes se prêtent mutuellement assistance en facilitant les communications et d'autres mesures appropriées visant à mettre fin de manière rapide et sécurisée à cet incident ou à cette menace d'incident.

Article 16. Application des lois et règlements

1. Les lois et règlements d'une Partie contractante relatifs à l'entrée sur son territoire ou au départ de celui-ci d'un aéronef assurant des services aériens internationaux ou à l'exploitation et à la navigation d'un tel aéronef pendant leur présence sur ledit territoire s'appliquent aux compagnies aériennes désignées de l'autre Partie contractante.

2. Les lois et règlements d'une Partie contractante régissant l'entrée et le séjour sur son territoire ou le départ de celui-ci de passagers, d'équipages, de marchandises ou de courrier, telles que les formalités concernant l'entrée, la sortie, l'émigration, l'immigration, les douanes, les monnaies, la santé et la quarantaine, s'appliquent aux passagers, aux équipages, aux marchandises et au courrier transportés par l'aéronef des compagnies aériennes désignées de l'autre Partie contractante pendant leur séjour sur ledit territoire.

3. Les passagers, les bagages et les marchandises en transit direct à travers le territoire de l'une ou l'autre des Parties contractantes et qui ne quittent pas la zone de l'aéroport réservée à cet effet font uniquement l'objet d'un contrôle simplifié, sauf en ce qui concerne le respect des mesures de sûreté contre des actes de violence ou de piraterie aérienne.

4. Si un passager transporté omet de respecter les lois et règlements pour l'entrée dans le pays de l'autre Partie contractante, une compagnie aérienne est tenue de le ramener à son point de départ, à ses propres frais.

Article 17. Consultations

Dans un esprit d'étroite collaboration, les autorités aéronautiques des Parties contractantes se consultent de temps à autre en vue de s'assurer que les dispositions du présent Accord sont appliquées et respectées de façon satisfaisante.

Article 18. Règlement des différends

1. En cas de différend entre les Parties contractantes relatif à l'interprétation ou à l'application du présent Accord, celles-ci s'efforcent en premier lieu de le régler par voie de négociations.

2. Si les Parties contractantes ne parviennent pas à régler le différend par voie de négociations, elles peuvent convenir de le soumettre à la décision d'une personne ou d'un organisme ; si elles ne s'entendent pas à ce sujet, le différend est, à la demande de l'une ou l'autre des Parties contractantes, soumis à la décision d'un tribunal composé de trois arbitres, un désigné par chaque Partie contractante et le troisième nommé par les deux arbitres ainsi désignés. Chacune des Parties

contractantes désigne un arbitre dans les 60 jours suivant la date de réception par l'une d'elles d'une note diplomatique de l'autre demandant l'arbitrage du différend par un tel tribunal, et la désignation du troisième arbitre intervient dans un nouveau délai de 60 jours. Si une Partie contractante omet de désigner son arbitre dans le délai imparti, le Président du Conseil de l'Organisation de l'aviation civile internationale peut, à la demande d'une Partie contractante, désigner un ou plusieurs arbitres, suivant le cas. Dans tous les cas, le troisième arbitre est un ressortissant d'un État tiers et préside le tribunal arbitral.

3. Les Parties contractantes se conforment à toute décision rendue en application du paragraphe 2 du présent article.

4. Les frais d'arbitrage sont répartis à parts égales entre les Parties contractantes.

Article 19. Amendements

1. Si l'une des Parties contractantes estime souhaitable de modifier une des dispositions du présent Accord, elle peut demander des consultations avec l'autre Partie contractante. Ces consultations commencent dans les 60 jours suivant la date de la demande, à moins que les deux Parties contractantes ne conviennent d'une prolongation de ce délai. Toute modification convenue lors de ces consultations est approuvée par chaque Partie contractante conformément à ses procédures juridiques et entre en vigueur le premier jour du deuxième mois après que les Parties contractantes se sont notifié l'accomplissement de ces procédures.

2. Nonobstant les dispositions du paragraphe 1 du présent article, des amendements portant uniquement sur l'annexe peuvent être convenus entre les autorités aéronautiques des Parties contractantes et prennent effet selon les modalités convenues entre elles.

Article 20. Dénonciation

1. Le présent Accord est valide pour une durée indéterminée.

2. L'une ou l'autre des Parties contractantes peut à tout moment notifier à l'autre Partie contractante sa décision de dénoncer le présent Accord. Cette notification est adressée simultanément à l'Organisation de l'aviation civile internationale.

3. Dans ce cas, le présent Accord cesse de produire ses effets 12 mois après la date de réception de la notification par l'autre Partie contractante. Si l'autre Partie Contractante omet d'en accuser réception, la notification est réputée avoir été reçue 14 jours après sa réception par l'Organisation de l'aviation civile internationale.

Article 21. Conventions multilatérales

Si une convention aéronautique multilatérale de caractère général entre en vigueur pour les deux Parties contractantes, les dispositions de cette convention prévalent. Des consultations peuvent avoir lieu, conformément à l'article 17 du présent Accord, en vue de déterminer la mesure dans laquelle les dispositions de la convention multilatérale affectent le présent Accord.

Article 22. Enregistrement auprès de l'OACI

Le présent Accord et tous les amendements qui y sont apportés sont enregistrés auprès de l'Organisation de l'aviation civile internationale.

Article 23. Entrée en vigueur

Le présent Accord entrera en vigueur dès que les deux Parties contractantes se sont notifié mutuellement, par un échange de notes transmises par voie diplomatique, l'accomplissement de leurs formalités constitutionnelles respectives.

FAIT à Riga, le 9 avril 1998, en double exemplaire en langue anglaise, les deux textes faisant également foi.

Pour le Gouvernement de la République de Lettonie :
[VLADIS BIRKAVS]

Pour le Gouvernement de la République slovaque :
[JANS JASOVSKY]

ANNEXE À L'ACCORD RELATIF AUX SERVICES AÉRIENS ENTRE LE GOUVERNEMENT DE LA RÉPUBLIQUE DE LETTONIE ET LE GOUVERNEMENT DE LA RÉPUBLIQUE SLOVAQUE

TABLEAU DE ROUTES

1. Tableau 1

Routes exploitées par la compagnie aérienne désignée de la République de Lettonie :

Origine	Points intermédiaires	Destination	Points au-delà
Points en Lettonie	À préciser	Points en Slovaquie	À préciser
Tous points		Tous points	

2. Tableau 2

Routes exploitées par la compagnie aérienne désignée de la République slovaque :

Origine	Points intermédiaires	Destination	Points au-delà
Points en Slovaquie	À préciser	Points en Lettonie	À préciser
Tous points		Tous points	

3. Les droits de trafic de cinquième liberté ne sont pas exercés entre les points intermédiaires ou les points au-delà et le territoire de l'autre Partie contractante, sauf accord contraire conclu à cet effet entre les deux autorités aéronautiques des Parties contractantes.

No. 54180

Latvia and Slovenia

Agreement between the Government of the Republic of Latvia and the Government of the Republic of Slovenia on International Road Transport (with additional protocol). Copenhagen, 26 May 1998

Entry into force: *provisionally on 26 May 1998 by signature and definitively on 16 April 2000, in accordance with article 18*

Authentic texts: *English, Latvian and Slovene*

Registration with the Secretariat of the United Nations: *Latvia, 4 January 2017*

Lettonie et Slovénie

Accord entre le Gouvernement de la République de Lettonie et le Gouvernement de la République de Slovénie relatif au transport routier international (avec protocole additionnel). Copenhague, 26 mai 1998

Entrée en vigueur : *provisoirement le 26 mai 1998 par signature et définitivement le 16 avril 2000, conformément à l'article 18*

Textes authentiques : *anglais, letton et slovène*

Enregistrement au Secrétariat de l'Organisation des Nations Unies : *Lettonie, 4 janvier 2017*

[TEXT IN ENGLISH – TEXTE EN ANGLAIS]

A G R E E M E N T

between

the Government of the Republic of Latvia and

the Government of the Republic of Slovenia

on International Road Transport

The Government of the Republic of Latvia and the Government of the Republic of Slovenia (hereinafter called "the Contracting Parties"), desirous to promote in the interest of developing mutually advantageous economic relations the transport of passengers and goods by road between the two countries and in transit through their territories and with the aim of protecting environment, whereby the vehicles which reduce noise and hazardous emissions and conform to high technical and safety standards shall be used

have agreed as follows:

Article 1

1. In accordance with the terms of this Agreement carriers of both the Contracting Parties by using vehicles registered in their home country may perform international carriage of passengers and goods by road for hire or reward or own account to, from or in transit through the territory of the other Contracting Party.

2. The present Agreement does not affect the rights and obligations of each Contracting Party resulting from the provisions of other international agreements in force for either Contracting Party.

Article 2

For the purpose of this Agreement:

1. The term "carrier" means any natural or legal person who is established in the territory of either Contracting Party and is authorized to engage in international carriage of passengers and goods by road in accordance with the relevant national laws and regulations.

2. The term "vehicle" means a motor vehicle registered in either territory of the Contracting Parties or a combination of vehicles of which

at least the motor vehicle is registered in one of the territories of the Contracting Parties and which is used and equipped exclusively for the carriage of passengers or goods, and in case of passenger service a passenger road vehicle (a bus) which has more than nine seats, including that of a driver.

3. The term "cabotage" means the operation of transport services between two or more points in the territory of one Contracting Party performed by a carrier established in the territory of the other Contracting Party.

PASSENGER TRANSPORT

Article 3

In accordance with this Agreement the passenger transport is the carriage of persons and their luggage by buses. It includes also unladen journeys by buses concerned with the aforementioned services.

Article 4

1. The term "regular bus services" shall mean a service where the journeys are carried out according to the beforehand agreed itinerary, time-table and fares tariff, passengers being taken up and set down at the beforehand agreed stopping points en route.

2. Regular bus services between the territories of the Contracting Parties or in transit through them shall be authorized, in mutual agreement, by the competent authorities of the Contracting Parties. The competent authority of each Contracting Party shall grant an authorization for the section of the itinerary operated in its territory.

3. The application in view to obtain the authorization for operating regular bus services shall be submitted to the competent authority of the

Contracting Party where the carrier is established and the respective vehicles are registered. In case the application does not arise any objection, the above competent authority shall communicate it together with its opinion to the competent authority of the other Contracting Party.

4. The procedure and requirements for submitting the applications and their content shall be agreed upon by the Joint Committee established under Article 16 of this Agreement.

5. The services stated in this Article shall be considered approved and can be started to operate once the competent authorities of both the Contracting Parties have exchanged the respective authorizations with all necessary enclosures.

During the journey the respective authorization or its authorized copy must be present in the vehicle.

Article 5

1. The term "shuttle services" means services whereby, by means of repeated outward and return journeys, previously formed groups of passengers are carried from a single place of departure to a single destination. Each group of passengers who have made the outward journey together shall subsequently be carried back to place of departure together. Passengers shall not be taken up or set down during the journey. The first return journey and the last outward journey shall be made unladen.

2. For services mentioned under paragraph 1 of this Article authorisations issued by the competent authorities of the other Contracting Party are required. The procedure and requirements for the submission of applications and their contents shall be agreed on by the Joint Committee under Article 16 of this Agreement.

Article 6

1. "The occasional passenger service" shall mean the transport services other than those referred to in paragraph 1 of Article 4 of this Agreement.

2. The occasional passenger service between the two territories of the Contracting Parties or in transit through them, carrying the same group of passengers, shall require no authorization if:

a) a round trip begins and it is intended to end in the country of registration of the vehicle providing that the group of passengers is brought back to the place of departure (closed door tour) by the same vehicle;

b) a journey with passengers starts at a place in the country of registration of the vehicle and ends in the territory of the other Contracting Party or any other country providing that the vehicle returns empty to the country of registration;

c) an outward journey is made unladen provided that all the passengers are taken up in the same place where they have been previously brought by the same carrier on a service referred to in subparagraph b) above, and are carried back into the country where the vehicle is registered.

3. In the vehicles used for performing services under paragraph 2 of this Article there shall be a properly completed waybill filled out by the carrier, containing the list of passengers which shall be certified by the journey organizer's or carrier's stamp and signature and stamped by the competent customs authorities. The waybill shall be completed while being in the territory of the home country and throughout the journey shall be kept in the vehicle for which it has been issued.

4. The occasional passenger services which do not meet the provisions of paragraph 2 of this Article are subject to an authorization of the competent authority of the other Contracting Party.

The Joint Committee referred to in Article 16 of this Agreement shall agree on the form of the authorization required for performing occasional passenger services and on other issues related to these services.

GOODS TRANSPORT

Article 7

1. A carrier of each Contracting Party shall have a permit in order to engage in the international carriage of goods by road between the two countries, in transit through the territory of the other Contracting Party as well as delivering goods to or from third countries if not otherwise provided by the Joint Committee mentioned in Article 16 of this Agreement.

A single permit shall authorize a carrier of one country to make one round journey.

2. A permit shall be used only by the carrier to whom it has been issued. It shall be valid for the use of a single motor vehicle or a coupled combination of vehicles (articulated vehicle or road train), without regard which is the country of registration of an accompanying semitrailer or trailer.

3. The competent authorities of both the Contracting Parties shall annually exchange the number of blank permits agreed upon by the Joint Committee mentioned in Article 16 of this Agreement.

Article 8

1. The permits referred to in Article 7 of this Agreement shall not be required for the:

a) carriage of goods in motor vehicles whose permitted gross laden weight, including trailers, does not exceed 6 tonnes, or whose permitted payload, including trailers, does not exceed 3,5 tonnes,

b) removals carriage performed by vehicles which have been equipped for this purpose,

c) carriage of objects, equipment and animals for theatrical, film, circus or musical performances or sporting events, exhibitions or fairs, or for making of radio or television broadcasts or films, provided that these objects and equipment are imported or exported temporarily,

d) funeral transport,

e) carriage of goods from a public airport or to a public airport in case of average or any other plane accident or in case of emergency landing due to divertion of route or in cases when air flights have been canceled,

f) carriage of mails,

g) carriage of vehicles which are damaged or have broken down,

h) carriage of humanitarian supplies needed for emergencies, notably in the event of natural disasters,

i) carriage of bees and fish fry,

j) unladen run of a relief vehicle used for transporting goods sent to replace a vehicle which has broken down in another country and continuation of the haul by the relief vehicle under cover of the permit issued for the vehicle which has broken down,

k) maintenance and service vehicles providing assistance to broken down or damaged vehicles.

2. A driver of the vehicle performing any of the transport operations listed in paragraph 1 of this Article shall have all necessary documents

clearly indicating that the transport is justified by any of provisions stated in this paragraph.

GENERAL PROVISIONS

Article 9

Cabotage transport is not permitted unless the competent authority of the respective Contracting Party has issued a special permit for this purpose.

Article 10

1. If the weight and/or dimensions of a laden or unladen vehicle when engaged in transport operations under the provisions of this Agreement exceed the permissible limits in force in the territory of the other Contracting Party, a special permit issued by the competent authority of that Contracting Party shall be required.

2. As regards the weight and dimensions of vehicles, each Contracting Party undertakes not to impose on vehicles registered in the territory of the other Contracting Party conditions which are more restrictive than those imposed on vehicles registered in its own country.

Article 11

The carriers established in both the Contracting Parties shall, when performing carriages of dangerous goods, comply with the provisions of the European Agreement Concerning the International Carriage of Dangerous Goods by Road (ADR).

Article 12

Both the Contracting Parties shall provide the necessary incentives to encourage the performance of combined transport operations and usage of the sea ports situated in their respective states.

Article 13

1. Subject to the provisions of this Agreement carriers of either Contracting Party and the crews of their vehicles shall, when in the territory of the other Contracting Party, comply with the laws and regulations in force in that country.

2. Permits and other necessary documents required in accordance with this Agreement shall be carried on the vehicles to which they relate and produced on demand of any authority respectively authorized to check them.

3. If a carrier or its crew seriously and repeatedly infringe legal regulations in force in the other country or the stipulations of this Agreement, the competent authority of the Contracting Party on the territory of which the vehicle has been registered and on request of the competent authority of the Contracting Party on the territory of which the infringement occurred, may adopt the following measures within the framework of regulations in force in the respective country:

a) warn the carrier that it is obliged to respect the regulations in force (warning);

b) temporary suspend the carrier from engaging in transport;

c) stop issuing permits to the relevant carrier or revoke any previously issued authorisation for the period for which the carrier has been suspended from engaging in transport by the competent authority of the other country.

The provisions of this Article shall be without prejudice to any lawful sanctions which may be applied in accordance with the laws and regulations of the country in which territory the infringement occurred.

4. The competent authority having taken any of the measures mentioned in paragraph 3 of this Article shall inform on it the competent authority of the other Contracting Party.

Article 14

1. Vehicles which are registered in the territory of one Contracting Party and are temporarily imported into the territory of the other Contracting Party to perform transport services in accordance with this Agreement shall be exempt, according to the reciprocity principle, from the levy of road use and traffic taxes.

2. However, this exemption shall not apply to the payment of road tolls, bridge tolls and other similar charges, which shall always be required on the basis of the principle of non discrimination.

3. On the vehicles mentioned in the paragraph 1 of this Article customs duties shall be exempted on:

a) the vehicles;

b) the fuel contained in the ordinary supply tanks of the vehicles;

c) spare parts imported into the territory of the other Contracting Party, intended for the breakdown service of a vehicle. Replaced parts shall be re-exported or destroyed under the control of competent customs authorities of the other Contracting Party.

Article 15

Pursuant to the preamble of this Agreement the Contracting Parties agree to support, when performing transport services, the usage of the modernly equipped and technically safe vehicles with low noise and emission of hazardous substances.

Article 16

In order to ensure the satisfactory implementation of this Agreement a Joint Committee shall be formed comprising the representatives of competent authorities of both the Contracting Parties. It shall meet at the request of either competent authority of the Contracting Parties alternately in the territories of the Contracting Parties.

Article 17

The Contracting Parties agree to lay down rules for the application of certain provisions of this Agreement in an Additional Protocol. The Additional Protocol shall form an integral part of the Agreement.

Article 18

This Agreement shall be applied provisionally as from the date of its signature. The Contracting Parties shall notify each other through diplomatic channels that the requirements regarding the procedure of entering into force of international agreements have been fulfilled.

This Agreement shall enter into force on the thirtieth day after the date of the later of these notifications.

Article 19

In case of necessity any amendment to the present Agreement shall be negotiated by the Contracting Parties and it shall enter into force according to the procedure as per Article 18.

Article 20

The Agreement shall remain in force unless it is terminated by either Contracting Party giving through diplomatic channels not later than three months prior the end of a calendar year written notice thereof to the other Contracting Party.

In witness whereof the undersigned, being duly authorized thereto, have signed this Agreement.

Done in two originals at Copenhagen on 26th May, 1998, each in the Latvian, Slovenian and English languages, each text being equally authentic and has equal legal force. In case of divergence of interpretation the English text shall prevail.

For the Government of the Republic of Latvia	For the Government of the Republic of Slovenia
[signature]	[signature]

ADDITIONAL PROTOCOL

to the Agreement between

the Government of the Republic of Latvia and

the Government of the Republic of Slovenia

on International Road Transport

In order to implement the Agreement in conformity with its Article 17 the Contracting Parties have agreed that for purposes of this Agreement the competent authorities are:

in the Republic of Latvia:
Ministry of Transport

in the Republic of Slovenia:
Ministry of Transport and Communications

Done in two originals at Copenhagen on 26th May, 1998, each in the Latvian, Slovenian and English languages, each text being equally authentic and has equal legal force.

For the Government
of the Republic of Latvia

For the Government
of the Republic of Slovenia

[TEXT IN LATVIAN – TEXTE EN LETTON]

Latvijas Republikas valdības
un
Slovēnijas Republikas valdības
NOLĪGUMS
par starptautiskajiem pārvadājumiem ar autotransportu

Latvijas Republikas valdība un Slovēnijas Republikas valdība (turpmāk tekstā - Līgumslēdzējas Puses),

nolūkā savstarpeji izdevīgu ekonomisko attiecību attīstības interesēs veicināt pasažieru un kravu pārvadājumus pa autoceļiem starp abām valstīm un tranzītā cauri to teritorijām, un saudzēt apkārtējo vidi, izmantojot pārvadājumiem autotransporta līdzekļus ar zemu trokšņu un kaitīgo vielu emisijas līmeni atbilstoši augstām tehnisko un drošības standartu prasībām,

vienojas par sekojošo:

1. pants

1. Saskaņā ar šā Nolīguma noteikumiem abu Līgumslēdzēju Pušu valstu pārvadātāji ar savās valstīs reģistrētiem autotransporta līdzekļiem drīkst veikt pasažieru un kravu starptautiskos pārvadājumus pēc nomas līguma, par atlīdzību vai savām vajadzībām uz otras Līgumslēdzējas Puses valsts teritoriju, no tās vai tranzītā cauri tai.

2. Šis Nolīgums neskar katras Līgumslēdzējas Puses tiesības un pienākumus, kas noteikti citos starptautiskajos līgumos, kuri ir saistoši vienai vai otrai Līgumslēdzējai Pusei.

2. pants

Šā Nolīguma ietvaros:

1. *"Pārvadātājs"* ir fiziska vai juridiska persona, kas reģistrēta vienas vai otras Līgumslēdzējas Puses valsts teritorijā un saskaņā ar savas valsts likumiem un noteikumiem ir tiesīga veikt starptautiskos pasažieru vai kravu pārvadājumus ar autotransportu.

2. *"Autotransporta līdzeklis"* ir jebkurš motorizēts autotransporta līdzeklis, kas reģistrēts viena no Līgumslēdzēju Pušu valstu teritorijām vai arī autotransporta līdzekļu kombinācija, no kuriem vismaz motorizētais autotransporta līdzeklis reģistrēts vienā no Līgumslēdzēju Pušu valstu teritorijām un kuru izmanto, un kurš paredzēts tikai vai nu pasažieru vai kravu pārvadāšanai, turklāt pasažieru pārvadāšanai paredzētos autotransporta līdzekļos (autobusos) ir vairāk par deviņām sēdvietām, autovadītāja sēdvietu ieskaitot.

3. *"Kabotāža"* ir pārvadājumi, ko veic vienas Līgumslēdzējas Puses valstī reģistrēts pārvadātājs starp diviem vai vairākiem otras Līgumslēdzējas Puses valsts teritorijas punktiem.

PASAŽIERU PĀRVADĀJUMI

3. pants

Saskaņā ar šo Nolīgumu pasažieru pārvadājumi ir personu un viņu bagāžas pārvadājumi ar autobusiem. Par tādiem uzskatāmi arī autobusu braucieni bez pasažieriem, kas saistīti ar šāda veida pakalpojumiem.

4. pants

1. *"Regulārie pasažieru pārvadājumi ar autobusiem"* ir pārvadājumi, kuros braucieni tiek veikti iepriekš noteiktā maršrutā atbilstoši iepriekš saskaņotam kustības sarakstam un braukšanas tarifam un kuru laikā pasažieri var iekāpt autobusā un izkāpt no tā iepriekš noteiktās pieturvietās.

2. Regulāriem pārvadājumiem ar autobusiem starp Līgumslēdzēju Pušu valstu teritorijām vai tranzītā cauri tām nepieciešama atļauja, ko, savstarpēji vienojoties, izdod Līgumslēdzēju Pušu kompetentās institūcijas. Katras Līgumslēdzējas Puses kompetentā institūcija izdod atļauju tai maršruta daļai, kas atrodas tās valsts teritorijā.

3. Lai saņemtu atļauju regulāriem pārvadājumiem, pārvadātājam jāiesniedz atbilstošs pieteikums tās Līgumslēdzējas Puses kompetentajai institūcijai, kuras valsts teritorijā pārvadātājs un attiecīgie transporta līdzekļi reģistrēti. Ja šī kompetentā institūcija pieteikumu akceptē, tā nosūta to kopā ar savu ieteikumu otras valsts kompetentajai institūcijai.

4. Šā Nolīguma 16. pantā minētā Kopējā komisija nosaka kārtību un prasības, kas jāizpilda, sastādot un iesniedzot pieteikumus.

5. Šajā pantā minētie pārvadājumi uzskatāmi par apstiprinātiem un tos var uzsākt, ja abu Līgumslēdzēju Pušu kompetentās institūcijas apmainījušās ar atļaujām, ieskaitot visu pārējo nepieciešamo dokumentāciju.

Brauciena laikā atļaujai vai tās apstiprinātai kopijai jāatrodas autotransporta līdzeklī.

5. pants

1. *"Sistemātiski turp un atpakaļ pārvadājumi"* ir pārvadājumi, kurus veicot, iepriekš izveidotas pasažieru grupas atkārtotu turp un atpakaļ braucienu laikā tiek pārvadātas no vienas brauciena sākuma vietas uz vienu brauciena galapunktu. Katra pasažieru grupa, kas veikusi braucienu turp, sekojošā atpakaļ braucienā tiek atvesta atpakaļ brauciena sākuma vietā nemainīgā sastāvā. Brauciena laikā pasažieri netiek uzņemti, ne arī izlaisti. Pirmajam braucienam atpakaļ uz brauciena sākuma vietu un pēdējam braucienam uz galapunktu jābūt bez pasažieriem.

2. Veicot šā panta 1. punktā minētos pārvadājumus, nepieciešama otras Līgumslēdzējas Puses kompetentās institūcijas izdota atļauja. Šā Nolīguma 16. pantā minētā Kopējā komisija vienojas par kārtību un prasībām, kas jāizpilda, sastādot un iesniedzot pieteikumu atļaujas saņemšanai.

6. pants

1. Neregulārie pasažieru pārvadājumi ir tādi pārvadājumi, kas neatbilst šā Nolīguma 4. panta 1. punktā noteiktajam regulāro pārvadājumu jēdzienam.

2. Neregulāriem pasažieru pārvadājumiem, pārvadājot vienu un to pašu pasažieru grupu starp abu Līgumslēdzēju Pušu valstu teritorijām vai tranzītā cauri tām, atļauja nav nepieciešama, ja:

a) brauciens sākas un to paredzēts beigt valstī, kurā transporta līdzeklis reģistrēts, turklāt pasažieru grupa tiek nogādāta atpakaļ brauciena sākuma vietā (brauciens ar slēgtām durvīm) ar vienu un to pašu transporta līdzekli;

b) brauciens ar pasažieriem sākas valstī, kurā transporta līdzeklis reģistrēts, un beidzas otras Līgumslēdzējas Puses vai citas valsts teritorijā, turklāt transporta līdzeklis atgriežas reģistrācijas valstī bez pasažieriem;

c) brauciens turp tiek veikts bez pasažieriem ar nosacījumu, ka visi pasažieri tiek uzņemti tajā pašā vietā, kur tos iepriekš aizvedis tas pats pārvadātājs šā punkta b) apakšpunktā minēto pārvadājumu ietvaros, lai atvestu atpakaļ uz valsti, kurā transporta līdzeklis reģistrēts.

3. Autotransporta līdzekļos, ar kuriem veic šā panta 2. punktā minētos pārvadājumus, jāatrodas pilnībā aizpildītam brauciena formulāram ar pasažieru sarakstu, ko ar parakstu un zīmogu apstiprinājis pārvadājuma organizētājs vai pārvadātājs un apzīmogojusi kompetenta muitas institūcija. Brauciena formulārs aizpildāms, pārvadātājam atrodoties savas valsts teritorijā, un visa brauciena laikā tam jāatrodas tajā transporta līdzeklī, kuram tas izsniegts.

4. Neregulāriem pasažieru pārvadājumiem, kas neatbilst šā panta 2. punkta noteikumiem, nepieciešama otras Līgumslēdzējas Puses kompetentās institūcijas izdota atļauja.

Šā Nolīguma 16. pantā minētā Kopējā komisija vienojas par atļauju formu, kas nepieciešama neregulāru pasažieru pārvadājumu veikšanai, un par citiem ar šo pakalpojumu saistītiem jautājumiem.

KRAVU PĀRVADĀJUMI

7. pants

1. Katras Līgumslēdzējas Puses pārvadatājam ir nepieciešama atļauja, lai veiktu starptautiskos kravu pārvadājumus starp abām valstīm, tranzītā cauri otras Līgumslēdzējas Puses valsts teritorijai, kā arī nogādājot kravu uz trešajām valstīm vai otrādi, ja vien šā Nolīguma 16. pantā minētā Kopēja komisija nav pieņēmusi citu lēmumu.

Vienreizēja atļauja dod tiesības vienas valsts pārvadātājam veikt vienu braucienu turp un atpakaļ.

2. Atļauju var izmantot tikai tas pārvadātājs, kuram tā izsniegta. Tā ir derīga vienam autotransporta līdzeklim bez piekabes vai vairāku autotransporta līdzekļu kombinācijai (vilcējam ar puspiekabi vai autovilcienam) neatkarīgi no tā, kādā valstī piekabe vai puspiekabe reģistrēta.

3. Abu Līgumslēdzēju Pušu kompetentās institūcijas ik gadus apmainās ar tādu atļauju veidlapu skaitu, par kādu vienojusies šā Nolīguma 16. pantā minētā Kopējā komisija.

8. pants

1. Šā Nolīguma 7. pantā minētās pārvadājumu atļaujas nav nepieciešamas:

a) kravu pārvadājumiem ar autotransporta līdzekļiem, kuru pilna masa, ieskaitot piekabes, nepārsniedz 6 tonnas vai kuru maksimālā celtspēja, ieskaitot piekabes, nepārsniedz 3,5 tonnas;

b) pārvadājumiem, kas saistīti ar dzīves vietas maiņu, veicot tos ar speciāliem šim nolūkam aprīkotiem autotransporta līdzekļiem;

c) pārvadājot piederumus, iekārtas un dzīvniekus, kas paredzēti teātra, kino, cirka vai mūzikas izrādēm, sporta pasākumiem, izstādēm vai gadatirgiem, kā arī radio un televīzijas raidījumu ierakstiem vai kinofilmu uzņemšanai, ja šie piederumi un iekārtas tiek ievestas vai izvestas uz laiku;

d) bēru pārvadājumiem;

e) kravu pārvadājumiem no publiskās lidostas vai uz publisko lidostu lidmašīnas avārijas vai cita veida lidmašīnas bojājuma gadījumā, vai arī piespiedu nosēšanās gadījumā, kad lidmašīna spiesta novirzīties no maršruta vai lidojumi atcelti;

f) pasta pārvadājumiem;

g) bojātu vai avarējušu transporta līdzekļu pārvadāšanai;

h) humāno kravu pārvadājumiem, kas nepieciešamas palīdzības sniegšanai ārkārtējās situācijās, īpaši dabas katastrofu gadījumos;

i) bišu saimju un zivju mazuļu pārvadājumiem;

j) autotransporta līdzekļa braucienam bez kravas palīdzības sniegšanai, lai nomainītu citā valstī bojātu transporta līdzekli un turpinātu pārvadājumu, izmantojot bojātajam autotransporta līdzeklim izsniegto atļauju;

k) tehniskās palīdzības transporta līdzekļiem, kas dodas sniegt palīdzību bojātiem vai avarējušiem transporta līdzekļiem.

2. Veicot šā panta 1. punktā minētos pārvadājumus, autotransporta līdzekļa vadītāja rīcībā jābūt visiem nepieciešamajiem dokumentiem, kas apliecina, ka attiecīgais pārvadājums atbilst kādam no šajā punktā uzskaitītajiem nosacījumiem.

VISPĀRĪGIE NOTEIKUMI

9. pants

Veikt kabotāžas pārvadājumus nav atļauts, ja nav saņemta speciāla, šim nolūkam izdota attiecīgās Līgumslēdzējas Puses kompetentās institūcijas atļauja.

10. pants

1. Ja, veicot pārvadājumus saskaņā ar šā Nolīguma noteikumiem, autotransporta līdzekļa ar kravu vai bez tās svars un(vai) izmēri pārsniedz pieļaujamās normas, kas ir spēkā otras Līgumslēdzējas Puses valsts teritorijā, nepieciešama šīs Līgumslēdzējas Puses kompetentās institūcijas izdota speciāla atļauja.

2. Attiecībā uz autotransporta līdzekļu svaru un izmēriem katra Līgumslēdzēja Puse apņemas neizvirzīt otras Līgumslēdzējas Puses valsts teritorijā reģistrētiem transporta līdzekļiem augstākas prasības nekā tās, kas noteiktas savā valstī reģistrētiem transporta līdzekļiem.

11. pants

Veicot bīstamo kravu pārvadājumus, abu Līgumslēdzēju Pušu valstīs reģistrētiem pārvadātājiem jāievēro Eiropas valstu Nolīguma par bīstamo kravu starptautiskajiem pārvadājumiem ar autotransportu (ADR) prasības.

12. pants

Abas Līgumslēdzējas Puses apņemas veikt nepieciešamos pasākumus, lai veicinātu kombinētos pārvadājumus un savās valstīs esošo jūras ostu izmantošanu.

13. pants

1. Veicot pārvadājumus saskaņā ar šā Nolīguma noteikumiem, vienas Līgumslēdzējas Puses pārvadātājiem un viņu autotransporta līdzekļu apkalpēm, atrodoties otras Līgumslēdzējas Puses valsts teritorijā, jāievēro šajā valstī spēkā esošie likumi un noteikumi.

2. Atļaujām un citiem nepieciešamajiem dokumentiem, kas paredzēti šajā Nolīgumā, jāatrodas autotransporta līdzeklī, uz kuru tie attiecas, un tie jāuzrāda pēc ikvienas amatpersonas pieprasījuma, kas atbilstoši pilnvarota veikt pārbaudi.

3. Ja pārvadātājs vai autotransporta līdzekļa apkalpe ir nopietni vai atkārtoti pārkāpusi šā Nolīguma noteikumus, kā arī otrā valstī spēkā esošos likumus un noteikumus, tās valsts, kurā reģistrēts transporta līdzeklis, kompetentā institūcija pēc valsts, kurā pārkāpums noticis, kompetentās institūcijas pieprasījuma var attiecīgajā valstī spēkā esošo noteikumu ietvaros piemērot šādas sankcijas:

a) aizrādīt pārvadātājam, ka viņam jāievēro spēkā esošie noteikumi (brīdinājums);

b) uz laiku aizliegt pārvadātājam iesaistīties pārvadājumu veikšanā;

c) pārtraukt atļauju izsniegšanu šim pārvadātājam vai anulēt iepriekš izsniegtu atļauju uz tādu laika periodu, uz kādu otras valsts kompetentā institūcija pārvadātājam aizliegusi veikt pārvadājumus.

Šā panta noteikumi neierobežo likumīgās sankcijas, ko var piemērot saskaņā ar tās valsts likumiem un noteikumiem, kuras teritorijā pārkāpums noticis.

4. Kompetentā institūcija, kas ir piemērojusi jebkuru no šā panta '. punktā minētajām sankcijām, par to paziņo otras Līgumslēdzējas Puses kompetentajai institūcijai.

14. pants

1. Vienas Līgumslēdzējas Puses valsts teritorijā reģistrēti autotransporta līdzekļi, kas uz laiku iebraukuši otras Līgumslēdzējas Puses valsts teritorijā, lai veiktu pārvadājumus saskaņā ar šo Nolīgumu, tiek abpusēji atbrīvoti no ceļu nodokļu un ar pārvadājumu veikšanu saistīto nodokļu maksājumiem.

2. Tomēr šis atbrīvojums neattiecas uz nodevām par maksas ceļu un tiltu lietošanu un citiem līdzīgiem maksājumiem, kuri iekasējami, pamatojoties uz nediskriminējošiem noteikumiem.

3. Kas attiecas uz autotransporta līdzekļiem, kas minēti šā panta 1. punktā, no muitas nodokļiem atbrīvojami:

a) autotransporta līdzekļi;

b) degviela, kas atrodas autotransporta līdzekļu standarta tvertnēs;

c) rezerves daļas, ko ieved otras Līgumslēdzējas Puses valsts teritorijā bojātu autotransporta līdzekļu remontam. Nomainītās detaļas ir jāizved vai jāiznīcina otras Līgumslēdzējas Puses kompetentu muitas amatpersonu klātbūtnē.

15. pants

Atbilstoši šā Nolīguma preambulai Līgumslēdzējas Puses vienojas atbalstīt tādu autotransporta līdzekļu izmantošanu pārvadājumos, kas ir moderni aprīkoti un tehniski droši ar zemu trokšņa un kaitīgo vielu emisijas līmeni.

16. pants

Lai nodrošinātu šā Nolīguma pienācīgu izpildi, izveidojama Kopējā komisija, kuras sastāvā ietilpst abu Līgumslēdzēju Pušu kompetento institūciju pārstāvji. Tā tiekas pēc jebkuras Līgumslēdzējas Puses kompetentās institūcijas lūguma pārmaiņus abu Līgumslēdzēju Pušu valstu teritorijās.

17. pants

Līgumslēdzējas Puses vienojas atsevišķu šā Nolīguma noteikumu piemērošanu atspoguļot Papildprotokolā. Papildprotokols ir šā Nolīguma neatņemama sastāvdaļa.

18. pants

Šis Nolīgums provizoriski piemērojams no tā parakstīšanas dienas. Līgumslēdzējas Puses viena otrai pa diplomātiskajiem kanāliem paziņo par to, ka visas ar starptautisko līgumu spēkā stāšanās kārtību saistītās prasības atbilstoši katras valsts tiesību normām ir izpildītas.

Šis Nolīgums stājas spēkā trīsdesmitajā dienā pēc pēdējā paziņojuma saņemšanas.

19. pants

Ja nepieciešams, Līgumslēdzējas Puses apspriež jebkura veida izmaiņas šajā Nolīgumā, un tās stājas spēkā šā Nolīguma 18. pantā noteiktajā kārtībā.

20. pants

Šis Nolīgums paliek spēkā tik ilgi, kamēr viena no Līgumslēdzējām Pusēm ne vēlāk kā trīs mēnešus pirms kalendāra gada beigām pa diplomātiskajiem kanāliem neiesniedz otrai Līgumslēdzējai Pusei rakstisku paziņojumu par savu nodomu izbeigt tā darbību.

TO APLIECINOT, apakšā parakstījušies, šim nolūkam pienācīgi pilnvaroti, ir parakstījuši šo Nolīgumu.

Parakstīts Kopenhāgenā 1998. gada "26." maijā divos oriģināleksemplāros, katrs latviešu, slovēņu un angļu valodā, turklāt visi teksti ir vienlīdz autentiski un tiem ir vienāds juridisks spēks. Domstarpību gadījumā noteicošais ir Nolīguma teksts angļu valodā.

Latvijas Republikas valdības vārdā:	Slovēnijas Republikas valdības vārdā:

Latvijas Republikas valdības
un Slovēnijas Republikas valdības
NOLĪGUMA
par starptautiskajiem pārvadājumiem ar autotransportu

PAPILDPROTOKOLS

Lai izpildītu Nolīgumu atbilstoši tā 17. pantam, Līgumslēdzējas Puses vienojās, ka šā Nolīguma ietvaros kompetentās institūcijas ir:

Latvijas Republikā:

Satiksmes ministrija;

Slovēnijas Republikā:

Transporta un sakaru ministrija.

Parakstīts Kopenhāgenā 1998. gada "26." maijā divos oriģināleksemplāros, katrs latviešu, slovēņu un angļu valodā, turklāt visi teksti ir vienlīdz autentiski un tiem ir vienāds juridisks spēks.

Latvijas Republikas valdības vārdā:	Slovēnijas Republikas valdības vārdā:

[TEXT IN SLOVENE – TEXTE EN SLOVÈNE]

S P O R A Z U M

med

Vlado Republike Latvije

in Vlado Republike Slovenije

o mednarodnem cestnem prevozu

Vlada Republike Latvije in Vlada Republike Slovenije (v nadaljnjem besedilu: pogodbenici) sta se v želji, da bi v interesu razvijanja vzajemno koristnih gospodarskih odnosov spodbujali cestni prevoz potnikov in blaga med državama in tranzit čez svoji ozemlji, ter z namenom varovanja okolja, pri čemer se uporabljajo vozila, ki zmanjšujejo hrup in nevarne emisije ter ustrezajo visokim tehničnim in varnostnim standardom,

sporazumeli, kot sledi:

1. člen

1. V skladu z določbami tega sporazuma lahko prevozniki obeh pogodbenic z uporabo vozil, registriranih v njihovi domači državi, opravljajo mednarodni prevoz potnikov in blaga po cesti za račun tretjega ali v svojem imenu na ozemlje druge pogodbenice, z njega ali v tranzitu čezenj.

2. Ta sporazum ne vpliva na pravice in obveznosti vsake pogodbenice, ki izhajajo iz določb drugih mednarodnih sporazumov, veljavnih za eno ali drugo pogodbenico.

2. člen

Za namen tega sporazuma:

1. je "prevoznik" katera koli fizična ali pravna oseba, ki ima sedež svojega podjetja na ozemlju ene od pogodbenic in je pooblaščena za opravljanje mednarodnega prevoza potnikov in blaga po cesti v skladu z ustreznimi državnimi zakoni in predpisi;

2. je "vozilo" motorno vozilo, registrirano na ozemlju ene od pogodbenic, ali kombinacija vozil, od katerih je vsaj motorno vozilo registrirano na ozemlju ene od pogodbenic in se uporablja ter je opremljeno izključno za prevoz potnikov ali blaga, in pri potniškem prevozu tudi vozilo za cestni prevoz potnikov (avtobus), ki ima več kot devet sedežev vključno z voznikovim;

3. je "kabotaža" prevoz med dvema ali več točkami na ozemlju ene pogodbenice, ki ga opravlja prevoznik, ki ima sedež svojega podjetja na ozemlju druge pogodbenice.

PREVOZ POTNIKOV

3. člen

Po tem sporazumu je prevoz potnikov prevoz oseb in njihove prtljage z avtobusi. Vključuje tudi prazno vožnjo avtobusov, ki opravljajo omenjene storitve.

4. člen

1. Izraz "linijski prevoz potnikov" je prevoz, ki se opravlja po vnaprej dogovorjeni progi, voznem redu in ceniku, potniki pa vstopajo in izstopajo na vnaprej dogovorjenih postajališčih.

2. Linijski prevoz potnikov med ozemljema pogodbenic ali tranzitno čez njuni ozemlji na podlagi doseženega soglasja dovolita pristojna organa pogodbenic. Pristojni organ vsake pogodbenice izda dovoljenje za del proge na svojem ozemlju.

3. Vloga za pridobitev dovoljenja za opravljanje linijskega prevoza potnikov se predloži pristojnemu organu pogodbenice, kjer ima prevoznik sedež svojega podjetja in so registrirana vozila. Če zoper vlogo ni ugovora, jo zgoraj navedeni pristojni organ pošlje skupaj s svojim mnenjem pristojnemu organu druge pogodbenice.

4. O postopku in zahtevah za predložitev vlog ter njihovi vsebini se dogovori skupni odbor, ustanovljen po 16. členu tega sporazuma.

5. Šteje se, da je prevoz iz tega člena odobren in se lahko začne opravljati, ko pristojna organa obeh pogodbenic izmenjata ustrezna dovoljenja z vsemi potrebnimi prilogami.

Dovoljenje oziroma njegova overjena kopija mora biti med vožnjo v vozilu.

5. člen

1. "Izmenični prevoz" je prevoz vnaprej oblikovanih skupin potnikov z več potovanji iz enega samega odhodnega kraja do enega samega namembnega kraja. Vsaka skupina, ki je odpotovala skupaj, se mora skupaj vrniti v odhodni kraj. Potniki med potovanjem ne smejo vstopati ali izstopati. Prva vožnja nazaj v odhodni kraj in zadnja vožnja v namembni kraj se opravita s praznim vozilom.

2. Za prevoze, omenjene v prvem odstavku tega člena, so potrebna dovoljenja, ki jih izdajo pristojni organi druge pogodbenice. O postopku in zahtevah za predložitev vlog ter o njihovi vsebini se dogovori skupni odbor, ustanovljen po 16. členu tega sporazuma.

6. člen

1. "Občasni prevoz potnikov" so prevozne storitve razen tistih, ki so navedene v prvem odstavku 4. člena tega sporazuma.

2. Za občasni prevoz potnikov med ozemljema pogodbenic ali v tranzitu čeznju z isto skupino potnikov ni potrebno dovoljenje, če:

a) se krožna vožnja začne in se namerava končati v državi registracije vozila pod pogojem, da isto vozilo pripelje skupino potnikov na odhodni kraj (vožnja zaprtih vrat),

b) se vožnja s potniki začne v kraju države registracije vozila in konča na ozemlju druge pogodbenice ali katere koli druge države pod pogojem, da se vozilo prazno vrne v državo registracije,

c) se opravi vožnja ob odhodu s praznim vozilom pod pogojem, da vsi potniki vstopijo na istem kraju, kamor jih je predhodno prepeljal isti prevoznik s prevozom iz pododstavka b) in jih prepelje nazaj v državo, kjer je vozilo registrirano.

3. V vozilih, ki se uporabljajo za prevoze po drugem odstavku tega člena, mora biti pravilno izpolnjena potniška spremnica, ki jo izpolni prevoznik ter vsebuje seznam potnikov in jo potrdi z žigom in podpisom organizator vožnje ali prevoznik in ima žig pristojnih carinskih organov. Potniška

spremnica se izpolni na ozemlju domače države in je ves čas vožnje v vozilu, za katero je bila izdana.

4. Za občasni prevoz potnikov, ki ne izpolnjuje določb drugega odstavka tega člena, je potrebno dovoljenje pristojnega organa druge pogodbenice.

Skupni odbor, naveden v 16. členu tega sporazuma, se dogovori o obliki dovoljenja, ki je potrebno za opravljanje občasnega prevoza potnikov, in o drugih vprašanjih, ki zadevajo ta prevoz.

PREVOZ BLAGA

7. člen

1. Prevoznik vsake pogodbenice mora imeti dovolilnico za mednarodni prevoz blaga po cesti med državama, v tranzitu čez ozemlje druge pogodbenice in za dostavo blaga v tretje države ali iz njih, če skupni odbor, omenjen v 16. členu tega sporazuma, ne določi drugače.

Posamezna dovolilnica dovoljuje prevozniku ene države eno krožno vožnjo.

2. Dovolilnico sme uporabiti samo prevoznik, kateremu je bila izdana. Veljavna je za uporabo enega motornega vozila ali spojene kombinacije vozil (sestavljeno vozilo ali cestni vlak) ne glede na to, v kateri državi je registriran spremljajoči priklopnik ali polpriklopnik.

3. Pristojni organi obeh pogodbenic letno izmenjajo število neizpolnjenih dovolilnic, o katerem se dogovori skupni odbor, omenjen v 16. členu tega sporazuma.

8. člen

1. Dovolilnice, navedene v 7. členu tega sporazuma, niso potrebne za:

a) prevoz blaga z motornimi vozili, katerih skupna dovoljena masa, vključno s priklopniki, ne presega 6 ton ali pri katerih dovoljena nosilnost, vključno s priklopniki, ne presega 3,5 tone,

b) selitveni prevoz z vozili, ki so opremljena v ta namen,

c) prevoz predmetov, opreme in živali za gledališke, filmske, cirkuške ali glasbene predstave ali športne prireditve, razstave ali sejme ali za snemanje radijskih ali televizijskih oddaj ali filmov pod pogojem, da se ti predmeti ali oprema uvažajo ali izvažajo začasno,

d) prevoz posmrtnih ostankov,

e) prevoz blaga z javnega letališča ali na javno letališče ob havariji ali kakšni drugi letalski nesreči ali ob zasilnem pristanku zaradi spremenjene smeri poleta ali ob odpovedanih letih,

f) prevoz poštnih pošiljk,

g) prevoz poškodovanih ali pokvarjenih vozil,

h) prevoz človekoljubnih pošiljk ob nujnih primerih, še posebej ob naravnih nesrečah,

i) prevoz čebel in ribjega podmladka,

j) prazno vožnjo nadomestnega vozila, ki se uporablja za prevoz blaga in nadomesti vozilo, ki se je pokvarilo v drugi državi, in nadaljuje prevoz v okviru dovolilnice, izdane za vozilo, ki se je pokvarilo,

k) vozila tehnične pomoči za popravilo pokvarjenih ali poškodovanih vozil.

2. Voznik vozila, ki opravlja kateri koli prevoz iz prvega odstavka tega člena, mora imeti vse potrebne dokumente, ki jasno kažejo upravičenost prevoza po kateri koli izmed določb, navedenih v tem odstavku.

SPLOŠNE DOLOČBE

9. člen

Kabotaža ni dovoljena, razen če je pristojni organ pogodbenice v ta namen izdal posebno dovolilnico.

10. člen

1. Če masa in/ali dimenzije naloženega ali praznega vozila pri opravljanju prevoza po določbah tega sporazuma presega dovoljene omejitve, ki veljajo na ozemlju druge pogodbenice, se zahteva posebna dovolilnica, ki jo izda pristojni organ te pogodbenice.

2. Glede mase in dimenzij vozil se vsaka pogodbenica zavezuje, da za vozila, ki so registrirana na ozemlju druge pogodbenice, ne bo postavljala pogojev, ki so strožji od tistih, ki veljajo za vozila, registrirana v njeni državi.

11. člen

Prevozniki, ki imajo sedež svojega podjetja v pogodbenicah, morajo pri prevozih nevarnega blaga spoštovati določbe Evropskega sporazuma o mednarodnem cestnem prevozu nevarnega blaga (ADR).

12. člen

Pogodbenici zagotavljata potrebne spodbude za pospeševanje kombiniranega prevoza in uporabo pomorskih pristanišč v svojih državah.

13. člen

1. V skladu z določbami tega sporazuma morajo prevozniki vsake pogodbenice in osebje njihovih vozil, kadar so na ozemlju druge pogodbenice, spoštovati zakone in predpise, ki veljajo v tej državi.

2. Dovolilnice in drugi potrebni dokumenti, ki se zahtevajo v skladu s tem sporazumom, morajo biti v vozilu, na katero se nanašajo, in jih je treba pokazati na zahtevo katerega koli organa pogodbenice, ki je pristojen za njihovo preverjanje.

3. Če prevoznik ali njegovo vozno osebje težje in večkrat krši veljavne pravne predpise v drugi državi ali določbe tega sporazuma, lahko pristojni organ pogodbenice, na ozemlju katere je bilo vozilo registrirano, in na prošnjo pristojnega organa pogodbenice, na ozemlju katere je bil storjen

prekršek, sprejme naslednje ukrepe v okviru veljavnih predpisov svoje države:

a) opozori prevoznika, da mora upoštevati veljavne predpise (opomin);

b) mu začasno prepove opravljati prevoz;

c) preneha izdajati dovolilnice temu prevozniku ali prekliče že izdano dovoljenje za obdobje, za katero mu je pristojni organ druge države začasno prepovedal opravljati prevoz.

Določbe tega člena ne vplivajo na zakonite sankcije, ki se uporabljajo v skladu z zakoni in predpisi države, na ozemlju katere je prišlo do kršitve.

4. Pristojni organ, ki je sprejel kakršne koli ukrepe, omenjene v tretjem odstavku tega člena, o tem obvesti pristojni organ druge pogodbenice.

14. člen

1. Vozila, ki so registrirana na ozemlju ene pogodbenice in se začasno uvozijo na ozemlje druge pogodbenice za opravljanje prevoznih storitev v skladu s tem sporazumom, so po načelu vzajemnosti oproščena plačila pristojbin za uporabo cest in dajatev na promet z vozilom.

2. Ta oprostitev pa ne velja za plačilo cestnin, mostnin in drugih podobnih pristojbin, ki se vedno zahtevajo na podlagi načela nediskriminacije.

3. Pri vozilih, omenjenih v prvem odstavku tega člena, so carinskih dajatev oproščeni:

a) vozila,

b) gorivo, vsebovano v serijsko vgrajenih rezervoarjih vozil,

c) rezervni deli, uvoženi na ozemlje druge pogodbenice in namenjeni za popravilo pokvarjenega vozila. Zamenjani deli se ponovno izvozijo ali uničijo pod nadzorom pristojnih carinskih organov druge pogodbenice.

15. člen

V skladu s preambulo tega sporazuma se pogodbenici dogovorita, da bosta pri opravljanju prevoznih storitev spodbujali uporabo sodobno opremljenih in tehnično varnih vozil z nizko ravnijo hrupa in emisijo nevarnih snovi.

16. člen

Za uspešno izvajanje tega sporazuma se oblikuje skupni odbor, ki ga sestavljajo predstavniki pristojnih organov obeh pogodbenic. Odbor se sestaja na željo pristojnega organa pogodbenic izmenično na ozemlju pogodbenic.

17. člen

Pogodbenici se dogovorita o določitvi pravil za uporabo posameznih določb tega sporazuma v dodatnem protokolu. Dodatni protokol je sestavni del sporazuma.

18. člen

Ta sporazum se uporablja začasno od datuma podpisa. Pogodbenici se po diplomatski poti medsebojno obvestita, da so izpolnjene zahteve v zvezi s postopkom za začetek veljavnosti mednarodnih sporazumov.

Ta sporazum začne veljati trideseti dan po datumu zadnjega od teh obvestil.

19. člen

Če je potrebno, se pogodbenici pogajata o kakršni koli spremembi tega sporazuma, sprememba pa začne veljati skladno s postopki iz 18. člena.

20. člen

Ta sporazum velja, dokler ga pogodbenica ne odpove, tako da po diplomatski poti najkasneje tri mesece pred iztekom koledarskega leta o tem pisno obvesti drugo pogodbenico.

V potrditev tega sta podpisana, pravilno pooblaščena v ta namen, podpisala ta sporazum.

Sestavljeno v dveh izvirnikih v Kopenhagnu dne 26. maja 1998, vsak v latvijskem, slovenskem in angleškem jeziku, pri čemer je vsako besedilo enako verodostojno in enako pravno veljavno. Ob razhajanjih pri razlagi je odločilno angleško besedilo.

Za Vlado
Republike Latvije

Za Vlado
Republike Slovenije

DODATNI PROTOKOL

k Sporazumu med

Vlado Republike Latvije

in Vlado Republike Slovenije

o mednarodnem cestnem prevozu

Za izvajanje tega sporazuma v skladu z njegovim 17. členom sta se pogodbenici dogovorili, da sta za namen tega sporazuma pristojna organa:

za Republiko Latvijo:
Ministrstvo za promet

za Republiko Slovenijo:
Ministrstvo za promet in zveze

Sestavljeno v dveh izvirnikih v Kopenhagnu dne 26. maja 1998, vsak v latvijskem, slovenskem in angleškem jeziku, pri čemer je vsako besedilo enako verodostojno in enako pravno veljavno.

Za Vlado
Republike Latvije

Za Vlado
Republike Slovenije

[TRANSLATION IN FRENCH – TRADUCTION EN FRANÇAIS]

ACCORD ENTRE LE GOUVERNEMENT DE LA RÉPUBLIQUE DE LETTONIE ET LE GOUVERNEMENT DE LA RÉPUBLIQUE DE SLOVÉNIE RELATIF AU TRANSPORT ROUTIER INTERNATIONAL

Le Gouvernement de la République de Lettonie et le Gouvernement de la République de Slovénie (ci-après dénommés « Parties contractantes »), désireux de promouvoir, en vue de développer des relations économiques mutuellement avantageuses, le transport routier de passagers et de marchandises entre les deux pays et en transit à travers leurs territoires, et dans le but de protéger l'environnement, en utilisant des véhicules moins bruyants, qui produisent moins d'émissions dangereuses et qui sont conformes à des normes techniques et de sécurité élevées,

Sont convenus de ce qui suit :

Article premier

1. Conformément aux dispositions du présent Accord, les transporteurs des deux Parties contractantes peuvent, au moyen de véhicules immatriculés dans leur pays d'origine, effectuer des opérations de transport routier international de passagers et de marchandises, pour leur propre compte ou pour le compte d'autrui, à destination ou en provenance du territoire de l'autre Partie contractante ou en transit à travers celui-ci.

2. Le présent Accord ne porte pas atteinte aux droits et obligations de chaque Partie contractante découlant des dispositions d'autres accords internationaux en vigueur pour l'une ou l'autre Partie contractante.

Article 2

Aux fins du présent Accord :

1. Le terme « transporteur » désigne toute personne physique ou morale établie sur le territoire de l'une ou l'autre Partie contractante et autorisée à effectuer des opérations de transport routier international de passagers et de marchandises, conformément aux lois et règlements nationaux pertinents ;

2. Le terme « véhicule » désigne un véhicule à moteur immatriculé sur le territoire de l'une ou l'autre Partie contractante ou un ensemble de véhicules dont au moins un véhicule à moteur est immatriculé sur le territoire de l'une ou l'autre Partie contractante et qui est utilisé et équipé exclusivement pour le transport de passagers ou de marchandises, et en cas de transport de passagers, un véhicule routier pour le transport de passagers (autobus) comptant plus de neuf sièges, y compris celui du chauffeur ;

3. Le terme « cabotage » désigne l'exploitation de services de transport entre deux points, ou plus, sur le territoire d'une Partie contractante par un transporteur établi sur le territoire de l'une ou l'autre Partie contractante.

TRANSPORT DE PASSAGERS

Article 3

Aux fins du présent Accord, le transport de passagers s'entend du transport de personnes et de leurs bagages par autobus. Il inclut également des trajets à vide effectués par les bus proposant les services susmentionnés.

Article 4

1. L'expression « services réguliers d'autobus » s'entend d'un service dont les trajets sont effectués selon un itinéraire, un horaire et un tarif convenus à l'avance, les passagers étant pris en charge et déposés aux points d'arrêt convenus à l'avance le long de l'itinéraire.

2. Les services réguliers d'autobus entre les territoires des Parties contractantes ou en transit à travers ceux-ci sont autorisés, d'un commun accord, par les autorités compétentes des Parties contractantes. L'autorité compétente de chaque Partie contractante accorde une autorisation pour la section de l'itinéraire exploitée sur son territoire.

3. La demande visant à obtenir l'autorisation d'exploiter des services réguliers d'autobus est soumise à l'autorité compétente de la Partie contractante dans laquelle le transporteur est établi et dans laquelle les véhicules concernés sont immatriculés. Si la demande ne soulève aucune objection, l'autorité compétente susmentionnée communique la demande et sa décision à son égard à l'autorité compétente de l'autre Partie contractante.

4. La procédure et les exigences relatives à la présentation des demandes ainsi que leur contenu sont convenus par la Commission mixte établie en application de l'article 16 du présent Accord.

5. Les services mentionnés au présent article sont considérés comme approuvés et peuvent commencer à être exploités dès que les autorités compétentes des deux Parties contractantes ont échangé les autorisations pertinentes accompagnées de toutes les pièces nécessaires.

Pendant le voyage, l'autorisation pertinente ou sa copie certifiée doit se trouver à bord du véhicule.

Article 5

1. L'expression « services de navette » s'entend des services par lesquels, au moyen de voyages aller et retour répétés, des groupes de passagers préalablement constitués sont transportés d'un lieu de départ donné à un lieu de destination donné. Chaque groupe de passagers ayant effectué ensemble le trajet à l'aller est par la suite ramené ensemble au point de départ. Les passagers ne peuvent être ni pris en charge ni débarqués pendant le trajet. Le premier voyage retour et le dernier voyage aller sont effectués à vide.

2. Pour les services visés au paragraphe 1 du présent article, il convient de disposer des autorisations délivrées par les autorités compétentes de l'autre Partie contractante. La procédure et les exigences relatives à la présentation des demandes ainsi qu'à leur contenu sont convenues par la Commission mixte établie en application de l'article 16 du présent Accord.

Article 6

1. L'expression « service occasionnel de transport de passagers » s'entend des services de transport autres que ceux visés au paragraphe 1 de l'article 4 du présent Accord.

2. Les services occasionnels de transport de passagers effectués entre les territoires des deux Parties contractantes ou en transit à travers ceux-ci et transportant le même groupe de passagers ne requièrent aucune autorisation si :

a) Un voyage aller et retour débute et est censé se terminer dans le pays d'immatriculation du véhicule, à condition que le groupe de passagers soit ramené au lieu de départ (circuit à portes fermées) par le même véhicule ;

b) Un voyage avec des passagers débute à un endroit situé dans le pays d'immatriculation du véhicule et se termine sur le territoire de l'autre Partie contractante ou de tout autre pays, à condition que le véhicule retourne à vide dans le pays d'immatriculation ;

c) Un voyage aller est effectué à vide, à condition que tous les passagers soient pris en charge au même endroit que celui où ils ont précédemment été déposés par le même transporteur dans le cadre d'un service visé à l'alinéa b) ci-dessus et à condition qu'ils soient ramenés dans le pays d'immatriculation du véhicule.

3. Les véhicules utilisés pour les services visés au paragraphe 2 du présent article disposent d'une lettre de voiture dûment remplie par le transporteur contenant la liste des passagers, certifiée par le cachet et la signature de l'organisateur du voyage ou du transporteur et par le cachet des autorités douanières compétentes. La lettre de voiture est remplie lorsque le véhicule se trouve sur le territoire du pays d'origine et est conservée pendant tout le voyage dans le véhicule pour lequel elle a été délivrée.

4. Les services occasionnels de transport de passagers qui ne répondent pas aux dispositions du paragraphe 2 du présent article doivent obtenir une autorisation de l'autorité compétente de l'autre Partie contractante.

La Commission mixte visée à l'article 16 du présent Accord convient de la forme que prend l'autorisation requise pour l'exécution de services occasionnels de transport de passagers et d'autres questions intéressant ces services.

TRANSPORT DE MARCHANDISES

Article 7

1. Un transporteur de chaque Partie contractante est titulaire d'un permis lui permettant d'effectuer des opérations de transport routier international de marchandises entre les deux pays ou en transit à travers le territoire de l'autre Partie contractante, ainsi que de livrer des marchandises à destination ou en provenance de pays tiers, sauf disposition contraire de la Commission mixte visée à l'article 16 du présent Accord.

Un permis unique autorise le transporteur d'un pays à effectuer un seul voyage aller et retour.

2. Un permis ne peut être utilisé que par le transporteur auquel il a été délivré. Il est valable pour l'utilisation d'un seul véhicule à moteur ou d'un ensemble de véhicules couplés (véhicule articulé ou train routier), quel que soit le pays d'immatriculation de la semi-remorque ou de la remorque qui y est attachée.

3. Les autorités compétentes des deux Parties contractantes s'informent mutuellement chaque année du nombre d'autorisations en blanc convenu par la Commission mixte visée à l'article 16 du présent Accord.

Article 8

1. Les autorisations visées à l'article 7 du présent Accord ne sont pas nécessaires pour :

a) Le transport de marchandises dans des véhicules à moteur dont le poids total roulant autorisé, remorques comprises, ne dépasse pas 6 tonnes, ou dont la charge utile autorisée, remorques comprises, ne dépasse pas 3,5 tonnes ;

b) Les opérations de déménagement effectuées par des véhicules équipés à cet effet ;

c) Le transport d'objets, d'équipements et d'animaux destinés à être utilisés dans le cadre de représentations théâtrales, cinématographiques, de cirque ou musicales, de manifestations sportives, d'expositions ou de foires, ou destinés à la réalisation d'émissions de radio ou de télévision ou de films, pour autant que ces objets et équipements soient importés ou exportés temporairement ;

d) Le transport funéraire ;

e) Le transport de marchandises au départ ou à destination d'un aéroport public en cas d'accident d'avion, y compris de gravité modérée, en cas d'atterrissage d'urgence en raison d'un changement d'itinéraire ou en cas d'annulation de vols ;

f) Le transport du courrier ;

g) Le transport de véhicules endommagés ou en panne ;

h) Le transport des fournitures humanitaires nécessaires en situation d'urgence, notamment en cas de catastrophe naturelle ;

i) Le transport d'abeilles et de fretin ;

j) Le trajet à vide d'un véhicule de secours utilisé pour le transport de marchandises et envoyé pour remplacer un véhicule en panne dans un autre pays et la poursuite du transport par le véhicule de secours sous couvert de l'autorisation délivrée pour le véhicule en panne ;

k) Les véhicules d'entretien et de service venant en aide aux véhicules en panne ou endommagés.

2. Le chauffeur du véhicule effectuant une ou plusieurs opérations de transport visées au paragraphe 1 du présent article dispose de tous les documents nécessaires, lesquels indiquent clairement que le transport est justifié en application de l'une quelconque des dispositions énoncées dans ledit paragraphe.

DISPOSITIONS GÉNÉRALES

Article 9

Les opérations de cabotage ne sont pas autorisées, sauf si l'autorité compétente de la Partie contractante concernée a délivré un permis spécial à cet effet.

Article 10

1. Si le poids et/ou les dimensions d'un véhicule en charge ou à vide, lorsqu'il effectue des opérations de transport en vertu des dispositions du présent Accord, dépassent les limites autorisées en vigueur sur le territoire de l'autre Partie contractante, un permis spécial délivré par l'autorité compétente de ladite Partie contractante est requis.

2. S'agissant du poids et des dimensions des véhicules, chacune des Parties contractantes s'engage à ne pas imposer aux véhicules immatriculés sur le territoire de l'autre Partie contractante des conditions qui seraient plus restrictives que celles imposées aux véhicules immatriculés sur son propre territoire.

Article 11

Les transporteurs établis dans les deux Parties contractantes sont tenus, lorsqu'ils effectuent des transports de marchandises dangereuses, de se conformer aux dispositions de l'Accord européen relatif au transport international des marchandises dangereuses par route.

Article 12

Les deux Parties contractantes fournissent les mesures incitatives nécessaires pour encourager l'exécution d'opérations de transport combiné et le recours aux ports maritimes situés sur leur territoire respectif.

Article 13

1. Sous réserve des dispositions du présent Accord, les transporteurs d'une Partie contractante et l'équipage de leurs véhicules sont tenus, sur le territoire de l'autre Partie contractante, de se conformer aux lois et règlements en vigueur dans ce pays.

2. Les autorisations et autres documents nécessaires requis en vertu du présent Accord, se trouvent à bord des véhicules auxquels ils se rapportent et sont présentés à la demande de toute autorité de l'une ou l'autre Partie compétente habilitée à les vérifier.

3. Si un transporteur ou son équipage enfreint de manière grave et répétée les dispositions juridiques en vigueur dans l'autre pays ou les dispositions du présent Accord, l'autorité compétente de la Partie contractante sur le territoire de laquelle le véhicule est immatriculé et sur demande de l'autorité compétente de la Partie contractante sur le territoire de laquelle l'infraction a eu lieu, peut adopter les mesures suivantes dans le cadre des règlements en vigueur dans le pays concerné :

a) Avertir le transporteur qu'il est tenu de respecter les règlements en vigueur (avertissement) ;

b) Suspendre temporairement le transporteur de ses activités de transporteur ;

c) Cesser de délivrer des autorisations au transporteur concerné ou révoquer toute autorisation précédemment délivrée pour la période pendant laquelle le transporteur est suspendu de toute activité de transport par l'autorité compétente de l'autre pays.

Les dispositions du présent article sont sans préjudice des sanctions légales qui peuvent être appliquées conformément aux lois et règlements du pays sur le territoire duquel l'infraction est commise.

4. L'autorité compétente qui a pris l'une quelconque des mesures visées au paragraphe 3 du présent article en informe l'autorité compétente de l'autre Partie contractante.

Article 14

1. Les véhicules immatriculés sur le territoire d'une Partie contractante et temporairement importés sur le territoire de l'autre Partie contractante afin d'exécuter des services de transport conformément au présent Accord sont exemptés, selon le principe de réciprocité, des taxes d'utilisation des routes et de circulation.

2. Toutefois, ces exemptions ne s'appliquent pas au paiement des droits de péage pour les routes et les ponts et autres redevances analogues, dont la perception repose toujours sur le principe de non-discrimination.

3. S'agissant des véhicules visés au paragraphe 1 du présent article, sont exemptés du paiement de droits de douane :

a) Les véhicules ;

b) Le carburant contenu dans les réservoirs ordinaires des véhicules ;

c) Les pièces de rechange importées sur le territoire de l'autre Partie contractante et destinées au dépannage d'un véhicule. Les pièces remplacées sont réexportées ou détruites sous le contrôle des autorités douanières compétentes de l'autre Partie contractante.

Article 15

Conformément au préambule du présent Accord, les Parties contractantes conviennent d'encourager, lors de l'exécution des services de transport, l'utilisation de véhicules modernes et sûrs d'un point de vue technique, peu bruyants et qui émettent peu de substances dangereuses.

Article 16

Aux fins de la bonne mise en œuvre du présent Accord, une commission mixte, composée de représentants des autorités compétentes des deux Parties contractantes, est mise sur pied. Elle se réunit à la demande de l'autorité compétente de l'une ou l'autre Partie contractante, alternativement sur les territoires des Parties contractantes.

Article 17

Les Parties contractantes conviennent d'établir, dans un protocole additionnel, les modalités d'application de certaines dispositions du présent Accord. Le protocole additionnel fait partie intégrante de l'Accord.

Article 18

Le présent Accord s'applique à titre provisoire à compter de la date de sa signature. Les Parties contractantes s'informent mutuellement, par la voie diplomatique, de l'accomplissement des exigences relatives à la procédure d'entrée en vigueur des accords internationaux.

Le présent Accord entre en vigueur le trentième jour suivant la date de la dernière notification en ce sens.

Article 19

Si nécessaire, tout amendement au présent Accord fait l'objet de négociations entre les Parties contractantes et entre en vigueur conformément à la procédure prévue à l'article 18.

Article 20

L'Accord reste en vigueur à moins qu'il ne soit dénoncé par l'une des Parties contractantes, par la voie diplomatique, au plus tard trois mois avant la fin d'une année civile, par notification écrite à l'autre Partie contractante.

EN FOI DE QUOI, les soussignés, à ce dûment autorisés, ont signé le présent Accord.

FAIT à Copenhague, le 26 mai 1998, en deux exemplaires originaux chacun en langues lettone, slovène et anglaise, chaque texte faisant également foi et ayant la même force juridique. En cas de divergence d'interprétation, le texte anglais prévaut.

Pour le Gouvernement de la République de Lettonie :
[VILIS KRIŠTOPANS]

Pour le Gouvernement de la République de Slovénie :
[ANTON BERGAUER]

PROTOCOLE ADDITIONNEL À L'ACCORD ENTRE LE GOUVERNEMENT DE LA RÉPUBLIQUE DE LETTONIE ET LE GOUVERNEMENT DE LA RÉPUBLIQUE DE SLOVÉNIE RELATIF AU TRANSPORT ROUTIER INTERNATIONAL

Afin de mettre en œuvre l'Accord conformément à son article 17, les Parties contractantes conviennent que les autorités compétentes aux fins du présent Accord sont :

Pour la République de Lettonie : le Ministère des transports ;

Pour la République de Slovénie : le Ministère des transports et des communications.

FAIT à Copenhague, le 26 mai 1998, en deux exemplaires originaux chacun en langues lettone, slovène et anglaise, chaque texte faisant également foi et ayant la même valeur juridique.

Pour le Gouvernement de la République de Lettonie :
[VILIS KRIŠTOPANS]

Pour le Gouvernement de la République de Slovénie :
[ANTON BERGAUER]

No. 54181

Latvia and Switzerland

Agreement between the Government of Latvia and the Swiss Federal Council on International Road Transport of Passengers and Goods (with protocol). Riga, 28 April 1998

Entry into force: *9 December 1998, in accordance with article 12*

Authentic texts: *German and Latvian*

Registration with the Secretariat of the United Nations: *Latvia, 4 January 2017*

Only the authentic German and Latvian texts of the Agreement and its protocol, and their translations into English and French, are published in this volume. The technical Annex included in the protocol is not published herein, in accordance with article 12 (2) of the General Assembly Regulations to give effect to Article 102 of the Charter of the United Nations, as amended, and the publication practice of the UN Secretariat.

Lettonie et Suisse

Accord entre le Gouvernement de la République de Lettonie et le Conseil fédéral Suisse relatif au transport international de passagers et de marchandises par route (avec protocole). Riga, 28 avril 1998

Entrée en vigueur : *9 décembre 1998, conformément à l'article 12*

Textes authentiques : *allemand et letton*

Enregistrement au Secrétariat de l'Organisation des Nations Unies : *Lettonie, 4 janvier 2017*

Seuls les textes authentiques en allemand et en letton de l'Accord et de son protocole, ainsi que leurs traductions en anglais et en français, sont publiés dans ce volume. L'annexe technique faisant partie du protocole, n'est pas publiée dans le présent volume, conformément aux dispositions de l'article 12, paragraphe 2, du règlement de l'Assemblée générale destiné à mettre en application l'Article 102 de la Charte des Nations Unies, tel qu'amendé, et à la pratique du Secrétariat en matière de publication.

[TEXT IN GERMAN – TEXTE EN ALLEMAND]

A b k o m m e n

zwischen der Regierung der Republik Lettland und dem Schweizerischen Bundesrat

über den grenzüberschreitenden Personen- und Güterverkehr auf der Strasse

---

Die Regierung der Republik Lettland und der Schweizerische Bundesrat, nachfolgend Vertragsparteien genannt, haben im Bestreben, die Personen - und Güterbeförderungen auf der Strasse zwischen den beiden Staaten und im Transit durch ihr Staatsgebiet zu erleichtern, folgendes vereinbart:

Artikel 1 Anwendungsbereich

Die Bestimmungen dieses Abkommens sind anwendbar auf Personen- und Güterbeförderungen, die von oder nach dem Staatsgebiet einer der Vertragsparteien oder im Transit durch eines dieser Staatsgebiete mit Fahrzeugen ausgeführt werden, die im Staatsgebiet der andern Vertragspartei zum Verkehr zugelassen sind.

Art. 2 Begriffsbestimmungen

Im Sinne dieses Abkommens bezeichnet:

1 der Begriff "Unternehmer" eine natürliche oder juristische Person, die entweder in der Republik Lettland oder in der Schweiz gemäss den in ihrem Staat geltenden Vorschriften berechtigt ist, Personen oder Güter im grenzüberschreitenden Verkehr auf der Strasse zu befördern;

2 der Begriff "Fahrzeug" ein Strassenfahrzeug mit mechanischem Antrieb sowie gegebenenfalls dessen Anhänger oder Sattelanhänger, das für die Beförderung

a) von mehr als neun sitzenden Reisenden, Fahrer eingeschlossen,

b) von Gütern

eingerichtet und zugelassen ist;

3 der Begriff "Genehmigung" jede Bewilligung, Konzession oder Genehmigung, die gemäss den nationalen Vorschriften der Vertragsparteien verlangt wird und welche die Unternehmer dazu berechtigt, den Personen- oder Güterverkehr im Sinne dieses Abkommens auszuführen.

Art. 3 Personenbeförderungen

1 Die gelegentlichen Personenbeförderungen, die unter den nachfolgenden Voraussetzungen ausgeführt werden, sind von der Genehmigungspflicht ausgenommen:

a) die Beförderung der gleichen Personen mit demselben Fahrzeug während der gesamten Reise, deren Ausgangs- und Endpunkt in dem Staat gelegen sind, in dem das Fahrzeug zum Verkehr zugelassen ist, sofern unterwegs oder bei Halten ausserhalb dieses Staatsgebietes Personen weder aufgenommen noch abgesetzt werden (Rundfahrten mit geschlossenen Türen); oder

b) die Beförderung von Personengruppen von einem Ort des Staates, in dem das Fahrzeug zum Verkehr zugelassen ist, an einen Ort im Staatsgebiet der anderen Vertragspartei, sofern das Fahrzeug leer in den Staat zurückkehrt, in dem es zum Verkehr zugelassen ist; oder

c) die Beförderung von Personengruppen von einem Ort im Staatsgebiet der anderen Vertragspartei, zu einem Ort des Staates, in dem das Fahrzeug zugelassen ist, sofern dieser Dienstleistung eine Leerfahrt in das Staatsgebiet der anderen Vertragspartei vorausgegangen ist und die Reisenden

- vor der Ankunft im Staatsgebiet, in dem sie aufgenommen werden, mit einem Beförderungsvertrag in Gruppen zusammengefasst werden; oder
- vorher von demselben Verkehrsunternehmer nach den unter b genannten Bedingungen in den anderen Vertragsstaat befördert worden sind und jetzt in ein anderes Land befördert werden; oder
- eingeladen werden, sich in das Staatsgebiet der andern Vertragspartei zu begeben, wobei der Einladende die Beförderungskosten trägt. Die Reisenden müssen einen zusammengehörenden Personenkreis bilden, der nicht nur zum Zweck der Fahrt zusammengestellt wurde.

d) Transitfahrten mit geschlossenen Türen durch das Staatsgebiet der anderen Vertragspartei.

2 Die regelmässigen Personenbeförderungen, die unter den nachfolgenden Voraussetzungen ausgeführt werden, sind von der Genehmigungspflicht ausgenommen:

- die Pendelfahrten mit Unterbringung im Transit oder nach dem Staatsgebiet der andern Vertragspartei; sowie
- die Leerfahrten der Fahrzeuge, die in Zusammenhang mit den Pendelfahrten durchgeführt werden.

3 Bei den in Ziffer 1 und 2 dieses Artikels genannten Beförderungen ist ein Kontrollpapier mitzuführen.

4 Andere als die in Ziffer 1 und 2 dieses Artikels erwähnten Beförderungen sind nach Massgabe des nationalen Rechts der Vertragsparteien genehmigungspflichtig. Die Genehmigungen werden unter Wahrung der Gegenseitigkeit erteilt.

Art. 4 Güterbeförderungen

Jeder im Staat einer Vertragspartei zugelassene Unternehmer ist berechtigt, vorübergehend ein leeres oder beladenes Fahrzeug in das Staatsgebiet der andern Vertragspartei einzuführen, um Güter zu befördern:

a) zwischen einem Ort im Staatsgebiet der einen Vertragspartei und einem beliebigen Ort im Staatsgebiet der anderen Vertragspartei; oder

b) vom Staatsgebiet der anderen Vertragspartei nach einem Drittstaat oder von einem Drittstaat nach dem Staatsgebiet der anderen Vertragspartei; oder

c) im Transit durch das Staatsgebiet der anderen Vertragspartei.

Art. 5 Anwendung nationalen Rechts

In allen Belangen, die dieses Abkommen nicht regelt, haben die Unternehmer und die Fahrzeugführer einer Vertragspartei bei Fahrten im Staatsgebiet der anderen Vertragspartei die dort geltenden Gesetze und Reglemente, die nicht diskriminierend angewendet werden, einzuhalten.

Art. 6 Verbot landesinterner Beförderungen

Die Cabotagebeförderungen von Personen und Gütern, d.h. Beförderungen zwischen zwei oder mehreren Orten innerhalb des Staatsgebietes der einen Vertragspartei durch

Unternehmer der anderen Vertragspartei, sind nicht erlaubt. Die in Art. 10 vorgesehene Gemischte Kommission kann diesbezügliche Erleichterungen vereinbaren.

Art. 7 Widerhandlungen

1 Die zuständigen Behörden der Vertragsparteien sind dafür besorgt, dass die Bestimmungen dieses Abkommens von den Unternehmern eingehalten werden.

2 Gegen Unternehmer und Fahrzeugführer, die auf dem Staatsgebiet der anderen Vertragspartei Bestimmungen des Abkommens oder dort geltende Gesetze und Reglemente über die Strassenbeförderungen oder den Strassenverkehr verletzt haben, können auf Verlangen der zuständigen Behörden dieses Staates folgende Massnahmen angeordnet werden, die durch die Behörden des Staates, in dem das Fahrzeug zum Verkehr zugelassen ist, zu vollziehen sind:

a) Verwarnung;

b) befristeter, teilweiser oder vollständiger Entzug der Berechtigung, Beförderungen auf dem Gebiet der Vertragspartei, in der die Widerhandlung begangen wurde, auszuführen.

3 Die Behörde, die eine solche Massnahme getroffen hat, unterrichtet hierüber die zuständigen Behörden der anderen Vertragspartei.

4 Vorbehalten bleiben Sanktionen, die gestützt auf das nationale Recht durch die Gerichte oder die zuständigen Behörden der Vertragspartei ergriffen werden können, auf deren Staatsgebiet solche Widerhandlungen begangen wurden.

Art. 8 Zuständige Behörden

Die Vertragsparteien geben gegenseitig die Behörden bekannt, die zur Durchführung dieses Abkommens ermächtigt sind. Diese Behörden verkehren direkt miteinander.

Art. 9 Ausführungsbestimmungen

Die Ausführungsbestimmungen zu diesem Abkommen werden von den Vertragsparteien in einem Protokoll vereinbart, das integrierenden Bestandteil dieses Abkommens bildet.

Art. 10 Gemischte Kommission

[1] Die Vertragsparteien setzen eine Gemischte Kommission für den Vollzug dieses Abkommens ein.

[2] Diese Kommission ist auch für die Anpassung des in Artikel 9 dieses Abkommens erwähnten Protokolls zuständig.

[3] Die zuständigen Behörden einer Vertragspartei können die Einberufung dieser Gemischten Kommission verlangen; diese tritt abwechslungsweise auf dem Staatsgebiet jeder Vertragspartei zusammen.

Art. 11 Anwendung auf das Fürstentum Liechtenstein

Dem formellen Wunsch des Fürstentums Liechtenstein entsprechend, erstreckt sich das Abkommen auch auf das Fürstentum Liechtenstein, solange dasselbe mit der Schweiz durch einen Zollanschlussvertrag verbunden ist.

Art. 12 Inkrafttreten und Geltungsdauer

[1] Die Vertragsparteien werden einander auf diplomatischem Wege durch einen Notenaustausch darüber in Kenntnis setzen, dass alle für die Inkrafttretung dieses Abkommens nötigen Bedingungen der nationalen Vorschriften erfüllt sind. Dieses Abkommen tritt am 30. Tag nach dem Datum der auf diplomatischem Wege gesandten letzten Note über seine Gutheissung im Einklang mit den gemäss den nationalen Vorschriften vorgesehenen Bedingungen in Kraft. Es wird vorläufig ab dem Datum seiner Unterzeichnung angewendet.

[2] Das Abkommen gilt für eine unbestimmte Dauer; es kann von jeder Vertragspartei unter Einhaltung einer Kündigungsfrist von mindestens 3 Monaten auf das Ende eines Kalenderjahres der anderen Vertragspartei schriftlich gekündigt werden.

Zu Urkund dessen haben die von ihren Regierungen gehörig Bevollmächtigten dieses Abkommen unterzeichnet.

Geschehen zu Riga am 28. April 1998

in zwei Originalausfertigungen, jedes davon in lettischer und deutscher Sprache, wobei jeder Wortlaut gleichermassen verbindlich ist. Im Falle von Abweichungen zwischen den Texten ist die deutsche Fassung massgebend.

Für die
Regierung der Republik Lettland:

Für den
Schweizerischen Bundesrat:

Protokoll

Gestützt auf Artikel 9 des am in unterzeichneten Abkommens zwischen der Regierung der Republik Lettland und dem Schweizerischen Bundesrat über den grenzüberschreitenden Personen- und Güterverkehr auf der Strasse

wird folgendes vereinbart:

1. Personenbeförderungen (Artikel 3)

Die in Artikel 3 Absätze 1 und 2 des Abkommens vorgesehenen Beförderungen werden unter Benützung eines Fahrtenblattes und einer Passagierliste durchgeführt. Muster dieser Dokumente liegen bei und bilden integrierenden Bestandteil dieses Protokolls.

Genehmigungsgesuche für Beförderungen, welche die in Artikel 3 Absätze 1 und 2 des Abkommens erwähnten Bedingungen nicht erfüllen (zum Beispiel Linienverkehr), sind der zuständigen Behörde des Staates zu unterbreiten, in dem das Fahrzeug zum Verkehr zugelassen ist; diese übermittelt die bewilligten Gesuche der zuständigen Behörde der anderen Vertragspartei oder informiert sie über allfällige negative Entscheide.

Die Unternehmer haben in ihren Anträgen den Fahrplan, die Tarife, die Linienführung wie auch andere Angaben auf Verlangen der zuständigen Behörde bekannt zu geben. Das Verfahren der Genehmigungsausstellung und andere ähnliche Fragen werden die zuständigen Behörden der Vertragsparteien gemeinsam aufgrund der Reziprozität regeln.

Die Behörde, die eine Genehmigung erteilt hat, unterrichtet hierüber die zuständige Behörde der anderen Vertragspartei durch Zustellung einer Kopie der erteilten Genehmigung.

Die Genehmigungen sind auf den Fahrzeugen mitzuführen und auf Verlangen der Kontrollorgane vorzuweisen.

Bei Leertransitfahrten hat der Unternehmer nachzuweisen, dass er das Staatsgebiet der anderen Vertragspartei leer durchfährt.

Wird ein entsprechender Nachweis vorgelegt, bedürfen Fahrzeuge, die als Ersatz für einen beschädigten oder in Panne geratenen Autobus bestimmt sind, keiner Leereinfahrtsgenehmigung.

2. Güterbeförderungen (Artikel 4)

Bei Beförderungen durch eine Fahrzeuggruppe, die sich aus verschiedenen Elementen (so z.B. Anhänger oder Sattelauflieger) zusammensetzt, werden die Bestimmungen dieses Abkommens auf die ganze Fahrzeuggruppe angewendet, sofern der Lastwagen oder der Sattelschlepper in einem der Vertragsstaaten zugelassen ist.

3. Anwendung nationalen Rechts (Artikel 5)

Die Vertragsparteien stellen fest, dass sich die Bestimmungen des Artikels 5 des Abkommens insbesondere auf die Gesetzgebung über die Strassenbeförderungen, den Strassenverkehr, die Masse und Gewichte der Fahrzeuge, die Arbeits- und Ruhezeit der Fahrzeugbesatzung, die Lenkzeit sowie die Abgaben, die Mauten und die Verwaltungsgebühren bezieht. Die Kraftfahrzeugsteuer, für die das Prinzip der Nationalität gilt, kann von einem Unternehmer der anderen Vertragspartei nicht verlangt werden.

4. **Zuständige Behörden (Artikel 8)**

Zuständige Behörden für die Durchführung des Abkommens sind:

für die Republik Lettland:

das Ministerium für Verkehr der Republik Lettland
Gogola 3
LV - 1743 Riga

für die Schweiz:

Eidgenössisches Departement für Umwelt,
Verkehr, Energie und Kommunikation
Bundesamt für Verkehr
CH - 3003 Bern

5. **Zugelassene Abmessungen und Gewichte der Fahrzeuge**

In bezug auf Abmessungen und Gewichte der Strassenfahrzeuge verpflichtet sich jede Vertragspartei, Fahrzeuge, die im Staatsgebiet der anderen Vertragspartei zum Verkehr zugelassen sind, keinen strengeren Bedingungen zu unterstellen als Fahrzeuge, die im eigenen Gebiet zum Verkehr zugelassen sind.

Für den Fall, dass die Fahrzeuge die Abmessungen und/oder Gewichte übersteigen, die im nationalen Recht jeder Vertragspartei festgesetzt sind, finden die folgenden Verfahren Anwendung:

für die Republik Lettland:

Die in der Schweiz zugelassenen Fahrzeuge dürfen in das Staatsgebiet der Republik Lettland mit einer Sonderbewilligung einfahren, die von der Direktion für Strassenverkehrssicherheit des Verkehrsministeriums ausgestellt wird (Adresse: Direktion für Strassenverkehrssicherheit, Miera-Strasse 25, LV - 1001 Riga; Fax Nr. +371 828 301). Die Gesuche zur Erteilung der Bewilligungen sind an die genannte Behörde mindestens 10 Tage vor der Verkehrsaufnahme zu schicken.

für die Schweiz:

Die in der Republik Lettland zugelassenen Fahrzeuge dürfen mit einer von einem schweizerischen Zollamt oder vom Bundesamt für Strassen, Hauptabteilung Strassenverkehr, Bern, ausgestellten Bewilligung in die vom Eidgenössischen Justiz- und Polizeidepartement festgelegte Grenzzone einfahren. Bei Grenzzonen handelt es sich in der Regel um das Gebiet im Umkreis von 10 Kilometern einer Zollstelle.

Für Beförderungen über diese Grenzzone hinaus erteilt das Bundesamt für Strassen, Hauptabteilung Strassenverkehr, CH - 3003 Bern (Telefax + 31 963 43 03) Sonderbewilligungen nur für die unteilbaren Ladegüter, sofern die Strassenverhältnisse die Erteilung der Bewilligung gestatten. Die Gesuche sind dieser Behörde im voraus zu unterbreiten.

Das im Fahrzeugausweis eingetragene Gesamtgewicht darf in keinem Fall überschritten werden.

6. **Zoll**

Der Treibstoff, der sich in den normalen Fahrzeugtanks der vorübergehend eingeführten Fahrzeuge befindet, wird ohne Einfuhrabgaben, Einfuhrverbote und Einfuhrbeschränkungen zugelassen.

Ersatzteile, die zur Instandsetzung eines bestimmten, bereits vorübergehend eingeführten Fahrzeuges dienen, werden ohne Einfuhrabgaben, Einfuhrverbote und Einfuhrbeschränkungen zur vorübergehenden Einfuhr zugelassen. Die Vertragsparteien können für diese Ersatzteile die Abfertigung mit Ausweis für die vorübergehende Einfuhr vorsehen. Die ersetzten Teile sind zu verzollen, wieder auszuführen oder unter Aufsicht der Zollorgane zu vernichten.

Geschehen zu Riga am 28. April 1998

in zwei Originalausfertigungen, jedes davon in deutscher und lettischer Sprache, wobei jeder Wortlaut gleichermassen verbindlich ist. Im Falle von Abweichungen zwischen den Texten ist die deutsche Fassung massgebend.

Für die
Regierung der Republik Lettland:

Für den
Schweizerischen Bundesrat:

[TEXT IN LATVIAN – TEXTE EN LETTON]

Latvijas Republikas valdības un Šveices Konfederācijas Federālās padomes

NOLĪGUMS

par pasažieru un kravu starptautiskajiem pārvadājumiem ar autotransportu

Latvijas Republikas valdība un Šveices Konfederācijas Federālā padome (turpmāk tekstā - "Līgumslēdzējas Puses"),

vēloties sekmēt pasažieru un kravu pārvadājumus ar autotransportu starp abām valstīm un tranzītā cauri to teritorijām, vienojās par sekojošo:

1. pants
Darbības sfēra

Šā Nolīguma noteikumi piemērojami pasažieru un kravu pārvadājumiem, kuri tiek veikti no jebkuras Līgumslēdzējas Puses valsts teritorijas, uz to vai arī tranzītā cauri šīs valsts teritorijai ar transporta līdzekļiem, kuri reģistrēti otras Līgumslēdzējas Puses valsts teritorijā.

2. pants
Definīcijas

Šā Nolīguma ietvaros:

1. *"Pārvadātājs"* ir fiziska persona vai juridiska persona, kura vai nu Latvijas Republikā, vai Šveicē saskaņā ar savā valstī spēkā esošajiem tiesību aktiem ir tiesīga veikt pasažieru vai kravu starptautiskos pārvadājumus ar autotransportu.

2. *"Transporta līdzeklis"* ir jebkurš motorizēts autotransporta līdzeklis, ieskaitot ar to savienotu piekabi vai puspiekabi, kas paredzēts:

a) vairāk par deviņu pasažieru (vadītāja vietu ieskaitot),

b) kravu

pārvadāšanai.

3. *"Atļauja"* ir jebkurš dokuments, kas nepieciešams saskaņā ar vienas vai otras Līgumslēdzējas Puses nacionālajiem tiesību aktiem un dod pārvadātājiem tiesības veikt pasažieru vai kravu pārvadājumus atbilstoši šā Nolīguma noteikumiem.

3. pants
Pasažieru pārvadājumi

1. Atļaujas nav nepieciešamas neregulāriem pasažieru pārvadājumiem, kas atbilst šādiem noteikumiem:

a) visa brauciena laikā, kas sākas un beidzas valstī, kurā transporta līdzeklis reģistrēts, ar vienu un to pašu transporta līdzekli tiek pārvadāti vieni un tie paši pasažieri un brauciena laikā vai, pieturot ārpus šīs valsts teritorijas, pasažieri netiek ne uzņemti, ne izsēdināti (braucieni "ar slēgtām durvīm"); vai

b) pasažieru grupa no kādas vietas valstī, kurā transporta līdzeklis reģistrēts, tiek pārvadāta uz kādu vietu otras Līgumslēdzējas Puses valsts teritorijā un transporta līdzeklis bez pasažieriem atgriežas valstī, kurā tas reģistrēts; vai

c) pasažieru grupa no kādas vietas otras Līgumslēdzējas Puses valsts teritorijā tiek pārvadāta uz kādu vietu valstī, kurā transporta līdzeklis reģistrēts, ja pirms šā pakalpojuma uz otras Līgumslēdzējas Puses valsts teritoriju tiek veikts brauciens bez pasažieriem un

- pasažieru grupas saskaņā ar pārvadājuma līgumu tiek izveidotas pirms ierašanās tās valsts teritorijā, kurā tās tiek uzņemtas; vai
- pasažieru grupas, kuras iepriekš uz otras Līgumslēdzējas Puses valsts teritoriju saskaņā ar "b" apakšpunkta nosacījumiem aizvedis tas pats pārvadātājs, tagad tiek nogādātas uz citu valsti; vai
- pasažieri ir tikuši ielūgti braucienam uz otras Līgumslēdzējas Puses valsts teritoriju, turklāt persona, kura ielūdz, sedz pārvadāšanas izmaksas. Pasažieri ir savstarpēji vienota personu grupa, kura nav izveidota tikai ar mērķi veikt šo braucienu;

d) ja cauri otras Līgumslēdzējas Puses valsts teritorijai tiek veikti tranzīta braucieni "ar slēgtām durvīm".

2. Atļaujas nav nepieciešamas regulāriem pasažieru pārvadājumiem, kas atbilst šādiem noteikumiem:

- tiek veikti sistemātiski turp un atpakaļ pārvadājumi uz otras Līgumslēdzējas Puses valsts teritoriju vai tranzītā cauri tai ar pasažieru izvietošanu naktsmītnēs; kā arī
- sistemātisko turp un atpakaļ pārvadājumu ietvaros tiek veikti transporta līdzekļu braucieni bez pasažieriem.

3. Veicot šā panta 1. un 2. punktā minētos pārvadājumus, jāved līdzi kontroles dokuments.

4. Pārvadājumiem, kas neatbilst šā panta 1. un 2. punkta noteikumiem, atļaujas nepieciešamas saskaņā ar Līgumslēdzēju Pušu nacionālo tiesību aktu prasībām. Atļaujas tiek izdotas, ievērojot savstarpības principu.

4. pants
Kravu pārvadājumi

Jebkuram vienas Līgumslēdzējas Puses valstī reģistrētam pārvadātājam ir tiesības uz laiku iebraukt otras Līgumslēdzējas Puses valsts teritorijā ar transporta līdzekļiem ar kravu vai bez tās, kravu pārvadāšanai:

a) no vietas, kas atrodas vienas Līgumslēdzējas Puses valsts teritorijā uz jebkuru vietu otras Līgumslēdzējas Puses valsts teritorijā; vai

b) no otras Līgumslēdzējas Puses valsts teritorijas uz kādu trešo valsti vai no trešās valsts uz otras Līgumslēdzējas Puses valsts teritoriju; vai

c) tranzītā cauri otras Līgumslēdzējas Puses valsts teritorijai.

5. pants
Nacionālo tiesību normu piemērošana

Visos jautājumos, kurus neregulē šis Nolīgums, vienas Līgumslēdzējas Puses pārvadātājiem un viņu transporta līdzekļu apkalpēm, veicot pārvadājumus otras Līgumslēdzējas Puses valsts teritorijā, ir jāievēro tur spēkā esošie likumi un citi normatīvie akti, kuri netiek piemēroti diskriminējoši.

6. pants
Kabotāžas pārvadājumu aizliegums

Nav atļauti pasažieru un kravu kabotāžas pārvadājumi, t.i. pārvadājumi, kurus vienas Līgumslēdzējas Puses pārvadātāji veic starp divām vai vairākām vietām otras Līgumslēdzējas Puses valsts teritorijā. Šā Nolīguma 10. pantā minētā Kopējā Komisija var vienoties par atvieglojumiem šajā jautājumā.

7. pants
Pārkāpumi

1. Līgumslēdzēju Pušu kompetentās institūcijas sekmē to, lai pārvadātāji ievērotu šā Nolīguma noteikumus.

2. Pret pārvadātājiem un transporta līdzekļu vadītājiem, kuri, atrodoties otras Līgumslēdzējas Puses valsts teritorijā, ir pārkāpuši šā Nolīguma noteikumus vai šajā valstī spēkā esošo, ar autotransporta pārvadājumiem saistīto likumu un citu normatīvo aktu vai ceļu satiksmes noteikumu prasības, pēc šīs valsts kompetento institūciju pieprasījuma transporta līdzekļa reģistrācijas valsts institūcijas veic šādus pasākumus:

a) izsaka brīdinājumu;

b) uz laiku, daļēji vai pilnīgi aizliedz veikt pārvadājumus tās Līgumslēdzējas Puses valsts teritorijā, kurā izdarīts pārkāpums.

3. Institūcija, kas veikusi kādu no minētajiem pasākumiem, informē par to otras Līgumslēdzējas Puses kompetentās institūcijas.

4. Tās Līgumslēdzējas Puses valsts tiesām vai citām pilnvarotām institūcijām, kuras teritorijā izdarīti pārkāpumi, ir tiesības piemērot sankcijas saskaņā ar savām nacionālajiem tiesību aktiem.

8. pants
Kompetentās institūcijas

Līgumslēdzējas Puses informē viena otru par savas valsts kompetentajām institūcijām, kuras ir pilnvarotas īstenot šo Nolīgumu. Šīs institūcijas strādā tiešā sadarbībā viena ar otru.

9. pants
Nolīguma izpildes noteikumi

Par šā Nolīguma izpildes noteikumiem Līgumslēdzējas Puses vienojas Protokolā, kas ir šā Nolīguma neatņemama sastāvdaļa.

10. pants
Kopējā Komisija

1. Šā Nolīguma izpildes nodrošināšanai Līgumslēdzējas Puses izveido Kopējo Komisiju.

2. Kopējā Komisija risina arī jautājumus par šā Nolīguma 9. pantā minētā Protokola piemērošanu.

3. Jebkuras Līgumslēdzējas Puses kompetentās institūcijas var pieprasīt šīs Kopējās Komisijas sasaukšanu; tās sēdes notiek pārmaiņus katras Līgumslēdzējas Puses valsts teritorijā.

11. pants
Pielietošana Lihtenšteinas hercogistē

Saskaņā ar Lihtenšteinas hercogistes formālo vēlēšanos Nolīguma noteikumi attiecas arī uz Lihtenšteinas hercogisti, kamēr tā ar Šveici ir saistīta ar vienotu muitas līgumu.

12. pants
Stāšanās spēkā un darbības ilgums

1. Abas Līgumslēdzējas Puses pa diplomātiskajiem kanāliem, apmainoties notām, paziņos viena otrai, ka izpildītas visas nacionālajos tiesību aktos paredzētās prasības attiecībā uz šā Nolīguma stāšanos spēkā. Šis Nolīgums stājas spēkā 30. dienā pēc tam, kad nosūtīta pēdējā no diplomātiskajām notām par tā akceptēšanu saskaņā ar nacionālajos tiesību aktos paredzētajām prasībām. Provizoriski šis Nolīgums tiek piemērots no tā parakstīšanas dienas.

2. Nolīgums noslēgts uz nenoteiktu laiku; katra Līgumslēdzēja Puse var izbeigt tā darbību, ne vēlāk kā trīs mēnešus pirms kalendārā gada beigām rakstiski paziņojot par to otrai Līgumslēdzējai Pusei.

TO APLIECINOT, savu valdību pienācīgi pilnvarotas personas ir parakstījušas šo Nolīgumu.

Parakstīts Rīgā 1998. gada 28. aprīlī divos oriģināleksemplāros, katrs no tiem latviešu un vācu valodā, turklāt abiem tekstiem ir vienāds juridisks spēks. Tekstu atšķirīgas interpretācijas gadījumā noteicošais ir teksts vācu valodā.

Latvijas Republikas
valdības vārdā:

Šveices Konfederācijas
Federālās padomes vārdā:

PROTOKOLS

Saskaņā ar Rīgā 1998. gada 28. aprīlī parakstītā Latvijas Republikas valdības un Šveices Konfederācijas Federālās padomes Nolīguma par pasažieru un kravu starptautiskajiem pārvadājumiem ar autotransportu 9. pantu

tiek nolemts sekojošais:

1. Pasažieru pārvadājumi (3. pants)

Veicot Nolīguma 3. panta 1. un 2. punktā minētos pārvadājumus, nepieciešams brauciena formulārs ar pasažieru sarakstu. Šo dokumentu paraugi pievienoti pielikumā un ir šā Protokola neatņemama sastāvdaļa.

Iesniegumi atļauju piešķiršanai pārvadājumiem, kuri neatbilst Nolīguma 3. panta 1. un 2. punktā minētajiem noteikumiem (piemēram, regulāri pasažieru pārvadājumi), ir jāiesniedz kompetentajai institūcijai valstī, kurā transporta līdzeklis reģistrēts; tā nosūta akceptētos iesniegumus otras Līgumslēdzējas Puses kompetentajai institūcijai vai informē to par atteikumu.

Pārvadātājiem savos iesniegumos jāuzrāda kustības saraksts, braukšanas tarifi, maršruts, kā arī cita informācija pēc kompetentās institūcijas pieprasījuma. Atļauju izsniegšanas kārtību un citus ar to saistītos jautājumus nosaka Līgumslēdzēju Pušu kompetentās institūcijas, kopīgi vienojoties uz savstarpības principiem.

Institūcija, kas izsniegusi atļauju, informē par to otras Līgumslēdzējas Puses kompetento institūciju, nosūtot tai izsniegtās atļaujas kopiju.

Atļaujas ir jāved līdzi transporta līdzekļos un jāuzrāda pēc kontrolējošo institūciju pārstāvju pieprasījuma.

Veicot tranzīta braucienus bez pasažieriem, pārvadātājam ir jāpierāda, ka viņš šķērso otras Līgumslēdzējas Puses valsts teritoriju bez pasažieriem.

Transporta līdzekļiem, kas ir paredzēti bojāta vai avārijā cietuša autobusa aizstāšanai, nav nepieciešama atļauja braucienam bez pasažieriem, ja tiek uzrādīts atbilstošs dokuments.

2. Kravu pārvadājumi (4. pants)

Veicot pārvadājumus ar transporta līdzekli, kura sastāvā ietilpst atsevišķi elementi (piem., piekabes vai puspiekabes), šā Nolīguma nosacījumi attiecināmi uz visu šo transporta līdzekļu grupu, ja kravas automobilis vai vilcējs ir reģistrēts vienā no Līgumslēdzēju Pušu valstīm.

3. Nacionālo tiesību normu piemērošana (5. pants)

Līgumslēdzējas Puses vienojas, ka Nolīguma 5. panta noteikumi īpaši attiecas uz tiesību normām par pārvadājumiem ar autotransportu, ceļu satiksmi, transporta līdzekļu pieļaujamajiem izmēriem un svaru, transporta līdzekļu apkalpju darba un atpūtas režīmu, braukšanas laiku kā arī nodokļiem, ceļa nodevām un administratīvajām nodevām. No otras Līgumslēdzējas Puses pārvadātāja nevar tikt iekasēta transporta līdzekļa valsts nodeva, kas attiecas tikai uz savā valstī reģistrētiem transporta līdzekļiem.

4. Kompetentās institūcijas (8. pants)

Kompetentās institūcijas šā Nolīguma īstenošanai:

Latvijas Republikā:
Satiksmes ministrija
Gogoļa iela - 3
LV - 1743 Rīga

Šveicē:
Eidgenössisches Departement für Umvelt, Verkehr, Energie und Kommunikation
Bundesamt für Verkehr
CH - 3003 Bern
(Šveices Konfederācijas Vides, satiksmes, enerģijas un sakaru departaments; Federālais satiksmes dienests)

5. Transporta līdzekļu pieļaujamie izmēri un svars.

Attiecībā uz transporta līdzekļu izmēriem un svaru katra Līgumslēdzēja Puse apņemas neizvirzīt otras Līgumslēdzējas Puses valstī reģistrētiem transporta līdzekļiem augstākas prasības par tām, kas ir spēkā attiecībā uz savā valstī reģistrētiem transporta līdzekļiem.

Gadījumā, ja transporta līdzekļu izmēri un/vai svars pārsniedz Līgumslēdzējas Puses nacionālo tiesību aktos noteiktos pieļaujamos lielumus, pārvadājumu veikšanai tiek noteikta šāda kārtība:

Šveicē:

Latvijas Republikā reģistrētie transporta līdzekļi drīkst iebraukt Konfederācijas juridiskā un policijas departamenta noteiktajā robežzonā ar Šveices muitas dienesta vai Federālās Autoceļu pārvaldes Ceļu satiksmes departamenta Bernē izdotu speciālu atļauju. Par robežzonu uzskatāma teritorija 10 kilometru attālumā ap muitas punktu.

Pārvadājumiem ārpus šīs robežzonas Federālās Autoceļu pārvaldes Ceļu satiksmes departaments (adrese: Bundesamt für Strassen, Hauptabteilung Strassenverkehr, CH - 3003 Bern; telefakss: + 31 963 43 03) izsniedz īpašas atļaujas tikai nedalāmo kravu pārvadājumiem, ja ceļa apstākļi pieļauj šādas atļaujas piešķiršanu. Pieprasījumi atļaujas saņemšanai iepriekš jāiesniedz minētajai institūcijai.

Transporta līdzekļa reģitrācijas dokumentā norādītā pilnā masa nekādā gadījumā nedrīkst tikt pārsniegta.

Latvijas Republikā:

Šveices Konfederācijas teritorijā reģistrētie transporta līdzekļi drīkst iebraukt Latvijas Republikas teritorijā ar Satiksmes ministrijas Ceļu satiksmes drošības direkcijas (adrese: Ceļu satiksmes drošības direkcija, Miera ielā 25, Rīga LV - 1001; fakss: + 371 7 828301) izdotu speciālu atļauju. Pieprasījumi atļauju saņemšanai jānosūta minētajai institūcijai vismaz 10 dienas pirms pārvadājuma uzsākšanas.

6. Muitas noteikumi

Nemaksājot muitas nodevas, bez ievešanas aizliegumiem un ierobežojumiem atļauts ievest otras Līgumslēdzējas Puses valsts teritorijā degvielu, kas atrodas uz laiku iebraucošu transporta līdzekļu standarta degvielas tvertnēs.

Nemaksājot muitas nodevas, bez ievešanas aizliegumiem un ierobežojumiem atļauts uz laiku ievest otras Līgumslēdzējas Puses valsts teritorijā rezerves daļas, kas paredzētas jau iepriekš uz laiku iebraukuša konkrēta transporta līdzekļa remontam.

Līgumslēdzējas Puses var paredzēt šīm rezerves daļām ievešanas formalitāšu kārtošanu, noformējot atļauju pagaidu ievešanai. Nomainītās detaļas ir jāmuito un jāizved vai jāiznīcina muitas iestāžu uzraudzībā.

Parakstīts Rīgā 1998. gada 28. aprīlī divos oriģināleksemplāros, katrs no tiem latviešu un vācu valodā, turklāt abiem tekstiem ir vienāds juridisks spēks. Tekstu atšķirīgas interpretācijas gadījumā noteicošais ir teksts vācu valodā.

Latvijas Republikas
valdības vārdā:

Šveices Konfederācijas
Federālās padomes vārdā:

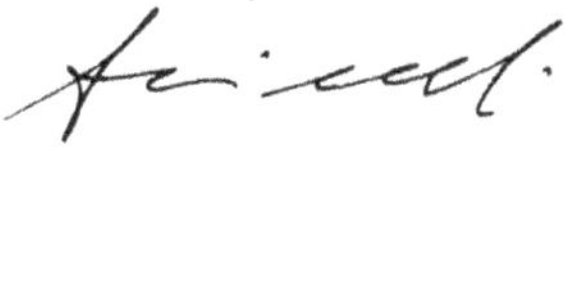

[TRANSLATION IN ENGLISH – TRADUCTION EN ANGLAIS]

AGREEMENT BETWEEN THE GOVERNMENT OF THE REPUBLIC OF LATVIA AND THE SWISS FEDERAL COUNCIL CONCERNING THE INTERNATIONAL ROAD TRANSPORT OF PASSENGERS AND GOODS

The Government of the Republic of Latvia and the Swiss Federal Council, hereinafter referred to as the Contracting Parties, in an effort to facilitate the carriage of passengers and goods by road between both States and in transit through their territories, have agreed as follows:

Article 1. Scope of application

The provisions of the present Agreement shall apply to the carriage of passengers and goods to or from the territory of one of the Contracting Parties or in transit through one of these territories by vehicles registered in the territory of the other Contracting Party.

Article 2. Definitions

For the purposes of the present Agreement:

1. The term "carrier" means a natural or legal person who, either in the Republic of Latvia or in Switzerland, is authorized, in accordance with the regulations applicable in that person's State, to carry persons or goods by road in international transport;

2. The term "vehicle" means a mechanically propelled road vehicle and, where applicable, its trailer or semi-trailer used for the carriage of:

(a) More than nine seated passengers, including the driver;

(b) Goods;

3. The term "authorization" means any permit, licence or authorization that is required under the national regulations of the Contracting Parties and that entitles operators to transport passengers or goods as covered by the present Agreement.

Article 3. Passenger transport

1. Occasional passenger transport operations carried out under the following conditions are exempt from the authorization requirement:

(a) The carriage of the same persons in the same vehicle throughout a journey whose point of departure and point of arrival are situated in the country of registration of the vehicle, provided that no persons are picked up or dropped off during the journey or at stops outside the territory of that country (closed-door round trips); or

(b) The carriage of groups of passengers from a point situated in the country of registration of the vehicle to a point in the territory of the other Contracting Party, provided that the vehicle returns empty to its country of registration; or

(c) The carriage of groups of passengers from a point in the territory of the other Contracting Party to a point in the country of registration of the vehicle, provided that such carriage is preceded by an unladen journey to the territory of the other Contracting Party and the passengers:

- Constitute a group formed under a transport contract prior to their arrival on the territory of the State in which they are picked up;
- Or have previously been brought by the same carrier to the other Contracting State in accordance with the conditions specified in (b) and are now being carried to another country; or
- Have been invited to travel to the territory of the other Contracting Party, the transport costs being borne by the inviting party. The passengers must constitute a cohesive group of persons not assembled solely for the purpose of the journey;

(d) Closed-door transit through the territory of the other Contracting Party.

2. Regular passenger transport operations carried out under the following conditions shall be exempt from the authorization requirement:

- Shuttle journeys with accommodation in transit or to the territory of the other Contracting Party; and
- Unladen journeys of the vehicles carried out in connection with the shuttle services.

3. The transport operations referred to in paragraphs 1 and 2 of the present article shall be accompanied by a control document.

4. Carriage operations other than those referred to in paragraphs 1 and 2 of this article shall be subject to authorization in accordance with the national law of the Contracting Parties. Authorizations shall be granted on the basis of reciprocity.

Article 4. Transport of goods

Any operator registered in the State of a Contracting Party shall be entitled to temporarily import a laden or unladen vehicle into the territory of the other Contracting Party for the purpose of transporting goods:

(a) Between a point in the territory of the one Contracting Party and any point in the territory of the other Contracting Party; or

(b) From the territory of the other Contracting Party to a third country or from a third country to the territory of the other Contracting Party; or

(c) In transit through the territory of the other Contracting Party.

Article 5. Application of national law

In all matters not covered by the present Agreement, operators and drivers from a Contracting Party shall, when travelling in the territory of the other Contracting Party, comply with locally applicable laws and regulations that are applied in a non-discriminatory manner.

Article 6. Restriction of intra-State transport

Cabotage transport of passengers and goods, which is transport between two or more places within the territory of one Contracting Party by operators of the other Contracting Party, is not permitted. The Joint Commission provided for in article 10 may agree on facilitation measures in this respect.

Article 7. Violations

1. The competent authorities of the Contracting Parties shall ensure that operators comply with the provisions of the present agreement.

2. The following measures may be imposed, at the request of the competent authorities of a Contracting Party, on operators and drivers who have infringed the provisions of the Agreement or the laws and regulations concerning road transport or road traffic in force in that Contracting Party, and shall be enforced by the authorities of the country of registration of the vehicle:

(a) Warning;

(b) Temporary, partial or total withdrawal of the entitlement to carry out transport operations in the territory of the Contracting Party in which the offence was committed.

3. The authority which has taken such a measure shall inform the competent authorities of the other Contracting Party thereof.

4. This shall be without prejudice to sanctions which may be imposed under national law by the courts or competent authorities of the Contracting Party on whose territory such offences have been committed.

Article 8. Competent authorities

The Contracting Parties shall notify each other of the authorities responsible for the application of the present Agreement. These authorities shall communicate directly with each other.

Article 9. Implementing provisions

Provisions for the implementation of the present Agreement shall be agreed upon by the Contracting Parties in a protocol which shall form an integral part of the Agreement.

Article 10. Joint Commission

1. The Contracting Parties shall establish a Joint Commission for the implementation of the present Agreement.

2. Said Commission shall also be responsible for amending or supplementing the protocol referred to in article 9 of the present Agreement.

3. The competent authorities of one Contracting Party may request the convening of this Joint Commission; the Commission shall meet alternately in the territory of each Contracting Party.

Article 11. Application in the Principality of Liechtenstein

In accordance with the formal request by the Principality of Liechtenstein, the Agreement shall also cover the Principality of Liechtenstein for as long as it remains linked to Switzerland by a customs union treaty.

Article 12. Entry into force and period of validity

1. The Contracting Parties shall notify each other by an exchange of notes through diplomatic channels that all conditions in national legislation required for the entry into force of the present Agreement have been fulfilled. The Agreement shall enter into force on the thirtieth day following the date of the last note of acceptance sent through diplomatic channels, in accordance with the conditions laid down by national law. It shall be applied provisionally from the date of its signature.

2. The Agreement shall apply for an indefinite period; it may be terminated in writing by either Contracting Party by giving at least three months of notice to the other Contracting Party, with termination taking effect at the end of a calendar.

IN WITNESS WHEREOF the undersigned plenipotentiaries, duly authorized by their Governments, have signed the present Agreement.

DONE at Riga on 28 April 1998 in two originals, each in the Latvian and German languages, both texts being equally authentic. In the event of any discrepancies between the texts, the German version shall prevail.

For the Government of the Republic of Latvia:
[VILIS KRIŠTOPANS]

For the Swiss Federal Council:
[MAX FRIEDLI]

PROTOCOL

On the basis of article 9 of the Agreement between the Government of the Republic of Latvia and the Swiss Federal Council concerning the international road transport of passengers and goods, signed at ... on ... ,

The following is agreed:

1. Passenger transport (article 3)

The transport operations provided for in article 3, paragraphs 1 and 2 of the Agreement shall be carried out using a journey form and a passenger list. Copies of these documents are attached hereto and shall form an integral part of the present Protocol.

Applications for the authorization of transport operations which do not fulfil the conditions mentioned in article 3, paragraphs 1 and 2 of the Agreement (for example, scheduled services) shall be submitted to the competent authority of the State in which the vehicle is registered; the latter shall forward the approved applications to the competent authority of the other Contracting Party or inform it of any negative decisions.

Operators shall include the timetable, fares, routing and other information requested by the competent authority in their applications. The procedure for issuing authorizations and other similar matters shall be determined jointly by the competent authorities of the Contracting Parties on the basis of reciprocity.

The authority which has granted an authorization shall inform the competent authority of the other Contracting Party thereof by forwarding a copy of the authorization granted.

The authorizations must be carried in the vehicles and presented upon request by the control authorities.

For unladen transit journeys, the operator must prove that he or she is passing unladen through the territory of the other Contracting Party.

Vehicles intended to replace a damaged or inoperable bus do not require an authorization for unladen entry, if appropriate proof is provided.

2. Transport of goods (article 4)

For transport by a combination of vehicles comprising different elements (such as trailers or semi-trailers), the provisions of the present Agreement shall apply to the whole combination of vehicles, provided that the lorry or the towing vehicle is registered in one of the Contracting States.

3. Application of national law (article 5)

The Contracting Parties note that the provisions of article 5 of the Agreement relate in particular to legislation on road transport, road traffic, the masses and weights of vehicles, working time and rest periods for vehicle crews, driving time, and also to taxes, tolls and administrative charges. Vehicle tax, which is subject to the principle of nationality, cannot be levied on an operator of the other Contracting Party.

4. Competent authorities (article 8)

The authorities responsible for the implementation of the Agreement are:

For the Republic of Latvia:

Ministry of Transport of the Republic of Latvia,

Gogola 3,

LV-1743 Riga

For Switzerland:

Federal Department of the Environment,

Transport, Energy and Communications,

Federal Office of Transport,

CH-3003 Bern

5. Approved dimensions and weights of vehicles

Where the dimensions and weights of road vehicles are concerned, each Contracting Party shall undertake not to subject vehicles registered for circulation in the territory of the other Contracting Party to more stringent conditions than those applicable to vehicles registered for circulation in its own territory.

Where vehicles exceed the dimensions and/or weights laid down in the national law of each Contracting Party, the following procedures shall apply:

For the Republic of Latvia:

Vehicles registered in Switzerland may enter the territory of the Republic of Latvia with a special authorization issued by the Road Traffic Safety Directorate of the Ministry of Transport (address: Road Traffic Safety Directorate, 25 Miera Street, LV-1001 Riga; Fax No. +371 828 301). Applications for authorizations must be sent to the above-mentioned authority at least 10 days before the start of operations.

For Switzerland:

Vehicles registered in the Republic of Latvia may enter the border zone defined by the Federal Department of Justice and Police with an authorization issued by a Swiss customs office or by the Federal Roads Office, Road Traffic Division, Bern. The border zone is usually the area within a 10-kilometre radius of a customs office.

For transport beyond area border zone, the Federal Roads Office, Road Traffic Division, CH-003 Berne (fax +31 963 43 03), issues special authorizations only for indivisible loads, provided that road conditions permit the issue of the authorization. Applications must be submitted to this authority in advance.

The total weight entered in the vehicle registration document must not be exceeded under any circumstances.

6. Customs

The fuel contained in the normal vehicle tanks of the temporarily imported vehicles shall be admitted free of import duties, import prohibitions and import restrictions.

Spare parts used for the repair of a specific vehicle already temporarily imported shall be admitted for temporary importation free of import duties, import prohibitions and import restrictions. The Contracting Parties may provide for these spare parts to be subject to clearance with a temporary importation card. The replaced parts shall be cleared through customs, re-exported or destroyed under the supervision of the customs authorities.

[TRANSLATION IN FRENCH – TRADUCTION EN FRANÇAIS]

ACCORD ENTRE LE GOUVERNEMENT DE LA RÉPUBLIQUE DE LETTONIE ET LE CONSEIL FÉDÉRAL SUISSE RELATIF AU TRANSPORT INTERNATIONAL PAR ROUTE DE PASSAGERS ET DE MARCHANDISES

Le Gouvernement de la République de Lettonie et le Conseil fédéral suisse, ci-après dénommés « Parties contractantes », désireux de faciliter le transport par route de passagers et de marchandises entre les deux États et en transit à travers leurs territoires, sont convenus de ce qui suit :

Article premier. Champ d'application

Les dispositions du présent Accord s'appliquent au transport de passagers et de marchandises à destination ou en provenance du territoire de l'une des Parties contractantes ou en transit à travers l'un desdits territoires par des véhicules immatriculés sur le territoire de l'autre Partie contractante.

Article 2. Définitions

Au sens du présent Accord :

1. Le terme « transporteur » désigne une personne physique ou morale qui, en République de Lettonie ou en Suisse, est autorisée, conformément aux réglementations en vigueur dans l'État de ladite personne, à effectuer le transport routier international de personnes ou de marchandises ;

2. Le terme « véhicule » désigne un véhicule routier à propulsion mécanique ainsi que, le cas échéant, sa remorque ou semi-remorque, construit et approuvé aux fins du transport :

   a) De plus de neuf passagers assis, y compris le chauffeur ;

   b) De marchandises ;

3. Le terme « autorisation » désigne tout permis, concession ou autorisation requis selon les réglementations nationales des Parties contractantes qui confère aux opérateurs le droit d'effectuer le transport de passagers et de marchandises couvert par le présent Accord.

Article 3. Transport de passagers

1. Le transport occasionnel de passagers remplissant les conditions suivantes est exempt d'autorisations :

   a) Le transport des mêmes personnes dans le même véhicule pendant tout un voyage dont le point de départ et le point d'arrivée sont situés dans le pays d'immatriculation du véhicule, à condition qu'aucune personne ne soit embarquée ou débarquée pendant le voyage ou au cours d'arrêts en dehors du territoire dudit pays (circuits à portes fermées) ; ou

   b) Le transport de groupes de passagers d'un point situé dans le pays d'immatriculation du véhicule à un point situé sur le territoire de l'autre Partie contractante, à condition que le véhicule retourne à vide dans son pays d'immatriculation ; ou

c) Le transport de groupes de passagers d'un point situé sur le territoire de l'autre Partie contractante à un point situé dans le pays d'immatriculation du véhicule, à condition que ledit transport soit précédé d'un trajet à vide vers le territoire de l'autre Partie contractante et que les passagers :

- Soient groupés en vertu d'un contrat de transport conclu avant leur arrivée sur le territoire de l'État dans lequel ils sont embarqués ; ou
- Aient été transportés préalablement par le même transporteur vers l'autre État contractant, conformément aux conditions visées à l'alinéa b) du présent paragraphe, et soient désormais transportés vers un autre pays ; ou
- Aient été invités à voyager sur le territoire de l'autre Partie contractante, les frais de transport étant pris en charge par la Partie invitante. Les passagers doivent constituer un groupe cohérent de personnes et ne pas être rassemblés dans le seul objectif d'effectuer ce trajet ;

d) Les trajets de transit à portes fermées à travers le territoire de l'autre Partie contractante.

2. Le transport occasionnel de passagers remplissant les conditions suivantes est exempt d'autorisations :

- Les services de navette avec hébergement en transit ou à destination du territoire de l'autre Partie contractante ;
- Les trajets à vide de véhicules effectués dans le cadre des services de navettes.

3. Les transports visés aux paragraphes 1 et 2 du présent article sont accompagnés d'un document de contrôle.

4. Les transports autres que ceux visés aux paragraphes 1 et 2 du présent article sont soumis à autorisation, conformément au droit interne des Parties contractantes. Les autorisations sont accordées sous réserve de réciprocité.

Article 4. Transport de marchandises

Tout transporteur enregistré dans l'État d'une Partie contractante dispose du droit d'importer temporairement un véhicule chargé ou à vide sur le territoire de l'autre Partie contractante afin de transporter des marchandises :

a) Entre un point situé sur le territoire de l'une des Parties contractantes et tout point situé sur le territoire de l'autre Partie contractante ; ou

b) Depuis le territoire de l'autre Partie contractante vers un pays tiers, ou depuis un pays tiers vers le territoire de l'autre Partie contractante ; ou

c) En transit à travers le territoire de l'autre Partie contractante.

Article 5. Application du droit interne

Pour toutes les questions non couvertes par le présent Accord, les transporteurs et les chauffeurs d'une Partie contractante, lorsqu'ils voyagent sur le territoire de l'autre Partie contractante, se conforment aux lois et réglementations applicables localement et appliquées de façon non discriminatoire.

Article 6. Interdiction des transferts à l'intérieur d'un pays

Le cabotage de passagers et de marchandises, c'est-à-dire le transport entre deux ou plusieurs points sur le territoire de l'une des Parties contractantes par des transporteurs de l'autre Partie contractante, n'est pas autorisé. La Commission mixte visée à l'article 10 du présent Accord peut convenir de mesures de facilitation à cet égard.

Article 7. Infractions

1. Les autorités compétentes des Parties contractantes s'assurent que les transporteurs se conforment aux dispositions du présent Accord.

2. Les mesures suivantes peuvent être imposées, sur demande des autorités compétentes de l'autre Partie contractante, aux transporteurs et aux chauffeurs ayant enfreint les dispositions du présent Accord ou les lois et réglementations relatives au transport routier ou à la circulation routière en vigueur dans cette autre Partie contractante, et sont appliquées par les autorités du pays dans lequel le véhicule est immatriculé :

   a) Avertissement ;

   b) Retrait, à titre temporaire, partiel ou total de l'autorisation d'effectuer des transports sur le territoire de la Partie contractante sur lequel l'infraction a été commise.

3. L'autorité qui a pris une mesure de ce type en informe les autorités compétentes de l'autre Partie contractante.

4. Cette disposition s'applique sans préjudice des sanctions qui peuvent être imposées en vertu du droit interne par les tribunaux ou les autorités compétentes de la Partie contractante sur le territoire de laquelle les infractions ont été commises.

Article 8. Autorités compétentes

Les Parties contractantes s'informent mutuellement des autorités responsables de l'application du présent Accord. Lesdites autorités communiquent directement entre elles.

Article 9. Dispositions de mise en œuvre

Les dispositions de mise en œuvre du présent Accord sont convenues par les Parties contractantes dans un protocole, qui fait partie intégrante du présent Accord.

Article 10. Commission mixte

1. Les Parties contractantes établissent une commission mixte chargée de la mise en œuvre du présent Accord.

2. La Commission mixte est également compétente pour modifier ou compléter le protocole visé à l'article 9 du présent Accord.

3. Les autorités compétentes de l'une des Parties contractantes peuvent exiger la convocation de réunions de la Commission mixte, alternativement sur le territoire de chacune des Parties contractantes.

Article 11. Application à la Principauté du Liechtenstein

Conformément à la demande formelle de la Principauté du Liechtenstein, le présent Accord couvre également la Principauté du Liechtenstein aussi longtemps que celle-ci demeure liée à la Suisse par un traité d'union douanière.

Article 12. Entrée en vigueur et durée de validité

1. Les Parties contractantes s'informent mutuellement par la voie diplomatique, au moyen d'un échange de notes, de l'accomplissement de toutes les conditions prévues par leurs législations internes et nécessaires à l'entrée en vigueur du présent Accord. L'Accord entre en vigueur le trentième jour suivant la date de la dernière note d'acceptation envoyée par la voie diplomatique, conformément aux conditions prévues par le droit interne. Le présent Accord s'applique à titre provisoire à compter de la date de sa signature.

2. Le présent Accord s'applique pour une durée indéterminée. Il peut être dénoncé par écrit par l'une ou l'autre des Parties contractantes, la dénonciation prenant effet à la fin de l'année civile, moyennant l'envoi d'une notification à l'autre Partie contractante au moins trois mois à l'avance.

EN FOI DE QUOI, les plénipotentiaires soussignés, à ce dûment autorisés par leurs Gouvernements, ont signé le présent Accord.

FAIT à Riga, le 28 avril 1998, en deux exemplaires originaux, chacun en langues lettone et allemande, les deux textes faisant également foi. En cas de divergence entre les textes, le texte allemand prévaut.

Pour le Gouvernement de la République de Lettonie :

[VILIS KRIŠTOPANS]

Pour le Conseil fédéral suisse :

[MAX FRIEDLI]

PROTOCOLE

Conformément à l'article 9 de l'Accord entre le Gouvernement de la République de Lettonie et le Conseil fédéral suisse relatif au transport international par route de passagers et de marchandises, signé à Riga le 28 avril 1998,

Il est convenu de ce qui suit :

1. Transport de passagers (article 3)

Les transports visés aux paragraphes 1 et 2 de l'article 3 de l'Accord sont effectués au moyen d'une feuille de route et d'une liste de passagers. Des modèles de ces documents sont joints au présent Protocole et en font partie intégrante.

Les demandes d'autorisation relatives aux transports ne remplissant pas les conditions énoncées aux paragraphes 1 et 2 de l'article 3 de l'Accord (par exemple, les services réguliers) sont soumises à l'autorité compétente de l'État dans lequel le véhicule est immatriculé, et cette autorité compétente transfère les demandes approuvées à l'autorité compétente de l'autre Partie contractante ou l'informe de toute décision négative.

Les transporteurs joignent à leurs demandes d'autorisation les horaires, les tarifs, l'itinéraire et toute autre information requise par l'autorité compétente. Les autorités compétentes des Parties contractantes conviennent conjointement de la procédure de délivrance des autorisations et de toute autre question similaire sous réserve de réciprocité.

L'autorité qui a accordé une autorisation en informe l'autorité compétente de l'autre Partie contractante en transmettant une copie de l'autorisation accordée.

Les autorisations doivent se trouver à bord des véhicules et doivent être présentées sur demande des autorités de contrôle.

Dans le cas des trajets de transit à vide, le transporteur doit prouver qu'il traverse à vide le territoire de l'autre Partie contractante.

Si des preuves sont fournies, l'entrée à vide de véhicules destinés à remplacer un bus endommagé ou en panne n'est pas soumise à autorisation.

2. Transport de marchandises (article 4)

Dans le cas d'un transport effectué par une combinaison de véhicules composée de différents éléments (par exemple, des remorques ou semi-remorques), les dispositions du présent Accord s'appliquent à la combinaison de véhicules dans son ensemble, à condition que le camion ou véhicule tracteur soit immatriculé dans l'un des États contractants.

3. Application du droit interne (article 5)

Les Parties contractantes prennent acte du fait que les dispositions de l'article 5 de l'Accord se rapportent notamment à la législation relative au transport routier, à la circulation routière, aux masses et poids des véhicules, au temps de travail et de repos de l'équipage des véhicules, à la durée de conduite, ainsi qu'aux taxes, péages et redevances administratives. La taxe sur les véhicules, soumise au principe de nationalité, ne peut être imposée à un transporteur de l'autre Partie contractante.

4. Autorités compétentes (article 8)

Les autorités responsables de la mise en œuvre de l'Accord sont :

Pour la République de Lettonie :

Ministère des transports de la République de Lettonie

Gogola 3

LV-1743 Riga

Pour la Suisse :

Département fédéral de l'environnement, des transports, de l'énergie et de la communication

Office fédéral des transports

CH-3003 Berne

5. Dimensions et poids approuvés des véhicules

En ce qui concerne les dimensions et le poids des véhicules routiers, chaque Partie contractante s'engage à ne pas soumettre les véhicules immatriculés à des fins de circulation sur le territoire de l'autre Partie contractante à des conditions plus strictes que celles applicables aux véhicules immatriculés à des fins de circulation sur son propre territoire.

Dans le cas où des véhicules excèdent les dimensions et/ou les poids définis dans le droit interne de chaque Partie contractante, les procédures énoncées ci-après s'appliquent.

Pour la République de Lettonie :

Les véhicules immatriculés en Suisse peuvent entrer sur le territoire de la République de Lettonie au moyen d'une autorisation spéciale délivrée par la Direction de la sécurité routière du Ministère des transports (adresse : Direction de la sécurité routière, Miera ielā 25, LV-1001 Riga ; fax : +371 828 301). Les demandes d'autorisations doivent être envoyées à l'autorité susmentionnée au moins 10 jours avant le début des opérations ;

Pour la Suisse :

Les véhicules immatriculés en République de Lettonie peuvent entrer dans la zone frontalière telle que définie par le Département fédéral de justice et de police au moyen d'une autorisation délivrée par un bureau de douane suisse ou par l'Office fédéral des routes de la Division de la circulation routière, à Berne. La zone frontalière couvre généralement la zone située dans un rayon de 10 kilomètres autour d'un bureau de douane.

En ce qui concerne les transports au-delà de ladite zone frontalière, l'Office fédéral des routes de la Division de la circulation routière, CH-003 Berne (fax : +31 963 43 03) délivre des autorisations spéciales uniquement pour les charges indivisibles, à condition que les conditions routières permettent la délivrance pour ces autorisations. Les demandes doivent être préalablement soumises à ladite autorité.

Le poids total consigné dans le document d'immatriculation du véhicule ne doit en aucune circonstance être excédé.

6. Douanes

Le carburant contenu dans le réservoir d'origine des véhicules temporairement importés est admis en franchise des droits de douane, prohibitions d'importation et restrictions à l'importation.

Les pièces de rechange utilisées pour la réparation d'un véhicule précis temporairement importé au préalable sont admises à l'importation temporaire en franchise des droits de douane, prohibitions d'importation et restrictions à l'importation. Les Parties contractantes peuvent prévoir que lesdites pièces de rechange soient soumises au dédouanement avec une carte d'importation temporaire. Les pièces remplacées sont dédouanées, réexportées ou détruites sous la supervision des autorités douanières.

No. 54182

Latvia
and
Turkey

International Road Transport Agreement between the Government of the Republic of Latvia and the Government of the Republic of Turkey. Ankara, 15 September 1995

Entry into force: *provisionally on 15 September 1995 by signature and definitively on 5 June 1996, in accordance with article 26*

Authentic texts: *English, Latvian and Turkish*

Registration with the Secretariat of the United Nations: *Latvia, 4 January 2017*

Lettonie
et
Turquie

Accord sur le transport routier international entre le Gouvernement de la République de Lettonie et le Gouvernement de la République turque. Ankara, 15 septembre 1995

Entrée en vigueur : *provisoirement le 15 septembre 1995 par signature et définitivement le 5 juin 1996, conformément à l'article 26*

Textes authentiques : *anglais, letton et turc*

Enregistrement au Secrétariat de l'Organisation des Nations Unies : *Lettonie, 4 janvier 2017*

[TEXT IN ENGLISH – TEXTE EN ANGLAIS]

International Road Transport

AGREEMENT

between
The Government of The Republic of Latvia
and
The Government of The Republic of Turkey

The Government of the Republic of Latvia and the Government of the Republic of Turkey, hereinafter referred to as "Contracting Parties",

Being desirous to facilitate transportation of passengers and goods by road between the two countries, as well as in transit through their territories,

Have agreed as follows:

Article 1

The provisions of this Agreement shall apply to the international carriage of passengers and goods by road, to or from the territory of one Contracting Party, and in transit through the territory of the other Contracting Party by using vehicles registered in the territories of the Contracting Parties.

Article 2

For the purpose of this Agreement:

The term *"carrier"* means any physical or legal person who is authorized to engage in the international carriage of passengers and goods in conformity with the laws, regulations and rules of the Contracting Parties.

The term *"vehicle"* means:

a) Any power driven road vehicle built either for carriage of passengers more than eight excluding the driver or goods or towing such vehicles, or

b) A combination comprising a vehicle as defined above in paragraph (a) and a trailer or a semi-trailer connected to it built for the carriage of passengers or goods.

The term *"permit"* means the permits issued to a road vehicle registered in the territory of one of the Contracting Parties by the competent authorities of the other Contracting Party to permit the vehicle to enter and leave or travel through the territory of the latter as well as other permits provided for by the present Agreement.

The term *"quota"* means the number of permits issued annually by the competent authorities of the each Contracting Party.

The term *"regular bus service"* means the carriage of passengers between the territories of the two Contracting Parties on a prescribed route in accordance with national schedules and tariffs.

The term *"regular transit bus service"* means a regular bus service: beginning in the territory of one Contracting Party, crossing the territory of the other Contracting Party without leaving or taking passengers and terminating in the territory of a third country.

The term *"shuttle service"* means an organized international transport of passengers previously grouped in accordance with their length of stay from one and the same point of departure to one and the same point of destination and their return to the point of departure at the end of a pre-scheduled period (passengers travelling in a group, are all required to return in the same group, the first return journey from and the last journey to the point of destination will be without passengers).

The term *"closed- door service"* means international carriage of one and the same group of passengers in one and the same vehicle in a tour, starting from a point in the territory of one of the Contracting Parties and terminating in the territory of the same Contracting Party without taking or leaving passengers.

The term *"transit transport"* means international carriage of passengers and goods through the territory of one Contracting Party, between points of departure and destination located outside the territory of that Contracting Party.

Article 3

Each Contracting Party, in conformity with the provisions of this Agreement, shall recognize the right of transit if carriers of the other Contracting Party perform transport of passengers, their personal effects, commercial goods and vehicles by road over the routes to be determined by the competent authorities of each Contracting Party.

Article 4

Subject to its national legislation, each Contracting Party shall grant authorization to the carriers of the other Contracting Party to establish offices and/or to appoint representatives and/or agencies in its own territory at places to be mutually agreed upon by the competent authorities of the Contracting Parties.

A carrier shall not act as a travel agency in the territory of the other Contracting Party.

Article 5

Either Contracting Party shall not levy any import or export tax or charge (including customs tax) on vehicles of the other Contracting Party, which are in transit in its territory other than:

a) the charges for using road network infrastructure (road and bridge tolls),

b) the charges for to meet the expenses relating to the maintenance, protection and administration of roads and transport,

c) fees, on a non - discriminatory basis, to cover the difference between the national and the international price of fuel, for the fuel purchased in the territory of the other Contracting Party,

d) charges levied, if weight, dimensions or load of the vehicle exceed the prescribed limits in the national legislation of the Contracting Parties.

The authorized carriage in transit through the territories of the Contracting Parties may be exempted on reciprocal basis from the charges stipulated in paragraph (b) of this Article.

Either Contracting Party shall not have the charges mentioned in paragraph (b) for the vehicles which are not passing transit.

Article 6

In the event that a carrier or the staff on board of the vehicle of one Contracting Party have not observed the legislation in force on the territory of the other Contracting Party, the provisions of this Agreement or the conditions mentioned in the permit, the competent authority of the country where the vehicle is registered, could at the demand of the competent authority of the other Contracting Party, take the following measures:

a) to issue a warning for the carrier who committed the infringement;

b) to cancel or to withdraw the permits allowing the right for the carrier to perform transports in the territory of the Contracting Party, where the infringement was committed.

The competent authority which has taken such a measure, shall notify the competent authority of the other Contracting Party about this.

The provisions of this Article shall not exclude the lawful sanctions which may be applied by the courts or administration authorities of the country where the infringement occurred.

Article 7

The Mixed Commission consisting of the representatives of the two competent authorities of the Contracting Parties shall be formed. The objectives of the Mixed Commission are:

a) to supervise the proper implementation of this Agreement,

b) to determine the form, the time and the ways of exchange of permits,

c) to study and make proposals for the solution of possible problems not settled directly between the competent authorities referred to in Article 24 of this Agreement,

d) to review all other relevant issues that fall within the scope of this Agreement and make recommendations thereof for settlement,

e) to consider any other matters to be mutually agreed upon relating to transportation.

The Mixed Commission shall meet when required at the request of the competent authorities of one of the Contracting Parties alternately in the Republic of Latvia and the Republic of Turkey.

The agenda to be discussed at the Mixed Commission meeting shall be prepared in advance in the light of the objectives mentioned above by the competent authorities of the Contracting Parties and agreed upon by means of diplomatic channels.

The Mixed Commission can recommend to amend any Article of this Agreement and submit to the competent authorities for approval.

Article 8

The vehicles registered in the territory of one Contracting Party shall not carry passengers and goods between any two points within the territory of the other Contracting Party.

Unless a special permit from the competent authority of the other Contracting Party is obtained, a carrier from one Contracting Party shall not carry passengers and goods from the territory of the other Contracting Party to third countries.

Article 9

An unloaded vehicle, registered in one Contracting Party shall not enter the territory of the other Contracting Party for the purpose of collecting passengers and goods destinated to the territory of the other Contracting Party or destinated to a third country, unless a special permit is issued for this purpose by the competent authority of the other Contracting Party.

CARRIAGE OF PASSENGERS

Article 10

A carrier of one Contracting Party shall operate a regular passenger service to or a regular transit passenger service through the territory of the other Contracting Party by obtaining a yearly permit in advance from the competent authority of the other Contracting Party.

Article 11

a) The closed- door journey service and full outgoing and empty return service to be performed by vehicle registered in the territory of one Contracting Party to or from the territory of the other Contracting Party shall not be subject to obtaining permit.

b) The shuttle transportation service of passengers require the separate permit, issued by competent authority of the other Contracting Party.

The application in view to obtain the authorization for the shuttle transportation service shall be submitted to the competent authority of the other Contracting Party 30 days before beginning of this transportation.

CARRIAGE OF GOODS

Article 12

The carriage of goods between the territories of the Contracting Parties and in transit through the territories of the Contracting Parties shall be subject to prior permit based on quota except the cases defined below:

a) Carriage of deceased (especially by vehicles designed for this purpose);

b) Carriage of decorative articles for theatrical performance;

c) Carriage of goods, equipments and animals needed for musical performances and cinema, circus and folkloric shows, sports activities and recording TV and radio programmes;

d) Carriage of works of art;

e) Carriage of animals other than those for slaughtering;

f) Carriage of damaged vehicles or vehicles out of operation;

g) Postal carriage;

h) Occasional carriage of goods to or from airports as a result of change in flight itineraires;

i) Carriage of aid material in case of emergencies and natural disasters;

j) Carriage of materials for fairs and exhibitions;

k) For transport services carried out by motor vehicles with a maximum total weight of 6 tons including trailer, or a maximum loading capacity of 3.5 tons, including trailer;

l) Carriage of household removal goods;

m) Other cases to be mutually agreed upon by the Mixed Commission.

Article 13

Permits shall be valid for one year and permits of the next year will be exchanged in November of every year. Some additional permits shall be exchanged whenever needed to meet the requirements of the competent authorities of the Contracting Parties on the basis of mutual agreement.

A permit shall be valid for one round trip to the territory of the other Contracting Party and/or in transit through the territory of the other Contracting Party.

It shall also be valid for one vehicle and only for the carrier to whom it is issued and shall not be transferable.

Article 14

A vehicle registered in the territory of one Contracting Party can collect return load to its territory only after delivery of goods to the territory of the other Contracting Party.

Article 15

The carriage of arms, ammunitions and military equipment and explosives between two Contracting Parties or transit through each Contracting Party's territory is subject to a special permit obtained for this purpose.

Transportation of goods, prohibited by national laws and regulations is allowed in the territories of the Contracting Parties according to their national laws and regulations with special permits issued by competent authorities.

Goods, which are prohibited to transport by international law are not permitted to transport to the territories of the Contracting Parties.

Article 16

The Contracting Parties shall take all the measures which they deem necessary in order to facilitate, simplify and accelerate to the greatest extent possible the customs and other formalities relating to carriage of passengers and goods.

Article 17

The international transport of goods by road in accordance with this Agreement shall be subject to the requirements of the Convention on the International Transport of Goods under cover of TIR Carnets and/or national laws and regulations.

Article 18

Fuel contained in the standard fuel tanks of vehicles shall be exempted from customs duties and all other taxes and duties. The standard fuel tank, is a tank provided by the manufacturers of vehicles technologically connected to the feed system of vehicles.

Article 19

The spare parts imported to the territory of the other Contracting Party in view to repair a vehicle already temporarily imported will be admitted without any custom duties and taxes.

A part which has not applied or been replaced shall either be re-exported or destroyed under the supervision of the customs authorities.

Article 20

a) A third- party- liability insurance complying with the laws and regulations in force in each of the Contracting Parties shall be applied to a vehicle used in the international carriage of passengers, baggages and/or goods between and/or in transit through the territory of the Contracting Parties.

b) Any kind of insurance complying with the laws and regulations in force in the Contracting Party in which the vehicle is registered shall be applied to passengers, baggages and/or goods, against damages that they will have during the carriage.

Article 21

The payments between the Contracting Parties concerning transport and transit operations shall be made in convertible currency to be accepted by the authorized banks of the Contracting Parties in accordance with currency laws, regulations and rules in force in the Contracting Parties.

Article 22

In cases of traffic accidents, breakdowns and violations of laws and regulations the competent authorities of the Contracting Party in whose territory such an incident occurs, shall provide the competent authorities of the other Contracting Party with reports and other information and the results of inquiry immediately.

Article 23

Carriers and crew of the vehicles registered in one Contracting Party, shall comply with laws and regulations governing the road traffic of the other Contracting Party.

Any other matters pertaining to transportation which are not covered by this Agreement, shall be subject to the laws, regulations and rules of the Contracting Parties.

Article 24

If the weight, dimensions or axle load of the vehicle exceed the maximum limits in force in the territory of one Contracting Party, the national laws and regulations are applied.

Article 25

The competent authorities which are responsible for the implementation of this Agreement are:

a) In the Republic of Latvia:

Ministry of Transport
of the Republic of Latvia
Road Department

b) In the Republic of Turkey:

Ministry of Transport
General Directorate of Road Transport
(Ulastirma Bakanliği
Kara Ulastirmasi Genel Müdürlüğü)
ANKARA

Article 26

This Agreement will be applied as provisional from the day of signing and will enter into force from the date of exchange of notes attesting its ratification in accordance with the national legislation of the Contracting Parties and shall remain in force for a period of one year.

This Agreement shall be automatically renewed for periods of one year unless either Contracting Party expresses its wish in writing to the other Contracting Party to terminate it at least three months prior to the date of expiry.

Done in Ankara on "15" September, 1995 in two original copies each of them in the Latvian, Turkish and English languages, all texts being equally authentic having equal legal force.

In case of any divergence of interpretation, the English text shall prevail.

For the Government
of the Republic of Latvia:

For the Government
of the Republic of Turkey:

[TEXT IN LATVIAN – TEXTE EN LETTON]

Latvijas Republikas Valdības un Turcijas Republikas Valdības

LĪGUMS

par starptautiskajiem pārvadājumiem ar autotransportu

Latvijas Republikas Valdība un Turcijas Republikas Valdība, turpmāk tekstā "Līgumslēdzējas Puses",

lai veicinātu pasažieru un kravu pārvadājumus ar autotransportu starp abām valstīm, kā arī tranzītā cauri to teritorijām, vienojās par sekojošo:

1. pants

Šā Līguma nosacījumi attiecas uz starptautiskajiem pasažieru un kravu pārvadājumiem ar autotransportu uz jebkuras Līgumslēdzējas Puses valsts teritoriju vai no tās, kā arī tranzītā cauri otras Līgumslēdzējas Puses valsts teritorijai, izmantojot Līgumslēdzēju Pušu valstu teritorijās reģistrētus autotransporta līdzekļus.

2. pants

Šā Līguma ietvaros:

"Pārvadātājs" - jebkura fiziska vai juridiska persona, kas saskaņā ar katras Līgumslēdzējas Puses likumiem un noteikumiem ir tiesīga veikt starptautiskos pasažieru un kravu pārvadājumus.

"Autotransporta līdzeklis":

a) jebkurš motorizēts autotransporta līdzeklis, kas paredzēts vairāk nekā astoņu pasažieru, tā vadītāju neskaitot, pārvadāšanai, vai kravu pārvadāšanai, kā arī šādu autotransporta līdzekļu vilkšanai;

b) autotransporta līdzekļu kombinācija, kas sastāv no a) apakšpunktā minētā autotransporta līdzekļa un piekabes vai puspiekabes, kas paredzēta pasažieru vai kravu pārvadāšanai.

"Atļaujas" - visas tās atļaujas, kuras vienas Līgumslēdzējas Puses kompetentā institūcija izsniegusi otras Līgumslēdzējas Puses valsts teritorijā reģistrētiem autotransporta līdzekļiem to iebraukšanai, izbraukšanai vai tās teritorijas šķērsošanai, kā arī citas šajā Līgumā paredzētās atļaujas.

"Kvota" - atļauju skaits, ko gada laikā izsniegušas katras Līgumslēdzējas Puses kompetentās institūcijas.

"Regulāri pārvadājumi ar autobusiem" - pasažieru pārvadājumi pa noteiktu maršrutu starp Līgumslēdzēju Pušu valstu teritorijām, saskaņā ar katrā valstī noteiktajiem kustības sarakstiem un tarifiem.

"Regulāri tranzīta pārvadājumi ar autobusiem" - regulāri pārvadājumi ar autobusiem, kas sākas vienas Līgumslēdzējas Puses valsts teritorijā, šķērso otras Līgumslēdzējas Puses valsts teritoriju, neizlaižot un neuzņemot tajā pasažierus, un beidzas trešās valsts teritorijā.

"Sistemātiski turp un atpakaļ pārvadājumi" - iepriekš nokomplektētu pasažieru grupu starptautiskie pārvadājumi, kas organizēti, ņemot vērā viņu uzturēšanās laiku, no vienas un tās pašas brauciena sākuma vietas uz vienu un to pašu galapunktu ar noteikumu, ka grupai iepriekš noteikta termiņa beigās jāatgriežas brauciena sākuma vietā (pasažieru grupai jāatgriežas nemainīgā sastāvā un pirmajam braucienam atpakaļ uz brauciena sākuma vietu un pēdējam braucienam uz galapunktu jābūt bez pasažieriem).

"Pārvadājumi ar slēgtām durvīm" - vienas un tās pašas pasažieru grupas starptautiskie pārvadājumi ar vienu un to pašu autotransporta līdzekli braucienā, kas sākas vienas Līgumslēdzējas Puses valsts teritorijā un beidzas tās pašas Līgumslēdzējas Puses valsts teritorijā, neizlaižot un neuzņemot pasažierus visa brauciena laikā.

"Tranzīta pārvadājumi" - pasažieru un kravu starptautiskie pārvadājumi caur jebkuras Līgumslēdzējas Puses valsts teritoriju, ja brauciena sākuma punkts un galapunkts atrodas ārpus attiecīgās Līgumslēdzējas Puses valsts teritorijas.

3. pants

Saskaņā ar šā Līguma nosacījumiem, katrai Līgumslēdzējai Pusei jāatzīst otras Līgumslēdzējas Puses pārvadātāju tiesības braukt tranzītā ar autotransporta līdzekļiem un pārvadāt tranzītā pasažierus, viņu personīgās lietas un komerciālas kravas pa maršrutiem, ko nosaka attiecīgās Līgumslēdzējas Puses kompetentās institūcijas.

4. pants

Katrai Līgumslēdzējai Pusei saskaņā ar savas valsts likumdošanu jāizdod atļauja otras Līgumslēdzējas Puses pārvadātājiem biroju un/vai aģentūru izveidošanai un/vai pārstāvju iecelšanai tās valsts teritorijā vietās, par kurām abpusēji vienojušās Līgumslēdzēju Pušu kompetentās institūcijas.

Pārvadātājs otras Līgumslēdzējas Puses valsts teritorijā nedrīkst darboties kā tūrisma aģents.

5. pants

Jebkura Līgumslēdzēja Puse neiekasēs nekādus importa vai eksporta nodokļus un maksājumus (muitas nodokli ieskaitot) par otras Līgumslēdzējas Puses autotransporta līdzekļiem, kas brauc tranzītā cauri tās teritorijai, izņemot:

a) maksu par ceļu tīkla izmantošanu (nodevas par ceļu un tiltu lietošanu);

b) maksu, lai segtu ar transporta un ceļu uzturēšanu, aizsardzību un pārvaldi saistītos izdevumus;

c) samaksu uz nediskriminējošiem noteikumiem, lai segtu starpību starp valsts un starptautisko cenu degvielai, kas nopirkta otras Līgumslēdzējas Puses valsts teritorijā;

d) maksājumus, ko iekasē, ja autotransporta līdzekļa svars, izmēri vai krava pārsniedz Līgumslēdzēju Pušu valstu likumdošanā paredzētos ierobežojumus.

Saskaņā ar atļaujām veicamos tranzīta pārvadājumus cauri Līgumslēdzēju Pušu valstu teritorijām, savstarpēji vienojoties, var atbrīvot no šī panta b) apakšpunktā paredzētās maksas.

Līgumslēdzējas Puses neiekasēs šī panta b) apakšpunktā minēto maksu no autotransporta līdzekļiem, kas neveic tranzīta pārvadājumus.

6. pants

Ja vienas Līgumslēdzējas Puses pārvadātājs vai viņa autotransporta līdzekļa apkalpe nav ievērojusi otras Līgumslēdzējas Puses valsts teritorijā spēkā esošo likumdošanu, šā Līguma nosacījumus vai atļaujā minētos noteikumus, tās valsts kompetentā institūcija, kurā šis autotransporta līdzeklis reģistrēts, pēc otras Līgumslēdzējas Puses kompetentās institūcijas pieprasījuma var piemērot sekojošas sankcijas:

a) brīdināt pārvadātāju, kurš izdarījis pārkāpumu;

b) anulēt vai atņemt atļaujas, kas pārvadātājam dod tiesības veikt pārvadājumus tās Līgumslēdzējas Puses valsts teritorijā, kurā pārkāpums noticis.

Kompetentajai institūcijai, kas piemērojusi kādu no šīm sankcijām, jāpaziņo par to otras Līgumslēdzējas Puses kompetentajai institūcijai.

Šā panta nosacījumi neizslēdz likumīgas sankcijas, kuras var piemērot tās valsts tiesas vai administratīvās institūcijas, kurā pārkāpums noticis.

7. pants

Jāizveido Kopējā Komisija, kas sastāv no abu Līgumslēdzēju Pušu kompetento institūciju pārstāvjiem. Kopējās Komisijas uzdevumos ietilpst:

a) kontrolēt šā Līguma pareizu izpildi;

b) noteikt atļauju formu, to apmaiņas veidu un termiņu;

c) izskatīt un izstrādāt priekšlikumus, to iespējamo jautājumu risināšanai, par kuriem nav tieši vienojušās šā Līguma 24. pantā minētās kompetentās institūcijas;

d) izskatīt visus pārējos jautājumus, kas saistīti ar šo Līgumu, un izstrādāt ieteikumus to risināšanai;

e) apspriest jebkurus citus ar pārvadājumiem saistītos jautājumus, par kuriem savstarpēji jāvienojas.

Kopējai Komisijai jātiekas pēc jebkuras Līgumslēdzējas Puses kompetentās institūcijas pieprasījuma pārmaiņus Latvijas Republikā un Turcijas Republikā.

Kopējās Komisijas sēdes darba kārtība minēto uzdevumu ietvaros Līgumslēdzēju Pušu kompetentajām institūcijām jāizstrādā iepriekš, saskaņojot to pa diplomātiskajiem kanāliem.

Kopējā Komisija var ierosināt labojumus jebkuram šā Līguma pantam un tie jāiesniedz kompetentajām institūcijām apstiprināšanai.

8. pants

Transporta līdzekļi, kas reģistrēti vienas Līgumslēdzējas Puses valsts teritorijā, nedrīkst veikt pasažieru un kravu pārvadājumus starp diviem punktiem otras Līgumslēdzējas Puses valsts teritorijā.

Vienas Līgumslēdzējas Puses pārvadātājs nedrīkst veikt pasažieru un kravu pārvadājumus no otras Līgumslēdzējas Puses valsts teritorijas uz trešajām valstīm, ja nav saņemta otras Līgumslēdzējas Puses kompetentās institūcijas speciāla atļauja.

9. pants

Autotransporta līdzeklis bez pasažieriem vai kravas, kas reģistrēts vienas Līgumslēdzējas Puses valsts teritorijā, nedrīkst iebraukt otras Līgumslēdzējas Puses valsts teritorijā, lai uzņemtu pasažierus vai kravu nogādāšanai uz savas valsts teritoriju vai uz trešo valsti, ja vien otras valsts kompetentās institūcijas šim nolūkam nav izsniegušas speciālu atļauju.

PASAŽIERU PĀRVADĀJUMI

10. pants

Lai veiktu regulārus pasažieru pārvadājumus uz otras Līgumslēdzējas Puses valsts teritoriju vai regulārus pasažieru tranzīta pārvadājumus cauri tai, jebkuras Līgumslēdzējas Puses pārvadātājam iepriekš jāsaņem otras Līgumslēdzējas Puses kompetentās institūcijas izsniegta gada atļauja.

11. pants

1. Atļauja nav nepieciešama pārvadājumiem ar "slēgtām durvīm" un pārvadājumiem, kad brauciens turp notiek ar pasažieriem, bet atpakaļceļš - bez pasažieriem, veicot tos ar vienā no Līgumslēdzēju Pušu valstu teritorijās reģistrētiem autotransporta līdzekļiem uz otras Līgumslēdzējas Puses valsts teritoriju vai no tās.

2. Sistemātiskiem pasažieru turp un atpakaļ pārvadājumiem nepieciešama otras Līgumslēdzējas Puses kompetentās institūcijas izsniegta īpaša atļauja.

Iesniegums atļauju saņemšanai sistemātisku turp un atpakaļ pārvadājumu veikšanai jāiesniedz otras Līgumslēdzējas Puses kompetentajai institūcijai 30 dienas pirms paredzēts uzsākt šos pārvadājumus.

KRAVU PĀRVADĀJUMI

12. pants

Kravu pārvadājumu veikšanai starp Līgumslēdzēju Pušu valstu teritorijām un tranzītā cauri Līgumslēdzēju Pušu valstu teritorijām nepieciešama uz noteikto kvotu pamata iepriekš izsniegta pārvadājumu atļauja, izņemot gadījumus, ja pārvadā:

a) mirstīgās atliekas (īpaši ar šim nolūkam paredzētiem autotransporta līdzekļiem);

b) dekorācijas, kas paredzētas teātra izrādēm;

c) priekšmetus, iekārtas un dzīvniekus, kas paredzēti muzikāliem uzvedumiem, kino, cirka un folkloras izrādēm, sporta pasākumiem, kā arī televīzijas un radio raidījumu ierakstiem;

d) mākslas priekšmetus;

e) dzīvniekus, kas nav paredzēti nokaušanai;

f) avarējušus un bojātus autotransporta līdzekļus;

g) pasta sūtījumus;

h) neregulāri - kravas uz vai no lidostām, ja mainīts lidojuma maršruts;

i) pirmās palīdzības piederumus ārkārtēju situāciju un dabas katastrofu gadījumos;

j) materiālus gadatirgiem un izstādēm;

k) kravas ar autotransporta līdzekli, kura kopējā masa, piekabi ieskaitot, nepārsniedz 6 tonnas vai maksimāla celtspēja, piekabi ieskaitot, nepārsniedz 3,5 tonnas;

l) iedzīves priekšmetus, pārceļoties uz pastāvīgu dzīvi citur;

m) citos gadījumos, par kuriem savstarpēji vienojusies Kopējā Komisija.

13. pants

Atļaujas ir derīgas vienu gadu un ar nākošā gada atļaujām jāapmainās katra gada novembrī. Nepieciešamības gadījumā pēc Līgumslēdzēju Pušu kompetento institūciju pieprasījuma, iespējams apmainīties ar papildus atļaujām uz savstarpējas vienošanas pamata.

Atļauja ir derīga vienam turp un atpakaļ braucienam uz otras Līgumslēdzējas Puses valsts teritoriju vai tranzītā cauri otras Līgumslēdzējas Puses valsts teritorijai.

Tā ir derīga tikai vienam autotransporta līdzeklim un tikai tam pārvadātājam, kam tā izsniegta. Tā nav nododama citai personai.

14. pants

Vienas Līgumslēdzējas Puses valsts teritorijā reģistrēts autotransporta līdzeklis drīkst uzņemt kravu nogādāšanai uz savas valsts teritoriju tikai tad, ja pirms tam veikts kravas pārvadājums uz otras Līgumslēdzējas Puses valsts teritoriju.

15. pants

Ieroču, munīcijas, militāro iekārtu un sprāgstvielu pārvadāšanai starp abu Līgumslēdzēju Pušu valstu teritorijām vai tranzītā cauri katras Puses teritorijai nepieciešama speciāla šim nolūkam paredzēta atļauja.

Kravu pārvadāšana, kas Līgumslēdzēju Pušu valstu teritorijās ir aizliegta ar tur spēkā esošajiem likumiem un noteikumiem, ir pieļaujama tikai, saņemot šajos likumos un noteikumos paredzētās kompetento institūciju izdotas speciālas atļaujas.

Uz Līgumslēdzēju Pušu valstu teritorijām nedrīkst pārvadāt kravas, kuru pārvadāšana ir aizliegta saskaņā ar starptautiskajiem noteikumiem.

16. pants

Līgumslēdzējām Pusēm jāveic visi pasākumi, ko tās uzskata par nepieciešamu, lai pēc iespējas atvieglotu, vienkāršotu un paātrinātu ar pasažieru un kravu pārvadājumiem saistīto muitas un citu formalitāšu kārtošanu.

17. pants

Saskaņā ar šo Līgumu veicamie starptautiskie kravu pārvadājumi ar autotransportu pakļauti Konvencijas par starptautiskajiem kravu pārvadājumiem prasībām, ņemot vērā TIR grāmatiņu izmantošanas un/vai attiecīgās valsts likumu un noteikumu prasības.

18. pants

Degviela, kas atrodas autotransporta līdzekļu standarta degvielas tvertnēs, tiek atbrīvota no muitas un visiem citiem nodokļiem un nodevām. Standarta degvielas tvertne ir tvertne, ko uzstādījusi autotransporta līdzekļa rūpnīca izgatavotāja un kas tehnoloģiski saistīta ar tā barošanas sistēmu.

19. pants

Rezerves daļas, ko ieved otras Līgumslēdzējas Puses valsts teritorijā jau iepriekš uz laiku iebraukuša autotransporta līdzekļa remontam, nav apliekamas ar muitas nodokļiem un nodevām.

Rezerves daļas, kas nav izmantotas, vai nomainītās detaļas izvedamas atpakaļ vai iznīcināmas pilnvarotu muitas ierēdņu klātbūtnē.

20. pants

1. Atbildības apdrošināšana par kaitējuma nodarīšanu trešajām personām, kas veikta saskaņā ar katras Līgumslēdzējas Puses valstī spēkā esošajiem likumiem un noteikumiem, attiecināma uz autotransporta līdzekļiem, kurus izmanto starptautiskajiem pasažieru, bagāžas un/vai kravu pārvadājumiem starp un/vai tranzītā cauri Līgumslēdzēju Pušu valstu teritorijām;

2. Jebkura veida apdrošināšana, kas veikta saskaņā ar katras Līgumslēdzējas Puses valsts teritorijā, kurā autotransporta līdzeklis reģistrēts, spēkā esošajiem likumiem un noteikumiem, attiecināma uz pasažieriem, bagāžu un/vai kravu kā atlīdzība par brauciena laikā iespējamiem nodarītajiem zaudējumiem.

21. pants

Līgumslēdzēju Pušu savstarpējie maksājumi par transporta un tranzīta operācijām izdarāmi tādā konvertējamā valūtā, kādu akceptējušas Līgumslēdzēju Pušu valstu pilnvarotās bankas, saskaņā ar Līgumslēdzēju Pušu valstu teritorijās spēkā esošajiem valūtas norēķinu likumiem un noteikumiem.

22. pants

Avāriju, autotransporta līdzekļu bojājumu, likumu un noteikumu pārkāpumu gadījumos tās Līgumslēdzējas Puses kompetentajām institūcijām, kuras valsts teritorijā starpgadījums noticis, nekavējoties par to jāsniedz otras Līgumslēdzējas Puses kompetentajām institūcijām ziņojums un cita informācija, kā arī izmeklēšanas rezultāti.

23. pants

Līgumslēdzēju Pušu pārvadātājiem un to valstu teritorijās reģistrēto autotransporta līdzekļu apkalpēm jāievēro otras Līgumslēdzējas Puses valsts teritorijā spēkā esošie likumi un noteikumi, kas reglamentē ceļu satiksmi.

Jebkuri citi jautājumi, kas saistīti ar pārvadājumiem un nav ietverti šajā Līgumā, risināmi saskaņā ar katras Līgumslēdzējas Puses valstī spēkā esošajiem likumiem un noteikumiem.

24. pants

Ja autotransporta līdzekļa svars, izmēri vai slodze uz ass pārsniedz vienas Līgumslēdzējas Puses valsts teritorijā spēkā esošās normas, jāvadās pēc šīs valsts likumiem un noteikumiem.

25. pants

Kompetentās institūcijas, kas atbildīgas par šā Līguma izpildi, ir:

a) Latvijas Republikā:
Latvijas Republikas Satiksmes ministrija
Autoceļu departaments

b) Turcijas Republikā:
Ministry of Transport
General Directorate of Road Transport
(Ulaştirma Bakanliği
Kara Ulastirmasi Genel Müdürlüğü)
ANKARA

26. pants

Šis Līgums provizoriski piemērojams no tā parakstīšanas dienas un stājas spēkā dienā, kad abas puses apmainījušās ar notām, kas apliecina Līguma ratifikāciju saskaņā ar katras Līgumslēdzējas Puses valsts likumdošanu, un tas paliek spēkā vienu gadu.

Turpmāk šā Līguma darbības termiņš automātiski pagarinās gadu no gada, ja vien viena no Līgumslēdzējām Pusēm ne vēlāk kā trīs mēnešus pirms tā darbības termiņa beigām nav rakstiski paziņojusi par savu nodomu izbeigt Līguma darbību.

Parakstīts Ankarā, 1995.gada "15." septembrī divos oriģināleksemplāros, katrs latviešu, turku un angļu valodās, turklāt visi teksti ir vienlīdz autentiski un tiem ir vienāds juridisks spēks.

Atšķirīgas interpretācijas gadījumā noteicošais ir teksts angļu valodā.

Latvijas Republikas
Valdības vārdā:

Turcijas Republikas
Valdības vārdā:

[TEXT IN TURKISH – TEXTE EN TURC]*

LETONYA CUMHURİYETİ HÜKÜMETİ İLE

TÜRKİYE CUMHURİYETİ HÜKÜMETİ

ARASINDA

ULUSLARARASI KARAYOLU TAŞIMACILIĞI

ANLAŞMASI

Bundan böyle Akit Taraflar olarak anılan,
Letonya Cumhuriyeti Hükümeti ile,
Türkiye Cumhuriyeti Hükümeti,

İki ülke arasında ve ülkeleri üzerinden transit olarak yolcu ve eşya taşımacılığını kolaylaştırmak arzusu ile ; aşağıdaki hususlarda mutabık kalmışlardır.

MADDE 1

Bu anlaşma hükümleri, yolcu ve eşyanın, diğer Akit Taraf ülkesinde tescil edilmiş taşıtlar ile, bir Akit Taraf ülkesine veya ülkesinden ve Akit Taraflardan biri üzerinden transit olarak Karayoluyla Uluslararası taşımasına uygulanır.

TANIMLAMALAR

MADDE 2

Bu Anlaşma'da:

"Taşımacı" terimi; Akit Tarafların kanun ve nizamlarına göre yolcu ve eşya taşımaya yetkili kılınmış gerçek ve tüzel kişiyi,

"Taşıt" terimi;

a) Şoför hariç sekizden fazla yolcu veya eşya taşımak üzere, veya bu taşıtları çekmek üzere imal edilmiş ve kendi gücüyle hareket eden bir karayolu taşıtını,

veya

b)Yukarıdaki paragraf (a) da belirlenen taşıtlar ile yolcu veya eşya taşımak amacıyla römork veya yarı römorklardan oluşan bir taşıt kombinasyonunu,

"İzin belgesi" terimi, Akit Taraflardan birinde kayıtlı taşıta diğer Akit Tarafa girip-çıkabilmesi veya transit geçebilmesi için bir Akit Tarafın yetkili makamlarınca verilen izin belgesi ile bu Anlaşma'da öngörülen diğer izin belgelerini,

* Published as submitted – Publié tel que soumis.

"Kota" terimi, Akit Tarafların yetkili makamları tarafından yıllık olarak verilecek izin belgeleri sayısını,

"Düzenli Otobüs Servisi" terimi, iki Akit Taraf toprakları arasında ulusal zaman ve ücret tarifesine bağlı olarak, önceden belirlenen güzergah üzerinde yolcu taşımacılığını,

"Düzenli transit otobüs servisi" terimi, bir Akit Taraf ülkesinde başlayan ve diğer Akit Taraf ülkesini yolcu indirmeden ve bindirmeden geçen ve üçüncü bir Devlet topraklarında sona eren düzenli servisi,

"Mekik Servis" terimi, bir ve aynı kalkış noktasından, planlanmış kalma süresine göre gruplandırılmış yolcuların bir ve aynı yere taşınması ve planlanan kalma süresi sonunda her bir grubun kalkış noktasına getirilmesini (Birlikte dışa seyahat eden yolcuların tümü, birlikte geri dönmek zorundadır. İlk dönüş seyahati ile en son gidiş seyahati boş olarak yapılır.)

"Kapalı-kapı servis " terimi, yolcu indirip bindirmeden, aynı yolcu grubunun aynı taşıtla, taşıtın tescil edildiği, Akit Taraf ülkesindeki bir noktadan başlayan ve bu ülkede sona eren tur taşımasını,

"Transit taşıma" terimi, kalkış ve varış noktaları bir Akit Taraf ülkesinin dışında olan noktalar arasında o Akit Taraf ülkesi üzerinden yapılan yolcu ve eşya taşımalarını,

ifade eder.

MADDE 3

Akit Taraflardan her biri, bu Anlaşma hükümlerine uymak kaydıyla, diğer Akit Taraf yolcuları, bunların kişisel eşyaları ile ticari eşya ve taşıtlarına kendi yetkili makamlarınca tesbit edilmiş güzergahlardan geçiş hakkını tanıyacaktır.

MADDE 4

Her Akit Taraf, kendi milli mevzuatına göre, diğer Akit Tarafın taşımacılarına, kendi topraklarında, karşılıklı olarak mutabık kalınan yerlerde büro açma, temsilcilik verme ve/veya acentalar atama izni verecektir.

Taşımacı diğer Akit Taraf ülkesinde seyahat acentası olarak faaliyet gösteremeyecektir.

MADDE 5

Akit Taraflar, toprakları üzerinden transit geçen diğer Akit Tarafın taşıtlarından,

a) Karayolu alt yapısının kullanılmasından alınan ücretler (paralı karayolu ve köprüler)

b) Karayolunun bakım ve korunmasını, karayolu ve taşımanın yönetimine ilişkin giderleri karşılamak için alınan ücretler,

c) Yakıtın ulusal ve uluslararası fiyatları arasındaki farkı karşılamak üzere, ayrıcalık gözetmeksizin alınacak ücretler,

d) Taşıtın ağırlığı, boyutları veya yükü Akit Tarafların milli mevzuatında belirtilen sınırları aştığı takdirde alınan ücretler,

dışındaki herhangi bir ithal veya ihraç vergisi veya resmi (gümrük vergisi dahil) almayacaklardır.

Akit Tarafların toprakları üzerinden transit taşımalar, karşılıklılık esasına göre yukarıda (b) paragrafında belirtilen ücretlerden muaf tutulabilir.

Her Akit Taraf, paragraf (b) de bahsedilen ücretleri, transit geçmeyen taşıtlardan almayacaklardır.

MADDE 6

1. Bir Akit Tarafta kayıtlı taşıtın mürettebatı veya taşımacısının, diğer Akit Tarafın topraklarında yürürlükte olan mevzuatı, bu Anlaşmanın hükümlerini veya izin belgesinde belirtilen koşulları ihlal etmesi durumunda; diğer Akit Tarafın yetkili makamının istemi üzerine, taşıtın kayıtlı olduğu ülkenin yetkili makamı, aşağıdaki önlemleri alabilir.

a) İhlali yapan taşımacıya ihtar vermek;

b) Taşımacıya ihlalin yapıldığı Akit Tarafın topraklarında taşıma yapma hakkı veren izin belgelerini iptal etmek veya geri almak.

Bu tip bir önlem uygulayan yetkili makam, diğer Akit Tarafın yetkili makamına, almış olduğu önlem hakkında bilgi verecektir.

Bu maddenin hükümleri, ihlalin yapıldığı ülkenin mahkemeleri veya idari makamları tarafından uygulanabilecek kanuni müeyyidelere mani olmayacaktır.

MADDE 7

Akit Tarafların temsilcilerinden teşkil olunan bir Karma Komisyon kurulacaktır. Karma Komisyonun görevleri şunlardır:

a) Bu Anlaşma'nın gereği veçhile uygulanmasına nezaret etmek,

b) İzin belgelerinin sayısı ve şekli ile belgelerin teati zamanı ve usullerini saptamak,

c) Bu Anlaşma'nın 24.maddesinde belirtilen yetkili makamlar arasında doğrudan çözümlenemeyecek muhtemel meseleleri incelemek ve çözümleri için tekliflerde bulunmak,

d) Bu Anlaşma kapsamına giren diğer tüm hususları gözden geçirmek ve bu hususların çözümleri ile ilgili tavsiyelerde bulunmak,

e) Taşımacılıkla ilgili olarak üzerinde mutabık kalınacak diğer hususları incelemek.

Karma Komisyon gerektiği takdirde Akit Tarafların birinin talebi üzerine sıra ile Türkiye ve Letonya da toplanacaktır.

Karma Komisyon toplantısında görüşülecek gündem yukarıda belirtilen görevler ışığında, Akit Taraflar arasında diplomatik yoldan önceden hazırlanacaktır.

Karma Komisyon işbu Anlaşmanın herhangi bir maddesinde değişiklik yapmayı önerebilir. Bu öneriler Akit Tarafların yetkili makamlarının onayına sunulur.

MADDE 8

Akit Taraflardan birinin ülkesinde tescil edilmiş taşıtlar diğer Akit Taraf topraklarındaki iki nokta arasında yolcu ve eşya taşıyamayacaktır.

Diğer Akit Taraf ülkesinin yetkili makamlarından özel izin belgesi alınmadıkça bir Akit Taraf taşımacısı diğer Akit Taraf topraklarından üçüncü ülkelere yolcu ve eşya taşıyamayacaktır.

MADDE 9

Bir Akit Taraf ülkesinde tescil edilmiş boş bir taşıt, yetkili makamlarca bu amaçla bir özel izin belgesi verilmedikçe, kendi ülkesine veya üçüncü bir ülkeye yolcu ve eşya almak üzere, diğer Akit Taraf ülkesine giremeyecektir.

YOLCU TAŞIMALARI

MADDE 10

Akit taraflardan birinin taşımacısı, diğer Akit Taraf yetkili makamından, önceden yıllık izin belgesi alarak diğer Taraf ülkesine düzenli servis veya diğer Tarafın ülkesi üzerinden düzenli transit servisi işletebilir.

MADDE 11

a) Akit Taraflardan birinin ülkesinde tescil edilmiş bir taşıtla yapılacak kapalı kapı servisi, dolu gidiş boş dönüş ve mekik servis izin belgesine tabi olmayacaktır.

b) Yolcuların mekik sefer ile taşımacılığı, için diğer Akit Tarafın yetkili makamlarınca verilecek ayrı bir izin belgesi gereklidir. Mekik sefer taşımacılığı için izin belgesi başvurusu, bu taşımacılığın başlamasından 60 gün önce diğer Akit Tarafın yetkili makamına yapılır.

EŞYA TAŞIMALARI

MADDE 12

Aşağıda belirtilen haller dışında, Akit Tarafların ülkeleri arasında ve üzerinden yapılacak transit eşya taşımaları, kotaya dayanan izin belgesine tabi olacaktır.

a) Cenaze taşımaları (özellikle bu amaçla teçhiz edilmiş taşıtlarla),
b) Tiyatro dekor ve malzemesi taşımalar,
c) Müzik, sinema, folklor ve sirk gösterileri, spor faaliyetleri ve radyo programları düzenlenmesi, televizyon ve sinema çekimleri için veya teçhizat ve hayvanların taşınması,
d) Sanat eserlerinin taşınması,
e) Kesim hayvanları dışındaki hayvanların taşınması,
f) Bozulmuş veya hasara uğramış taşıtların taşınması,
g) Posta taşımaları,
h) Hava taşıma güzergahlarının değiştirilmesi halinde hava limanlarından arızi olarak mal taşımaları,
i) Tabii afetler halinde yardım malzemesi taşımaları,
J) Sergi ve fuar malzemeleri taşımaları,
k) Toplam ağırlığı maksimum 6 ton veya yükleme kapasitesi maksimum 3,5 ton olan motorlu ticari taşıtlarla yapılan taşımalar,
ı) Ev eşyası taşımacılığı (taşınma amacıyla)
m) Karma Komisyon tarafından karşılıklı mutabakata varılacak diğer haller.

MADDE 13

İzin belgeleri yıllık olacak ve her yılın Kasım ayında bir sonraki yılın belgeleri teati edilecektir. Gerektiği hallerde, Akit tarafların ihtiyaçlarını karşılamak amacıyla ve karşılıklı mutabakat üzerine ek izin belgeleri de teati edilebilir.

Bir izin belgesi, diğer Akit Tarafın topraklarına bir gidiş-dönüş seferi ve/veya diğer Akit Tarafın topraklarından transit seferi için geçerli olacaktır.

Belge, bir taşıt ve adına düzenlenmiş taşımacı için geçerli olacak ve devredilemeyecektir.

MADDE 14

Bir Akit Tarafın ülkesinde kayıtlı bir taşıt, sadece, yükünü diğer Akit Tarafın topraklarına boşalttıktan sonra, kendi ülkesine dönüş yükü alabilir.

MADDE 15

Silah, cephane, askeri malzeme, patlayıcı maddeler ile diğer tehlikeli maddelerin iki ülke arasında veya Akit Tarafların birinin ülkesinden transit taşınması özel izne bağlıdır.

Ulusal kanun ve nizamnamelerle taşınması yasaklanmış malların Akit Tarafların topraklarında ulusal kanun ve nizamlara göre nakline, yetkili makamlardan alınacak özel izin belgesiyle müsaade edilir.

Uluslararası yasalarca taşınması yasaklanmış malların Akit Taraf ülkelerine taşınması yasaktır.

MADDE 16

Akit Taraflar, yolcu ve eşya taşımacılığına ilişkin gümrük ve diğer formalitelerin mümkün olduğu kadar kolaylaştırılması, basitleştirilmesi ve çabuklaştırılması için gerekli gördükleri bütün tedbirleri alacaklardır.

MADDE 17

İşbu Anlaşmaya göre eşyanın karayolu ile uluslararası taşınması, TIR Karnesi Teminatında Eşyanın Uluslararası Taşınması sözleşmesi gereklerine ve/veya tarafların ulusal kanun ve nizamlarına tabi olacaktır.

MADDE 18

Taşıtların standart depolarındaki akaryakıt, gümrük vergisi ile diğer vergi ve resimlerden muaf olacaktır. Standart depo, taşıtı imal eden fabrikanın taşıta koyduğu depodur.

MADDE 19

Bir taşıtın tamiri için geçici olarak ithal edilen yedek parçalar, gümrük vergisi ve resimlerden muaf tutulacaklardır.

Taşıtların arıza nedeniyle değiştirilen parçaları ile kullanılmamış parçalar ya ülke dışına çıkarılacak veya gümrük makamlarının gözetiminde imha edilecektir.

MADDE 20

a) Yolcular, bagaj ve/veya eşyanın, Akit Tarafların toprakları arasında ve/veya üzerinden transit olarak uluslararası taşınmasında kullanılan bir taşıtla taşınması sırasında, üçüncü şahıslara verilecek zararları karşılamak üzere, her bir Akit Tarafta yürürlükteki kanun ve nizamlara uygun sigorta yaptırılacaktır.

b) Yolcuların, bagaj ve/veya eşyanın taşınması sırasında uğrayacağı zararları karşılamak üzere, taşıtın tescil edildiği Akit Taraf topraklarında yürürlükteki kanun ve nizamlara uygun sigorta yaptırılacaktır.

MADDE 21

Akit Taraflar arasında taşıma ve transit faaliyetlerinden doğan ödemeler Akit Taraflarda yürürlükte bulunan, paraya ilişkin kanun, nizam ve kurallara göre Akit Taraf yetkili Bankalarınca kabul edilen serbest döviz ile yapılacaktır.

MADDE 22

Kaza, bozulma ve ülke yasalarının ihlali halinde, bu olayların ülkesi üzerinde vuku bulduğu Akit Taraf yetkili makamları bu konudaki rapor ve tahkikat sonuçlarını diğer Akit Tarafa ivedilikle ileteceklerdir.

MADDE 23

Akit Taraflardan birinde tescil edilmiş taşıtların personeli ve taşımacılar diğer Akit Taraf ülkesinde karayolu trafiğini düzenleyen kanun ve nizamlara uyacaklardır.

İşbu Anlaşma kapsamına girmeyen, taşımacılıkla ilgili diğer hususlar, Akit Trafların kanun, nizam ve kurallarına tabi olacaktır.

MADDE 24

Eğer taşıtın ağırlığı, ebad veya dingil ağırlığı, bir Akit Tarafta yürürlükte olan maksimum limitleri geçerse, ulusal kanun ve mevzuatları uygulanır.

MADDE 25

İşbu Anlaşma'nın uygulanmasından sorumlu yetkili makamlar :

a) Türkiye Cumhuriyetinde;
Ulaştırma Bakanlığı
Kara Ulaştırması Genel Müdürlüğü
ANKARA

b) Letonya Cumhuriyetinde ;
Road Department
Ministry of Transport
of the Republic of Latvia

MADDE 26

Bu Anlaşma, imza tarihinden itibaren geçici olarak uygulanır ve Akit Tarafların milli mevzuatına göre onay işlemlerinin tamamlandığını belirten notaların teati edildiği tarihte yürürlüğe girecek ve bir yıl süre ile yürürlükte kalacaktır.

Bu süre sona ermeden üç ay önce Akit Taraflardan biri Anlaşma'yı sona erdirmek istediğini diğer Akit Taraf'a yazılı olarak bildirmedikçe, Anlaşma kendiliğinden birer yıllık süreler için yenilenecektir.

15.9.1995 tarihinde Ankara'da iki orijinal nüsha halinde Türkçe, Letonyaca ve İngilizce dillerinde bütün nüshalar aynı derecede geçerli olarak düzenlenmiştir. Herhangi bir anlaşmazlık durumunda İngilizce metin geçerlidir.

Letonya Cumhuriyeti Hükümeti
Adına

Dr. Andris GUTMANIS
Ulaştırma Bakanı

Türkiye Cumhuriyeti Hükümeti
Adına

Ali Şevki EREK
Ulaştırma Bakanı

[TRANSLATION IN FRENCH – TRADUCTION EN FRANÇAIS]

ACCORD SUR LE TRANSPORT ROUTIER INTERNATIONAL ENTRE LE GOUVERNEMENT DE LA RÉPUBLIQUE DE LETTONIE ET LE GOUVERNEMENT DE LA RÉPUBLIQUE TURQUE

Le Gouvernement de la République de Lettonie et le Gouvernement de la République turque, ci-après dénommés « Parties contractantes »,

Désireux de faciliter le transport routier de passagers et de marchandises entre les deux pays, ainsi qu'en transit à travers leurs territoires,

Sont convenus de ce qui suit :

Article premier

Les dispositions du présent Accord s'appliquent au transport international par route de passagers et de marchandises en provenance ou à destination du territoire d'une Partie contractante et en transit à travers le territoire de l'autre Partie contractante, en utilisant des véhicules immatriculés dans le territoire respectif des Parties contractantes.

Article 2

Aux fins du présent Accord :

Le terme « transporteur » désigne toute personne physique ou morale autorisée à effectuer des transports internationaux de passagers et de marchandises conformément aux lois, règlements et règles des Parties contractantes ;

Le terme « véhicule » désigne :

a) Tout véhicule routier à moteur conçu soit pour le transport de passagers (plus de huit personnes, exception faite du chauffeur) ou de marchandises, soit pour le remorquage de tels véhicules ; ou

b) Un ensemble composé d'un véhicule tel que défini à l'alinéa a) du présent article et d'une remorque ou d'une semi-remorque qui lui est attelée, conçu pour le transport de passagers ou de marchandises ;

Le terme « autorisation » désigne toute autorisation délivrée pour un véhicule routier immatriculé sur le territoire de l'une des Parties contractantes par les autorités compétentes de l'autre Partie contractante, afin de permettre au véhicule d'entrer sur le territoire de cette dernière, d'en sortir ou de s'y déplacer, ainsi que toute autre autorisation mentionnée dans le présent Accord ;

Le terme « quota » désigne le nombre d'autorisations délivrées annuellement par les autorités compétentes de chaque Partie contractante ;

L'expression « service régulier par autobus » désigne le transport de passagers entre les territoires des deux Parties contractantes le long d'un itinéraire défini, conformément aux horaires et aux tarifs établis à l'échelle nationale ;

L'expression « service régulier de transit par autobus » désigne tout service régulier par autobus qui commence sur le territoire de l'une des Parties contractantes et se termine sur le territoire d'un pays tiers, en traversant le territoire de l'autre Partie contractante, sans y embarquer, ni y débarquer de passagers ;

L'expression « service de navette » désigne le transport international organisé de passagers groupés préalablement selon la durée de leur séjour, d'un seul et même point de départ à destination d'un seul et même point d'arrivée, et le retour de ces voyageurs à leur point de départ à la fin d'une période prédéterminée (les passagers se déplaçant avec un groupe retournent ensemble à leur point de départ, et le premier voyage retour et le dernier voyage aller se font à vide) ;

L'expression « circuit à portes fermées » désigne le transport international d'un seul et même groupe de passagers à bord d'un seul et même véhicule pour un voyage débutant à un point situé sur le territoire de l'une des Parties contractantes et se terminant sur le territoire de la même Partie contractante, sans embarquer ni débarquer de passagers ;

L'expression « transport en transit » désigne le transport international de passagers ou de marchandises à travers le territoire de l'une des Parties contractantes, entre un point de départ et un point d'arrivée situés en dehors du territoire de ladite Partie contractante.

Article 3

Chaque Partie contractante, conformément aux dispositions du présent Accord, reconnaît le droit de transit si les transporteurs de l'autre Partie contractante effectuent le transport routier de passagers, de leurs effets personnels, de marchandises commerciales ou de véhicules le long d'itinéraires qui seront fixés par les autorités compétentes de chaque Partie contractante.

Article 4

Sous réserve de sa législation interne, chaque Partie contractante accorde aux transporteurs de l'autre Partie contractante l'autorisation d'ouvrir des bureaux et/ou de désigner des représentants et/ou de créer des agences sur son propre territoire en des lieux convenus d'un commun accord par les autorités compétentes des Parties contractantes.

Le transporteur ne fait pas office d'agence de voyage sur le territoire de l'autre Partie contractante.

Article 5

Les Parties contractantes ne prélèvent aucune taxe à l'importation ou à l'exportation, ni aucune redevance (y compris les taxes douanières) sur les véhicules de l'autre Partie contractante qui sont en transit sur son territoire, à l'exception :

a) Des redevances d'utilisation des infrastructures du réseau routier (péages des routes et des ponts) ;

b) Des redevances perçues aux fins de l'entretien, de la protection et de l'administration des routes et des transports ;

c) Des redevances perçues, sur une base non discriminatoire, pour couvrir la différence entre le prix national et le prix international du carburant, en ce qui concerne le carburant acheté sur le territoire de l'autre Partie contractante ;

d) Des redevances applicables si le poids, les dimensions ou la charge du véhicule dépassent les limites autorisées par la législation de la Partie contractante.

Le transport en transit autorisé à travers les territoires des Parties contractantes peut être exonéré, sur une base de réciprocité, des redevances visées à l'alinéa b) du présent article.

Aucune des Parties contractantes ne perçoit les redevances visées à l'alinéa b) pour les véhicules qui ne sont pas en transit.

Article 6

Dans le cas où le transporteur ou le personnel à bord d'un véhicule immatriculé dans l'une des Parties contractantes enfreint la législation en vigueur sur le territoire de l'autre Partie contractante, les dispositions du présent Accord ou les conditions énoncées dans l'autorisation, l'autorité compétente du pays d'immatriculation du véhicule peut, à la demande de l'autorité compétente de l'autre Partie contractante, prendre les mesures énoncées ci-après :

a) Adresser un avertissement au transporteur ayant commis une infraction ;

b) Annuler ou retirer les autorisations donnant le droit au transporteur d'effectuer des transports sur le territoire de la Partie contractante où l'infraction a été commise.

Lorsqu'elle prend une telle mesure, l'autorité compétente en informe l'autorité compétente de l'autre Partie contractante.

Les dispositions du présent article ne sauraient exclure l'imposition de sanctions légales, telles qu'elles peuvent être appliquées par les tribunaux ou les autorités administratives du pays dans lequel l'infraction a été commise.

Article 7

Le Comité mixte, composé de représentants des deux autorités compétentes des Parties contractantes, est créé. Il a notamment pour objectifs :

a) De superviser la mise en œuvre du présent Accord ;

b) De déterminer la forme, le calendrier et les modalités d'échange des autorisations ;

c) D'examiner les éventuels différends non réglés directement entre les autorités compétentes au moyen de la procédure visée à l'article 24 du présent Accord, ainsi que de formuler des propositions aux fins de leur règlement ;

d) D'examiner toutes les autres questions pertinentes qui relèvent du champ d'application du présent Accord et de formuler des recommandations aux fins de leur règlement ;

e) D'examiner toute autre question relative au transport devant être réglée d'un commun accord par les Parties.

Le Comité mixte se réunit selon que de besoin, à la demande des autorités compétentes de l'une des Parties contractantes, alternativement en République de Lettonie et en République turque.

L'ordre du jour de la réunion du Comité mixte est établi au préalable, compte tenu des objectifs mentionnés ci-dessus, par les autorités compétentes des Parties contractantes et fait l'objet d'un accord par voie diplomatique.

Le Comité mixte peut recommander d'amender tout article du présent Accord et le soumettre aux autorités compétentes pour approbation.

Article 8

Les véhicules immatriculés sur le territoire d'une Partie contractante ne peuvent pas transporter de passagers ou de marchandises entre deux points situés sur le territoire de l'autre Partie contractante.

Sauf autorisation spéciale délivrée par l'autorité compétente de l'autre Partie contractante, un transporteur d'une Partie contractante ne peut pas transporter de passagers ou de marchandises depuis le territoire de l'autre Partie contractante à destination d'un pays tiers.

Article 9

Un véhicule non chargé, immatriculé dans une Partie contractante, ne peut pas entrer sur le territoire de l'autre Partie contractante afin d'embarquer des voyageurs ou des marchandises à destination du territoire de l'autre Partie contractante ou d'un pays tiers, à moins qu'une autorisation spéciale ne soit délivrée à cette fin par l'autorité compétente de l'autre Partie contractante.

TRANSPORT DE VOYAGEURS

Article 10

Un transporteur d'une Partie contractante exploite un service régulier de transport de passagers à destination du territoire de l'autre Partie contractante ou un service régulier de transport de passagers en transit à travers le territoire de l'autre Partie contractante et pour ce faire, il obtient au préalable une autorisation annuelle auprès de l'autorité compétente de l'autre Partie contractante.

Article 11

a) Les circuits à portes fermées, ainsi que les voyages aller et retour à vide effectués par un véhicule immatriculé sur le territoire d'une Partie contractante à destination ou en provenance du territoire de l'autre Partie contractante ne nécessitent pas d'autorisation.

b) Le transport de passagers en navettes nécessite une autorisation distincte, laquelle est délivrée par l'autorité compétente de l'autre Partie contractante.

La demande d'obtention d'une telle autorisation est soumise à l'autorité compétente de l'autre Partie contractante 30 jours avant la mise en service de ce type de transport.

TRANSPORT DE MARCHANDISES

Article 12

Le transport de marchandises entre les territoires des Parties contractantes et en transit à travers les territoires des Parties contractantes est soumis à l'obtention d'une autorisation préalable et à un quota, sauf dans les cas suivants :

a) Transport de défunts (notamment au moyen de véhicules conçus à cette fin) ;

b) Transport d'éléments décoratifs destinés à des représentations théâtrales ;

c) Transport de biens, matériels et animaux destinés à des représentations musicales et cinématographiques, à des cirques et représentations folkloriques, à des activités sportives et à l'enregistrement de programmes télévisés et radiophoniques ;

d) Transport d'œuvres d'art ;

e) Transport d'animaux non destinés à l'abattage ;

f) Transport de véhicules endommagés ou en panne ;

g) Transports postaux ;

h) Transport occasionnel de marchandises à destination ou au départ d'un aéroport, en raison d'une modification de l'itinéraire de vol ;

i) Transport de matériel de secours en cas de situations d'urgence ou de catastrophes naturelles ;

j) Transport de matériel destiné à des foires ou à des expositions ;

k) Services de transport effectués par des véhicules à moteur d'un poids total maximal de 6 tonnes, remorque comprise, ou d'une capacité de chargement maximale de 3,5 tonnes, remorque comprise ;

l) Enlèvement des articles ménagers ;

m) Autres cas faisant l'objet d'un accord au sein du Comité mixte.

Article 13

Les autorisations sont valables pour un an et les autorisations pour l'année suivante sont échangées en novembre de chaque année. Des autorisations supplémentaires sont échangées lorsqu'il y a lieu, pour répondre aux exigences des autorités compétentes des Parties contractantes sur la base d'un commun accord.

L'autorisation est valable pour un voyage aller et retour à destination du territoire de l'autre Partie contractante et/ou pour un transport en transit à travers le territoire de l'autre Partie contractante.

Elle est valable pour un seul véhicule et uniquement pour le transporteur auquel elle est délivrée et ne peut être transférée.

Article 14

Un véhicule immatriculé sur le territoire d'une Partie contractante peut charger une cargaison pour son voyage retour uniquement après avoir livré les marchandises sur le territoire de l'autre Partie contractante.

Article 15

Le transport d'armes, de munitions, d'équipement militaire et d'explosifs entre les deux Parties contractantes ou en transit à travers le territoire de l'une ou l'autre Partie contractante fait l'objet d'une autorisation spéciale devant être obtenue à cet effet.

Le transport de marchandises interdites par les lois et règlements nationaux est autorisé sur les territoires des Parties contractantes conformément à leurs lois et règlements nationaux et fait l'objet d'autorisations spéciales délivrées par les autorités compétentes.

Il n'est pas autorisé de transporter vers les territoires des Parties contractantes des marchandises dont le transport est interdit par le droit international.

Article 16

Les Parties contractantes prennent toutes les mesures qu'elles jugent nécessaires pour faciliter, simplifier et accélérer, dans la mesure du possible, les formalités de douane et autres formalités relatives au transport de passagers et de marchandises.

Article 17

Le transport routier international de marchandises, conformément aux dispositions du présent Accord, est soumis aux dispositions de la Convention douanière relative au transport international de marchandises sous le couvert de carnets TIR et/ou aux lois et règlements nationaux.

Article 18

Le carburant contenu dans le réservoir d'origine des véhicules est exonéré des droits de douane et autres taxes et redevances. Le réservoir d'origine s'entend du réservoir fourni par le constructeur du véhicule et connecté, par des moyens technologiques, au système d'alimentation du véhicule.

Article 19

Les pièces de rechange importées sur le territoire de l'autre Partie contractante en vue de réparer un véhicule déjà importé temporairement seront exonérées de droits de douane et autres redevances.

Toute pièce n'ayant pas été utilisée ou toute pièce ayant été remplacée est soit réexportée, soit détruite sous le contrôle des autorités douanières.

Article 20

a) Tout véhicule utilisé pour le transport international de passagers, de bagages et/ou de marchandises entre les territoires des Parties contractantes ou en transit à travers les territoires des Parties contractantes est couvert par une assurance responsabilité civile conforme aux lois et règlements en vigueur dans chacune des Parties contractantes.

b) Les passagers, leurs bagages et/ou les marchandises sont couverts contre les dommages susceptibles de survenir durant le transport, moyennant une assurance conforme aux lois et règlements en vigueur dans la Partie contractante dans laquelle le véhicule est immatriculé.

Article 21

Les paiements entre les Parties contractantes concernant les opérations de transport et de transit s'effectuent dans une devise convertible acceptée par les banques agréées des Parties contractantes, conformément aux lois, règlements et règles monétaires en vigueur dans les Parties contractantes.

Article 22

En cas d'accidents de la circulation, de pannes ou d'infractions aux lois et règlements, les autorités compétentes de la Partie contractante sur le territoire de laquelle un tel incident se produit fournissent immédiatement aux autorités compétentes de l'autre Partie contractante les rapports et autres renseignements pertinents, ainsi que les conclusions de l'enquête.

Article 23

Les transporteurs et l'équipage des véhicules immatriculés dans une Partie contractante sont tenus de se conformer aux lois et règlements régissant la circulation routière de l'autre Partie contractante.

Toute autre question en matière de transport qui n'est pas couverte par le présent Accord est soumise aux lois, règlements et règles des Parties contractantes.

Article 24

Si le poids, les dimensions ou la charge par essieu du véhicule dépassent les limites maximales autorisées sur le territoire d'une Partie contractante, les lois et règlements nationaux s'appliquent.

Article 25

Les autorités compétentes chargées de la mise en œuvre du présent Accord sont les suivantes :

a) En République de Lettonie :
Département du réseau routier
du Ministère des transports
de la République de Lettonie

b) En République turque :
Direction générale du transport routier
du Ministère des transports
(Ulastirma Bakanliği
Kara Ulastirmasi Genel Müdürlüğü)
Ankara

Article 26

Le présent Accord sera appliqué à titre provisoire à compter du jour de sa signature et entrera en vigueur à compter de la date à laquelle les Parties contractantes s'informent, par un échange de notes, qu'elles ont ratifié l'Accord conformément à leur législation interne, et il reste en vigueur pendant une période d'un an.

Le présent Accord est automatiquement renouvelé pour des périodes d'un an, sauf si l'une des Parties contractantes exprime par écrit à l'autre Partie contractante son souhait de le dénoncer au moins trois mois avant la date d'expiration.

FAIT à Ankara, le 15 septembre 1995, en deux exemplaires originaux, chacun en langues lettone, turque et anglaise, tous les textes faisant également foi et ayant la même force juridique.

En cas de divergence d'interprétation, le texte anglais prévaut.

Pour le Gouvernement de la République de Lettonie :

[ANDRIS GŪTMANIS]

Pour le Gouvernement de la République turque :

[ALI SEVKI EREK]

No. 54183

New Zealand and Samoa

Agreement between the Government of New Zealand and the Government of Samoa for the elimination of double taxation with respect to taxes on income and the prevention of tax evasion and avoidance. Apia, 8 July 2015

Entry into force: *23 December 2015 by notification, in accordance with article 26*

Authentic text: *English*

Registration with the Secretariat of the United Nations: *New Zealand, 25 January 2017*

Nouvelle-Zélande et Samoa

Accord entre le Gouvernement de la Nouvelle-Zélande et le Gouvernement du Samoa portant sur l'élimination des doubles impositions en matière d'impôts sur le revenu et sur la prévention de la fraude et de l'évasion fiscales. Apia, 8 juillet 2015

Entrée en vigueur : *23 décembre 2015 par notification, conformément à l'article 26*

Texte authentique : *anglais*

Enregistrement au Secrétariat de l'Organisation des Nations Unies : *Nouvelle-Zélande, 25 janvier 2017*

[TEXT IN ENGLISH – TEXTE EN ANGLAIS]

Agreement
between
the Government of New Zealand
and
the Government of Samoa
for the Elimination of Double Taxation with Respect to Taxes on Income and the Prevention of Tax Evasion and Avoidance

The Government of New Zealand and the Government of Samoa,

Desiring to further develop their economic relationship and to enhance their cooperation in tax matters,

Intending to conclude an Agreement for the elimination of double taxation with respect to taxes on income without creating opportunities for non-taxation or reduced taxation through tax evasion or avoidance (including through treaty-shopping arrangements aimed at obtaining reliefs provided in this Agreement for the indirect benefit of residents of third States)

Have agreed as follows:

CHAPTER I
SCOPE OF THE AGREEMENT

Article 1
Persons Covered

This Agreement shall apply to persons who are residents of one or both of the Contracting States.

Article 2
Taxes Covered

1. The taxes to which the Agreement shall apply are:
   (a) In New Zealand:
   the income tax (hereinafter referred to as "New Zealand tax");
   (b) In Samoa:
   the income tax (hereinafter referred to as "Samoa tax").

2. The Agreement shall apply also to any identical or substantially similar taxes that are imposed after the date of signature of the Agreement in addition to, or in place of, the taxes listed in paragraph 1. The competent authorities of the Contracting States shall notify each other of any significant changes that have been made in their taxation laws.

3. Notwithstanding the provisions of paragraphs 1 and 2, the taxes covered by the Agreement do not include any amount which represents a penalty or interest imposed under the laws of either Contracting State.

CHAPTER II
DEFINITIONS

Article 3
General Definitions

1. For the purposes of this Agreement, unless the context otherwise requires:

(a) the term "person" includes an individual, a company and any other body of persons;

(b) the term "company" means any body corporate or any entity that is treated as a body corporate for tax purposes;

(c) the term "enterprise" applies to the carrying on of any business;

(d) the terms "enterprise of a Contracting State" and "enterprise of the other Contracting State" mean respectively an enterprise carried on by a resident of a Contracting State and an enterprise carried on by a resident of the other Contracting State;

(e) the term "international traffic" means any transport by a ship or aircraft operated by an enterprise of a Contracting State, except when the ship or aircraft is operated solely between places in the other Contracting State;

(f) the term "competent authority" means:

(i) in the case of New Zealand, the Commissioner of Inland Revenue or an authorised representative; and

(ii) in the case of Samoa, the CEO of the Ministry for Revenue or an authorised representative;

(g) the term "national", in relation to a Contracting State, means:

(i) any individual possessing the nationality or citizenship of that Contracting State; and

(ii) any legal person, partnership or association deriving its status as such from the laws in force in that Contracting State;

(h) the term "business" includes the performance of professional services and of other activities of an independent character;

(i) the terms "a Contracting State" and "the other Contracting State" mean New Zealand or Samoa as the context requires; and

(j) (i) the term "New Zealand" means the territory of New Zealand but does not include Tokelau; it also includes any area beyond the territorial sea designated under New Zealand legislation and in accordance with international law as an area in which New Zealand may exercise sovereign rights with respect to natural resources; and

(ii) the term "Samoa" means the Independent State of Samoa and its territorial waters.

2. For the purposes of Articles 10, 11 and 12, dividends, interest or royalties arising in a Contracting State and derived by or through a trust shall be deemed to be beneficially owned by a resident of the other Contracting State where:

(a) such income is subject to tax in that other State in the hands of the trustee of that trust;

(b) with reference to dividends, the income would be subject to tax in the hands of the trustee of that trust but for an exemption that applies to those dividends under the laws of that other State.

3. As regards the application of the Agreement at any time by a Contracting State, any term not defined therein shall, unless the context otherwise requires, have the meaning that it has at that time under the law of that State for the purposes of the taxes to which the Agreement applies, any meaning under the applicable tax laws of that State prevailing over a meaning given to the term under other laws of that State.

Article 4
Resident

1. For the purposes of this Agreement, the term "resident of a Contracting State" means any person who, under the laws of that State, is liable to tax therein by reason of their domicile, residence, place of management or any other criterion of a similar nature, and also includes that State and any political subdivision or local authority thereof. This term, however, does not include any person who is liable to tax in that State in respect only of income from sources in that State.

2. Where by reason of the provisions of paragraph 1 an individual is a resident of both Contracting States, then their status shall be determined as follows:

(a) the individual shall be deemed to be a resident only of the State in which a permanent home is available to the individual; if a permanent home is available to the individual in both States, the individual shall be deemed to be a resident only of the State with which the individual's personal and economic relations are closer (centre of vital interests);

(b) if the State in which the individual has their centre of vital interests cannot be determined, or if a permanent home is not available to the individual in either State, the individual shall be deemed to be a resident only of the State in which the individual has an habitual abode;

(c) if the individual has an habitual abode in both States or in neither of them, the individual shall be deemed to be a resident only of the State of which the individual is a national;

(d) if the individual is a national of both States or of neither of them, the competent authorities of the Contracting States shall settle the question by mutual agreement.

3. Where by reason of the provisions of paragraph 1 a person other than an individual is a resident of both Contracting States, the competent

authorities of the Contracting States shall endeavour to determine by mutual agreement the Contracting State of which such person shall be deemed to be a resident for the purposes of the Agreement, having regard to its place of effective management, the place where it is incorporated or otherwise constituted and any other relevant factors. In the absence of such agreement, such person shall not be entitled to any relief or exemption from tax provided by this Agreement except to the extent and in such manner as may be agreed upon by the competent authorities of the Contracting States.

Article 5
Permanent Establishment

1. For the purposes of this Agreement, the term "permanent establishment" means a fixed place of business through which the business of an enterprise is wholly or partly carried on.

2. The term "permanent establishment" includes especially:
   (a) a place of management;
   (b) a branch;
   (c) an office;
   (d) a factory;
   (e) a workshop, and
   (f) a mine, an oil or gas well, a quarry or any other place of extraction of natural resources.

3. A building site, or a construction, installation or assembly project, or supervisory activities in connection with that building site or construction, installation or assembly project, constitutes a permanent establishment if it lasts more than 6 months.

4. An enterprise shall be deemed to have a permanent establishment in a Contracting State and to carry on business through that permanent establishment if for more than 183 days in any twelve month period:

(a) it carries on activities in that State which consist of, or which are connected with, the exploration for or exploitation of natural resources, including standing timber, situated in that State; or

(b) it operates substantial equipment in that State.

5. Notwithstanding the provisions of paragraphs 1, 2 and 3, where an enterprise of a Contracting State performs services in the other Contracting State:

(a) through an individual who is present in that other State for a period or periods exceeding in the aggregate 183 days in any twelve month period, and where the services performed in that other State through that individual are professional services or other activities of an independent nature, or

(b) for a period or periods exceeding in the aggregate 183 days in any twelve month period, and these services are performed for the same project or for connected projects through one or more individuals who are present and performing such services in that other State

the activities carried on in that other State in performing these services shall be deemed to be carried on through a permanent establishment of the enterprise situated in that other State, unless these services are limited to those mentioned in paragraph 7 which, if performed through a fixed place of business, would not make the fixed place of business a permanent establishment under the provisions of that paragraph. For the purposes of this paragraph, services performed by an individual on behalf of one enterprise shall not be considered to be performed by another enterprise through that individual unless that other enterprise supervises, directs or controls the manner in which these services are performed by the individual.

6. For the purposes of determining the duration of activities under paragraphs 3, 4 and 5, the period during which activities are carried on in a Contracting State by an enterprise associated with another enterprise shall be aggregated with the period during which activities are carried on by the enterprise with which it is associated if the first-mentioned activities are connected with and are identical or substantially similar to the activities carried on in that State by the last-mentioned enterprise, provided that any period during which two or more associated enterprises are carrying on concurrent activities is counted only once. An enterprise shall be deemed to be associated with another enterprise if one is controlled directly or indirectly by the other, or if both are controlled directly or indirectly by a third person or persons.

7. Notwithstanding the preceding provisions of this Article, the term "permanent establishment" shall be deemed not to include:

(a) the use of facilities solely for the purpose of storage, display or delivery of goods or merchandise belonging to the enterprise;

(b) the maintenance of a stock of goods or merchandise belonging to the enterprise solely for the purpose of storage, display or delivery;

(c) the maintenance of a stock of goods or merchandise belonging to the enterprise solely for the purpose of processing by another enterprise;

(d) the maintenance of a fixed place of business solely for the purpose of purchasing goods or merchandise or of collecting information, for the enterprise;

(e) the maintenance of a fixed place of business solely for the purpose of carrying on, for the enterprise, any other activity of a preparatory or auxiliary character;

(f) the maintenance of a fixed place of business solely for any combination of activities mentioned in subparagraphs (a) to (e), provided that the overall activity of the fixed place of business resulting from this combination is of a preparatory or auxiliary character.

8. Notwithstanding the provisions of paragraphs 1 and 2, where a person – other than an agent of an independent status to whom paragraph 9 applies – is acting on behalf of an enterprise and:

(a) has, and habitually exercises, in a Contracting State an authority to conclude contracts on behalf of the enterprise; or

(b) manufactures or processes in a Contracting State for the enterprise goods or merchandise belonging to the enterprise,

that enterprise shall be deemed to have a permanent establishment in that State in respect of any activities which that person undertakes for the enterprise, unless the activities of such person are limited to those mentioned in paragraph 7 which, if exercised through a fixed place of business, would not make this fixed place of business a permanent establishment under the provisions of that paragraph.

9. An enterprise shall not be deemed to have a permanent establishment in a Contracting State merely because it carries on business in that State through a broker, general commission agent or any other agent of an independent status, provided that such persons are acting in the ordinary course of their business.

10. The fact that a company which is a resident of a Contracting State controls or is controlled by a company which is a resident of the other Contracting State, or which carries on business in that other State (whether through a permanent establishment or otherwise), shall not of itself constitute either company a permanent establishment of the other.

CHAPTER III
TAXATION OF INCOME

Article 6
Income from Immovable Property

1. Income derived by a resident of a Contracting State from immovable property (including income from agriculture, forestry or fishing) situated in the other Contracting State may be taxed in that other State.

2. The term "immovable property" shall have the meaning which it has under the law of the Contracting State in which the property in question is situated. The term shall in any case include any natural resources, property accessory to immovable property, livestock and equipment used in agriculture and forestry, rights to which the provisions of general law respecting immovable property apply, usufruct of immovable property, rights to explore for or exploit natural resources or standing timber, and rights to variable or fixed payments either as consideration for or in respect of the exploitation of, or the right to explore for or exploit natural resources or standing timber; ships, boats and aircraft shall not be regarded as immovable property.

3. The provisions of paragraph 1 shall apply to income derived from the direct use, letting, or use in any other form of immovable property.

4. The provisions of paragraphs 1 and 3 shall also apply to the income from immovable property of an enterprise.

5. Any right referred to in paragraph 2 of this Article shall be regarded as situated where the property to which it relates is situated or where the exploration or exploitation may take place.

Article 7

Business Profits

1. The profits of an enterprise of a Contracting State shall be taxable only in that State unless the enterprise carries on business in the other Contracting State through a permanent establishment situated therein. If the enterprise carries on business as aforesaid, the profits of the enterprise may be taxed in the other State but only so much of them as is attributable to that permanent establishment, or sales in that other Contracting State of goods or merchandise of the same or similar kind as those sold through that permanent establishment. It is understood that the profits of an enterprise shall include profits attributable to sales of goods and merchandise referred to in this subparagraph only when the competent authority of the Contracting State in which a permanent establishment of the enterprise is situated considers that the enterprise has entered into an arrangement in relation to the sales of those goods or merchandise to avoid taxation of those profits in that Contracting State.

2. Subject to the provisions of paragraph 3, where an enterprise of a Contracting State carries on business in the other Contracting State through a permanent establishment situated therein, there shall in each Contracting State be attributed to that permanent establishment the profits which it might be expected to make if it were a distinct and separate enterprise engaged in the same or similar activities under the same or similar conditions and dealing wholly independently with the enterprise of which it is a permanent establishment.

3. In determining the profits of a permanent establishment, there shall be allowed as deductions expenses which are incurred for the purposes of the permanent establishment, including executive and general administrative expenses so incurred, whether in the State in which the permanent establishment is situated or elsewhere.

4. For the purposes of the preceding paragraphs, the profits to be attributed to the permanent establishment shall be determined by the same method year by year unless there is good and sufficient reason to the contrary.

5. Where:

(a) a resident of a Contracting State beneficially owns (whether as a direct beneficiary of a trust or through one or more interposed trusts) a share of the profits of a business of an enterprise carried on in the other Contracting State by the trustee of a trust other than a trust which is treated as a company for tax purposes; and

(b) in relation to that enterprise, that trustee has or would have, if it were a resident of the first-mentioned State, a permanent establishment in the other State,

then the business of the enterprise carried on by the trustee through such permanent establishment shall be deemed to be a business carried on in the other State by that resident through a permanent establishment situated in that other State and the resident's share of profits may be taxed in the other State but only so much of them as is attributable to that permanent establishment.

6. Where profits include items of income which are dealt with separately in other Articles of this Agreement, then the provisions of those Articles shall not be affected by the provisions of this Article.

7. Nothing in this Article shall affect any provisions of the laws of either Contracting State at any time in force as they affect the taxation of any income from any form of insurance.

Article 8

Ship and Air Transport

1. Profits of an enterprise of a Contracting State from the operation of ships or aircraft in international traffic shall be taxable only in that State.

2. Notwithstanding the provisions of paragraph 1 and Article 7, profits of an enterprise of a Contracting State derived from carriage by ship or aircraft of passengers, livestock, mail, goods or merchandise which are shipped or embarked in the other Contracting State and are discharged at a place in that other State, or for leasing on a full basis of a ship or aircraft for purposes of such carriage, may be taxed in that other State.

3. The provisions of paragraphs 1 and 2 shall also apply to profits from the participation in a pool, a joint business or an international operating agency.

Article 9

Associated Enterprises

1. Where

(a) an enterprise of a Contracting State participates directly or indirectly in the management, control or capital of an enterprise of the other Contracting State, or

(b) the same persons participate directly or indirectly in the management, control or capital of an enterprise of a Contracting State and an enterprise of the other Contracting State,

and in either case conditions are made or imposed between the two enterprises in their commercial or financial relations which differ from those which would be made between independent enterprises, then any profits which would, but for those conditions, have accrued to one of the enterprises, but, by reason of those conditions, have not so accrued, may be included in the profits of that enterprise and taxed accordingly.

2. Where a Contracting State includes in the profits of an enterprise of that State - and taxes accordingly - profits on which an enterprise of the other Contracting State has been charged to tax in that other State and the profits so included are profits which would have accrued to the enterprise of the first-mentioned State if the conditions made between the two enterprises had been those which would have been made between independent enterprises, then that other State shall make an appropriate adjustment to the amount of the tax charged therein on those profits. In determining such adjustment, due regard shall be had to the other provisions of this Agreement and the competent authorities of the Contracting States shall if necessary consult each other.

Article 10

Dividends

1. Dividends paid by a company which is a resident of a Contracting State to a resident of the other Contracting State may be taxed in that other State.

2. However, such dividends may also be taxed in the Contracting State of which the company paying the dividends is a resident and according to the laws of that State, but if the beneficial owner of the dividends is a resident of the other Contracting State, the tax so charged shall not exceed:

(a) 5 per cent of the gross amount of the dividends if the beneficial owner is a company which holds directly at least 10 per cent of the voting power in the company paying the dividends; and

(b) 15 per cent of the gross amount of the dividends in all other cases.

This paragraph shall not affect the taxation of the company in respect of the profits out of which the dividends are paid.

3. The term "dividends" as used in this Article means income from shares and other income treated as income from shares by the laws of the State of which the company making the distribution is a resident.

4. The provisions of paragraphs 1 and 2 shall not apply if the beneficial owner of the dividends, being a resident of a Contracting State, carries on business in the other Contracting State of which the company paying the dividends is a resident through a permanent establishment situated therein and the holding in respect of which the dividends are paid is effectively connected with such permanent establishment. In such case the provisions of Article 7 shall apply.

5. Where a company which is a resident of a Contracting State derives profits or income from the other Contracting State, that other State may not impose any tax on the dividends paid by the company, except insofar as such dividends are paid to a resident of that other State or insofar as the holding in respect of which the dividends are paid is effectively connected with a permanent establishment situated in that other State, nor subject the company's undistributed profits to a tax on the company's undistributed profits, even if the dividends paid or the undistributed profits consist wholly or partly of profits or income arising in such other State.

Article 11
Interest

1. Interest arising in a Contracting State and paid to a resident of the other Contracting State may be taxed in that other State.

2. However, such interest may also be taxed in the Contracting State in which it arises and according to the laws of that State, but if the beneficial owner of the interest is a resident of the other Contracting State, the tax so charged shall not exceed 10 per cent of the gross amount of the interest.

3. The term "interest" as used in this Article means income from debt-claims of every kind, whether or not secured by mortgage and whether or not carrying a right to participate in the debtor's profits, and in particular, income from government securities and income from bonds or debentures, including premiums and prizes attaching to such securities, bonds or debentures, as well as all other income treated as income from money lent by the laws, relating to tax, of the Contracting State in which the income arises, but does not include any income which is treated as a dividend under Article 10.

4. The provisions of paragraphs 1 and 2 shall not apply if the beneficial owner of the interest, being a resident of a Contracting State, carries on business in the other Contracting State in which the interest arises through a permanent establishment situated therein and the debt-claim in respect of which the interest is paid is effectively connected with such permanent establishment. In such case the provisions of Article 7 shall apply.

5. Interest shall be deemed to arise in a Contracting State when the payer is a resident of that State. Where, however, the person paying the interest, whether the person is a resident of a Contracting State or not, has in a Contracting State a permanent establishment in connection with which the indebtedness on which the interest is paid was incurred, and such interest is deductible in determining the profits attributable to such permanent establishment, then such interest shall be deemed to arise in the State in which the permanent establishment is situated.

6. Where, by reason of a special relationship between the payer and the beneficial owner or between both of them and some other person, the amount of the interest, having regard to the debt-claim for which it is paid, exceeds the amount which would have been agreed upon by the payer and the beneficial owner in the absence of such relationship, the provisions of this Article shall apply only to the last-mentioned amount. In such case, the excess part of the payments shall remain taxable according to the laws of each Contracting State, due regard being had to the other provisions of this Agreement.

Article 12
Royalties

1. Royalties arising in a Contracting State and paid to a resident of the other Contracting State may be taxed in that other State.

2. However, such royalties may also be taxed in the Contracting State in which they arise, and according to the laws of that State, but if the beneficial owner of the royalties is a resident of the other Contracting State, the tax so charged shall not exceed 10 per cent of the gross amount of the royalties.

3. The term "royalties" as used in this Article means payments of any kind received as a consideration for:

(a) the use of, or the right to use, any copyright, patent, design or model, plan, secret formula or process, trademark or other like property or right;

(b) the use of, or the right to use:

(i) motion picture films,

(ii) films or audio or video tapes or disks, or any other means of image or sound reproduction or transmission for use in connection with television, radio, internet or other broadcasting;

(c) the use of, or the right to use any industrial, scientific or commercial equipment;

(d) knowledge or information concerning technical, industrial, commercial or scientific experience;

(e) any assistance that is ancillary and subsidiary to, and is furnished as a means of enabling the application or enjoyment of, any such property or right as is mentioned in subparagraph (a) or (b), any such equipment as is mentioned in subparagraph (c) or any such knowledge or information as is mentioned in subparagraph (d);

(f) any forbearance in respect of the use or supply of any property or right referred to in this paragraph.

4. The provisions of paragraphs 1 and 2 shall not apply if the beneficial owner of the royalties, being a resident of a Contracting State, carries on business in the other Contracting State in which the royalties arise through a permanent establishment situated therein and the right or property in respect of which the royalties are paid is effectively connected with such permanent establishment. In such case the provisions of Article 7 shall apply.

5. Royalties shall be deemed to arise in a Contracting State when the payer is a resident of that State. Where, however, the person paying the royalties, whether the person is a resident of a Contracting State or not, has in a Contracting State a permanent establishment in connection with which the liability to pay the royalties was incurred, and the royalties are deductible in determining the profits attributable to such permanent establishment, then the royalties shall be deemed to arise in the State in which the permanent establishment is situated.

6. Where, by reason of a special relationship between the payer and the beneficial owner or between both of them and some other person, the amount of the royalties, having regard to the use, right or information for which they are paid, exceeds the amount which would have been agreed upon by the payer and the beneficial owner in the absence of such relationship, the provisions of this Article shall apply only to the last-mentioned amount. In such case, the excess part of the payments shall remain taxable according to the laws of each Contracting State, due regard being had to the other provisions of this Agreement.

Article 13
Alienation of Property

1. Income or gains derived by a resident of a Contracting State from the alienation of immovable property referred to in Article 6 and situated in the other Contracting State may be taxed in that other State.

2. Income or gains from the alienation of movable property forming part of the business property of a permanent establishment which an enterprise of a Contracting State has in the other Contracting State, including such income or gains from the alienation of such a permanent establishment (alone or with the whole enterprise), may be taxed in that other State.

3. Income or gains derived by an enterprise of a Contracting State from the alienation of ships or aircraft operated in international traffic, or movable property pertaining to the operation of such ships or aircraft, shall be taxable only in that State.

4. Income or gains derived by a resident of a Contracting State from the alienation of shares deriving more than 50 per cent of their value directly or indirectly from immovable property situated in the other Contracting State may be taxed in that other State.

5. Nothing in this Agreement affects the application of the laws of a Contracting State relating to the taxation of gains of a capital nature derived from the alienation of any property other than that to which any of the preceding paragraphs of this Article apply.

Article 14
Income from Employment

1. Subject to the provisions of Articles 15, 17 and 18, salaries, wages and other similar remuneration derived by a resident of a Contracting State in respect of an employment shall be taxable only in that State unless the employment is exercised in the other Contracting State. If the employment is so exercised, such remuneration as is derived therefrom may be taxed in that other State.

2. Notwithstanding the provisions of paragraph 1, remuneration derived by a resident of a Contracting State in respect of an employment exercised in the other Contracting State shall be taxable only in the first-mentioned State if:

(a) the recipient is present in the other State for a period or periods not exceeding in the aggregate 183 days in any twelve month period commencing or ending in the income year concerned, and

(b) the remuneration is paid by, or on behalf of, an employer who is not a resident of the other State, and

(c) the remuneration is not deductible in determining the profits attributable to a permanent establishment which the employer has in the other State.

3. Notwithstanding the preceding provisions of this Article, remuneration derived by a resident of a Contracting State in respect of an employment exercised aboard a ship or aircraft operated in international traffic shall be taxable only in that State.

Article 15

Directors' Fees

Directors' fees and other similar payments derived by a resident of a Contracting State in that person's capacity as a member of the board of directors of a company which is a resident of the other Contracting State may be taxed in that other State.

Article 16

Entertainers and Sportspersons

1. Notwithstanding the provisions of Articles 7 and 14, income derived by a resident of a Contracting State as an entertainer, such as a theatre, motion picture, radio or television artiste, or a musician, or as a sportsperson, from that person's personal activities as such exercised in the other Contracting State, may be taxed in that other State.

2. Where income in respect of personal activities exercised by an entertainer or a sportsperson in that person's capacity as such accrues not to the entertainer or sportsperson but to another person, that income may, notwithstanding the provisions of Articles 7 and 14, be taxed in the Contracting State in which the activities of the entertainer or sportsperson are exercised.

Article 17

Pensions

1. Pensions (including government service pensions) and other similar remuneration paid to a resident of a Contracting State in consideration of past employment shall be taxable only in that State.

2. Pensions and other payments made under the social security legislation of a Contracting State to a resident of the other Contracting State shall be taxable only in that other State.

Article 18
Government Service

1. (a) Salaries, wages and other similar remuneration (other than pensions) paid by the Government of a Contracting State to an individual in respect of services rendered to that Government shall be taxable only in that State.

   (b) However, such payments shall be taxable only in the other Contracting State if the services are rendered in that State and the individual is a resident of that State who:

   (i) is a national of that State; or

   (ii) did not become a resident of that State solely for the purpose of rendering the services.

2. The provisions of Articles 14, 15 or 16 shall apply to payments in respect of services rendered in connection with a business carried on by a Government referred to in paragraph 1.

Article 19
Students

Payments which a student or business apprentice who is or was immediately before visiting a Contracting State a resident of the other Contracting State and who is present in the first-mentioned State solely for the purpose of their education or training receives for the purpose of their maintenance, education or training shall not be taxed in that State, provided that such payments arise from sources outside that State.

Article 20

Other Income

1. Items of income of a resident of a Contracting State, wherever arising, not dealt with in the foregoing Articles of this Agreement shall be taxable only in that State.

2. The provisions of paragraph 1 shall not apply to income, other than income from immovable property as defined in paragraph 2 of Article 6, if the recipient of such income, being a resident of a Contracting State, carries on business in the other Contracting State through a permanent establishment situated therein and the right or property in respect of which the income is paid is effectively connected with such permanent establishment. In such case, the provisions of Article 7 shall apply.

3. Notwithstanding the provisions of paragraphs 1 and 2, items of income of a resident of a Contracting State not dealt with in the foregoing Articles of this Agreement and arising in the other Contracting State may also be taxed in that other State.

Article 21

Entitlement to Benefits

Notwithstanding the other provisions of this Agreement, a benefit under this Agreement shall not be granted in respect of an item of income if it is reasonable to conclude, having regard to all relevant facts and circumstances, that obtaining that benefit was one of the principal purposes of any arrangement or transaction that resulted directly or indirectly in that benefit, unless it is established that granting that benefit in these circumstances would be in accordance with the object and purpose of the relevant provisions of this Agreement.

CHAPTER IV
ELIMINATION OF DOUBLE TAXATION

Article 22
Elimination of Double Taxation

1. Subject to the provisions of the laws of New Zealand which relate to the allowance of a credit against New Zealand tax of tax paid in a country outside New Zealand (which shall not affect the general principle of this Article), Samoa tax paid under the laws of Samoa and consistent with this Agreement, in respect of income derived by a resident of New Zealand from sources in Samoa (excluding, in the case of a dividend, tax paid in respect of the profits out of which the dividend is paid) shall be allowed as a credit against New Zealand tax payable in respect of that income.

2. Subject to the provisions of the laws of Samoa from time to time in force which relate to the allowance of a credit against Samoa tax of tax paid in a country outside Samoa (which shall not affect the general principle of this Article), New Zealand tax paid under the laws of New Zealand and consistent with this Agreement, in respect of income derived by a resident of Samoa from sources in New Zealand shall be allowed as a credit against Samoa tax payable in respect of that income.

3. For the purpose of paragraph 1, Samoa tax paid shall include an amount equivalent to the amount of any Samoa tax forgone.

4. In paragraph 3, the term "Samoa tax forgone" means an amount which, under the law of Samoa relating to Samoa tax and in accordance with this Agreement, would have been payable as Samoa tax on income but for an exemption from, or a reduction of, Samoa tax on that income resulting from the operation of those provisions of the laws of Samoa which the Government of New Zealand and the Government of Samoa agree from time to time in letters exchanged for this purpose to be provisions to which this paragraph applies; and subject to its terms, such an agreement on applicable provisions

shall be valid for as long as those provisions are not modified after the date of that agreement or have been modified only in minor respects so as not to affect their general character.

5. Paragraphs 3 and 4 shall apply only in relation to those years of income that may be agreed by the Government of Samoa and the Government of New Zealand in letters exchanged for this purpose.

6. Notwithstanding paragraphs 3, 4 and 5, a New Zealand resident deriving income from Samoa, being income referred to in those paragraphs, shall not be deemed to have paid Samoa tax in respect of such income where:

(a) the New Zealand resident is a financial institution or is associated with a financial institution;

(b) the competent authority of New Zealand considers, after consultation with the competent authority of Samoa, that it is inappropriate to do so having regard to:

(i) whether any prearrangements have been entered into by any person for the purpose of taking advantage of paragraph 3 for the benefit of that person or any other person;

(ii) whether any benefit accrues or may accrue to a person who is neither a New Zealand resident nor a Samoa resident;

(iii) the prevention of fraud or the avoidance of the taxes to which this Agreement applies;

(iv) any other matter which either competent authority considers relevant in the particular circumstances of the case, including any submissions from the New Zealand resident concerned.

7. The provisions of paragraphs 3, 4, 5 and 6 shall only apply for a period of 10 years commencing on the date in which the Agreement enters into force.

CHAPTER V
SPECIAL PROVISIONS

Article 23
Mutual Agreement Procedure

1. Where a person considers that the actions of one or both of the Contracting States result or will result for that person in taxation not in accordance with the provisions of this Agreement, that person may, irrespective of the remedies provided by the domestic law of those States, present a case to the competent authority of the Contracting State of which the person is a resident. The case must be presented within three years from the first notification of the action resulting in taxation not in accordance with the provisions of the Agreement.

2. The competent authority shall endeavour, if the objection appears to it to be justified and if it is not itself able to arrive at a satisfactory solution, to resolve the case by mutual agreement with the competent authority of the other Contracting State, with a view to the avoidance of taxation which is not in accordance with the Agreement. Any agreement reached shall be implemented notwithstanding any time limits in the domestic law of the Contracting States.

3. The competent authorities of the Contracting States shall endeavour to resolve by mutual agreement any difficulties or doubts arising as to the interpretation or application of the Agreement. They may also consult together for the elimination of double taxation in cases not provided for in the Agreement.

4. The competent authorities of the Contracting States may communicate with each other directly, including through a joint commission consisting of themselves or their representatives, for the purpose of reaching an agreement in the sense of the preceding paragraphs.

Article 24
Exchange of Information

1. The competent authorities of the Contracting States shall exchange such information as is foreseeably relevant for carrying out the provisions of this Agreement or to the administration or enforcement of the domestic laws concerning taxes of every kind and description imposed on behalf of the Contracting States, or of their political subdivisions or local authorities, insofar as the taxation thereunder is not contrary to the Agreement. The exchange of information is not restricted by Articles 1 and 2.

2. Any information received under paragraph 1 by a Contracting State shall be treated as secret in the same manner as information obtained under the domestic laws of that State and shall be disclosed only to persons or authorities (including courts and administrative bodies) concerned with the assessment or collection of, the enforcement or prosecution in respect of, the determination of appeals in relation to the taxes referred to in paragraph 1, or the oversight of the above. Such persons or authorities shall use the information only for such purposes. They may disclose the information in public court proceedings or in judicial decisions. Notwithstanding the foregoing, information received by a Contracting State may be used for other purposes when such information may be used for such other purposes under the laws of both States and the competent authority of the supplying State authorises such use.

3. In no case shall the provisions of paragraphs 1 and 2 be construed so as to impose on a Contracting State the obligation:

(a) to carry out administrative measures at variance with the laws and administrative practice of that or of the other Contracting State;

(b) to supply information which is not obtainable under the laws or in the normal course of the administration of that or of the other Contracting State;

(c) to supply information which would disclose any trade, business, industrial, commercial or professional secret or trade process, or information the disclosure of which would be contrary to public policy (ordre public).

4. If information is requested by a Contracting State in accordance with this Article, the other Contracting State shall use its information gathering measures to obtain the requested information, even though that other State may not need such information for its own tax purposes. The obligation contained in the preceding sentence is subject to the limitations of paragraph 3 but in no case shall such limitations be construed to permit a Contracting State to decline to supply information solely because it has no domestic interest in such information.

5. In no case shall the provisions of paragraph 3 be construed to permit a Contracting State to decline to supply information solely because the information is held by a bank, other financial institution, nominee or person acting in an agency or a fiduciary capacity or because it relates to ownership interests in a person.

Article 25

Members of Diplomatic Missions and Consular Posts

Nothing in this Agreement shall affect the fiscal privileges of members of diplomatic missions or consular posts under the general rules of international law or under the provisions of special agreements.

CHAPTER VI
FINAL PROVISIONS

Article 26
Entry into Force

1. Each of the Contracting States shall notify the other through diplomatic channels of the completion of the procedures required by its law for the bringing into force of this Agreement. The Agreement shall enter into force on the date of the later of these notifications and its provisions shall have effect:

(a) in New Zealand:

(i) in respect of withholding tax on income, profits or gains derived by a non-resident, for amounts paid or credited on or after the first day of the second month next following the date on which the Agreement enters into force;

(ii) in respect of other New Zealand tax, for any income year beginning on or after 1 April next following the date on which the Agreement enters into force;

(b) In Samoa:

(i) in respect of withholding tax on income that is derived by a non-resident, in relation to income derived on or after the first day of the second month next following the date on which the Agreement enters into force;

(ii) in respect of any other Samoa tax, in relation to income of any year of income beginning on or after 1 January next following that in which the Agreement enters into force.

2. The Agreement between the Government of New Zealand and the Government of Samoa for the Allocation of Taxing Rights with respect to Certain Income of Individuals and to Establish a Mutual Agreement Procedure in respect of Transfer Pricing Adjustments signed at Apia on 24 August 2010 shall terminate and cease to have effect from the date upon which this

Agreement has effect in respect of the taxes to which this Agreement applies in accordance with the provisions of paragraph 1 of this Article.

3. The Agreement between the Government of New Zealand and the Government of Samoa on the Exchange of Information with Respect to Taxes signed at Apia on 24 August 2010 shall terminate and cease to have effect from the date upon which Article 24 of this Agreement has effect in accordance with the provisions of paragraph 1 of this Article. Notwithstanding the termination of the Tax Information Exchange Agreement, the Contracting States shall remain bound by the provisions of Article 8 of that Agreement with respect to any information obtained under that Agreement.

Article 27

Termination

This Agreement shall remain in force until terminated by a Contracting State. Either Contracting State may terminate the Agreement, through diplomatic channels, by giving notice of termination at least six months before the end of any calendar year after the year beginning after the expiration of 5 years from the date of its entry into force. In such event, the Agreement shall cease to have effect:

(a) in New Zealand:

  (i) in respect of withholding tax on income, profits or gains derived by a non-resident, for amounts paid or credited on or after the first day of the second month next following that in which the notice of termination is given;

  (ii) in respect of other New Zealand tax, for any income year beginning on or after 1 April in the calendar year next following that in which the notice of termination is given;

(b) in Samoa:

(i) in respect of withholding tax on income that is derived by a non-resident, in relation to income derived on or after the first day of the second month next following the date on which the notice of termination is given;

(ii) in respect of any other Samoa tax, for any income year beginning on or after 1 January in the calendar year next following that in which the notice of termination is given.

IN WITNESS WHEREOF the undersigned, duly authorised by their respective Governments, have signed this Agreement.

DONE in duplicate at Apia this 8th day of July 2015 in the English language.

For the Government of New Zealand	For the Government of Samoa
Right Honourable John Key	Honourable Tuilaepa Lupesoliai Sailele Malielegaoi
Prime Minister of New Zealand	Prime Minister of Samoa

[TRANSLATION IN FRENCH – TRADUCTION EN FRANÇAIS]

ACCORD ENTRE LE GOUVERNEMENT DE LA NOUVELLE-ZÉLANDE ET LE GOUVERNEMENT DU SAMOA PORTANT SUR L'ÉLIMINATION LES DOUBLES IMPOSITIONS EN MATIÈRE D'IMPÔTS SUR LE REVENU ET SUR LA PRÉVENTION DE LA FRAUDE ET L'ÉVASION FISCALES

Le Gouvernement de la Nouvelle-Zélande et le Gouvernement du Samoa,

Désireux de développer davantage leurs relations économiques et de renforcer leur coopération en matière fiscale,

Déterminés à conclure un accord en vue d'éliminer les doubles impositions en matière d'impôts sur le revenu sans pour autant créer de possibilités de non-imposition ou d'imposition réduite au moyen de la fraude ou de l'évasion fiscale (notamment par le biais du chalandage de traités en vue d'obtenir les allégements prévus dans le présent Accord au bénéfice indirect de résidents d'États tiers),

Sont convenus de ce qui suit :

CHAPITRE I. CHAMP D'APPLICATION DU PRÉSENT ACCORD

Article premier. Personnes visées

Le présent Accord s'applique aux personnes qui sont des résidentes d'un État contractant ou des deux États contractants.

Article 2. Impôts visés

1. Les impôts auxquels s'applique le présent Accord sont :

a) En Nouvelle-Zélande :

L'impôt sur le revenu (ci-après dénommé « impôt néo-zélandais ») ;

b) Au Samoa :

L'impôt sur le revenu (ci-après dénommé « impôt samoan »).

2. Le présent Accord s'applique aussi à tous les impôts identiques ou analogues qui seraient établis après la date de sa signature et qui s'ajouteraient aux impôts énumérés au paragraphe 1 ou qui les remplaceraient. Les autorités compétentes des États contractants se communiquent mutuellement toute modification significative apportée à leur législation fiscale.

3. Nonobstant les dispositions des paragraphes 1 et 2, les impôts visés par l'Accord ne comprennent pas les montants qui représentent des pénalités ou des intérêts imposés par la législation de l'un ou l'autre des États contractants.

CHAPITRE II. DÉFINITIONS

Article 3. Définitions générales

1. Aux fins du présent Accord, à moins que le contexte n'exige une autre interprétation :

a) Le terme « personne » s'entend d'une personne physique, d'une société et de tout autre groupement de personnes ;

b) Le terme « société » désigne toute personne morale ou toute entité considérée comme une personne morale à des fins d'imposition ;

c) Le terme « entreprise » s'applique à l'exercice de toute activité commerciale ;

d) Les expressions « entreprise d'un État contractant » et « entreprise de l'autre État contractant » désignent respectivement une entreprise exploitée par un résident d'un État contractant et une entreprise exploitée par un résident de l'autre État contractant ;

e) L'expression « trafic international » désigne tout transport effectué par un navire ou un aéronef exploité par une entreprise d'un État contractant, sauf lorsque le navire ou l'aéronef est exploité uniquement entre des points situés dans l'autre État contractant ;

f) L'expression « autorité compétente » désigne :

i) En Nouvelle-Zélande, le Commissaire de l'Administration fiscale ou son représentant autorisé ; et

ii) Au Samoa, le Directeur du Ministère du revenu ou son représentant autorisé ;

g) Le terme « ressortissant », au regard d'un État contractant, désigne :

i) Toute personne physique possédant la nationalité ou la citoyenneté de cet État contractant ; et

ii) Toute personne morale, société de personnes ou association constituée conformément à la législation en vigueur dans cet État contractant ;

h) Le terme « activité » comprend l'exercice d'une profession libérale ou d'autres activités de caractère indépendant ;

i) Les expressions « un État contractant » et « l'autre État contractant » désignent soit la Nouvelle-Zélande, soit le Samoa, selon le contexte ;

j) i) Le terme « Nouvelle-Zélande » désigne le territoire de la Nouvelle-Zélande, mais ne comprend pas les Tokélaou ; il comprend également toute zone située au-delà de la mer territoriale désignée, en vertu de la législation néo-zélandaise et conformément au droit international, comme une zone dans laquelle la Nouvelle-Zélande peut exercer des droits souverains eu égard aux ressources naturelles ; et

ii) Le terme « Samoa » désigne l'État indépendant du Samoa et ses eaux territoriales.

2. Au sens des articles 10, 11 et 12, les dividendes, intérêts ou redevances provenant d'un État contractant et obtenus par ou à travers une fiducie sont considérés comme ayant pour bénéficiaire effectif un résident de l'autre État contractant lorsque :

a) Ces revenus sont soumis à l'impôt dans cet autre État entre les mains du mandataire de cette fiducie ;

b) En ce qui concerne les dividendes, le revenu serait soumis à l'impôt entre les mains du mandataire de cette fiducie, sauf si une exemption s'applique à ces dividendes en vertu de la législation de cet autre État.

3. Pour l'application de l'Accord à un moment donné par un État contractant, toute expression ou tout terme qui n'y est pas défini a, à moins que le contexte n'exige une interprétation différente, le sens que lui attribue, à ce moment-là, le droit de cet État concernant les impôts auxquels s'applique l'Accord, le sens attribué à ce terme ou à cette expression par le droit fiscal applicable de cet État prévalant sur le sens que lui attribuent les autres branches du droit de cet État.

Article 4. Résident

1. Aux fins de la présente Convention, l'expression « résident d'un État contractant » désigne toute personne qui, selon la législation de cet État, est assujettie à l'impôt dans cet État en raison de son domicile, de sa résidence, de son siège de direction ou de tout autre critère de nature analogue, et s'applique aussi à cet État ainsi qu'à toutes ses subdivisions politiques ou à ses collectivités locales. Toutefois, cette expression ne comprend pas les personnes qui ne sont assujetties à l'impôt dans cet État que pour les revenus de sources situées dans cet État.

2. Lorsque, selon les dispositions du paragraphe 1, une personne physique est résidente des deux États contractants, sa situation est réglée de la manière suivante :

a) Cette personne est considérée comme étant résidente seulement de l'État où elle dispose d'un foyer d'habitation permanent ; si elle dispose d'un foyer d'habitation permanent dans les deux États, elle est considérée comme étant résidente seulement de l'État avec lequel elle a les liens personnels et économiques les plus étroits (centre des intérêts vitaux) ;

b) Si l'État où cette personne a le centre de ses intérêts vitaux ne peut pas être déterminé, ou si elle ne dispose d'un foyer d'habitation permanent dans aucun des États, elle est considérée comme étant résidente seulement de l'État où elle séjourne de façon habituelle ;

c) Si cette personne séjourne de façon habituelle dans les deux États, ou si elle ne séjourne de façon habituelle dans aucun d'entre eux, elle est considérée comme étant résidente seulement de l'État dont elle possède la nationalité ;

d) Si cette personne possède la nationalité des deux États ou si elle ne possède la nationalité d'aucun d'eux, les autorités compétentes des États contractants tranchent la question d'un commun accord.

3. Lorsque, selon les dispositions du paragraphe 1, une personne autre qu'une personne physique est résidente des deux États contractants, les autorités compétentes des États contractants s'efforcent de déterminer d'un commun accord l'État contractant dont la personne est considérée comme résidente aux fins du présent Accord, en tenant compte de son siège de direction effectif, du lieu où elle est enregistrée ou constituée, et de tout autre élément pertinent. En l'absence d'un tel accord, cette personne n'a droit à aucun des allégements ou exonérations d'impôt prévus par le présent Accord, sauf dans la mesure et selon les modalités convenues par les autorités compétentes des États contractants.

Article 5. Établissement stable

1. Aux fins du présent Accord, l'expression « établissement stable » désigne une installation fixe d'affaires par l'intermédiaire de laquelle une entreprise exerce tout ou partie de son activité.

2. L'expression « établissement stable » comprend notamment :

a) Un siège de direction ;

b) Une succursale ;

c) Un bureau ;

d) Une usine ;

e) Un atelier ;

f) Une mine, un puits de pétrole ou de gaz, une carrière ou tout autre lieu d'extraction de ressources naturelles.

3. Un chantier de construction, ou un projet de construction, d'installation ou de montage, ou des activités de supervision en rapport avec ce chantier ou ce projet de construction, d'installation ou de montage, constituent un établissement stable si leur durée est supérieure à six mois.

4. Une entreprise est considérée comme ayant un établissement stable dans un État contractant et comme exerçant son activité par l'intermédiaire de cet établissement stable si, pendant plus de 183 jours au cours de toute période de 12 mois :

a) Elle exerce dans cet État des activités qui consistent en ou qui sont liées à l'exploration ou à l'exploitation de ressources naturelles, y compris le bois sur pied, situées dans cet État ; ou

b) Elle exploite des équipements d'envergure dans cet État.

5. Nonobstant les dispositions des paragraphes 1, 2 et 3, lorsqu'une entreprise d'un État contractant fournit des services dans l'autre État contractant :

a) Par l'intermédiaire d'une personne physique séjourne dans cet autre État pendant une période ou plusieurs périodes dépassant au total 183 jours au cours de toute période de 12 mois, et lorsque les services fournis dans cet autre État par l'intermédiaire de cette personne physique sont des services professionnels ou d'autres activités de nature indépendante ; ou

b) Pendant une période ou plusieurs périodes dépassant au total 183 jours au cours de toute période de 12 mois, que ces services sont exécutés pour le même projet ou pour des projets connexes par l'intermédiaire d'une ou de plusieurs personnes physiques qui séjournent dans cet autre État et y exécutent ces services ;

les activités exécutées dans cet autre État dans le cadre de la prestation de ces services sont considérées comme étant exécutées par l'intermédiaire d'un établissement stable de l'entreprise situé dans cet autre État, à moins que ces services ne se limitent à ceux mentionnés au paragraphe 7 et qui, s'ils étaient exécutés par l'intermédiaire d'une installation fixe d'affaires, ne permettraient pas de considérer cette installation comme un établissement stable selon les dispositions de ce paragraphe. Aux fins du présent paragraphe, les services exécutés par une personne physique pour le compte d'une entreprise ne sont pas considérés comme étant exécutés par une autre entreprise par l'intermédiaire de cette personne physique, sauf si cette autre entreprise supervise, dirige ou contrôle la manière dont ces services sont exécutés par la personne physique.

6. Pour déterminer la durée des activités en vertu des paragraphes 3, 4 et 5, la période au cours de laquelle des activités sont exercées dans un État contractant par une entreprise associée à une autre entreprise se cumule avec la période au cours de laquelle des activités sont exercées par l'entreprise à laquelle elle est associée, si les premières activités sont liées et identiques ou analogues aux activités exercées dans cet État par la dernière entreprise mentionnée, à condition que toute période au cours de laquelle deux ou plusieurs entreprises associées exercent des activités concurrentes ne soit comptée qu'une seule fois. Une entreprise est considérée comme associée à une autre entreprise si l'une est contrôlée directement ou indirectement par l'autre, ou si les deux sont contrôlées directement ou indirectement par une ou plusieurs tierces personnes.

7. Nonobstant les dispositions précédentes du présent article, il est considéré qu'un « établissement stable » ne comprend pas :

a) L'utilisation d'installations aux seules fins d'entreposage, d'exposition ou de livraison de marchandises appartenant à l'entreprise ;

b) L'exploitation d'un stock de biens et de marchandises appartenant à l'entreprise aux seules fins d'entreposage, d'exposition ou de livraison ;

c) L'exploitation d'un stock de biens et de marchandises appartenant à l'entreprise aux seules fins de transformation par une autre entreprise ;

d) L'exploitation d'une installation fixe d'affaires aux seules fins d'acheter des marchandises ou de réunir des informations pour l'entreprise ;

e) L'exploitation d'une installation fixe d'affaires aux seules fins d'exercer, pour l'entreprise, toute autre activité de caractère préparatoire ou auxiliaire ;

f) L'exploitation d'une installation fixe d'affaires aux seules fins de l'exercice cumulé d'activités mentionnées aux alinéas a) à e), à condition que l'activité d'ensemble de l'installation fixe d'affaires résultant de ce cumul ait un caractère préparatoire ou auxiliaire.

8. Nonobstant les dispositions des paragraphes 1 et 2, lorsqu'une personne, autre qu'un agent jouissant d'un statut indépendant auquel s'applique le paragraphe 9, agit pour le compte d'une entreprise et :

a) Dispose dans cet État de pouvoirs, qu'elle y exerce habituellement, lui permettant de conclure des contrats au nom de l'entreprise ;

b) Fabrique ou transforme dans un État contractant pour l'entreprise des biens ou des marchandises appartenant à l'entreprise ;

cette entreprise est considérée comme ayant un établissement stable dans cet État en ce qui concerne les activités que cette personne entreprend pour cette entreprise, à moins que les activités de cette personne ne se limitent à celles qui sont mentionnées au paragraphe 7 et qui, si elles étaient exercées par l'intermédiaire d'une installation fixe d'affaires, ne permettraient pas de considérer cette installation comme un établissement stable selon les dispositions de ce paragraphe.

9. Une entreprise n'est pas considérée comme ayant un établissement stable dans un État contractant du seul fait qu'elle y exerce son activité par l'entremise d'un courtier, d'un commissionnaire général ou de tout autre agent jouissant d'un statut indépendant, à condition que ces personnes agissent dans le cadre ordinaire de leur activité.

10. Le fait qu'une société qui est résidente d'un État contractant contrôle ou est contrôlée par une société qui est résidente de l'autre État contractant ou qui y exerce son activité (que ce soit par

l'intermédiaire d'un établissement stable ou non) ne suffit pas, en lui-même, à faire de l'une quelconque de ces sociétés un établissement stable de l'autre.

CHAPITRE III. IMPOSITION DES REVENUS

Article 6. Revenus immobiliers

1. Les revenus qu'une personne résidente d'un État contractant tire de biens immobiliers (y compris les revenus d'exploitations agricoles ou forestières) situés dans l'autre État contractant sont imposables dans cet autre État.

2. L'expression « biens immobiliers » a le sens que lui attribue le droit de l'État contractant où les biens considérés sont situés. En tout état de cause, cette expression comprend les ressources naturelles, les biens accessoires aux biens immeubles, le cheptel et le matériel utilisé dans les exploitations agricoles et forestières, les droits auxquels s'appliquent les dispositions du droit privé concernant les biens immeubles, l'usufruit des biens immeubles, les droits d'exploration ou d'exploitation des ressources naturelles ou du bois sur pied, ainsi que les droits à des paiements variables ou fixes, soit en contrepartie, soit au titre de l'exploitation ou du droit d'exploration ou d'exploitation des ressources naturelles ou du bois sur pied. Les navires, bateaux et aéronefs ne sont pas considérés comme des biens immobiliers.

3. Les dispositions du paragraphe 1 s'appliquent aux revenus provenant de l'exploitation directe, de la location ou de l'affermage, ainsi que de toute autre forme d'exploitation des biens immobiliers.

4. Les dispositions des paragraphes 1 et 3 s'appliquent également aux revenus provenant des biens immobiliers d'une entreprise.

5. Tout droit visé au paragraphe 2 du présent article est considéré comme étant situé à l'endroit où se trouve le bien sur lequel il porte ou à l'endroit où l'exploration ou l'exploitation peut avoir lieu.

Article 7. Bénéfices des entreprises

1. Les bénéfices d'une entreprise d'un État contractant ne sont imposables que dans cet État, à moins que l'entreprise n'exerce son activité dans l'autre État contractant par l'intermédiaire d'un établissement stable qui y est situé. Si l'entreprise exerce son activité de la manière susmentionnée, les bénéfices de l'entreprise sont imposables dans l'autre État, mais uniquement dans la mesure où ils sont imputables à cet établissement stable, ou aux ventes réalisées, dans cet autre État contractant, de biens ou de marchandises de nature identique ou analogue à ceux vendus par l'intermédiaire de cet établissement stable. Il est entendu que les bénéfices d'une entreprise n'incluent les bénéfices imputables aux ventes de biens et de marchandises visées au présent paragraphe que lorsque l'autorité compétente de l'État contractant où est situé un établissement stable de l'entreprise considère que l'entreprise a conclu un arrangement relatif aux ventes de ces biens ou marchandises pour éviter l'imposition de ces bénéfices dans cet État contractant.

2. Sous réserve des dispositions du paragraphe 3, lorsqu'une entreprise d'un État contractant exerce son activité dans l'autre État contractant par l'intermédiaire d'un établissement stable qui y est situé, il est imputé, dans chaque État contractant, à cet établissement stable les bénéfices qu'il aurait pu réaliser s'il avait constitué une entreprise distincte exerçant des activités identiques ou

analogues dans des conditions identiques ou analogues et traitant en toute indépendance avec l'entreprise dont il constitue un établissement stable.

3. Pour déterminer les bénéfices d'un établissement stable, sont admises en déduction les dépenses exposées aux fins poursuivies par cet établissement stable, y compris les dépenses de direction et les frais généraux d'administration ainsi enregistrés, soit dans l'État où est situé cet établissement stable, soit ailleurs.

4. Aux fins des paragraphes précédents, les bénéfices à imputer à l'établissement stable sont déterminés chaque année selon la même méthode, à moins qu'il n'existe des motifs valables et suffisants de procéder autrement.

5. Lorsque :

a) Un résident d'un État contractant est le bénéficiaire effectif (que ce soit en tant que bénéficiaire direct d'une fiducie ou par l'intermédiaire d'une ou de plusieurs fiducies interposées) d'une part des bénéfices d'une activité d'une entreprise exercée dans l'autre État contractant par le mandataire d'une fiducie autre qu'une fiducie qui est considérée comme une société aux fins d'imposition ; et

b) En ce qui concerne cette entreprise, ce mandataire a ou aurait, s'il était un résident du premier État, un établissement stable dans l'autre État ;

alors l'activité de l'entreprise exercée par le mandataire par l'intermédiaire de cet établissement stable est considérée comme une activité exercée dans l'autre État par ce résident par l'intermédiaire d'un établissement stable situé dans cet autre État, et la part des bénéfices de ce résident est imposable dans l'autre État, mais seulement dans la mesure où elle est imputable à cet établissement stable.

6. Lorsque les bénéfices comprennent des éléments de revenu qui sont traités séparément dans d'autres articles du présent Accord, les dispositions de ces articles ne sont pas affectées par les dispositions du présent article.

7. Les dispositions du présent article ne portent pas atteinte aux dispositions de la législation de l'un ou l'autre État contractant en vigueur à tout moment, qui concernent l'imposition des revenus provenant de toute forme d'assurance.

Article 8. Transport maritime et aérien

1. Les bénéfices qu'une entreprise d'un État contractant tire de l'exploitation, en trafic international, de navires ou d'aéronefs, ne sont imposables que dans cet État.

2. Nonobstant les dispositions du paragraphe 1 et de l'article 7, les bénéfices d'une entreprise d'un État contractant provenant du transport par navire ou aéronef de passagers, de bétail, de courrier, de biens ou de marchandises qui sont embarqués dans l'autre État contractant et sont déchargés en un lieu situé dans cet autre État, ou de la location d'un navire ou d'un aéronef affrété aux fins d'un tel transport, sont imposables dans cet autre État.

3. Les dispositions des paragraphes 1 et 2 s'appliquent aussi aux bénéfices provenant de la participation à un consortium, à une coentreprise ou à un organisme d'exploitation internationale.

Article 9. Entreprises associées

1. Lorsque :

a) Une entreprise d'un État contractant participe directement ou indirectement à la direction, au contrôle ou au capital d'une entreprise de l'autre État contractant ; ou que

b) Les mêmes personnes participent directement ou indirectement à la direction, au contrôle ou au capital d'une entreprise d'un État contractant et d'une entreprise de l'autre État contractant ;

et que, dans l'un et l'autre cas, les deux entreprises sont, dans leurs relations commerciales ou financières, liées par des conditions convenues ou imposées, qui diffèrent de celles qui seraient convenues entre des entreprises indépendantes, les bénéfices qui, sans ces conditions, auraient été réalisés par l'une des entreprises, mais n'ont pu l'être en fait à cause de ces conditions, peuvent être inclus dans les bénéfices de cette entreprise et imposés en conséquence.

2. Lorsqu'un État contractant inclut dans les bénéfices d'une entreprise de cet État, et impose en conséquence, des bénéfices sur lesquels une entreprise de l'autre État contractant a été imposée dans cet autre État, et que les bénéfices ainsi inclus sont des bénéfices qui auraient été réalisés par l'entreprise du premier État si les conditions convenues entre les deux entreprises avaient été celles qui auraient été convenues entre des entreprises indépendantes, alors cet autre État procède à un ajustement approprié du montant de l'impôt qui y a été perçu sur ces bénéfices. Pour déterminer cet ajustement, il est tenu compte des autres dispositions du présent Accord, et si nécessaire, les autorités compétentes des États contractants se concertent.

Article 10. Dividendes

1. Les dividendes payés par une société qui est résidente d'un État contractant à un résident de l'autre État contractant sont imposables dans cet autre État.

2. Toutefois, ces dividendes sont aussi imposables dans l'État contractant dont la société qui paie les dividendes est résidente, et selon la législation de cet État, mais si le bénéficiaire effectif des dividendes est un résident de l'autre État contractant, l'impôt ainsi établi ne peut excéder :

a) 5 % du montant brut des dividendes si le bénéficiaire effectif est une société qui détient directement au moins 10 % des parts avec droit de vote de la société qui paie les dividendes ; et

b) 15 % du montant brut des dividendes, dans tous les autres cas.

Le présent paragraphe n'affecte pas l'imposition de la société au titre des bénéfices qui servent au paiement des dividendes.

3. Le terme « dividendes » employé dans le présent article désigne les revenus d'actions et les autres revenus soumis au même régime fiscal que les revenus d'actions par la législation de l'État dont la société distributrice est résidente.

4. Les dispositions des paragraphes 1 et 2 ne s'appliquent pas lorsque le bénéficiaire effectif des dividendes, résident d'un État contractant, exerce dans l'autre État contractant dont la société qui paie les dividendes est résidente, une activité industrielle ou commerciale par l'intermédiaire d'un établissement stable qui y est situé, et que la participation génératrice des dividendes s'y rattache effectivement. Dans ce cas, les dispositions de l'article 7 sont applicables.

5. Lorsqu'une société qui est résidente d'un État contractant tire des bénéfices ou des revenus de l'autre État contractant, cet autre État ne peut percevoir aucun impôt sur les dividendes payés par la société, sauf dans la mesure où ces dividendes sont payés à un résident de cet autre État, ou dans la mesure où la participation génératrice des dividendes se rattache effectivement à un établissement stable situé dans cet autre État, ni prélever aucun impôt, au titre de l'imposition des bénéfices non distribués, sur les bénéfices non distribués de la société, même si les dividendes payés ou les bénéfices non distribués consistent en tout ou en partie en bénéfices ou revenus provenant de cet autre État.

Article 11. Intérêts

1. Les intérêts provenant d'un État contractant et payés à un résident de l'autre État contractant sont imposables dans cet autre État.

2. Toutefois, ces intérêts sont aussi imposables dans l'État contractant d'où ils proviennent et selon la législation de cet État, mais si le bénéficiaire effectif des intérêts est un résident de l'autre État contractant, l'impôt ainsi établi ne peut excéder 10 % du montant brut des intérêts.

3. Le terme « intérêts » employé dans le présent article désigne les revenus de créances de toute nature, assorties ou non de garanties hypothécaires ou d'une clause de participation aux bénéfices du débiteur, et notamment les revenus de fonds publics ou d'obligations d'emprunts, y compris les primes et lots attachés à ces titres, ainsi que de tout autre revenu traité comme un revenu de sommes prêtées par la législation en matière d'impôt de l'État contractant dans lequel les revenus sont générés. Sont exclus les revenus traités comme des dividendes au titre de l'article 10.

4. Les dispositions des paragraphes 1 et 2 ne s'appliquent pas lorsque le bénéficiaire effectif des intérêts, résident d'un État contractant, exerce dans l'autre État contractant d'où proviennent les intérêts, une activité industrielle ou commerciale par l'intermédiaire d'un établissement stable qui y est situé, et que la créance génératrice des intérêts s'y rattache effectivement. Dans ce cas, les dispositions de l'article 7 sont applicables.

5. Les intérêts sont considérés comme provenant d'un État contractant lorsque le débiteur est un résident de cet État. Toutefois, lorsque le débiteur des intérêts, qu'il soit ou non un résident d'un État contractant, a dans un État contractant un établissement stable pour lequel la dette donnant lieu au paiement des intérêts a été contractée, et que ces intérêts sont déductibles, pour la détermination des bénéfices imputables à cet établissement stable, ceux-ci sont considérés comme provenant de l'État contractant où l'établissement stable est situé.

6. Lorsque, en raison de relations spéciales existant entre le débiteur et le bénéficiaire effectif ou que l'un et l'autre entretiennent avec de tierces personnes, le montant des intérêts, compte tenu de la créance pour laquelle ils sont payés, excède celui dont seraient convenus le débiteur et le bénéficiaire effectif en l'absence de pareilles relations, les dispositions du présent article ne s'appliquent qu'à ce dernier montant. Dans ce cas, la partie excédentaire des paiements reste imposable selon la législation de chaque État contractant, compte tenu des autres dispositions du présent Accord.

Article 12. Redevances

1. Les redevances générées dans un État contractant et payées à un résident de l'autre État contractant sont imposables dans cet autre État.

2. Toutefois, ces redevances sont aussi imposables dans l'État contractant de la source et selon la législation de cet État, mais si le bénéficiaire effectif des redevances est un résident de l'autre État contractant, l'impôt ainsi établi ne peut excéder 10 % du montant brut des redevances.

3. Le terme « redevances » employé dans le présent article désigne les sommes de toute nature payées pour :

a) L'usage ou la concession de l'usage d'un droit d'auteur, d'un brevet, d'un dessin ou modèle, d'un plan, d'une formule ou d'un procédé secrets, d'une marque de commerce ou autre propriété ou droit similaire ;

b) L'usage ou la concession de l'usage :

i) De films cinématographiques ;

ii) De films ou de bandes ou disques audio ou vidéo, ou tout autre moyen de reproduction ou de transmission d'images ou de sons destinés à être utilisés dans le cadre d'une diffusion télévisée, à la radio, sur Internet ou autre ;

c) L'usage ou la concession de l'usage de tout équipement industriel, commercial ou scientifique ;

d) Des connaissances ou des informations ayant trait à une expérience acquise dans le domaine industriel, commercial ou scientifique ;

e) Toute aide accessoire et subsidiaire fournie en vue de permettre l'application ou la jouissance d'un bien ou d'un droit visé à l'alinéa a) ou b), d'un équipement visé à l'alinéa c) ou de connaissances ou d'informations visées à l'alinéa d) ;

f) Toute abstention concernant l'usage ou la fourniture de tout bien ou droit visé au présent paragraphe.

4. Les dispositions des paragraphes 1 et 2 ne s'appliquent pas lorsque le bénéficiaire effectif des redevances, résident d'un État contractant, exerce dans l'autre État contractant source des redevances une activité industrielle ou commerciale par l'intermédiaire d'un établissement stable qui y est situé et que le droit ou le bien générateur des redevances s'y rattache effectivement. Dans ce cas, les dispositions de l'article 7 sont applicables.

5. Les redevances sont considérées comme provenant d'un État contractant lorsque le débiteur est un résident de cet État. Toutefois, lorsque le débiteur des redevances, qu'il soit ou non un résident d'un État contractant, a dans un État contractant un établissement stable pour lequel l'engagement donnant lieu aux redevances a été contracté, et que ces redevances sont déductibles, pour la détermination des bénéfices imputables à cet établissement stable, celles-ci sont considérées comme provenant de l'État où l'établissement stable est situé.

6. Lorsque, en raison de relations spéciales existant entre le débiteur et le bénéficiaire effectif ou que l'un et l'autre entretiennent avec de tierces personnes, le montant des redevances, compte tenu de la prestation pour laquelle elles sont payées, excède celui dont seraient convenus le débiteur et le bénéficiaire effectif en l'absence de pareilles relations, les dispositions du présent article ne s'appliquent qu'à ce dernier montant. Dans ce cas, la partie excédentaire des paiements reste imposable selon la législation de chaque État contractant, compte tenu des autres dispositions du présent Accord.

Article 13. Aliénation de biens

1. Les revenus ou gains qu'un résident d'un État contractant tire de l'aliénation de biens immobiliers visés à l'article 6 et situés dans l'autre État contractant sont imposables dans cet autre État.

2. Les revenus ou gains provenant de l'aliénation de biens mobiliers qui font partie de l'actif d'un établissement stable qu'une entreprise d'un État contractant a dans l'autre État contractant, y compris de tels revenus ou gains dégagés de l'aliénation de cet établissement stable (seul ou avec l'ensemble de l'entreprise), sont imposables dans cet autre État.

3. Les revenus ou gains provenant de l'aliénation de navires ou d'aéronefs exploités en trafic international par une entreprise d'un État contractant ou de biens meubles affectés à l'exploitation de ces navires ou aéronefs ne sont imposables que dans cet État.

4. Les revenus ou gains qu'un résident d'un État contractant tire de l'aliénation d'actions qui tirent directement ou indirectement plus de 50 % de leur valeur de biens immobiliers situés dans l'autre État contractant sont imposables dans cet autre État.

5. Aucune disposition du présent Accord ne porte atteinte à l'application de la législation d'un État contractant relative à l'imposition des gains en capital provenant de l'aliénation d'un bien autre que ceux auxquels s'applique l'un des paragraphes précédents du présent article.

Article 14. Revenus d'emploi

1. Sous réserve des dispositions des articles 15, 17 et 18, les salaires, traitements et autres rémunérations similaires qu'un résident d'un État contractant reçoit au titre d'un emploi salarié ne sont imposables que dans cet État, à moins que l'emploi ne soit exercé dans l'autre État contractant. Si l'emploi y est exercé, les rémunérations reçues à ce titre sont imposables dans cet autre État.

2. Nonobstant les dispositions du paragraphe 1, les rémunérations qu'un résident d'un État contractant reçoit au titre d'un emploi salarié exercé dans l'autre État contractant ne sont imposables que dans le premier État si :

a) Le bénéficiaire séjourne dans l'autre État pendant une période ou des périodes n'excédant pas au total 183 jours au cours de toute période de 12 mois commençant ou se terminant durant l'année fiscale considérée ; et

b) Les rémunérations sont payées par un employeur, ou pour le compte d'un employeur, qui n'est pas un résident de l'autre État ; et

c) La charge des rémunérations n'est pas déductible pour déterminer les bénéfices imputables à un établissement stable que l'employeur a dans l'autre État.

3. Nonobstant les dispositions précédentes du présent article, les rémunérations qu'un résident d'un État contractant tire d'un emploi salarié exercé à bord d'un navire ou d'un aéronef exploité en trafic international ne sont imposables que dans cet État.

Article 15. Tantièmes

Les tantièmes et autres rétributions similaires qu'un résident d'un État contractant reçoit en sa qualité de membre du conseil d'administration d'une société qui est un résident de l'autre État contractant sont imposables dans cet autre État.

Article 16. Artistes du spectacle et sportifs

1. Nonobstant les dispositions des articles 7 et 14, les revenus qu'un résident d'un État contractant tire de ses activités personnelles exercées dans l'autre État contractant en tant qu'artiste du spectacle, tel qu'un artiste de théâtre, de cinéma, de la radio ou de la télévision, ou un musicien, ou en tant que sportif sont imposables dans cet autre État.

2. Lorsque les revenus d'activités qu'un artiste du spectacle ou un sportif exerce personnellement et en cette qualité sont attribués non pas à l'artiste du spectacle ou au sportif lui-même, mais à une autre personne, ces revenus sont, nonobstant les dispositions des articles 7 et 14, imposables dans l'État contractant où les activités de l'artiste du spectacle ou du sportif sont exercées.

Article 17. Pensions

1. Les pensions (y compris les pensions de fonctionnaires) et autres rémunérations similaires payées à un résident d'un État contractant au titre d'un emploi antérieur ne sont imposables que dans cet État.

2. Les pensions et autres paiements payés en vertu de la législation relative au régime de sécurité sociale d'un État contractant à un résident de l'autre État contractant ne sont imposables que dans cet autre État.

Article 18. Fonction publique

1. a) Les salaires, traitements et autres rémunérations analogues, autres que les pensions, payés par le Gouvernement d'un État contractant à une personne physique au titre de services fournis à cet État ne sont imposables que dans cet État ;
   b) Toutefois, ces paiements ne sont imposables que dans l'autre État contractant si les services sont fournis dans cet État et si la personne physique est un résident de cet État qui :
      i) Possède la nationalité de cet État ; ou
      ii) N'est pas devenu un résident de cet État à seule fin d'exécuter les services en question.

2. Les dispositions des articles 14, 15 et 16 s'appliquent aux montants versés au titre de services fournis dans le cadre d'une activité industrielle ou commerciale exercée par le Gouvernement mentionné dans le paragraphe 1.

Article 19. Étudiants

Les sommes qu'un étudiant ou un stagiaire qui est, ou qui était immédiatement avant de se rendre dans un État contractant, un résident de l'autre État contractant et qui séjourne dans le premier État à seule fin d'y poursuivre ses études ou sa formation, reçoit pour couvrir ses frais d'entretien, d'études ou de formation ne sont pas imposables dans cet État, à condition qu'elles proviennent de sources situées en dehors de cet État.

Article 20. Autres revenus

1. Les éléments du revenu d'un résident d'un État contractant, d'où qu'ils proviennent, qui ne sont pas traités dans les articles précédents du présent Accord ne sont imposables que dans cet État.

2. Les dispositions du paragraphe 1 ne s'appliquent pas aux revenus autres que ceux provenant de biens immobiliers tels qu'ils sont définis au paragraphe 2 de l'article 6, lorsque le bénéficiaire de ces revenus, résident d'un État contractant, exerce dans l'autre État contractant une activité industrielle ou commerciale par l'intermédiaire d'un établissement stable qui y est situé et que le droit ou le bien générateur des revenus s'y rattache effectivement. Dans ce cas, les dispositions de l'article 7 sont applicables.

3. Nonobstant les dispositions des paragraphes 1 et 2 du présent article, les éléments de revenu d'un résident d'un État contractant qui ne sont pas traités dans les articles précédents du présent Accord et qui proviennent de l'autre État contractant sont aussi imposables dans cet autre État.

Article 21. Droit à prestations

Nonobstant les autres dispositions du présent Accord, un avantage au titre du présent Accord n'est pas accordé à l'égard d'un élément de revenu s'il est raisonnable de conclure, compte tenu de tous les faits et circonstances pertinents, que l'obtention de cet avantage était l'un des principaux objectifs de tout arrangement ou de toute transaction qui a donné lieu directement ou indirectement à cet avantage, à moins qu'il ne soit établi que l'octroi de cet avantage dans ces circonstances serait conforme à l'objet et au but des dispositions pertinentes du présent Accord.

CHAPITRE IV. ÉLIMINATION DES DOUBLES IMPOSITIONS

Article 22. Élimination des doubles impositions

1. Sous réserve des dispositions de la législation de la Nouvelle-Zélande concernant l'imputation sur l'impôt néo-zélandais de l'impôt payé dans un pays autre que la Nouvelle-Zélande (qui n'affectent pas le principe général du présent article), l'impôt samoan payé en vertu de la législation du Samoa et conformément au présent Accord, à l'égard des revenus qu'un résident de la Nouvelle-Zélande tire de sources situées au Samoa (à l'exclusion, dans le cas de dividendes, de l'impôt payé au titre des bénéfices qui servent au paiement des dividendes) est imputé sur l'impôt néo-zélandais dû, à hauteur de ces revenus.

2. Sous réserve des dispositions de la législation du Samoa en vigueur concernant l'imputation sur l'impôt du Samoa de l'impôt payé dans un pays autre que le Samoa (qui n'affectent pas le principe général du présent article), l'impôt néo-zélandais payé en vertu de la législation de la Nouvelle-Zélande et conformément au présent Accord, au titre des revenus qu'un résident du Samoa tire de sources situées en Nouvelle-Zélande, est imputé sur l'impôt du Samoa dû au titre de ces revenus.

3. Aux fins du paragraphe 1, l'impôt samoan payé comprend un montant équivalent au montant de tout impôt samoan non perçu.

4. Au paragraphe 3, l'expression « impôt samoan non perçu » désigne un montant qui, en vertu de la législation samoane relative à l'impôt samoan et conformément au présent Accord, aurait

été payable au titre de l'impôt samoan sur le revenu si ce n'était une exonération ou une réduction de l'impôt samoan sur ce revenu résultant de l'application des dispositions de la législation samoane que le Gouvernement de la Nouvelle-Zélande et le Gouvernement du Samoa conviennent de temps à autre, dans des lettres échangées à cette fin, comme étant des dispositions auxquelles s'applique le présent paragraphe, et, sous réserve de ses termes, un tel accord sur les dispositions applicables est valide aussi longtemps que ces dispositions ne sont pas modifiées après la date de cet accord ou n'ont été modifiées que sur des points mineurs de manière à ne pas en affecter le caractère général.

5. Les paragraphes 3 et 4 ne s'appliquent qu'aux années de revenu qui peuvent être convenues par le Gouvernement du Samoa et le Gouvernement de la Nouvelle-Zélande dans des lettres échangées à cette fin.

6. Nonobstant les paragraphes 3, 4 et 5, un résident de Nouvelle-Zélande qui perçoit des revenus au Samoa, qui sont des revenus visés à ces paragraphes, n'est pas considéré comme ayant payé l'impôt du Samoa au titre de ces revenus lorsque :

- a) Le résident de Nouvelle-Zélande est une institution financière ou est associé à une institution financière ;
- b) L'autorité compétente de la Nouvelle-Zélande considère, après consultation de l'autorité compétente du Samoa, que cela est inapproprié, en raison de ce qui suit :
    - i) Des arrangements préalables ont été conclus par une personne dans le but de tirer parti du paragraphe 3 au profit de cette personne ou de toute autre personne ;
    - ii) Un avantage quelconque revient ou peut revenir à une personne qui n'est résidente ni de Nouvelle-Zélande ni du Samoa ;
    - iii) La prévention de la fraude ou l'évasion relatives aux impôts auxquelles le présent Accord s'applique ;
    - iv) Toute autre question que l'une ou l'autre des autorités compétentes considère comme pertinente dans les circonstances particulières du cas, y compris toute observation du résident néo-zélandais concerné.

7. Les dispositions des paragraphes 3, 4, 5 et 6 ne s'appliquent que pendant une période de 10 ans à compter de la date d'entrée en vigueur de l'Accord.

CHAPITRE V. DISPOSITIONS PARTICULIÈRES

Article 23. Procédure amiable

1. Lorsqu'une personne estime que les mesures prises par un État contractant ou par les deux États contractants entraînent ou entraîneront pour elle une imposition non conforme aux dispositions du présent Accord, elle peut, indépendamment des recours prévus par le droit interne de ces États, soumettre son cas à l'autorité compétente de l'État contractant dont elle est un résident. Le cas doit être soumis dans un délai de trois ans à compter de la première notification de la mesure qui entraîne une imposition non conforme aux dispositions de l'Accord.

2. Les autorités compétentes s'efforcent, si la réclamation lui paraît fondée et, si elle n'est pas elle-même en mesure d'y apporter une solution satisfaisante, de résoudre le cas par voie d'accord amiable avec les autorités compétentes de l'autre État contractant en vue d'éviter une imposition non conforme à l'Accord. Tout accord est appliqué quels que soient les délais prévus par le droit interne des États contractants.

3. Les autorités compétentes des États contractants s'efforcent, par voie d'accord amiable, de résoudre les difficultés ou de dissiper les doutes auxquels peuvent donner lieu l'interprétation ou l'application de l'Accord. Elles peuvent également se concerter en vue d'éliminer les doubles impositions dans les cas non prévus par l'Accord.

4. Les autorités compétentes des États contractants peuvent communiquer directement entre elles, y compris au sein d'une commission mixte composée de ces autorités ou de leurs représentants, en vue de parvenir à un accord au sens des paragraphes précédents.

Article 24. Échange de renseignements

1. Les autorités compétentes des États contractants échangent les renseignements vraisemblablement pertinents pour appliquer les dispositions du présent Accord ou celles de la législation interne relative aux impôts de toute nature ou dénomination prélevés pour le compte des États contractants, de leurs subdivisions politiques ou de leurs collectivités locales, à condition que l'imposition qu'elle prévoit ne soit pas contraire au présent Accord. L'échange de renseignements n'est pas limité par les articles premier et 2.

2. Les renseignements reçus en vertu du paragraphe 1 par un État contractant sont tenus secrets de la même manière que les renseignements obtenus en application de la législation interne de cet État et ne sont communiqués qu'aux personnes ou autorités (y compris les tribunaux et organes administratifs) concernées par l'établissement ou le recouvrement des impôts mentionnés au paragraphe 1, par les procédures ou poursuites concernant ces impôts, par les décisions sur les recours relatifs à ces impôts, ou par le contrôle de ce qui précède. Ces personnes ou autorités n'utilisent les renseignements qu'à ces fins. Elles peuvent faire état de ces renseignements dans des procédures judiciaires publiques ou dans des décisions judiciaires. Nonobstant ce qui précède, les renseignements reçus par un État contractant peuvent être utilisés à d'autres fins si la législation des deux États l'autorise et si l'autorité compétente de l'État qui fournit ces renseignements autorise cette utilisation.

3. Les dispositions des paragraphes 1 et 2 ne peuvent en aucun cas être interprétées comme imposant à un État contractant l'obligation :

a) De prendre des mesures administratives dérogeant à sa législation et à sa pratique administrative ou à celles de l'autre État contractant ;

b) De fournir des renseignements qui ne pourraient être obtenus sur la base de sa législation ou dans le cadre de sa pratique administrative normale ou de celles de l'autre État contractant ;

c) De fournir des renseignements qui révéleraient un secret commercial, industriel, professionnel ou un procédé commercial, ou des renseignements dont la divulgation serait contraire à l'ordre public.

4. Si des renseignements sont demandés par un État contractant conformément au présent article, l'autre État contractant utilise ses mesures de collecte de renseignement pour obtenir les renseignements demandés, quand bien même il n'aurait pas besoin de ces renseignements à ses propres fins fiscales. L'obligation contenue dans la phrase précédente est soumise aux limitations prévues au paragraphe 3, mais en aucun cas ces limitations ne doivent être interprétées comme autorisant un État contractant à refuser de fournir des renseignements au seul motif qu'il ne détient aucun intérêt national dans ces renseignements.

5. En aucun cas les dispositions du paragraphe 3 ne peuvent être interprétées comme autorisant un État contractant à refuser de communiquer des renseignements uniquement parce que ceux-ci sont détenus par une banque, une autre institution financière, un mandataire ou une personne agissant en tant qu'agent ou à titre fiduciaire, ou parce que ces renseignements se rattachent aux droits de propriété d'une personne.

Article 25. Membres des missions diplomatiques et des postes consulaires

Aucune disposition du présent Accord ne porte atteinte aux privilèges fiscaux dont bénéficient les membres des missions diplomatiques ou des représentations consulaires en vertu des règles générales du droit international ou des dispositions d'accords particuliers.

Chapitre VI. Dispositions finales

Article 26. Entrée en vigueur

1. Les États contractants se notifient mutuellement, par la voie diplomatique, l'accomplissement des procédures internes requises par leur législation pour l'entrée en vigueur du présent Accord. L'Accord entre en vigueur à la date de réception de la dernière de ces notifications, et ses dispositions s'appliquent :

a) En Nouvelle-Zélande :

i) En ce qui concerne la retenue d'impôt sur les revenus, bénéfices ou gains réalisés par un non-résident, aux montants payés ou crédités à partir du premier jour du deuxième mois suivant la date d'entrée en vigueur de l'Accord, inclus ;

ii) En ce qui concerne les autres impôts néo-zélandais, à tout exercice fiscal commençant le 1er avril qui suit immédiatement la date à laquelle l'Accord entre en vigueur, ou après cette date ;

b) Au Samoa :

i) En ce qui concerne la retenue d'impôt sur les revenus réalisés par un non-résident, aux revenus obtenus à partir du premier jour du deuxième mois suivant la date d'entrée en vigueur de l'Accord, inclus ;

ii) En ce qui concerne les autres impôts samoans, aux revenus de tout exercice fiscal commençant le 1er janvier qui suit immédiatement la date à laquelle l'Accord entre en vigueur, ou après cette date.

2. L'Accord entre le Gouvernement de la Nouvelle-Zélande et le Gouvernement du Samoa sur la répartition des droits d'imposition à l'égard de certains revenus des personnes physiques et l'établissement d'une procédure amiable en matière d'ajustement des prix de transfert, signé à Apia le 24 août 2010, prend fin et cesse de produire ses effets à la date à laquelle le présent Accord prend effet à l'égard des impôts auxquels s'applique le présent Accord conformément aux dispositions du paragraphe 1 du présent article.

3. L'Accord entre le Gouvernement de la Nouvelle-Zélande et le Gouvernement du Samoa relatif à l'échange de renseignements en matière fiscale, signé à Apia le 24 août 2010, prend fin et cesse de produire ses effets à la date à laquelle l'article 24 du présent Accord prend effet conformément aux dispositions du paragraphe 1 du présent article. Nonobstant l'abrogation de l'Accord relatif à l'échange de renseignements en matière fiscale, les États contractants restent liés

par les dispositions de l'article 8 du présent Accord pour tout renseignement obtenu dans le cadre de cet Accord.

Article 27. Dénonciation

Le présent Accord demeure en vigueur tant qu'il n'a pas été dénoncé par un État contractant. Chaque État contractant peut dénoncer le présent Accord par la voie diplomatique moyennant une notification adressée au moins six mois avant la fin de toute année civile après l'expiration d'un délai de cinq ans à compter de la date de son entrée en vigueur. Dans ce cas, l'Accord cesse de produire ses effets :

a) En Nouvelle-Zélande :

i) En ce qui concerne la retenue d'impôt sur les revenus, bénéfices ou gains réalisés par un non-résident, à l'égard des montants payés ou crédités à partir du premier jour du deuxième mois suivant la date à laquelle la notification de dénonciation est donné ;

ii) En ce qui concerne les autres impôts néo-zélandais, à l'égard de tout exercice fiscal commençant le 1er avril suivant immédiatement la date à laquelle la notification de dénonciation est donné, ou après cette date ;

b) Au Samoa :

i) En ce qui concerne la retenue d'impôt sur les revenus réalisés par un non-résident, à l'égard des revenus obtenus à partir du premier jour, inclus, du deuxième mois suivant la date à laquelle la notification de dénonciation est donné ;

ii) En ce qui concerne les autres impôts samoans, à l'égard de tout exercice fiscal commençant le 1er janvier qui suit immédiatement la date à laquelle la notification de dénonciation est donné, ou après cette date.

EN FOI DE QUOI, les soussignés, à ce dûment autorisés par leurs Gouvernements respectifs, ont signé le présent Accord.

FAIT à Apia, le 8 juillet 2015, en double exemplaire en langue anglaise.

Pour le Gouvernement de la Nouvelle-Zélande :

JOHN KEY
Premier Ministre de Nouvelle-Zélande

Pour le Gouvernement du Samoa :

TUILAEPA LUPESOLIAI SAILELE MALIELEGAOI
Premier Ministre du Samoa